Black Political Thought

In *Black Political Thought: From David Walker to the Present,* Sherrow O. Pinder has brought together the writings and discourses central to black political thought and African American politics, compiling a unique anthology of speeches and articles from over 150 years of African American history.

Providing in-depth examinations and critical analyses of topics such as slavery, reconstruction, race and racism, Black Nationalism and Black Feminism – from a range of perspectives – students are equipped with a comprehensive and informative account of how these issues have fundamentally shaped and continue to shape black political thinking. Each of the six thematic parts is framed by an introduction written by black scholars working in the field, and a list of further readings is provided. Individual chapters are then enhanced by end of chapter questions and author biographies.

Written for the interdisciplinary field of Black Studies, and other social science and humanities disciplines, this textbook offers a unique resource for political scientists, sociologists, historians, feminists, and the general reader of black political thought.

Sherrow O. Pinder, Professor of Political Science at California State University, Chico is the author of several books and serves as the "Race Politics in the United States" Book Series Editor at Anthem Press, London. She works primarily in the areas of race, gender, and ethnic politics in the United States, social welfare policy, black political thought, globalization studies and whiteness studies. In 2018, Pinder was invited to present her work, "The Liminality of Whiteness and its Problematics for Race Politics in the United States," at the Newberry Scholarly Seminar in American Literature.

Black Political Thought

From David Walker to the Present

Edited by

Sherrow O. Pinder

California State University, Chico

CAMBRIDGE
UNIVERSITY PRESS

CAMBRIDGE
UNIVERSITY PRESS

University Printing House, Cambridge CB2 8BS, United Kingdom

One Liberty Plaza, 20th Floor, New York, NY 10006, USA

477 Williamstown Road, Port Melbourne, VIC 3207, Australia

314–321, 3rd Floor, Plot 3, Splendor Forum, Jasola District Centre, New Delhi – 110025, India

79 Anson Road, #06–04/06, Singapore 079906

Cambridge University Press is part of the University of Cambridge.

It furthers the University's mission by disseminating knowledge in the pursuit of
education, learning, and research at the highest international levels of excellence.

www.cambridge.org
Information on this title: www.cambridge.org/9781107199729
DOI: 10.1017/9781108185875

© Sherrow O. Pinder 2020

First published 2020

Printed in the United Kingdom by TJ International Ltd, Padstow, Cornwall

A catalogue record for this publication is available from the British Library.

Library of Congress Cataloging-in-Publication Data
Names: Pinder, Sherrow O., editor.
Title: Black political thought from David Walker to the present / edited by
Sherrow O. Pinder, California State University, Chico.
Description: Cambridge, United Kingdom ; New York, NY, USA : Cambridge University Press,
[2020] | Includes bibliographical references and index.
Identifiers: LCCN 2019019741 | ISBN 9781107199729 (hardback) |
ISBN 9781316648995 (paperback)
Subjects: LCSH: African Americans – Politics and government – Sources. |
African Americans – Social conditions – Sources. | United States – Race relations – Political
aspects – Sources.
Classification: LCC E185.61 .B594 2020 | DDC 305.896/073–dc23
LC record available at https://lccn.loc.gov/2019019741

ISBN 978-1-107-19972-9 Hardback
ISBN 978-1-316-64899-5 Paperback

Contents

Notes on the Contributors

Nikki L. M. Brown is the Raphael Cassimere Professor of History at the University of New Orleans. Brown's first book, *Private Politics and Public Voices: African American Women's Politics from World War I to the New Deal* (2006), explored the attempts made by African American women to shape public policy between 1915 and 1920. *Private Politics and Public Voices* was awarded the 2007 Letitia Woods Brown Memorial Book Prize as best book in African American women's history. Brown has written several articles on African American women and political reform in the Progressive Era, African American men and masculinity in New Orleans, and the impact of racial segregation laws on contemporary American politics. Her second book is on the photographs of Louisiana's civil rights movement.

Charisse Burden-Stelly is an Assistant Professor and Mellon Faculty Fellow of Africana Studies and Political Science at Carleton College. She is a scholar of political theory, political economy, and intellectual history with a substantive focus on racial capitalism and the black radical tradition. She has just completed *W. E. B. Du Bois: A Life in American History,* a co-authored book project with Gerald Horne, and is working on a single-authored manuscript titled *The Radical Horizon of Black Betrayal: Antiradicalism, Antiblackness, and the U.S. Capitalist State.* She received the National Conference of Black Political Scientists' Alex Willingham Best Political Theory Paper Award in 2017 and in 2018 she became a regular contributor to *Black Perspectives,* the blog of the African American Intellectual History Society. Dr. Burden-Stelly's published work appears in journals including *Souls, The CLR James Journal, The International Journal of Africana Studies, The Du Bois Review*, and *Socialism & Democracy.*

Erica F. Cooper is a co-director of the African and African American Studies program at East Carolina University. Previously, she was an Associate Professor of Communication Studies at Roanoke College. She received her PhD from Indiana University in Communication and Culture, with a special emphasis in Law. Her research examines the interracial communication and identity formation as well as examining the methods of argumentation in legal and political discourse. Recent works include a rhetorical history of the development of the one-drop rule in US jurisprudence.

Babacar M'Baye is a Professor of English at Kent State University. A native of Senegal, Professor M'Baye received his PhD from Bowling Green State University in Ohio. His research interests vary from Pan-African literatures, cultures, music, films, gender expressions, and sexualities to black Atlantic studies, transnationalism, and postcolonialism. Professor M'Baye is the author of *Black Cosmopolitanism and Anticolonialism: Pivotal Moments* (2017), *The Trickster Comes West: Pan-African Influence in Early Black Diasporan Narratives* (2009), and the co-editor of *Crossing Traditions: American Popular Music in Local and Global Contexts* (2013). He is also the co-editor of Lexington Books' Critical African Studies in Gender and Sexuality Series.

Brenda E. Stevenson is the Nickoll Family Endowed Chair and Professor of History and African American Studies at UCLA. Her book length works include: *The Journals of Charlotte Forten Grimke* (1988), *Life in Black and White: Family and Community in the Slave South* (1996), *The Contested Murder of Latasha Harlins: Justice, Gender and the Origins of the L.A. Riots* (2013), and *What is Slavery?* (2015). She is a past John Simon Guggenheim Fellow, a recipient of the Organization of American Historian's Rawley Prize for the best book on race; the Carter G. Woodson Medallion from the Association for the Study of African American Life and History; and the John Blassingame Award from the Southern Historical Society.

Sherrow O. Pinder is Professor of Political Science and Multicultural and Gender Studies at California State University, Chico. She is the author of several books. Her latest book is *Black Women, Work, and Welfare in the Age of Globalization* (2018). Professor Pinder is also "Race Politics in the United States" Book Series Editor at Anthem Press, London. In 2018, Professor Pinder was invited to present her work, "The Liminality of Whiteness and its Problematics for Race Politics in the United States," at the Newberry Scholarly Seminar in American Literature. Her present book project, *Michael Jackson and the Quandary of a Black Identity* is under contract with State University of New York Press.

Preface

Black Political Thought: From David Walker to the Present has two main goals. One is to offer a standard textbook for undergraduate students and faculty working in the field of Black Studies and African American Studies as well as other disciplines in the humanities and social sciences, including Political Science, American Studies, Ethnic Studies, Women's Studies, and Sociology. The second is to provide the general reader with a collection that introduces the key concepts that have helped to shape and develop black political thought within the broader interdisciplinary field of Black Studies.

Black Studies represents an attractive and buoyant area of studies for students and scholars at American and international colleges and universities. However, there aren't many scholarly works published on black political thought. This book aims to contribute as well as expand the scholarship available for anyone interested in Black Studies. In addition, it offers new pedagogical tools that will prove indispensable to enhance Student Learning Outcomes. *Black Political Thought* was prompted by the urgent need for a primary text for a class on Black Political Thought that I am developing and will teach at the university where I am at present employed.

Black Political Thought is divided into six sections/parts: Part I, Slavery and Its Discontents; Part II, Reconstruction; Part III, Black Nationalism; Part IV, Race and Racism; Part V, Feminism and Difference; and Part VI, Past, Present, and Future Issues. Each part has a specific theme, which, all together describes and explains how blacks in the United States, as individuals and as a group, have, in various ways, addressed and responded to the unequal political, economic, and social underpinnings of the United States. While it draws on existing works that take into account the past, present, and future experiences of blacks in the United States, it opens up new ways to help in the analysis of the unequal positioning of blacks historically and at present.

The chief novelty of this textbook lies in its wide-ranging pedagogical approach to Black Studies. It begins with an introductory chapter titled "Key Concepts, Ideas, and Issues that have Formed Black Political Thought." Each part of the textbook starts with an introduction of around 3500 to 4500 words written by black scholars Brenda E. Stevenson, Nikki L. M. Brown, Babacar M'Baye, Charisse Burden-Stelly, Sherrow O. Pinder, and Erica F. Cooper respectively, working in the field of Black Studies. The introduction provides an overview of the topic presented under the border heading of, for example, Slavery and Its Discontents by highlighting the most important concepts, ideas, and purpose of each of the chapters in the section. This provides students with the context they need to read effectively. Key concepts, facts, and ideas are stressed in the text, and referred back to a glossary, which is included before the index. Cross-referencing is thus used throughout the text.

In addition, a short biography of the authors of the chapters is included at the beginning of each chapter so that students can become acquainted with the author and his/her work and understand his/her importance in the area. The short biography aims to encourage students to conduct their own research to learn more about an author and his/her other works. An annotated bibliography provided at the end of each part also guides students and instructors seeking additional information and lists further readings such as works of scholars that should be included in the book, but, because of limited space, could not be included.

Study questions at the end of each part and chapter are provided. The questions are, for the most part, conceptual and require answers that are provided in an essay format. Questions represent an important pedagogical tool. Many instructors find it very useful to have reflective questions following each part of a textbook that can help students think about the concepts and make meaningful connections with the materials provided in the book. Furthermore, the aim of these questions is to help students organize and process the objectives, ideas, argumentation, and concepts presented in the chapters. These questions will increase students' comprehension of the material and help them think critically about Black Studies. *Black Political Thought* has a sequence and is organizational but instructors do not have to follow the sequence and will be able to select their own reading sequences. In short, this volume constitutes a standard textbook that will contribute to the dissemination of further knowledge of black political thought.

Acknowledgments

The Editor would like to thank the following for their permission to reprint their material:

Anthony Joseph and Kathleen Neal Cleaver for permission to reprint Kathleen Neal Cleaver, "The Antidemocratic Power of Whiteness," *Chicago-Kent Law Review, Symposium on the Law of Freedom Part II: Freedom Beyond the United States*, vol. 70, issue 3 (April 1995), pp. 1375–1387.

Cambridge University Press for permission to reprint Barbara J. Fields, "Whiteness, Racism, and Identity," *International Labor and Working Class History* 60 (Fall 2001), pp. 48–56.

Cheryl I. Harris and Harvard Law Review Association for permission to reprint "Whiteness as Property," *Harvard Law Review* 106, no. 8 (June 1993), pp. 1737–1744.

Emily Wojcik for permission to reprint Stokely Carmichael, "Toward Black Liberation," *The Massachusetts Review* 7, no. 4 (Autumn 1966), pp. 639–651.

Gary L. Lemons and the *International Journal of Sociology and Social Policy* for permission to reprint Gary L. Lemons, "To Be Black, Male, and 'Feminist': Making Womanist Space for Black Men," *International Journal of Sociology and Social Policy* 17, no. 1/2 (1997).

Patricia Hill Collins and *The Black Scholar* for permission to reprint "WHAT's In A NAME? Womanism, Black Feminism and Beyond," *The Black Scholar* 26, no. 1 (1996), pp. 9–17.

Introduction
Key Concepts, Ideas, and Issues that have Formed Black Political Thought

SHERROW O. PINDER

> It is a peculiar sensation, this double-consciousness, this sense of always looking at oneself through the eyes of others, of measuring one's soul by the tape of a world that looks on in amused contempt and pity.
>
> —W. E. B. Du Bois, *The Souls of Black Folk*

In the United States, black political thought in its genealogical orientation, from slavery to present, is an appropriate mode of inquiry and analysis into the unequal positioning of blacks. In the form of a politically engaged critique, blacks' positionality as second-class citizens has produced and continues to produce an ongoing crisis of signification. In fact, the never-ending American issue is that, historically, blacks were not recognized as rights-bearing subjects. To put it differently, America's democratic creed of liberty and equality, which is equivalent to the exercise of freedom, a fundamental element of one's autonomy, was not extended to blacks, free or slaves. And today, blacks continue to be denied their rights of citizenship, wittingly amplified in the forms of racial profiling and institutionalized violence. When blacks' rights have been, or are curtailed, blacks are involved in public lectures, demonstrations, riots, and other forms of direct and performative actions, which are described and explained as actions "in crisis" or actions that are "provoking crisis." In this discussion, the term crisis designates a phenomenon that manifests itself when the systems and structures are called into question through oppositional strategies. Because of the radical ways in which blacks resist the normative working of institutionalized power and invoke alternatives, it is safe to say that these actions were and are crystallized into various forms of speaking and writing. Indeed, speaking and writing are acts of resistance. These are political practices.

Black Political Thought: From David Walker to the Present represents a critical compass to rearticulate the political based on the lived experiences of blacks in the United States, which cannot exist independent of past and present practices of inequality towards them. For this reason, this collection focuses on how and why blacks in the United States, as individuals and as a group, have historically conceptualized, analyzed, and responded to the ill will of ordinary whites and those in power who through laws, policies and customs, and cultural practice have made blacks into inferior beings as a justification to deny them their rights of equality, in such a way that the interests of the dominant class are upheld and preserved, and which today have not disappeared. This carries several implications for America's development into a nation where identity markers such as race, gender, and class determine who are the rights-bearing subjects.

To appreciate the *critique* of the unequal position of blacks presented by the scholars in this collection, it is useful to think of what Homi K. Bhabha calls "a third space"[1] for interpretation and counterhegemonic critique of the foundational and institutional racial oppression that permits all other forms of discrimination – sexism, classism, ableism, homophobia, Islamophobia, ageism, and xenophobia – to happen. Readers of Michel Foucault's "What is Critique?" will recognize that "critique only exists in relation to something other than itself."[2] Any critique of blacks' inequality needs to inquire into what renders this kind of discriminatory practice possible. The authors in this collection look at the lived experience of blacks historically and currently as a critique of America's discriminatory practice. Through the lived experience of blacks, black political thought has been materialized, concretized, and is sustained. What we can learn from such a critique is, at least for me, what make the writers in the collection particularly suited for any book on black political thought. What it means to be black in the face of institutional arrangements, systems and structures, ontologies, ideologies and epistemologies, and cultural expectations that promote the interests of the dominant group in the United States is indeed paramount.

Black Political Thought: From David Walker to the Present is divided into six parts. Each section examines some of the key questions that have informed black political thinking. This collection engages with systems, structures, epistemology, ideology, and the discourse of black unequal positioning. It examines slavery and its discontents, the Reconstruction period, Black Nationalism, race and racism, feminism and difference, and past, present, and future issues, and how these issues have motivated and continue to motivate black political thinking. In fact, black political thinking is motivated in the writings of many black scholars by very specific problems and situations – political, social, epistemological, sexual, and economic – that positioned blacks as second-class citizens. This is precisely the underlying motivation for the writers in this volume. It is to help us make sense of the past, present, and future concerns that have and continue to inform and shape the political in black thinking. Black scholars Brenda E. Stevenson, Nikki L. M. Brown, Babacar M'Baye, Charisse Burden-Stelly, Sherrow O. Pinder, and Erica F. Cooper provide introductory remarks for each section.

---

[1] Homi K. Bhabha, *The Location of Culture* (New York: Routledge, 1994).

[2] Michel Foucault, "What is Critique?" in *The Politics of Truth*, ed. Sylvère Lotringer and Lysa Hochroth (Los Angeles, CA: Semiotext(e), 1997), p. 23.

Part I: Slavery and Its Discontents

In this collection, slavery is the starting point for developing and shaping black political thinking. In the words of Brenda E. Stevenson, "black political thought in the nineteenth-century United States unequivocally centered on the inequality of African and African descended peoples, both enslaved and free." It has often been remarked that the brutality of the slave regime and the ways in which slaves were treated as disposable bodies – where power was exercised over slaves through the use of severe punishments such as whipping, and practices such as underfeeding, starving, breeding, and killing – cannot be disavowed. However, these punishments and practices were not enough to make slaves into something other than human beings. The laws that were in place recognized that the slaves were people.

When Frederick Douglass asks in "What to the Slave is the Fourth of July?": "must I undertake to prove that the slave is a man?," his question is obviously rhetorical and he does not intend to prove that the slaves were indeed people. The institution of the laws, ideology, and cultural practice, which continuously dehumanized the slaves and undermined their personhood by upholding the idea that their lives were unlivable and not grievable clearly assumed that they were people. In fact, the daily acts of violence against slaves were to convince blacks that they were *less* than whites. Through physical, psychic, epistemological, and ontological violence, the white man became a "man" by legally and culturally overpowering blacks to his *will*.

In the face of slavery, blacks' "vocation to be fully humans" and experience the rights and liberties that were accessible to whites was an endless fight. For the author of *The Pedagogy of the Oppressed*, Paulo Freire, dehumanization "marks not only those whose humanity has been stolen [slaves], but also (though in a different way) those who have stolen it [masters]."[3] But how long might the slaves be contented with their condition of servitude? It was inevitable that the slaves would eventually become disgruntled with their situation and struggle against the masters as was illustrated in the many slave riots. However, for the struggle to have any significance, the slaves must not become in turn masters of the masters but reestablish the humanity of both (themselves and their masters). In other words, by liberating themselves, the slaves would liberate their masters.[4]

Part I, "Slavery and Its Discontents," draws on the writers' diverse thought on slavery and its discontents based on their experience of slavery as a free or enslaved person. Stevenson in the introductory chapter explains how David Walker, Maria W. Stewart, Frederick Douglass, Henry Highland Garnet, and Martin Robison

---

[3] Paulo Freire, *Pedagogy of the Oppressed*, trans. Myra Bergman Ramos (New York: Continuum, 2002), p. 44.
[4] Ibid.

Delany, in varied ways, confronted the contradictions and tensions of their time. In fact, slavery became a living source of inspiration for blacks. Black scholars approached the subject from various critical perspectives. In her detailed analysis, Stevenson observes that "each work is meant to expose the varied and overlapping experiences, goals, and strategies of those men and women who dedicated their lives to the cause of racial equality." Importantly, this brings us to the observation that thinking and writing can materialize, in the words of Hannah Arendt, "out of incidents of living experience and must remain bound to them as the only guidepost by which to take its bearing."[5] In other words, experience is the foundation of the writings presented on slavery and its discontents. As slavery came to an end, the period of Reconstruction continued to cement blacks' inferior status. The following section expounds on some of the issues of the Reconstruction era.

Part II: Reconstruction

In 1865, the Thirteenth Amendment to the American Constitution brought an end to slavery. The United States entered the Reconstruction era (1865–77). In *Black Reconstruction in America*, W. E. B. Du Bois provocatively asks: "What is the object of writing the History of Reconstruction? Is it to wipe out the disgrace of a people which fought to make slaves of Negroes? Is it to show that the North had higher motives than freeing black men? Is it to prove that Negroes were black angels?"[6] In fact, the political, social, and economic effects of Reconstruction raise the most interesting and challenging questions. And while these questions await negative answers, Reconstruction, Du Bois tell us, was "simply to establish the Truth on which Right in the future may be built."[7] Indeed, it was important for those in power to extend, at least in theory, the principles of democratic governance to blacks and give them the basic educational skills and economic resources necessary for their future development. However, blacks remained at the mercy of popular prejudice arising from their previous condition of servitude. The unequal treatment that blacks experienced during slavery had been transformed into the Reconstruction era, an overriding issue for any collection on black political thought.

Nikki L. M. Brown in her introductory remarks on Reconstruction notes that the authors in this section, W. E. B. Du Bois, T. Thomas Fortune, and Booker T.

---

[5] Hannah Arendt, *Between Past and Future: Eight Exercises in Political Thought* (New York: Penguin, 1961), p. 14.

[6] W. E. B. Du Bois, *Black Reconstruction in America: An Essay Toward a History of the Part Which Black Folk Played in the Attempt to Reconstruct Democracy in America, 1860–1880* (New York: Russell & Russell, 1935), p. 775.

[7] Ibid.

Washington, are elite black men. In fact, this may generate some disapproval given that black women were, certainly, speaking and writing about women's condition during and after slavery, in the Reconstruction era. Fannie Barrier Williams, in "The Intellectual Progress of the Women of the United States since the Emancipation Proclamation," for one, draws our attention to the fact that black women worked hard to emancipate themselves from the ills of slavery and continued to suffer in silence and struggle "to keep hallowed their own person." And their struggle is not recorded in America's history. However, black women's "unwritten history is full of heroic struggles," Williams reminds us.[8]

Nonetheless, how can we truly comprehend the Reconstruction period without including Du Bois' "Of the Dawn of Freedom," which, as Brown acknowledges, "offered the most famous pronouncement about racism in modern US history: 'The problem of the 20th century is the problem of the color-line.'" Swedish economist and sociologist Gunnar Myrdal would later refer to this insoluble problem as the "American dilemma."[9] And even though blacks were no longer slaves, they remained segregated and lived on the social, economic, and political margin. Reconstruction did not solve blacks' unequal position. Indeed, with the enactment of the Thirteenth, Fourteenth, and Fifteenth Amendments, during the Reconstruction era, black inequality, in the words of Brown, "took shape, most disturbingly, in the form of extralegal violence – race riots, lynchings, and intimidation by terrorist groups." In other words, the actions of the Ku Klux Klan and state racist laws like the literacy test, the poll tax, and the grandfather clause in place to curtail black men from voting perpetuated blacks' inequality. Furthermore, according to Brown, "extremist groups, a weak federal government, and outbreaks of violence between southern whites and blacks were so numerous that they became impossible to solve."

On the other hand, Booker T. Washington, in his essay, in Brown's words, "considered himself an energetic optimist, and he was sure that African Americans would grow into economic self-sufficiency." However, it is T. Thomas Fortune who draws our attention to the fact that blacks, voting for Rutherford B. Hayes equipped the Hayes administration to turn, in Fortune's words, "the colored voters of the South over to the bloodthirsty minority." With President Hayes in power, the Compromise of 1877 brought an end to the Reconstruction period. The United States, according to Brown, "was a meaner, crueler country for African Americans after Reconstruction" with the Jim Crow Laws in place soon after. Blacks continued

---

[8] Fannie Barrier Williams, "The Intellectual Progress of the Women of the United States since the Emancipation Proclamation," in *The World Conference of Representative Women*, ed. May Wright Sewall (New York: Rand, McNally & Company, 1894), 711–715. Available at https://archive.org/stream/worldscongressof00worluoft/worldscongressof00worluoft_djvu.txt.

[9] Gunnar Myrdal, *An American Dilemma: The Negro Problem and Modern Democracy* (New York: Harper & Row, 1962).

to be treated as second-class citizens. In fact, the 1886 canonical landmark case, *Plessy v. Ferguson*, confirmed the status of second-class citizenry upon blacks, which corresponded to the readily available doctrine of "separate but equal" that equally carried the day. Blacks as well as whites fastened themselves to the doctrine, and blacks who failed to constitute themselves within its terms and posed an immediate threat to the white social body had to pay the consequences. For the most part, they died the victims of continued state violence and lynchings. Furthermore, blacks continued to be viewed as inferior to whites, were denied self-determination, and continued to experience relentless racism and its multidimensional forms of discriminatory practice. Black Nationalism, as an oppositional force against America's racism, is important for thinking about the scope of black political thought.

Part III: Black Nationalism

In time, Martin R. Delany, in his book *The Condition, Elevation, Emigration, and Destiny of the Colored People of the United States, Politically Considered*, advocated for the self-sufficiency of blacks and called for "emigration of the colored people of the United States" to Liberia. Also, in the years between Reconstruction and World War I, Bishop Henry McNeal Turner of the African Methodist Episcopal Church was one of the main advocates for the self-sufficiency of blacks in the United States. "These intellectuals," Babacar M'Baye notes, "were nationalists because they believed that the marginalization to which they were subjected in the United States from slavery time to the 1950s contradicted America's self-representation as a cosmopolitan nation that is founded on republicanism and democracy."

Part III focuses on "Black Nationalism" as one of the responses to address blacks' unequal position in a polity that professes democratic principles of equal justice and economic and political freedom within the rule of law for all citizens of the United States. The authors in this section are James Theodore Holly, Marcus Garvey, and Stokely Carmichael. M'Baye, in his introductory remarks points to the origins of Pan-Africanism as founded and consolidated within Black Nationalism, a long intellectual tradition "that is completely detached from black cosmopolitanism." In part, Black Nationalism focuses on cutting the cord that binds blacks to the United States and enhancing their capacity for self-representation. In the words of James Theodore Holly, "self-government and civilized progress" can only be achieved by black emigration, at least for Holly, to Haytia (Haiti).

M'Baye, drawing on the relevance of Black Nationalism, "a theory founded on the shared struggle against historical forces that have prevented many black communities from establishing either a collective entity such as a country, a meta-nation, or another geographic political and economic entity for themselves," is fundamental for black political thinking. Certainly, Black Nationalism, as Michael C. Dawson acknowledges, continues to be "the focus of contemporary debate within the black community."[10] More recently, the media's exposure of Chicago's Trinity United Church of Christ Reverend Jeremiah Wright's angry outbursts in opposition to racism was met with an enormous amount of hostility from the masses. Certainly, for Reverend Wright, racism is a facilitator for ills such as failing infrastructures, increasing joblessness, poverty, crime, violence, gangs, lack of access to adequate health care, and educational underachievement that decimate black communities and reduce poor blacks to a "death-in-life." The death-in-life is a condition that is described "as ontological death, that is, the loss of their personhood."[11]

Indeed, when Reverend Wright shouts from a pulpit, "God damn America," he criticizes the institutionalized violence and the criminal justice system that is too often "excessively punitive and destructive in black communities."[12] Far from uttering a cry of surprise, Reverend Wright offers an investigative account of America's racism. We can see clearly, like other Black Nationalists – Stokely Carmichael, Marcus Garvey, and James Theodore Holly – that Wright's obligation is not to the United States because the United States "is tainted by worldly sin – its imperialism (the Mexican-American War, the conquest of the Philippines, the occupation of Haiti and Cuba); its dispossession of the Indians; its subordination of blacks; its use of atomic weapons; its misadventures in Vietnam, Chile, and Nicaragua; and still other misdeeds about which all too many Americans are ignorant or indifferent."[13] To put it differently, like the fathers of Black Nationalism and Pan-Africanism, Reverend Wright's loyalty is not to the American people but to America's promises in the Declaration of Independence: "We hold these truths to be self-evident that all men are created equal." For Reverend Wright, America has not lived up to this promise because of its discriminatory treatment, not only of blacks, but other racialized ethnic groups such as First Nations, Mexicans, Muslims, and Asians in the United States, women, sexual minorities, senior citizens, the poor, and the disabled, which constitutes, in Reverend Wright's words, "a moral atrocity warranting God's damnation."[14] Reverend Wright hides nothing about race and racism in the United States.

---

[10] Michael C. Dawson, *Black Visons: The Roots of Contemporary Black Political Ideology* (University of Chicago Press, 2001), p. 45.

[11] Sherrow O. Pinder, *Black Women, Work, and Welfare in the Age of Globalization* (Lanham, MD: Lexington Books, 2018), p. viii.

[12] Randall Kennedy, *The Persistence of the Color Line: Racial Politics and the Obama Presidency* (New York: Pantheon, 2011), p. 187.

[13] Ibid., p. 188.

[14] Ibid., p. 187.

Part IV: Race and Racism

Because of the increasing range of books and journal articles addressing issues of race and racism from a variety of disciplinary and conceptual perspectives, the theorizing of race and racism must be included in any book on black political thought. Hence, how to theorize race, racism, and related topics, and develop conceptual tools for the analysis of the many ways in which race as a concept and racism as a system have shaped past and present black political thinking in the United States must be accounted for. Black political thought has to respond to this and draw on race and racism in such a way that the "black perspective" comes more to the forefront. On this note, it is paramount indeed to point to the problematics of substituting race for racism and the failure to examine the indispensability of race and racism as two overlying but sharply differentiated manifestations.

In fact, assigning racial categories to people is symptomatic of racism. Furthermore, because of how the body is racialized, blacks encounter the racist world through their bodies. The fact that a class analysis appears to get in the way of accepting such a claim does not make this self-evident certainty less certain. For sure, a black male lawyer on Wall Street will experience race differently than a black single mother on welfare living in the Bronx in New York City. Race is fixed on the body and it is a phenomenon that is both visual and psychical. It is the central marker confirming the ontology of race. Clearly, blacks assume the mark and burden of race, and have agitated in the name of race. In fact, some black male leaders have been presented as speaking as and for blacks. While we should dispute the obligation of black men to speak for all blacks, surely, we are cognizant of the masculinist ways in which representational politics operates.[15]

When Frantz Fanon, in his influential book *Black Skin, White Masks*, declares that "The Negro is not. No more than the white man,"[16] is he suggesting that there is no biological basis to race? So, what exactly is race? Given that blacks' lives are always conditioned by their race, an essential question is what relationship might there be between attitudes toward race and blacks? So how, exactly, can we account for "the declining significance of race"[17] and "the end of racism"[18] as is espoused by some scholars? To say that a black person is a slave not of the idea that others have of him/her but of his/her own appearance, to use Fanon's

---

[15] Sherrow O. Pinder, *The Politics of Race and Ethnicity in the United States: Americanization and De-Americanization of Racialized Ethnic Groups* (Basingstoke: Palgrave Macmillan, 2013).

[16] Frantz Fanon, *Black Skin, White Masks*, trans. Charles Lam Markmann (New York: Grove, 1967), p. 180.

[17] See William Julius Wilson, *The Declining Significance of Race* (University of Chicago Press, 1980).

[18] See Dinesh D'Souza, *The End of Racism: Principles for a Multicultural Society* (New York: Free Press, 1995).

language,[19] is to contend that race subjects blacks to an identification that is marked on the body. In other words, blacks are, in deconstructivist language, "always already overdetermined from the outside." Thus, differences among blacks stemming from identity markers such as gender, sexuality, disability, and class are overlooked. That race, as the outcome of racism, is the signifier that is pegged to other signifiers such as gender, class, sexuality, disability, and speech and language impairment cannot be denied. It is no wonder that Charisse Burden-Stelly draws our attention to "present programs for the cultivation of a vibrant black community: economic development, moral uplift, social organization, political protection, self-determination, race unity, cultural pride," which are deemed fitting for blacks' advancement.

Part IV, "Race and Racism," draws on the works of Alexander Crummell, W. E. B. Du Bois, and Ida B. Wells. "Their political thought," according to Burden-Stelly, which is "articulated through ethnological, evangelical, racial uplift, and Republican discourse," in extraordinary ways, confronts "the contradictions between idealized notions of American progress and the realities of the racial Nadir." It is important to remember that while Du Bois calls for the conservation of race because blacks have a lot of positive attributes that American society as a whole can benefit from, a "new" form of racism that pretends to omit race and views racism as over, has recently reared its head above the so-called "colorblindness" and "post-raciality" and has been redirected to the "old" blatant one against blacks. We need not look any further than the present political climate, in which with an antidemocratic American president holding the highest position of power, rights for racialized ethnic groups, sexual minorities, the poor, documented and undocumented workers, the disabled, women, and other marginalized groups have been severely curtailed. Indeed, when feminists across the board joined forces to protest the Trump administration's curtailing of women's hard-won rights, solidarity amongst women came to the forefront. But, as Sherrow O. Pinder reminds us, "'we' are not one in the same feminist struggle for a just society."

Part V: Feminism and Difference

"Women" as a category of analysis is important for feminism. When one thinks that "white is what women are," one needs to draw from the archetypal discussion on gender positioning. Since black women are not seen as women, in order for black women to break into the category of the woman, the racialization of women and its deleterious implications have to be prohibited. This, in turn, would open up new possibilities for women's subjectivity and varied positioning to be

---

[19] Fanon, *Black Skin, White Masks*, p. 116.

acceptable. The writings of Mary Church Terrell, Patricia Hill Collins, and Gary L. Lemons are included in Part V, "Feminism and Difference," and are valued for their profound theoretical underpinnings in relation to the political insights that these authors highlight in exposing the limits of acceptable womanhood and opening up a complex analysis for thinking differences, which is by no means to abandon the feminist goal of equality for all. While the experiences of women cannot be homogenized, Pinder draws on the fact that "there is a great continuity of feminist treatment of differences within gender to privilege the concerns of white women and ignore issues that are of importance to black women." Perhaps this is why so many black feminists debate abandoning the term feminism and employ "woman-ism" as a more compelling term to address their concerns.

"Womanists" and black feminists are both concerned with fights against racism, sexism, and other systems that promote inequality. Womanism is defined typically as a reaction to feminism for not incorporating issues that are important to black women. This notion thus takes into account Alice Walker's metaphoric use of *the garden* where room exists for all flowers to bloom equally and differently. *The garden* metaphor shows that differences within the very discourse of feminism cannot and should not be sidestepped. Feminists should find ways that allow for these differences to materialize and be addressed. To this end, employing womanism as a discourse of resistance is an appropriate strategy for taking into account the many forms that injustice and inequality take on individuals and groups that are outside of the recognizable norms. It allows for an analysis, which demonstrates that womanism is not limited to black women's concerns but can open up a space where black men, for example, as Pinder writes "can work to empower themselves in feminist solidarity" and broaden the concept to embrace the concerns of all people. The need to situate black women's inequality within the larger framework of black political thought becomes overriding.

Given that whiteness is the norm and white women are not positioned outside of whiteness, white privilege, as Pinder points out, might propel white women to "define and shape what feminist concerns should be and guide the development of feminist goals." If a broad feminist agenda is to be reimagined, white women would have to unlearn their privilege, which, in itself, constitutes a double recogni-tion—that is, white women gaining a certain kind of "other knowledge" not merely information that they have not yet acknowledged or received, but knowledge that they are not equipped to value.[20] This is symptomatic of how white women are positioned as a part of America's cultural norm defined by whiteness. Hence, unlearning dominant systems of knowledge and representation, which, for the postcolonial theorist Gayatri C. Spivak is a "transformation of consciousness – a

---

[20]Gayatri C. Spivak, *The Spivak Reader: Selected Works of Gayatri Chakravorty Spivak*, ed. Donna Landry and Gerald Maclean (New York: Routledge, 1995), p. 4.

changing mindset," inextricably comprises a dual acknowledgment.[21] This dual acknowledgment is necessary to dislocate white entitlement and destabilize whiteness presumptive hegemony.

Part VI: Past, Present, and Future Issues

With the election of the first black American president to date, the United States imagined itself as a "post-racial" society. "Post-racial" thinking suggests that there is a "declining significance of race" and, therefore, "an end to racism." Hence, "post-racial" was being organized as a discourse to explain and define new ways of thinking and understanding America's race politics. For this reason, when examining the past and present issues impacting black political thought one has to be aware of the fact that black political thought is not produced in a vacuum or only in relation to the previous body of works that historically developed and continues to shape black political thought. In Part VI, "Past, Present, and Future Issues," the final section of this book, Erica F. Cooper examines some of the issues, concerns, and problems that appear to be specific to America's past but are indeed extended to the present and hint to future concerns of blacks. These are the subjects explored by scholars Cheryl I. Harris, Barbara J. Fields, and Kathleen Neal Cleaver in the concluding section. Cooper indeed captures in the writings of these scholars the pathos of white supremacy in the context of the Marxist theorist Antonio Gramsci's notion of ideology in an attempt, as Cooper states, "to reveal the translucent processes of hegemony, marginalization, legitimization, and naturalization as they appear in social discourses." Indeed, white supremacy does not manifest itself in the same way as it did during indentured servitude, slavery, Reconstruction, the Jim Crow South, and the post-Civil Rights period. However, it still pervades society in discursive and nondiscursive practices, which, Cooper points out, W. E. B. Du Bois identifies as the "public and psychological wages" of whiteness, nonmaterial but psychical benefits that are bestowed on whites. And while the "psychological wages" associated with white supremacy encouraged the making of America's working class, white workers aggressively safeguarded themselves and their interests by holding on to their "whiteness as property." In other words, poor whites dissociated themselves from blacks. Indeed, poor whites were willing to accept low wages from their employer, in the words of Cooper, "masking the material reality of wage dependency among the white working class." In this sense, white privilege strengthens whites' continuing ascendancy, and the social ontology of whiteness is the fundamental structure responsible for providing

---

[21] Gayatri C. Spivak, *The Postcolonial Critic: Interviews, Strategies, Dialogue*, ed. Sarah Harasym (New York: Routledge, 1990), p. 20.

whites with privileges that are denied to blacks. However, one has to bear in mind that white supremacy is not the same as whiteness. Whiteness is interconnected to systems and structures that shape and uphold racial oppression and how whiteness is extended to race and racism is an overarching concern for authors in this section. It is precisely for this reason that whiteness makes use of, in Cooper's words, "a vocabulary of race to construct an arbitrary racial classification system."

In the United States, race cannot be understood or analyzed outside of whiteness. Whiteness is an ontological neutral category that upholds the white subject as raceless and unmarked and ensures that the benefits that accrue to whites not merely include economic, political, and social gains but also increase their self-sufficiency, ontological and epistemological sanctuary, and guarantee the satisfaction of their conscious as well as unconscious desires. In other words, whiteness instills in whites the conception of white privilege as a guarantee of power, that which blacks do not possess. Whiteness, as Cooper notes, "has been constructed in ways that reinforce the exclusion and invalidation of the experiences of those who fail to meet the criteria for acceptance into the powerful ruling class." In this sense, it is paramount to problematize the ways whiteness has shaped, continues to shape, and will continue to shape black political thought unless whiteness is denormalized.

Conclusion

To compile in a single book "black political thought" in its entirety is an enormous challenge because there are so many important scholars that must be included in such a book. Furthermore, to account for the multifaceted concerns, intellectual backgrounds, and the array of political theorizing that constitutes black political thought, it is important not to treat black political thought as if a "black perspective" is what makes it political. In fact, the chapters in each section are by no means an exhaustive account of black political thought. There are more details to add, subtract, refine, reformulate, and so forth. But, I am confident that the included writings will inspire the readers to think critically and engage with the challenges of black political thought. The upshot is that *Black Political Thought: From David Walker to the Present* is not directed only at students and instructors. It is compiled in such a way that it offers its readers a refreshing guide to black political thinking in the past, present, and future. At the same time, readers will find this text insightful, useful, and, most of all, engaging.

PART I
Slavery and Its Discontents

BRENDA E. STEVENSON

Let your motto be resistance! resistance! RESISTANCE!

Black political thought in the nineteenth-century United States unequivocally centered on the inequality of African and African descended peoples, both enslaved and free. There were other themes that were more specific in nature, particularly those associated with exemplars and conditions of a gendered black society. Black manhood, and to a much lesser extent black womanhood, were significant points of departure. So too was insisting on the importance of education, the availability of paid labor and humane working conditions, racial etiquette discourse and the lingering issue of colonization, or at least disparate emigration, recurrent in the speeches, sermons, conference agendas, and newspaper articles produced. Racial equality, however, remained the constant beat. It was manifestly pronounced and underscored, even more than the abolition of slavery. What good, after all, would it do to free slaves if their freedom was so narrow as to be unrecognizable?

The content, literary style, and even didactic deliverance of black political thought in the early nineteenth century derived from previous political iterations of black protest, resistance, and collective pathos in the Atlantic world passed down either orally or in print. The published poetry of Phillis Wheatley, along with the autobiographical accounts of Atlantic world freed slaves such as Ottobah Cugoano, Ukawsaw Gronniosaw, Olaudah Equiano, and Mary Prince and the letters of Ignacio Sancho, spoke boldly to a shared black consciousness of political, social, and economic oppression whether one was a slave, freed, or free. This consciousness included the black desire for freedom, equality, safety, material comfort, and human dignity, desires that are so painfully articulated in the writings presented here.

The African descended men and women who led black political thought movements and activist efforts for black freedom and equality lived in difficult, but hopeful times. Important outcomes regarding the legal end to the Atlantic slave trade; the gradual ending of slavery in the Northeast and its banning in the Northwest territory; along with its termination in many other places in the Americas and the Caribbean signaled an important shift in a hemispheric commitment to the institution.[1] Free people of color and the enslaved could take credit for much of this change.

Their efforts in a multiplicity of resistance forms – from armed rebellion and mass escapes to legislative petitions, lawsuits, and taking part in oral and print campaigns – fostered conditions that ended slavery in much of the nation and ignited a moral debate that concluded with the Thirteenth, Fourteenth, and Fifteenth Amendments. Eighteenth- and nineteenth-century blacks, along with allied whites and indigenous peoples, instituted the nation's first formal anti-slavery societies and campaigns for racial equality.[2]

These signs of progress, however, faced a steady stream of discouraging conditions. It certainly was not clear in 1829, when David Walker published his infamous *Appeal* – the first selection in this section – that slavery would end or free blacks would be given constitutional rights, all within the next half-century. Not only was the slave population growing rapidly, but the free black population endured mounting economic, political, and social discrimination, were outlawed in the South from gaining literacy, segregated in public facilities everywhere, disenfranchised in most places, and discouraged from taking up residence almost anywhere. North, south, east, and west, free people of color met legal and customary walls of opposition that kept them on the margins of an unwelcoming US society. The federal government offered no reprieve, but rather was itself an exemplar of racial inequality. It restricted the ability of free blacks to work in federal agencies, to become elected officials, and to participate in militias. The US Supreme Court acted likewise. It forbade the federal government from limiting slavery in the nation's territories and denied free blacks citizenship status.[3]

Anti-black race riots also were not unusual.[4] Likewise, the use of racial epithets was a common way to diminish free blacks who dared to live beyond their prescribed margins. Characterization of blacks as buffoons through minstrelsy and

---

[1] Brenda E. Stevenson, *What is Slavery?* (Cambridge: Polity Press, 2015), Kindle edition, Abolition Timeline Table, 163.

[2] Douglas Harper, "Emancipation in New York," in "Slavery in the North," http://slavenorth.com/nyemancip.htm, accessed December 12, 2013.

[3] Leon F. Litwack, *North of Slavery: The Negro in the Free States, 1790–1860* (University of Chicago Press, 1961), Kindle edition, Kindle location, Chapter 1, 32.

[4] Ibid., Chapter 3, 698–703, 951–958.

stereotypical images of blacks in political cartoons were equally popular.[5] So too was growing pro-slavery rhetoric – arguments couched in the idea that slavery was an ancient institution and part of a natural organization, or hierarchy, of mankind; i.e. blacks were slaves because they were meant to be.[6]

Is it little wonder then that the notion of free black colonization elicited a contentious national debate? Many whites supported the idea. Most free blacks did not. They believed that it was a blatant attempt to get rid of them, rather than to offer them equal rights in the land of their birth. The movement initially began as efforts by early black and white abolitionists who believed that African descended people would never be accepted as equals in American society. Some even believed that colonization could lead to a gradual end to slavery. Others hoped that blacks who returned to Africa would help to Christianize the region. Many white supporters' motives, however, derived from racist ideas of blacks' inferiority and their desire to rid their slave society altogether of the free black presence.[7]

David Walker's *Appeal* of 1829, followed closely by his compatriot Maria W. Stewart's four public lectures (1831–1833), marked the beginning of tremendous organized abolitionist and free black rights efforts that rapidly grew a national constituency. In 1830, forty free black men from eight states met to consider the condition of African Americans in the nation. One year later, William Lloyd Garrison, who would become the face of radical white abolitionism, began publishing the *Liberator Magazine* with black financial support. On January 6, 1832, Garrison formed the New England Anti-Slavery Society (NEASS). The American Anti-Slavery Society (AASS), a biracial "umbrella" organization of men and women, came into being the next year.[8] By 1838, the AASS had more than 1350 local auxiliaries and 250,000 members.[9]

Most of these men and women supported immediate abolition, not the gradualism that characterized late eighteenth-century emancipations in the Northern and middle states. This new generation of anti-slavery advocates also largely were pacifists who believed in tactics of moral suasion and non-violent protest. As the movement progressed in the nineteenth century, however, different factions developed varied strategies. Garrison's circle was considered radical because of its opposition to engaging the political process (voting, petitions to Congress, etc.) and

---

[5] Ibid., Chapter 3, 932–936, 941.

[6] Drew Gilpin Faust, *The Ideology of Slavery: Proslavery Thought in the Antebellum South, 1830–1860* (Baton Rouge, LA: Louisiana State University Press, 1981), Kindle edition, 12.

[7] Brenda E. Stevenson, *Life in Black and White: Family and Community in the Slave South* (New York: Oxford University Press), p. 277.

[8] Mark L. Kamrath, "American Anti-Slavery Society," in *Slavery in the United States: A Social, Political, and Historical Encyclopedia*, vol. 2, ed. Junius P. Rodriguez (Santa Barbara: ABC-Clio, 2007), pp. 161–162.

[9] Ibid.; Seymour Drescher, *Abolition: A History of Slavery and Antislavery* (Cambridge University Press, 2009), p. 304.

the inclusion of women as equals in membership and leadership.[10] The American and Foreign Anti-Slavery Society (AFAS), formed in 1840, perceived political participation as a viable, and valuable, strategy.[11] Many of their adherents went on to help create the pro-abolitionist Liberty Party in 1840, the Free Soil Party of 1848, and the Republican Party of 1856.[12]

Anti-slavery advocates affiliated with the AASS and the AFAS mostly agreed that the acquisition of free blacks' rights was vital to their abolitionist campaigns.[13] Free blacks, who were active participants in every faction of the abolitionist movement, certainly believed they should be equal citizens. Despite the early push to colonize them outside the nation, free people of color were a growing community in antebellum America, increasing in number from 313,000 in 1830, to 477,000 by 1860.[14] The path forward sometimes was a contentious one, with race and gender as worrisome wedges to overall solidarity.

Many of these organizations were segregated by race. African Americans believed that they had the most to gain, or lose, from the movement and, as such, always should be able to independently articulate an anti-slavery and free black civil rights plan of action. Not surprisingly, their agendas often were on the "left" of those of their most liberal white allies. Free African American men organized themselves into societies, held multi-state conventions, published newspapers, pamphlets, broadsides, biographies, and autobiographies, starred on the lecture circuits at home and abroad, and donated funds to the cause. Some also supported those political parties and activities associated with free soil and anti-slavery. The "Negro Convention" movements of the 1830s, 1840s, and 1850s, in particular, were unique sites of black, male anti-slavery strategizing, although a few women always attended.[15] While their specific agendas changed somewhat across time, delegates generally agreed that they should agitate for equal rights, educational and occupational opportunities, moral uplift, gendered responsibility, and abolition.[16] Many also supported other reforms of the day, particularly women's rights.[17]

---

[10] William Lloyd Garrison, "On the Constitution and the Union," in "The Great Crisis!," *The Liberator* 2, no. 52 (December 29, 1832), http://fair-use.org/the-liberator/1832/12/29/on-the-constitution-and-the-union, accessed July 19, 2014.

[11] Kamrath, "American Anti-Slavery Society," pp. 161–162.

[12] Eric Foner, *Free Soil, Free Labor, Free Men: The Ideology of the Republican Party before the Civil War* (New York: Oxford University Press, 1995), passim.

[13] Litwack, *North of Slavery*, Kindle location, Chapter 7, 2202–2214.

[14] Erin Bradford, "Free African American Population in the U.S., 1790–1860," www.ncpedia.org/sites/default/files/census_stats_1790–1860.pdf.

[15] Joel Schor, "The Rivalry between Frederick Douglass and Henry Highland Garnet," *The Journal of Negro History* 64, no. 1 (Winter 1979): 30–38. Also, see Litwack, *North of Slavery*, Kindle location, Chapter 7.

[16] Schor, "Rivalry."

[17] "(1888) Frederick Douglass on Women's Suffrage," *Woman's Journal* (April 14, 1888), www.blackpast.org/1888-frederick-douglass-woman-suffrage, accessed July 22, 2014.

Some anti-slavery societies also were gender segregated, or comprised mostly of youth. Massachusetts could boast of 183 local antebellum organizations, including 41 all-female societies and 13 youth groups.[18] As lecturers, petitioners, fundraisers, authors, biographers, editors, artists, sewing circle participants, fugitive slave supporters, free produce advocates, teachers, and letter writers, these women were active in every part of the abolitionist movement except as candidates for political office. They held three biracial conventions of their own at the end of the 1830s where they condemned slavery and racial prejudice, encouraged women to sign anti-slavery petitions, financially supported the movement, criticized churches for not joining the cause, and challenged other women to perceive slave females as their "sisters."[19]

The efforts of black anti-slavery female activists were folded into the larger agendas of self-help, moral uplift, and literacy for all US persons of African descent, not just slaves. They organized clubs such as the African Female Benevolent Society in Newport, Rhode Island, the Colored Female Religious and Moral Reform Society in Salem, Massachusetts, and the Minerva Literary Society of Philadelphia and were credited with founding the first women's abolition society in Salem, Massachusetts in 1832. They also helped organize biracial female societies. Likewise, many of the literary texts authored by this first significant generation of African American women authors promoted abolition.

The first half of the nineteenth century, therefore, was rife with abolitionist ideals, rhetoric, and political philosophies. The five authors featured in the following selections provide the very best examples that these literate black activists/abolitionists had to offer. Each work is meant to expose the varied and overlapping experiences, goals, and strategies of those men and women who dedicated their lives to the cause of racial equality. They paid heavy costs for their heroic work. David Walker lost his life. Henry Highland Garnet's life was threatened during the New York Draft Riots of 1863. Frederick Douglass had to relocate, for a time, to Canada and then Britain. Martin Robison Delany eventually moved his family to Canada. Maria Stewart lost her place in Boston free black society. They realized, of course, that not to act – and not to act boldly – was just as dangerous.

David Walker: Rejects Racist Ideas of Black Inferiority

"Our Wretchedness in Consequence of Slavery" is the first of four essays in David Walker's incendiary publication *Walker's Appeal, in Four Articles, Together With a Preamble to the Colored Citizens of the World, But in Particular and Very*

---

[18] Drescher, *Abolition*, p. 304.
[19] Ibid., pp. 93–94.

Expressly to Those of the United States of America ... Sept. 28th, 1829. David Walker was born of a free woman in Wilmington, North Carolina in 1785. His slave father is believed to have died before his birth. Walker left Wilmington as a young man, hoping to escape the brutality and hypocrisy of the slave South and traveled extensively in the United States before settling in Boston. There, he opened a second-hand clothing store, married, and became a noted figure in the city's free black community given his propertied status and his willingness to aid free people of color and, purportedly, fugitive slaves. Walker participated in an evangelical anti-slavery group that included, among others, Maria Stewart and William Lloyd Garrison. One year after his publication – the first book to call for slaves to mount armed resistance – David Walker was found dead in mysterious circumstances.[20]

Walker wrote "Our Wretchedness in Consequence of Slavery" in the style of a fiery sermon with many biblical references to overcoming adversity. There, he laid out clearly his reasons for his protest tract – the inhumane treatment of blacks, slave and free, in the United States. Black people, he explained, are denied economic opportunity and political rights and are taught that they are inferior to all other humans. He openly challenges the notion of black inferiority, insisting instead that the cruelty and non-Christian behavior of whites suggests that it is they who are actually inferior. In their actions, he concludes, they are more like "devils than accountable men." The author rallies blacks to be proud of their race and to fight for their freedom, a right "guaranteed to us by our Maker."

Henry Highland Garnet: The Plight of Free Blacks Intimately Tied to that of the Enslaved

Garnet first delivered his "An Address to the Slaves of the United States, 1843" at a colored convention being held in the Park Presbyterian Church in Buffalo, New York, the first of the Negro conventions to openly address the plight of slaves instead of just the free black condition. Later, Garland's "Address" appeared as an introduction to the second edition (1858) of David Walker's *Appeal*.[21] This was no coincidence since Garnet's address, like the *Appeal*, included a call to arm black men to gain their liberty. Organizers of the Buffalo convention, including William Lloyd Garrison and Frederick Douglass, worried that endorsing Garnet's "radical"

---

[20] John C. Inscoe, "David Walker, 1785–1830," *Documenting the American South*, http://docsouth.unc.edu/nc/walker/bio.html; *Dictionary of North Carolina Biography*, ed. William S. Powell (Chapel Hill, NC: University of North Carolina Press).

[21] Harrison Graves and Jake Asplaugh, "Henry Highland Garnet's 'Address to the Slaves'," *Colored Conventions: Bringing Nineteenth Century Black Organizing to Digital Life*, http://coloredconventions.org/exhibits/show/henry-highland-garnet-address.

speech as representative of their efforts would alarm their white audiences and supporters.[22]

There is no question that Garnet was especially concerned with slaves, and for good reason. He too was born a slave in Maryland in 1815 and escaped with his family ten years later.[23] Residing as fugitives in New York, the family was never secure. Garnet, however, did manage to acquire a sound education at a local African free school and later studied navigation. His travels, and his fragile hold on freedom given his fugitive status, framed his political ideology in support of colonization. Garnet made the decision to move to England in 1850, and two years later to Jamaica. As an ordained Presbyterian minister, he worked abroad as both an abolitionist and missionary. He desired to move to Africa to preach Christianity, forming the African Civilization Society in 1859. Like many black ex-patriates, Garnet returned to the United States at the beginning of the Civil War in order to advocate black emancipation as an outcome of the war. He preached before the House of Representatives in February 1865, becoming the first black person to do so. Henry Highland Garnet eventually did move to Liberia, dying there in 1882.[24]

His "Address to the Slaves" before the Buffalo convention begins with a denunciation of slavery as a moral wrong and connects the conditions of enslaved and free blacks. One could not be free without the other being free, he asserts, underscoring the existing familial ties between them. Like others, Garnet's speech emphasizes the hypocrisy of white Christians whose greed and lust are responsible for black oppression and dehumanization. Garnet also directly appeals to enslaved men, as men, to protect their women from rape and concubinage by the "unbridled lusts of incarnate devils." He urges them to always resist their enslavement, to refuse to work without compensation, and to be prepared to die for their freedom as did other heroic men, black and white, such as Denmark Vesey, Nat Turner, Toussaint L'Overture, George Washington, and the Marquis de Lafayette.

Frederick Douglass: The Hypocrisy of America's Democracy

There was no more famed abolitionist than Frederick Douglass, the great political thinker, orator, editor, reformer, author, and exemplar of black excellence in a generation of exceptional political activists. "What to the Slave is the Fourth of July?," which Douglass delivered before the Rochester Ladies Anti-Slavery Society on

---

[22] Graves and Asplaugh, "Henry Highland Garnet's 'Address to the Slaves'." Available at: http://coloredconventions.org/exhibits/show/henry-highland-garnet-address/context-of-the-address-.

[23] Anna Mae Duane and Thomas Thurston, "Henry Highland Garnet," The New York African Free School Collection, New York Public Library, www.nyhistory.org/web/africanfreeschool/bios/henry-highland-garnet.html.

[24] Ibid.

July 5, 1852, is a popular example of his political reasoning and concerns written at the peak of his anti-slavery activism.

Frederick Augustus Washington Bailey was born a slave in Talbot County on Maryland's eastern shore in 1818, but managed to escape from bondage at the age of 20. Douglass was "the" star on the abolitionist lecture circuit in the United States and abroad, not only because he offered the "authentic" voice of a slave, but also because of his growing eloquence, obvious intelligence, and handsome demeanor. He came to publish three important antebellum newspapers, *The North Star, Frederick Douglass' Paper*, and *The Douglass Monthly* and to author three autobiographies, among other works. Douglass also campaigned tirelessly to persuade President Lincoln to allow black troops to fight during the Civil War, and to use the war as a way to end slavery nationally.[25]

Frederick Douglass' "What to the Slave is the Fourth of July?" reiterates the themes of Walker and Garnet, particularly their denunciation of the ideals and morals of white Christian citizens in the United States. Taking to task the hypocrisy of a celebration of US independence from British "oppression," Douglass is clear that the idea of a "free" democratic America is a sham. The nation "is false to the past," the great orator asserts, "false to the present, and solemnly binds herself to be false to the future." Slavery is "the great sin and shame of America!"

Martin Robison Delany: Black Self-Determination is Essential

Martin Robison Delany's "Comparative Condition of the Colored People of the United States" is the second chapter of his 1852 monograph *The Condition, Elevation, Emigration, and Destiny of the Colored People of the United States, Politically Considered*. Like Garnet, Delany espoused colonization. Unlike Garnet, he rejected emigration to Liberia because he believed its leadership was corrupt. He promoted instead black movement to Central and South America.

Born in Virginia to a free, skilled, literate seamstress and an enslaved carpenter, Martin Delany moved with the free members of his family to Pennsylvania when his mother was found guilty of teaching her children, a crime in Virginia. In Pittsburgh, Delany was able to acquire a formal education, including courses in classical languages. He later apprenticed as a physician and was even admitted to Harvard Medical School, but was unable to attend because of protests from fellow

[25] Regarding Frederick Douglass see: Frederick Douglass, *Narrative of the Life of Frederick Douglass* (Edison, NJ: Chartwell Books, 2015); John Blassingame, John McKivigan, and Peter Hinks (eds.), *The Frederick Douglass Papers*, 4 vols. (New Haven, CT: Yale University Press, 1979–1991); Philip S. Foner (ed.), *The Life and Writings of Frederick Douglass*, 4 vols. (New York: International Publishers, 1955); David Blight, "Frederick Douglass, 1818–1895," http://docsouth .unc.edu/neh/douglass/bio.html.

white students. Delany also managed to travel widely in the Deep South, gaining a first-hand account of slavery there. He expressed his abolitionist sentiments as an author, lecturer, and newspaperman. Delany founded his own paper, *Mystery*, and later helped Frederick Douglass to edit the *North Star*. Unable to tolerate the treatment of blacks in the United States, he moved his family to Canada in 1856. Many regarded Martin Delany as a black separatist, but he was not alone in his views. Moreover, Delany did not give up completely on the United States. He returned to fight in the Civil War becoming, in 1865, the first black commissioned officer with the rank of major.[26]

Delany's "Comparative Condition of the Colored People of the United States" insists on a common theme found elsewhere in these writings assembled here – that there were few differences between the slave and free blacks in American society, with the exceptions that "we are defacto masters of ourselves and joint rulers of our own domestic society." In "Comparative Condition," Delany encourages his black audience to be both self-determinists and politicians, particularly in the effort to acquire equal rights and self-governance. Delany's emphasis on self-determination is important because some white abolitionists of the era worried that their black peers were not satisfied with white anti-slavery efforts. Delany confronts this concern openly, explaining in no uncertain terms that he believes that the cause of anti-slavery should be a black racial project. He reminds his audience in support of this conclusion that "Anti-slavery took its rise among colored men ... our [white] Anti-Slavery brethren were converts of the colored men, in behalf of their elevation." Consequently, black abolitionists should be able to speak and act for themselves and for the sake of this "holy" movement without "people thinking that they oppose or criticize white abolitionists."

Maria W. Stewart: Foundations of Female Political Activism

Maria W. Miller Stewart, the author of "Why Sit Ye Here and Die," a speech that she gave in 1832, became the first American-born woman to hold a series of public lectures before a gender-mixed audience. Stewart was born free in Connecticut, but orphaned young, she became the servant in a white minister's home in Hartford. There, she gained literacy skills, but not the formal education that she wanted. Stewart studied the Bible carefully, and after leaving Connecticut to move to Boston where she married a black seaman, she was able to study history and classical literature. She also became part of a Christian/abolitionist group of David Walker's. Inspired by her recent conversion to evangelical Christianity

---

[26] Eleanor Stanford, "Martin R. Delany (1812–1885)," *Encyclopedia Virginia*, www.encyclopediavirginia.org/Delany_Martin_R_1812–1885#start_entry.

and the work of her abolitionist friends, Stewart felt it was her duty to lecture, teach, preach, and bully, if necessary, free blacks into moral reform and political action – a difficult path for a female in the early 1830s. In so doing, however, Maria Stewart became an early symbol of female activism and reform that became so important in the decades before the Civil War. Stewart, who gave four public lectures between 1831 and 1833, distributing copies to her audience and others, spoke on almost every issue relevant to the black community at that time – colonization, emancipation, the expansion of rights for blacks, the role of women in free black political and social struggles, the necessity of educational and economic opportunities for blacks, racial unity, and black self-determination.[27]

In "Why Sit Ye Here and Die," given at Boston's Franklin Hall, Stewart centers her attention on the poor living and working conditions of urban free blacks. "Tell us no more of southern slavery," she pronounces boldly, given the economic marginality free people of color suffered. It is to black women, however, that she dedicates much of this speech. In it, Stewart asks her "sisters" to make certain that they adhere to the proper gender conventions of the day – to be "fair," "spotless," and "innocent" so that those around them can witness that black women are the intellectual and moral equals to white females, worthy of the same opportunities and protections.

QUESTIONS

(1) Based on the readings in this section, "Slavery and Its Discontents," describe and explain the impact of slavery on the slaves as well as their masters.

(2) There is a clear relation between the arguments for the end of slavery and Christian morality. What are some of the issues about slavery presented and discussed in the readings that go again Christian morality?

(3) Why was it not necessary to prove that the slave was a human being? Did the laws and customs in place that constantly dehumanized the slaves disprove such a claim?

(4) What are some of the concerns presented by the authors in this section on slavery and are the authors' concerns similar and/or different?

(5) What are some of the factors presented in this section that reinforced and upheld the second-class position of blacks during slavery?

FURTHER READINGS

- Booker T. Washington, *Up from Slavery: An Autobiography* (New York: Doubleday, 1909). Available at: www.bartleby.com/1004/.

---

[27] Brenda E. Stevenson, "Maria Stewart and the Public Domain of Female Abolitionism," unpublished manuscript, Wesleyan University "Imperatives of Leadership" Lecture Series, 1984.

- Delilah L. Beasley, "Slavery in California," *Journal of Negro History* 3, no. 1 (January 1918): 33–44.
- Edward W. Blyden, "The Call of Providence to the Descendants of Africa in America," in *Liberia's Offering* (New York: John A. Gray, 1862), pp. 67–91.
- Frederick Douglass, *The Narrative of the Life of Frederick Douglass, an American Slave* (Boston, MA: The Antislavery Office, 1845).
- H. Ford Douglas, "I Do Not Believe in the Antislavery of Abraham Lincoln," (1860). Available at: www.blackpast.org/1860-h-ford-douglas-i-do-not-believe-antislavery-abraham-lincoln.
- Harriet Jacobs, *Incidents in the Life of a Slave Girl* (Boston, 1861 and Detroit, MI: Negro History Press, 1969).
- Henry Highland Garnet, *The Past and Present Conditions, and the Destiny of the Colored Race: A Discourse Delivered at the Fifteenth Anniversary of the Female Benevolent Society of Troy N.Y. Feb. 14, 1858* (Troy, NY: Steam Press of JC ... and Company).
- Maria W. Stewart, "A Lecture on African Rights and Liberty." An address delivered at the African Masonic Hall (Boston, MA, February 27, 1833).
- Solomon Northup, *Twelve Years a Slave*, ed. Sue L. Eakin and Joseph Logsdon (Baton Rouge: Louisiana State University Press, 1968).
- William Wells Brown, *Narrative of William Wells Brown, a Fugitive Slave* (Boston: The Anti-Slavery Office, 1848).

1 Our Wretchedness in Consequence of Slavery

DAVID WALKER

The outspoken writer, anti-slavery activist, and abolitionist David Walker (1796–1830) was born free in Wilmington, North Carolina. His mother was free and his father was a slave who died before Walker was born. Despite the fact that Walker was a free black man, he felt suffocated growing up in a slave society and found the institution of slavery unbearable for all blacks. In 1827, he moved to Boston, Massachusetts, where after the American Revolutionary War (1775–1783) slavery was abolished. It was in Boston that Walker would become a writer for *Freedom's Journal*, the first black journal, which lasted for about two years (1827–1829). In 1830, Walker published *Walker's Appeal, in Four Articles, Together With a Preamble to the Colored Citizens of the World, But in Particular and Very Expressly to Those of the United States of America ... Sept. 28th, 1829*. The extract "Our Wretchedness in Consequence of Slavery" is taken from this publication in which he condemns the many atrocities of slavery and encourages blacks to take a role in fighting their oppression and rise up against their masters.

My beloved brethren: The Indians of North and of South America—the Greeks—the Irish, subjected under the king of Great Britain—the Jews, that ancient people of the Lord—the inhabitants of the islands of the sea—in fine, all the inhabitants of the earth, (except however, the sons of Africa) are called men, and of course are, and ought to be free. But we, (coloured people) and our children are brutes!! and of course are, and ought to be SLAVES to the American people and their children forever! to dig their mines and work their farms; and thus go on enriching them, from one generation to another with our blood and our tears!!!!

I promised in a preceding page to demonstrate to the satisfaction of the most incredulous, that we, (coloured people of the United States of America) are the most wretched, degraded and abject set of beings that ever lived since the world began, and that the white Americans having reduced us to the wretched state of slavery, treat us in that condition more cruel (they being an enlightened and Christian people) than any heathen nation did any people whom it had reduced to our condition. These affirmations are so well confirmed in the minds of all unprejudiced men, who have taken the trouble to read histories, that they need no elucidation from me. But to put them beyond all doubt, I refer you in the first place to the children of Jacob, or of Israel in Egypt, under Pharaoh and his people. Some of my brethren do not know who Pharaoh and the Egyptians were—I know it to be a fact, that some of them take the Egyptians to have been a gang of devils, not knowing any better, and that they (Egyptians) having got possession of the Lord's people, treated them nearly as cruel as Christians Americans do us, at the present day. For the information of such, I would only mention that the Egyptians were Africans or coloured people, such as we are—some of them yellow and others dark—a mixture of Ethiopians and the natives of Egypt—about the same as you see the coloured people of the United States at the present day,—I say, I call your attention then, to the children of Jacob, while I point out particularly to you his son Joseph, among the rest, in Egypt.

"And Pharaoh, said unto Joseph, thou shalt be over my house, and according unto thy word shall all my people be ruled; only in the throne will I be greater than thou."*

"And Pharaoh said unto Joseph, see, I have set thee over all the land of Egypt." †

"And Pharaoh said unto Joseph, I am Pharaoh, and without thee shall no man lift up his hand or foot in all of the land of Egypt." ‡

Now I appeal to heaven and to earth, and particularly to the American people themselves, who cease not to declare that our condition is not hard, and that we are comparatively satisfied to rest in wretchedness and misery, under them and their children. Not, indeed, to show me a coloured President, a Governor, a Legislator, a Senator, a Mayor, or an Attorney at the Bar.—But to show me a man of colour, who holds the low office of a Constable, or one who sits in a Juror Box, even on a case of one of his wretched brethren, throughout this great Republic !!—But let us pass Joseph the son of Israel a little farther in review, as he existed with that heathen nation.

"And Pharaoh called Joseph's name Zaphnath-paaneah; and he gave him to wife Asenath the daughter of Potipherah priest of On. And Joseph went out over all the land of Egypt." §

Compare the above, with the American institutions. Do they not institute laws to prohibit us from marrying among the whites? I would wish, candidly, however, before the Lord, to be understood, that I would not give a pinch of snuff to be married to any white person I ever saw in all the days of my life. And I do say it, that the black man, or man of colour, who will leave his own colour (provided he can get one, who is good for any thing) and marry a white woman, to be a double slave to her, just because she is white, ought to be treated by her as he surely will be, *viz*: as a NIGER!!! It is not, indeed, what I care about inter-marriages with the whites, which induced me to pass this subject in review; for the Lord knows, that there is a day coming when they will be glad enough to get into the company of the blacks, notwithstanding, we are, in this generation, levelled by them, almost on a level with the brute creation; and some of us they treat even worse than they

---

* See Genesis, chap. xli. v. 40. † v. 41. ‡v. 44. §v. 45.

do the brutes that perish. I only made this extract to show how much lower we are held, and how much more cruel we are treated by the Americans, than were the children of Jacob, by the Egyptians. We will notice the sufferings of Israel some further, under heathen Pharaoh, compared with ours under the enlightened Christians of America.

"And Pharaoh spake unto Joseph, saying, thy father and thy brethren are come unto thee: The land of Egypt is before thee: in the best of the land make thy father and brethren to dwell; in the land of Goshen let them dwell; and if thou knowest any men of activity among them, then make them rulers over cattle."*

I ask those people who treat us so well, Oh! I ask them, where is the most barren spot of land which they have given unto us? Israel had the most fertile land in all Egypt. Need I mention the very notorious fact, that I have known a poor man of colour, who laboured night and day, to acquire a little money, and having acquired it, he vested it in a small piece of land, and got him a house erected thereon, and having paid for the whole, he moved his family into it, where he was suffered to remain but nine months, when he was cheated out of his property by a white man, and driven out of door!—And is not this the case generally? Can a man of colour buy a piece of land and keep it peaceably? Will not some white man try to get it from him, even if it is in a mud hole? I need not comment any farther on a subject, which all, both black and white, will readily admit. But I must, really, observe that in this very city, when a man of colour dies, if he owned any real estate it most generally falls into the hands of some white person. The wife and children of the deceased may weep and lament if they please, but the estate will be kept snug enough by its white possessors.

But to prove farther that the condition of the Israelites was better under the Egyptians than ours is under the whites. I call upon the professing Christians, I call upon the philanthropist, I call upon the very tyrant himself, to show me a page of history, either sacred or profane, on which a verse can be found, which maintains, that the Egyptians heaped the insupportable insult upon the children of Israel, by telling them that they were not of the human family. Can the whites deny this charge? Have they not, after having reduced us to the deplorable con- dition of slaves under their feet, held us up as descending originally from the tribes of Monkeys or Orangutans? O! my God! I appeal to every man of feeling—is not this insupportable? Is it not heaping the most gross insult upon our miseries, because they have got us under their feet and we cannot help ourselves? Oh! pity us we pray thee, Lord Jesus, Master.—Has Mr. Jefferson declared to the world, that we are inferior to the whites, both in the endowments of our bodies and of minds? It is indeed surprising, that a man of such great learning, combined with such excellent natural parts, should speak so of a set of men in chains. I do not know

---

* Genesis, chap. xlvii. v. 5, 6.

what to compare it to, unless, like putting one wild deer in an iron cage, where it will be secured, and hold another by the side of the same, then let it go, and expect the one in the cage to run as fast as the one at liberty. So far, my brethren, were the Egyptians from heaping these insults upon their slaves, that Pharaoh's daughter took Moses, a son of Israel, for her own, as will appear by the following.

"And Pharaoh's daughter said unto her, [Moses' mother] take this child away, and nurse it for me, and I will pay thee thy wages. And the woman took the child [Moses] and nursed it. And the child grew, and she brought him unto Pharaoh's daughter and he became her son. And she called his name Moses: and she said because I drew him out of the water."*

In all probability, Moses would have become Prince Regent to the throne, and no doubt, in process of time but he would have been seated on the throne of Egypt. But he had rather suffer shame, with the people of God, than to enjoy pleasures with that wicked people for a season. O! that the coloured people were long since of Moses' excellent disposition, instead of courting favour with, and telling news and lies to our natural enemies, against each other—aiding them to keep their hellish chains of slavery upon us. Would we not long before this time, have been respectable men, instead of such wretched victims of oppression as we are? Would they be able to drag our mothers, our fathers, our wives, our children and ourselves, around the world in chains and hand-cuffs as they do, to dig up gold and silver for them and theirs? This question, my brethren, I leave for you to digest; and may God Almighty force it home to your hearts. Remember that unless you are united, keeping your tongues within your teeth, you will be afraid to trust your secrets to each other, and thus perpetuate our miseries under the Christians ! ! ! ! Addition,—Remember, also to lay humble at the feet of our Lord and Master Jesus Christ, with prayers and fastings. Let our enemies go on with their butcheries, and at once fill up their cup. Never make an attempt to gain our freedom of natural right, from under our cruel oppressors and murderers, until you see your way clear†; when that hour arrives and you move, be not afraid or dismayed; for be you assured that Jesus Christ the King of heaven and of earth who is the God of justice and of armies, will surely go before you. And those enemies who have for hundreds of years stolen our rights and kept us ignorant of Him and His

---

* See Exodus, chap ii. v. 9, 10.
† It is not to be understood here, that I mean for us to wait until God shall take us by the hair of our heads and drag us out of abject wretchedness and slavery, nor do I mean to convey the idea for us to wait until our enemies shall make preparations, and call us to seize those preparations, take it away from them, and put every thing before us to death, in order to gain our freedom which God has given us. For you must remember that we are men as well as they. God has been pleased to give us two eyes, two hands, two feet, and some sense in our heads as well as they. They have no more right to hold us in slavery than we have to hold them, we have just as much right, in the sight of God, to hold them and their children in slavery and wretchedness, as they have to hold us, and no more.

divine worship, he will remove. Millions of whom, are this day, so ignorant and avaricious, that they cannot conceive how God can have an attribute of justice, and show mercy to us because it pleased Him to make us black—which color, Mr. Jefferson calls unfortunate !!!!!! As though we are not as thankful to our God for having made us as it pleased himself, as they (the whites,) for having made them white. They think because they hold us in their infernal chains of slavery that we wish to be white, or of their color—but they are dreadfully deceived—we wish to be just as it pleased our Creator to have made us, and no avaricious and unmerciful wretches, have any business to make slaves of or hold us in slavery. How would they like for us to make slaves of, or hold them in cruel slavery, and murder them as they do us? But is Mr. Jefferson's assertions true? viz. "that it is unfortunate for us that our Creator has been pleased to make us black." We will not take his say so, for the fact. The world will have an opportunity to see whether it is unfortunate for us, that our Creator has made us darker than the whites.

Fear not the number and education of our *enemies*, against whom we shall have to contend for our lawful right; guaranteed to us by our Maker; for why should we be afraid, when God is, and will continue, (if we continue humble) to be on our side?

The man who would not fight under our Lord and Master Jesus Christ, in the glorious and heavenly cause of freedom and of God—to be delivered from the most wretched, abject and servile slavery, that ever a people was afflicted with since the foundation of the world, to the present day—ought to be kept with all of his children or family, in slavery, or in chains, to be butchered by his cruel enemies.

I saw a paragraph, a few years since, in a South Carolina paper, which, speaking of the barbarity of the Turks, it said: "The Turks are the most barbarous people in the world—they treat the Greeks more like *brutes* than human beings." And in the same paper was an advertisement, which said: "Eight well built Virginia and Maryland Negro fellows and four *wenches* will positively be *sold* this day, *to the highest bidder*!" And what astonished me still more was, to see in this same *humane paper*!! the cuts of three men, with clubs and budgets on their backs, and an advertisement offering a considerable sum of money for their apprehension and delivery. I declare, it is really so funny to hear the Southerners and Westerners of this country talk about *barbarity*, that it is positively, enough to make a man *smile*.

The sufferings of the Helots among the Spartans, were somewhat severe, it is true, but to say that theirs, were as severe as ours among the Americans I do most strenuously deny—for instance, can any man show me an article on a page of ancient history which specifies, that, the Spartans chained, and hand-cuffed the Helots, and dragged them from their wives and children, children from their parents, mothers from their suckling babes, wives from their husbands, driving them from one end of the country to the other? Notice the Spartans were heathens, who lived long before our Divine Master made his appearance in the flesh. Can Christian Americans deny these barbarous cruelties? Have you not, Americans, having subjected us under you, added to these miseries, by insulting us in telling us to our face, because we are helpless, that we are not of the human family? I ask you, O! Americans, I ask you, in the name of the Lord, can you deny these charges? Some perhaps may deny, by saying, that they never thought or said that we were not men. But do not actions speak louder than words?—have they not made provisions for the Greeks, and Irish? Nations who have never done the least thing for them, while *we*, who have enriched their country with our blood and tears—have dug up gold and silver for them and their children, from generation to generation, and are in more miseries than any other people under heaven, are not seen, but by comparatively, a handful of the American people? There are indeed, more ways to kill a dog, besides choking it to death with butter. Further. The Spartans or Lacedaemonians, had some frivolous pretext, for enslaving the Helots, for they (Helots) while being free inhabitants of Sparta, stirred up an intestine commotion, and were, by the Spartans subdued, and made prisoners of war. Consequently they and their children were condemned to perpetual slavery.*

I have been for years troubling the pages of historians, to find out what our fathers have done to the *white Christians of America*, to merit such condign punishment as they have inflicted on them, and do continue to inflict on us their children. But I must aver, that my researches have hitherto been to no effect. I have therefore, come to the immovable conclusion, that they (Americans) have, and do continue to punish us for nothing else, but for enriching them and their country. For I cannot conceive of any thing else. Nor will I ever believe otherwise, until the Lord shall convince me.

The world knows, that slavery as it existed among the Romans, (which was the primary cause of their destruction) was, comparatively speaking, no more than a *cypher*, when compared with ours under the Americans. Indeed, I should not have noticed the Roman slaves, had not the very learned and penetrating Mr. Jefferson said, "when a master was murdered, all his slaves in the same house, or within hearing, were condemned to death."† Here let me ask Mr. Jefferson, (but he is gone to answer at the bar of God, for the deeds done in his body while living,) I therefore ask the whole American people, had I not rather die, or be put to death, than to be a slave to any tyrant, who takes not only my own, but my wife and children's lives by the inches? Yea, would I meet death with avidity far! far!! in preference to such *servile submission* to the murderous hands of tyrants. Mr. Jefferson's very severe remarks on us have been so extensively argued upon by men whose attainments in literature, I shall never be able to reach, that I would

---

* See Dr. Goldsmith's *History of Greeks*—page 9. See also Plutarch's Lives. The Helots subdued by Agis, king of Sparta.

† See his notes on Virginia, page 210.

not have meddled with it, were it not to solicit each of my brethren, who has the spirit of a man, to buy a copy of Mr. Jefferson's "Notes on Virginia," and put it in the hand of his son. For let no one of us suppose that the refutations which have been written by our white friends are enough—they are *whites*—we are *blacks*. We, and the world wish to see the changes of Mr. Jefferson refuted by the blacks *themselves*, according to their chance; for we must remember that what the whites have written respecting this subject, is other men's labours, and did not emanate from the blacks. I know well, that there are some talents and learning among the coloured people of this country, which we have not a chance to develope, in consequence of oppression; but our oppression ought not to hinder us from acquiring all we can.—For we will have a chance to develope them by and by. God will not suffer us, always to be oppressed. Our sufferings will come to an *end*, in spite of all the Americans this side of *eternity*. Then we will want all the learning and talents among ourselves, and perhaps more, to govern ourselves.—"Every dog must have its day," the American's is coming to an end.

But let us review Mr. Jefferson's remarks respecting us some further. Comparing our miserable fathers, with the learned philosophers of Greece, he says:

> Yet notwithstanding these and other discouraging circumstances among the Romans, their slaves were often their rarest artists. They excelled too, in science, insomuch as to be usually employed as tutors to their master's children; Epictetus, Terence and Phædrus, were slaves,—but they were of the race of whites. It is not their *condition* then, but *nature*, which has produced the distinction.*

See this, my brethren!! Do you believe that this assertion is swallowed by millions of the whites? Do you know that Mr. Jefferson was one of as great characters as ever lived among the whites? See his writings for the world, and public labours for the United States of America. Do you believe that the assertions of such a man, will pass away into oblivion unobserved by this people and the world? If you do you are much mistaken—See how the American people treat us—have we souls in our bodies? Are we men who have any spirits at all? I know that there are many *swell-bellied* fellows among us, whose greatest object is to fill their stomachs. Such I do not mean—I am after those who know and feel, that we are MEN, as well as other people; to them, I say, that unless we try to refute Mr. Jefferson's arguments respecting us, we will only establish them.

But the slaves among the Romans. Every body who has read history, knows, that as soon as a slave among the Romans obtained his freedom, he could rise to the greatest eminence in the State, and there was no law instituted to hinder a slave from buying his freedom. Have not the Americans instituted laws to hinder us from obtaining our freedom? Do any deny this charge? Read the laws of

---

* See his notes on Virginia page 211.

Virginia, North Carolina, &c. Further: have not the Americans instituted laws to prohibit a man of colour from obtaining and holding any office whatever, under the government of the United States of America? Now, Mr. Jefferson tells us, that our condition is not so hard, as the slaves were under the Romans.

It is time for me to bring this article to a close. But before I close it, I must observe to my brethren that at the close of the first Revolution in this country, with Great Britain, there were but thirteen States in the Union, now there are twenty-four, most of which are slave-holding States, and the whites are dragging us around in chains and in handcuffs, to their new States and Territories to work their mines and farms, to enrich them and their children—and millions of them believing firmly that we being a little darker than they, were made by our Creator to be an inheritance to them and their children forever—the same as a parcel of *brutes.*

Are we MEN!!—I ask you, O my brethren! are we MEN? Did our Creator make us to be slaves to dust and ashes like ourselves? Are they not dying worms as well as we? Have they not to make their appearance before the tribunal of Heaven, to answer for the deeds done in the body, as well as we? Have we any other Master but Jesus Christ alone? Is he not their Master as well as ours?—What right then, have we to obey and call any other Master, but Himself? How we could be so *submissive* to a gang of men, whom we cannot tell whether they are as good as ourselves or not, I never could conceive. However, this is shut up with the Lord, and we cannot precisely tell—but I declare, we judge men by their works.

The whites have always been an unjust, jealous, unmerciful, avaricious and blood-thirsty set of beings, always seeking after power and authority.—We view them all over the confederacy of Greece, where they were first known to be anything, (in consequence of education) we see them there, cutting each other's throats—trying to subject each other to wretchedness and misery—to effect which, they used all kinds of deceitful, unfair, and unmerciful means. We view them next in Rome, where the spirit of tyranny and deceit raged still higher. We view them in Gaul, Spain, and in Britain. —In fine, we view them all over Europe, together with what were scattered about in Asia and Africa, as heathens, and we see them acting more like devils than accountable men. But some may ask, did not the blacks of Africa, and the mulattoes of Asia, go on in the same way as did the whites of Europe. I answer, no—they never were half so avaricious, deceitful and unmerciful as the whites, according to their knowledge.

But we will leave the whites or Europeans as heathens, and take a view of them as Christians, in which capacity we see them as cruel, if not more so than ever. In fact, take them as a body, they are ten times more cruel, avaricious and unmerciful than ever they were; for while they were heathens, they were bad enough it is true, but it is positively a fact that they were not quite so audacious as to go and take vessel loads of men, women and children, and in cold blood, and through devilishness, throw them into the sea, and murder them in all kind of ways. While they were heathens, they were too ignorant for such barbarity. But being Christians, enlightened and sensible, they are completely prepared for such hellish cruelties. Now suppose God were to give them more sense, what would they do? If it were possible, would they not *dethrone* Jehovah and seat themselves upon his throne? I therefore, in the name and fear of the Lord God of Heaven and of earth, divested of prejudice either on the side of my colour or that of the whites, advance my suspicion of them, whether they are as *good by nature* as we are or not. Their actions, since they were known as a people, have been the reverse, I do indeed suspect them, but this, as I before observed, is shut up with the Lord, we cannot exactly tell, it will be proved in succeeding generations.—The whites have had the essence of the gospel as it was preached by my master and his apostles—the Ethiopians have not, who are to have it in its meridian splendor—the Lord will give it to them to their satisfaction. I hope and pray my God, that they will make good use of it, that it may be well with them.*

QUESTIONS

(1) One of the main arguments presented by David Walker in "Our Wretchedness in Consequence of Slavery" is for the abolition of slavery. What were some of the impacts of Walker's appeal to end slavery on slaves, free blacks, and the abolitionist movement in the South?

(2) Given that God created blacks and whites as the same, why, for Walker, is it so worrisome for Thomas Jefferson in "Notes on Virginia" to speak of blacks as inferior to whites both physically and mentally?

(3) What is the significance of David Walker's "Our Wretchedness in Consequence of Slavery" for any discussion on slavery?

(4) Describe and explain how whites violated the Christian principles of equal justice for all by enslaving blacks?

(5) In examining slavery throughout the world, Walker discusses the bondage wreaked by Pharaoh on the Israelites and the slavery of the Romans and the Spartans. Is Walker justified to argue that slavery in the United States was the most wretched in comparison?

---

* It is my solemn belief, that if ever the world becomes Christianized, (which must certainly take place before long) it will be through the means, under God of the *Blacks*, who are now held in wretchedness, and degradation, by the white *Christians* of the world, who before they learn to do justice to us before our Maker—and be reconciled to us, and reconcile us to them, and by that means have clear consciences before God and man.—Send out Missionaries to convert the Heathens, many of whom after they cease to worship gods, which neither see nor hear, become ten times more the children of Hell, then ever they were, why what is the reason? Why the reason is obvious, they must learn to do justice at home, before they go into distant lands, to display their charity, Christianity, and benevolence; when they learn to do justice, God will accept their offering, (no man may think that I am against Missionaries for I am not, my object is to see justice done at home, before we go to convert the Heathens.)

2 An Address to the Slaves of the United States

HENRY HIGHLAND GARNET

Henry Highland Garnet (1815–1882) was an abolitionist, minister, and educator. He was born into slavery in New Market, Kent County, Maryland. He escaped with his family to Wilmington, Delaware. When he was ten years old, he moved with his family to New York City where, from 1826 to 1833, he attended the African Free School founded on November 2, 1787 by the New York Manumission Society to promote the abolition of slaves in New York State, which was made up of rich white men including John Jay and Alexander Hamilton. Later on, he attended the Phoenix High School for Colored Youth. Garnet, in 1834, along with William H. Day and David Ruggles, established the Garrison and Literary Benevolent Society for black men. In 1839, Garnet graduated from Oneida Theological Institute in Whitesboro, New York. During the Civil War, Garnet was adviser to President Abraham Lincoln. In 1872, Garnet helped to create the Cuban Anti-Slavery Society in New York City. He was appointed United States Minister to Liberia and died there in 1882. The extract, "An Address to the Slaves of the United States," was first read in 1843 at the National Convention held at Buffalo, NY, and was rejected twice by the National Convention. It was not until 1848 that "An Address to the Slaves of the United States" would appear as an introduction in the second edition of David Walker's *Appeal to the Colored Citizens of the World.*

Brethren and Fellow Citizens:—Your brethren of the North, East, and West have been accustomed to meet together in National Conventions, to sympathize with each other, and to weep over your unhappy condition. In these meetings we have addressed all classes of the free, but we have never, until this time, sent a word of consolation and advice to you. We have been contented in sitting still and mourning over your sorrows, earnestly hoping that before this day your sacred liberty would have been restored. But, we have hoped in vain. Years have rolled on, and tens of thousands have been borne on streams of blood and tears, to the shores of eternity. While you have been oppressed, we have also been partakers with you; nor can we be free while you are enslaved. We, therefore, write to you as being bound with you. Many of you are bound to us, not only by the ties of a common humanity, but we are connected by the more tender relations of parents, wives, husbands, children, brothers, and sisters, and friends. As such we most affectionately address you.

Slavery has fixed a deep gulf between you and us, and while it shuts out from you the relief and consolation which your friends would willingly render, it affects and persecutes you with a fierceness which we might not expect to see in the fiends of hell. But still the Almighty Father of mercies has left to us a glimmering ray of hope, which shines out like a lone star in a cloudy sky. Mankind are becoming wiser, and better—the oppressor's power is fading, and you, every day, are becoming better informed, and more numerous. Your grievances, brethren, are many. We shall not attempt, in this short address, to present to the world all the dark catalogue of this nation's sins, which have been committed upon an innocent people. Nor is it indeed necessary, for you feel them from day to day, and all the civilized world look upon them with amazement.

Two hundred and twenty-seven years ago, the first of our injured race were brought to the shores of America. They came not with glad spirits to select their homes in the New World. They came not with their own consent, to find an unmolested enjoyment of the blessings of this fruitful soil. The first dealings they had with men calling themselves Christians, exhibited to them the worst features of corrupt and sordid hearts; and convinced them that no cruelty is too great, no villainy and no robbery too abhorrent for even enlightened men to perform, when influenced by avarice and lust. Neither did they come flying upon the wings of Liberty, to a land of freedom. But they came with broken hearts, from their beloved native land, and were doomed to unrequited toil and deep degradation. Nor did the evil of their bondage end at their emancipation by death. Succeeding generations inherited their chains, and millions have come from eternity into time, and have returned again to the world of spirits, cursed and ruined by American slavery.

The propagators of the system, or their immediate ancestors, very soon discovered its growing evil, and its tremendous wickedness, and secret promises were made to destroy it. The gross inconsistency of a people holding slaves, who had themselves "ferried o'er the wave" for freedom's sake, was too apparent to be entirely overlooked. The voice of Freedom cried, "Emancipate your slaves." Humanity supplicated with tears for the deliverance of the children of Africa. Wisdom urged her solemn plea. The bleeding captive plead his innocence, and pointed to Christianity who stood weeping at the cross. Jehovah frowned upon the nefarious institution, and thunderbolts, red with vengeance, struggled to leap forth to blast the guilty wretches who maintained it. But all was in vain. Slavery had stretched its dark wings of death over the land, the Church stood silently by the priests prophesied falsely, and the people loved to have it so. Its throne is established, and now it reigns triumphant.

Nearly three millions of your fellow-citizens are prohibited by law and public opinion, (which in this country is stronger than law) from reading the Book of Life. Your intellect has been destroyed as much as possible, and every ray of light they have attempted to shut out from your minds. The oppressors themselves have become involved in the ruin. They have become weak, sensual, and rapacious—they have cursed you—they have cursed themselves—they have cursed the earth which they have trod.

The colonists threw the blame upon England. They said that the mother country entailed the evil upon them, and that they would rid themselves of it if they could. The world thought they were sincere, and the philanthropic pitied them. But time soon tested their sincerity. In a few years the colonists grew strong, and severed themselves from the British Government. Their independence was declared, and they took their station among the sovereign powers of the earth. The declaration was a glorious document. Sages admired it, and the patriotic of every nation reverenced the God-like sentiments which it contained. When the power of Government returned to their hands, did they emancipate the slaves? No; they rather added new links to our chains. Were they ignorant of the principles of Liberty? Certainly they were not. The sentiments of their revolutionary orators fell in burning eloquence upon their hearts, and with one voice they cried, *Liberty or Death*. Oh what a sentence was that! It ran from soul to soul like electric fire, and nerved the arm of thousands to fight in the holy cause of Freedom. Among the diversity of opinions that are entertained in regard to physical resistance, there are but a few found to gainsay that stern declaration. We are among those who do not.

Slavery! How much misery is comprehended in that single word. What mind is there that does not shrink from its direful effects? Unless the image of God be obliterated from the soul, all men cherish the love of Liberty. The nice discerning political economist does not regard the sacred right more than the untutored African who roams in the wilds of Congo. Nor has the one more right to the full enjoyment of his freedom than the other. In every man's mind the good seeds of liberty are planted, and he who brings his fellow down so low, as to make him contented with a condition of slavery, commits the highest crime against God and man. Brethren, your oppressors aim to do this. They endeavor to make you as much like brutes as possible. When they have blinded the eyes of your mind—when they have embittered the sweet waters of life— when they have shut out the light which shines from the word of God—then, and not till then, has American slavery done its perfect work.

To such Degradation it is sinful in the Extreme for you to make voluntary Submission. The divine commandments you are in duty bound to reverence and obey. If you do not obey them, you will surely meet with the displeasure of the Almighty. He requires you to love him supremely, and your neighbor as yourself— to keep the Sabbath day holy—to search the Scriptures—and bring up your children with respect for his laws, and to worship no other God but him. But slavery sets all these at nought, and hurls defiance in the face of Jehovah. The forlorn condition in which you are placed, does not destroy your moral obligation to God. You are not certain of heaven, because you suffer yourselves to remain in a state of slavery, where you cannot obey the commandments of the Sovereign of the universe. If the ignorance of slavery is a passport to heaven, then it is a blessing, and no curse, and you should rather desire its perpetuity than its abolition. God will not receive slavery, nor ignorance, nor any other state of mind, for love and obedience to him. Your condition does not absolve you from your moral obligation. The diabolical injustice by which your liberties are cloven down, *neither God; nor angels, or just men, command you to suffer for a single moment. Therefore it is your solemn and imperative duty to use every means, both moral; intellectual and physical that promises success.* If a band of heathen men should attempt to enslave a race of Christians, and to place their children under the influence of some false religion, surely Heaven would frown upon the men who would not resist such aggression, even to death. If, on the other hand, a band of Christians should attempt to enslave a race of heathen men, and to entail slavery upon them, and to keep them in heathenism in the midst of Christianity, the God of heaven would smile upon every effort which the injured might make to disenthral themselves.

Brethren, it is as wrong for your lordly oppressors to keep you in slavery, as it was for the man thief to steal our ancestors from the coast of Africa. You should therefore now use the same manner of resistance, as would have been just in our ancestors when the bloody foot prints of the first remorseless soul thief was placed upon the shores of our fatherland. The humblest peasant is as free in the sight of God as the proudest monarch that ever swayed a sceptre. Liberty is a spirit sent out from God, and like its great Author, is no respecter of persons.

Brethren, the time has come when you must act for yourselves. It is an old and true saying that, "if hereditary bondmen would be free, they must themselves strike the blow." You can plead your own cause, and do the work of emancipation better than any others. The nations of the world are moving in the great cause of universal freedom, and some of them at least will, ere long, do you justice. The combined powers of Europe have placed their broad seal of disapprobation upon the African slave trade. But in the slaveholding parts of the United States, the trade is as brisk as ever. They buy and sell you as though you were brute beasts. The North has done much—her opinion of slavery in the abstract is known. But in regard to the South, we adopt the opinion of the New York Evangelist—"We have advanced so far, that the cause apparently waits for a more effectual door to be thrown open than has been yet." We are about to point out that more effectual door. Look around you, and behold the bosoms of your loving wives heaving with untold agonies! Hear the cries of your poor children! Remember the stripes your fathers bore. Think of the torture and disgrace of your noble mothers. Think of your wretched sisters, loving virtue and purity, as they are driven into concubinage and are exposed to the unbridled lusts of incarnate devils. Think of the undying glory that hangs around the ancient name of Africa: —and forget not that you are native-born American citizens, and as such, you are justly entitled to all the rights that are granted to the freest. Think how many tears you have poured out upon the soil which you have cultivated with unrequited toil and enriched with your blood; and then go to your lordly enslavers and tell them plainly, that you *are determined to be free.* Appeal to their sense of justice, and tell them that they have no more right to oppress you, than you have to enslave them. Entreat them to remove the grievous burdens which they have imposed upon you, and to remunerate you for your labor. Promise them renewed diligence in the cultivation of the soil, if they will render to you an equivalent for your services. Point them to the increase of happiness and prosperity in the British West Indies since the Act of Emancipation. Tell them in language which they cannot misunderstand, of the exceeding sinfulness of slavery, and of a future judgment, and of the righteous retributions of an indignant God. Inform them that all you desire is *freedom*, and that nothing else will suffice. Do this, and for ever after cease to toil for the heartless tyrants, who give you no other reward but stripes and abuse. If they then commence the work of death, they, and not you, will be responsible for the consequences. You had better all die—*die immediately*, than live as slaves and entail your wretchedness upon your posterity. If you would be free in this generation, here is your only hope. However much you and all of us may desire it, there is not much hope of redemption without the shedding of blood. If you must bleed, let it all come at once—rather *die freemen, than live to be slaves.* It is impossible like the children of Israel, to make a grand exodus from the land of bondage. The Pharaohs are on both sides of the blood-red waters! You cannot move *en masse*, to the dominions of the British Queen—nor can you pass through Florida and overrun Texas, and at last find peace in Mexico. The propagators of American slavery are spending their blood and treasure, that they may plant the black flag in the heart of Mexico and riot in the halls of the Montezumas. In the language of the Rev. Robert Hall, when addressing the volunteers of Bristol, who were rushing forth to repel the invasion of Napoleon, who threatened to lay waste the fair homes of England, "Religion is too much interested in your behalf, not to shed over you her most gracious influences."

You will not be compelled to spend much time in order to become inured to hardships. From the first moment that you breathed the air of heaven, you have been accustomed to nothing else but hardships. The heroes of the American Revolution were never put upon harder fare than a peck of corn and a few herrings per week. You have not become enervated by the luxuries of life. Your sternest energies have been beaten out upon the anvil of severe trial. Slavery has done this, to make you subservient, to its own purposes; but it has done more than this, it has prepared you for any emergency. If you receive good treatment, it is what you could hardly expect; if you meet with pain, sorrow, and even death, these are the common lot of slaves.

Fellow-men! Patient sufferers! behold your dearest rights crushed to the earth! See your sons murdered, and your wives, mothers and sisters doomed to prostitution. In the name of the merciful God, and by all that life is worth, let it no longer be a debatable question whether it is better to choose *Liberty or death*.

In 1822, Denmark Veazie [Vesey], of South Carolina, formed a plan for the liberation of his fellow-men. In the whole history of human efforts to overthrow slavery, a more complicated and tremendous plan was never formed. He was betrayed by the treachery of his own people, and died a martyr to freedom. Many a brave hero fell, but history, faithful to her high trust, will transcribe his name on the same monument with Moses, Hampden, Tell, Bruce and Wallace, Toussaint L'Ouverture, Lafayette and Washington. That tremendous movement shook the whole empire of slavery. The guilty soul-thieves were overwhelmed with fear. It is a matter of fact, that at that time, and in consequence of the threatened revolution, the slave States talked strongly of emancipation. But they blew but one blast of the trumpet of freedom and then laid it aside. As these men became quiet, the slaveholders ceased to talk about emancipation; and now behold your condition today! Angels sigh over it, and humanity has long since exhausted her tears in weeping on your account!

The patriotic Nathaniel Turner followed Denmark Veazie [Vesey]. He was goaded to desperation by wrong and injustice. By despotism, his name has been recorded on the list of infamy, and future generations will remember him among the noble and brave.

Next arose the immortal Joseph Cinque, the hero of the *Amistad*. He was a native African, and by the help of God he emancipated a whole ship-load of his fellow-men on the high seas. And he now sings of liberty on the sunny hills of Africa and beneath his native palm trees, where he hears the lion roar and feels himself as free as that king of the forest.

Next arose Madison Washington that bright star of freedom, and took his station in the constellation of true heroism. He was a slave on board the brig *Creole*, of Richmond, bound to New Orleans, that great slave mart, with a hundred and four others. Nineteen struck for liberty or death. But one life was taken, and the whole were emancipated, and the vessel was carried into Nassau, New Providence.

Noble men! Those who have fallen in freedom's conflict, their memories will be cherished by the true hearted and the God-fearing in all future generations; those who are living, their names are surrounded by a halo of glory.

Brethren, arise, arise! Strike for your lives and liberties. Now is the day and the hour. Let every slave throughout the land do this, and the days of slavery are numbered. You cannot be more oppressed than you have been—you cannot suffer greater cruelties than you have already. *Rather die freemen, than live to be slaves*! It is impossible, like the children of Israel, to make a grand exodus from the land of bondage. Remember that you are *four millions*!

It is in your power so to torment the God-cursed slaveholders that they will be glad to let you go free. If the scale was turned, and black men were the masters and white men the slaves, every destructive agent and element would be employed to lay the oppressor low. Danger and death would hang over their heads day and night. Yes, the tyrants would meet with plagues more terrible than those of Pharaoh. But you are a patient people. You act as though you were made for the special use of these devils. You act as though your daughters were born to pamper the lusts of your masters and overseers. And worse than all, you tamely submit while your lords tear your wives from your embraces and defile them before your eyes. In the name of God, we ask, are you men? Where is the blood of your fathers? Has it all run out of your veins? Awake, awake; millions of voices are calling you! Your dead fathers speak to you from their graves. Heaven, as with a voice of thunder, calls on you to arise from the dust.

Let your motto be resistance! resistance! RESISTANCE! No oppressed people have ever secured their liberty without resistance. What kind of resistance you had better make, you must decide by the circumstances that surround you, and according to the suggestion of expediency. Brethren, adieu! Trust in the living God. Labor for the peace of the human race, and remember that you are *four millions*.

QUESTIONS

(1) Why is the enslavement of blacks such a great concern for Henry Highland Garnet?

(2) Garnet's argument against slavery appeals to the dignity of man. How for Garnet is manhood tied to civil rights and liberty?

(3) What are some of the concerns presented by Garnet against the institution of slavery?

(4) Why, for Garnet, is slavery "the highest crime against God and man"?

(5) What are some of the examples that Garnet draws upon to show why it is important for slaves to resist their masters and fight for their freedom?

3 | What to the Slave is the Fourth of July?

FREDERICK DOUGLASS

Frederick Douglass (1818–1895) was born in Maryland as a slave. It was illegal for slaves to read and write. Douglass, at first, was taught to read by his master Hugh Auld's wife. She was later influenced by her husband's notion that teaching slaves to read would encourage them to desire freedom and she stopped teaching Douglass to read. He continued to secretly learn to read and write. After escaping from slavery in 1838, Douglass worked as an agent for the Massachusetts Anti-Slavery Society. In 1845, Douglass authored *Narrative of the Life of Frederick Douglass, an American Slave*. Some of his other books included: *My Bondage and My Freedom*, 1881; and *Life and Times of Frederick Douglass*, 1892. After the publication of Douglass' autobiography, Douglass was forced to leave the United States. He lived for two years in Great Britain and visited Ireland where he gave many lectures. In 1847, Douglass returned to the United States. He later established the abolitionist newspaper *The North Star*, which was renamed *Frederick Douglass' Paper*. In 1848, he was the only black to attend the Seneca Falls Convention, the first women's rights convention. After the Civil War, Douglass became a central figure in the National Republican Party. In 1887, Douglass published "The Future of the Colored Race" in the *North American Review*. The extract below is taken from Douglass' speech, "What to the Slave is the Fourth of July?," which he delivered to the Anti-Slavery Society on July 5, 1852 at Rochester, New York. In this speech, he condemned slavery in America and advocated for freedom and equal rights for blacks.

Fellow-citizens, pardon me, and allow me to ask, why am I called upon to speak here to-day? What have I, or those I represent, to do with your national independence? Are the great principles of political freedom and of natural justice, embodied in that Declaration of Independence, extended to us? and am I, therefore, called upon to bring our humble offering to the national altar, and to confess the benefits, and express devout gratitude for the blessings, resulting from your independence to us?

Would to God, both for your sakes and ours, that an affirmative answer could be truthfully returned to these questions! Then would my task be light, and my burden easy and delightful. For who is there so cold that a nation's sympathy could not warm him? Who so obdurate and dead to the claims of gratitude, that would not thankfully acknowledge such priceless benefits? Who so stolid and selfish, that would not give his voice to swell the hallelujahs of a nation's jubilee, when the chains of servitude had been torn from his limbs? I am not that man. In a case like that, the dumb might eloquently speak, and the "lame man leap as an hart."

But, such is not the state of the case. I say it with a sad sense of the disparity between us. I am not included within the pale of this glorious anniversary! Your high independence only reveals the immeasurable distance between us. The blessings in which you this day rejoice, are not enjoyed in common. The rich inheritance of justice, liberty, prosperity, and independence, bequeathed by your fathers, is shared by you, not by me. The sunlight that brought life and healing to you, has brought stripes and death to me. This Fourth of July is *yours*, not mine. You may rejoice, I must mourn. To drag a man in fetters into the grand illuminated temple of liberty, and call upon him to join you in joyous anthems, were inhuman mockery and sacrilegious irony. Do you mean, citizens, to mock me, by asking me to speak to-day? If so, there is a parallel to your conduct. And let me warn you that it is dangerous to copy the example of a nation whose crimes, towering up to heaven, were thrown down by the breath of the Almighty, burying that nation in irrecoverable ruin! I can to-day take up the plaintive lament of a peeled and woe-smitten people.

"By the rivers of Babylon, there we sat down. Yea! we wept when we remembered Zion. We hanged our harps upon the willows in the midst thereof. For there, they that carried us away captive, required of us a song; and they who wasted us required of us mirth, saying, Sing us one of the songs of Zion. How can we sing the Lord's song in a strange land? If I forget thee, O Jerusalem, let my right hand forget her cunning. If I do not remember thee, let my tongue cleave to the roof of my mouth."

Fellow-citizens, above your national, tumultuous joy, I hear the mournful wail of millions, whose chains, heavy and grievous yesterday, are to-day rendered more intolerable by the jubilant shouts that reach them. If I do forget, if I do not faithfully remember those bleeding children of sorrow this day, "may my right hand forget her cunning, and may my tongue cleave to the roof of my mouth!" To forget them, to pass lightly over their wrongs, and to chime in with the popular theme, would be treason most scandalous and shocking, and would make me a reproach before God and the world. My subject, then, fellow-citizens, is AMERICAN SLAVERY. I shall see this day and its popular characteristics from the slave's point of view. Standing there, identified with the American bondman, making his wrongs mine, I do not hesitate to declare, with all my soul, that the character and conduct of this nation never looked blacker to me than on this Fourth of July! Whether we turn to the declarations of the past, or to the professions of the present, the conduct of the nation seems equally hideous and revolting. America is false to the past, false to the present, and solemnly binds herself to be false to the future. Standing with God and the crushed and bleeding slave on this occasion, I will, in the name of humanity which is outraged, in the name of liberty which is fettered, in the name of the constitution and the bible, which are disregarded and trampled upon, dare to call in question and to denounce, with all the emphasis I can command, everything that serves to perpetuate slavery—the great sin and shame of America! "I will not equivocate; I will not excuse;" I will use the severest language I can command; and yet not one word shall escape me that any man, whose judgment is not blinded by prejudice, or who is not at heart a slaveholder, shall not confess to be right and just.

But I fancy I hear some one of my audience say, it is just in this circumstance that you and your brother abolitionists fail to make a favorable impression on the public mind. Would you argue more, and denounce less, would you persuade more and rebuke less, your cause would be much more likely to succeed. But, I submit, where all is plain there is nothing to be argued. What point in the anti-slavery creed would you have me argue? On what branch of the subject do the people of this country need light? Must I undertake to prove that the slave is a man? That point is conceded already. Nobody doubts it. The slaveholders themselves acknowledge it in the enactment of laws for their government. They acknowledge it when they punish disobedience on the part of the slave. There are seventy-two crimes in the state of Virginia, which, if committed by a black man (no matter how ignorant he be), subject him to the punishment of death; while only two of these same crimes will subject a white man to the like punishment. What is this but the acknowledgement that the slave is a moral, intellectual, and responsible being. The manhood of the slave is conceded. It is admitted in the fact that southern statute books are covered with enactments forbidding, under severe fines and penalties, the teaching of the slave to read or write. When you can point to any such laws, in reference to the beasts of the field, then I may consent to argue the manhood of the slave. When the dogs in your streets, when the fowls of the air, when the cattle on your hills, when the fish of the sea, and the reptiles that crawl, shall be unable to distinguish the slave from a brute, *then* will I argue with you that the slave is a man!

For the present, it is enough to affirm the equal manhood of the Negro race. Is it not astonishing that, while we are plowing, planting, and reaping, using all kinds of mechanical tools, erecting houses, constructing bridges, building ships, working in metals of brass, iron, copper, silver, and gold; that, while we are reading, writing, and cyphering, acting as clerks, merchants, and secretaries, having among us lawyers, doctors, ministers, poets, authors, editors, orators, and teachers; that, while we are engaged in all manner of enterprises common to other men, digging gold in California, capturing the whale in the Pacific, feeding sheep and cattle on the hillside, living, moving, acting, thinking, planning, living in families as husbands, wives, and children, and, above all, confessing and worshiping the Christian's God, and looking hopefully for life and immortality beyond the grave, we are called upon to prove that we are men!

Would you have me argue that man is entitled to liberty? that he is the rightful owner of his own body? You have already declared it. Must I argue the wrongfulness of slavery? Is that a question for republicans? Is it to be settled by the rules of logic and argumentation, as a matter beset with great difficulty, involving a doubtful application of the principle of justice, hard to be understood? How should I look to-day in the presence of Americans, dividing and subdividing a discourse, to show that men have a natural right to freedom, speaking of it relatively and positively, negatively and affirmatively? To do so, would be to make myself ridiculous, and to offer an insult to your understanding. There is not a man beneath the canopy of heaven that does not know that slavery is *wrong for him.*

What, am I to argue that it is wrong to make men brutes, to rob them of their liberty, to work them without wages, to keep them ignorant of their relations to their fellow-men, to beat them with sticks, to flay their flesh with the lash, to load their limbs with irons, to hunt them with dogs, to sell them at auction, to sunder their families, to knock out their teeth, to burn their flesh, to starve them into obedience and submission to their masters? Must I argue that a system, thus marked with blood and stained with pollution, is *wrong*? No! I will not. I have better employment for my time and strength than such arguments would imply.

What, then, remains to be argued? Is it that slavery is not divine; that God did not establish it; that our doctors of divinity are mistaken? There is blasphemy in the thought. That which is inhuman cannot be divine. Who can reason on such a proposition! They that can, may; I cannot. The time for such argument is past.

At a time like this, scorching irony, not convincing argument, is needed. O! had I the ability, and could I reach the nation's ear, I would to-day pour out a fiery stream of biting ridicule, blasting reproach, withering sarcasm, and stern rebuke. For it is not light that is needed, but fire; it is not the gentle shower, but thunder. We need the storm, the whirlwind, and the earthquake. The feeling of the nation must be quickened; the conscience of the nation must be roused; the propriety of the nation must be startled; the hypocrisy of the nation must be exposed; and its crimes against God and man must be proclaimed and denounced.

What to the American slave is your Fourth of July? I answer: a day that reveals to him, more than all other days in the year, the gross injustice and cruelty to which he is the constant victim. To him, your celebration is a sham; your boasted liberty, an unholy license; your national greatness, swelling vanity; your sounds of rejoicing are empty and heartless; your denunciations of tyrants, brass-fronted impudence; your shouts of liberty and equality, hollow mockery; your prayers and hymns, your sermons and thanksgivings, with all your religious parade and solemnity, are to him mere bombast, fraud, deception, impiety, and hypocrisy—a thin veil to cover up crimes which would disgrace a nation of savages. There is not a nation on the earth guilty of practices more shocking and bloody, than are the people of these United States, at this very hour.

Go where you may, search where you will, roam through all the monarchies and despotisms of the old world, travel through South America, search out every abuse, and when you have found the last, lay your facts by the side of the every-day practices of this nation, and you will say with me, that, for revolting barbarity and shameless hypocrisy, America reigns without a rival.

QUESTIONS

(1) What did Frederick Douglass mean when he said: "the fourth of July is yours not mine"? Discuss.

(2) According to Douglass, how did slavery go against the American creed of liberty and equality for all and true Christian principles?

(3) The fourth of July celebration is about America's liberty and independence from British rule. However, for Douglass, this celebration is a good example of America's hypocrisy. Why?

(4) In spite of slavery, did Douglass feel hopeful for the future of blacks in America?

(5) For Douglass, what are some of the evils that are associated with slavery? And how does Douglass show that those in power did recognize that the slave is human?

4 | Comparative Condition of the Colored People of the United States

MARTIN ROBISON DELANY

Martin Robison Delany (1812–1885) was born in Charles Town, Virginia. He was an abolitionist, journalist, physician, and a major political architect of Black Nationalism. In 1843, Delany produced *The Mystery*, one of the earliest black newspapers. Also, Delany, from 1847 to 1849 with Frederick Douglass, worked on *The North Star*. In 1852, he published his book, *The Condition, Elevation, Emigration, and Destiny of the Colored People of the United States, "Politically Considered."* In his book, Delany put forward a program of racial separatism and advocated colonization as the only possibility to achieve freedom for blacks in the United States. In the Civil War, he was a major in the 104th US colored troops. During Reconstruction, he ran unsuccessfully for lieutenant governor of South Carolina. "Comparative Condition of the Colored People of the United States," is taken from the above mentioned book. In this extract, Delany points out that America did not extend the American creed of democracy and equal liberty to blacks in America. Instead it embarked on policies that degraded blacks. For Delany, the abolitionists' belief that moral suasion and racial uplift were needed for blacks' freedom was not enough. Blacks had to become politically active and understand the laws in order to morally persuade those in power that slavery was wrong.

The United States, untrue to her trust and unfaithful to her professed principles of republican equality, has also pursued a policy of political degradation to a large portion of her native born countrymen, and that class is the Colored People. Denied an equality not only of political but of natural rights, in common with the rest of our fellow citizens, there is no species of degradation to which we are not subject.

Reduced to abject slavery is not enough, the very thought of which should awaken every sensibility of our common nature; but those of their descendants who are freemen even in the non-slaveholding States, occupy the very same position politically, religiously, civilly and socially, (with but few exceptions,) as the bondman occupies in the slave States.

In those States, the bondman is disfranchised, and for the most part so are we. He is denied all civil, religious, and social privileges, except such as he gets by mere sufferance, and so are we. They have no part nor lot in the government of the country, neither have we. They are ruled and governed without representation, existing as mere nonentities among the citizens, and excrescences on the body politic—a mere dreg in community, and so are we. Where then is our political superiority to the enslaved? none, neither are we superior in any other relation to society, except that we are defacto masters of ourselves and joint rulers of our own domestic household, while the bondman's self is claimed by another, and his relation to his family denied him. What the unfortunate classes are in Europe, such are we in the United States, which is folly to deny, insanity not to understand, blindness not to see, and surely now full time that our eyes were opened to these startling truths, which for ages have stared us full in the face.

It is time that we had become politicians, we mean, to understand the political economy and domestic policy of nations; that we had become as well as moral theorists, also the practical demonstrators of equal rights and self-government. Except we do, it is idle to talk about rights, it is mere chattering for the sake of being seen and heard—like the slave, saying something because his so called "master" said it, and saying just what he told him to say. Have we not now sufficient intelligence among us to understand our true position, to realise our actual condition, and determine for ourselves what is best to be done? If we have not now, we never shall have, and should at once cease prating about our equality, capacity, and all that.

Twenty years ago, when the writer was a youth, his young and yet uncultivated mind was aroused, and his tender heart made to leap with anxiety in anticipation of the promises then held out by the prime movers in the cause of our elevation.

In 1830 the most intelligent and leading spirits among the colored men in the United States, such as James Forten, Robert Douglass, I. Bowers, A. D. Shadd, John Peck, Joseph Cassey, and John B. Vashon of Pennsylvania; John T. Hilton, Nathaniel and Thomas Paul, and James G. Barbodoes of Massachusetts; Henry Sipkins, Thomas Hamilton, Thomas L. Jennings, Thomas Downing, Samuel E. Cornish, and others of New York; R. Cooley and others of Maryland, and representatives from other States which cannot now be recollected, the data not being at hand, assembled in the city of Philadelphia, in the capacity of a National Convention, to "devise ways and means for the bettering of our condition." These Conventions determined to assemble annually, much talent, ability, and energy of character being displayed; when in 1831 at a sitting of the Convention in September, from their previous pamphlet reports, much interest having been created throughout the country, they were favored by the presence of a number of whites, some of whom were able and distinguished men, such as Rev. R. R. Gurley, Arthur Tappan, Elliot Cresson, John Rankin, Simeon Jocelyn and others, among them William Lloyd Garrison, then quite a young man, all of whom were staunch and ardent Colonizationists, young Garrison at that time, doing his mightiest in his favorite work.

Among other great projects of interest brought before the convention at a previous sitting, was that of the expediency of a general emigration, as far as it was practicable, of the colored people to the British Provinces of North America. Another was that of raising sufficient means for the establishment and erection of a College for the proper education of the colored youth. These gentlemen long accustomed to observation and reflection on the condition of their people saw at once, that there must necessarily be means used adequate to the end to be attained—that end being an unqualified equality with the ruling class of their fellow citizens. He saw that as a class, the colored people of the country were ignorant, degraded and oppressed, by far the greater portion of them being abject slaves in the South, the very condition of whom was almost enough, under the circumstances, to blast the remotest hope of success, and those who were freemen, whether in the South or North, occupied a subservient, servile, and menial position, considering it a favor to get into the service of the whites, and do their degrading offices. That the difference between the whites and themselves, consisted in the superior advantages of the one over the other, in point of attainments. That if a knowledge of the arts and sciences, the mechanical occupations, the industrial occupations, as farming, commerce, and all the various business enterprises, and learned professions were necessary for the superior position occupied by their rulers, it was also necessary for them. And very reasonably too, the first suggestion which occurred to them was, the advantages of a location, then the necessity of a qualification. They reasoned with themselves, that all distinctive differences made among men on account of their origin, is wicked, unrighteous, and cruel, and never shall receive countenance in any shape from us, therefore, the first acts of the measure entered into by them, was to protest, solemnly protest, against every unjust measure and policy in the country, having for its object the proscription of the colored people, whether state, national, municipal, social, civil, or religious.

But being far-sighted, reflecting, discerning men, they took a political view of the subject, and determined for the good of their people to be governed in their policy according to the facts as they presented themselves. In taking a glance at Europe, they discovered there, however unjustly, as we have shown in another part of this pamphlet, that there are and have been numerous classes proscribed and oppressed, and it was not for them to cut short their wise deliberations, and arrest their proceedings in contention, as to the cause, whether on account of language, the color of eyes, hair, skin, or their origin of country—because all this is contrary to reason, a contradiction to common sense, at war with nature herself, and at variance with facts as they stare us every day in the face, among all nations, in every country—this being made the pretext as a matter of *policy* alone—a fact worthy of observation, that wherever the objects of oppression are the most easily distinguished by any peculiar or general characteristics, these people are the more easily oppressed, because the war of oppression is the more easily waged against them. This is the case with the modern Jews and many other people who have strongly-marked, peculiar, or distinguishing characteristics. This arises in this wise. The policy of all those who proscribe any people, induces them to select as the objects of proscription, those who differed as much as possible, in some particulars, from themselves. This is to ensure the greater success, because it engenders the greater prejudice, or in other words, elicits less interest on the part of the oppressing class, in their favor. This fact is well understood in national conflicts, as the soldier or civilian, who is distinguished by his dress, mustache, or any other peculiar appendage, would certainly prove himself a madman, if he did not take the precaution to change his dress, remove his mustache, and conceal as much as possible his peculiar characteristics, to give him access among the repelling party.

This is mere policy, nature having nothing to do with it. Still, it is a fact, a great truth well worthy of remark, and as such as adduce it for the benefit of those of our readers, unaccustomed to an enquiry into the policy of nations.

In view of these truths, our fathers and leaders in our elevation, discovered that as a policy, we the colored people were selected as the subordinate class in this country, not on account of any actual or supposed inferiority on their part, but simply because, in view of all the circumstances of the case, they were the very best class that could be selected. They would have as readily had any other class as subordinates in the country, as the colored people, but the condition of society *at the time*, would not admit of it. In the struggle for American Independence, there were among those who performed the most distinguished parts, the most common-place peasantry of the Provinces. English, Danish, Irish, Scotch, and others, were among those whose names blazoned forth as heroes in the American Revolution. But a single reflection will convince us, that no course of policy could have induced the proscription of the parentage and relatives of such men as Benjamin Franklin the printer, Roger Sherman the cobbler, the tinkers, and others of the signers of the Declaration of Independence. But as they were determined to have a subservient class, it will readily be conceived, that according to the state of society at the time, the better policy on their part was, to select some class, who from their political position—however much they may have contributed their aid as we certainly did, in the general struggle for liberty by force of arms—who had the least claims upon them, or who had the *least chance*, or was the *least potent* in urging their claims. This class of course was the colored people and Indians.

The Indians who in the early settlement of the continent, before an African captive had ever been introduced thereon, were reduced to the most abject slavery, toiling day and night in the mines, under the relentless hands of heartless Spanish taskmasters, but being a race of people raised to the sports of fishing, the chase, and of war, were wholly unaccustomed to labor, and therefore sunk under the insupportable weight, two millions and a half having fallen victims to the cruelty of oppression and toil suddenly placed upon their shoulders. And it was only this that prevented their farther enslavement as a class, after the provinces were absolved from the British Crown. It is true that their general enslavement took place on the islands and in the mining districts of South America, where indeed, the Europeans continued to enslave them, until a comparatively recent period; still, the design, the feeling, and inclination from policy, was the same to do so here, in this section of the continent.

Nor was it until their influence became too great, by the political position occupied by their brethren in the new republic, that the German and Irish peasantry ceased to be sold as slaves for a term of years fixed by law, for the repayment of their passage-money, the descendants of these classes of people for a long time being held as inferiors, in the estimation of the ruling class, and it was not until they assumed the rights and privileges guaranteed to them by the established policy of the country, among the leading spirits of whom were their relatives, that the policy towards them was discovered to be a bad one, and accordingly changed. Nor was it, as is frequently very erroneously asserted, by colored as well as white persons, that it was on account of hatred to the African, or in other words, on account of hatred to his color, that the African was selected as the subject of oppression in this country. This is sheer nonsense; being based on policy and nothing else, as shown in another place. The Indians, who being the most foreign to the sympathies of the Europeans on this continent, were selected in the first place, who, being unable to withstand the hardships, gave way before them.

But the African race had long been known to Europeans, in all ages of the worlds history, as a long-lived, hardy race, subject to toil and labor of various kinds, subsisting mainly by traffic, trade, and industry, and consequently being as foreign to the sympathies of the invaders of the continent as the Indians, they were selected, captured, brought here as a laboring class, and as a matter of policy held as such. Nor was the absurd idea of natural inferiority of the African ever dreamed of, until recently adduced by the slave-holders and their abettors, in justification of the policy. This, with contemptuous indignation, we fling back into their face, as a scorpion to a vulture. And so did our patriots and leaders in the cause of regeneration know better, and never for a moment yielded to the base doctrine. But they had discovered the great fact, that a cruel policy was pursued towards our people, and that they possessed distinctive characteristics which made them the objects of proscription. These characteristics being strongly marked in the colored people, as in the Indians, by color, character of hair and so on, made them the more easily distinguished from other Americans, and the policies more effectually urged against us. For this reason they introduced the subject of emigration to Canada, and a proper institution for the education of the youth.

At this important juncture of their proceedings, the afore named white gentlemen were introduced to the notice of the Convention, and after gaining permission to speak, expressed their gratification and surprise at the qualification and talent manifested by different members of the Convention, all expressing their determination to give the cause of the colored people more serious reflection. Mr. Garrison, the youngest of them all, and none the less honest on account of his youthfulness, being but 26 years of age at the time, (1831) expressed his determination to change his course of policy at once, and espouse the cause of the elevation of the colored people here in their own country. We are not at present well advised upon this point, it now having escaped our memory, but we are under the impression that Mr. Jocelyn also, at once changed his policy.

During the winter of 1832, Mr. Garrison issued his "Thoughts on African Colonization" and near about the same time or shortly after, issued the first number of the "Liberator," in both of which, his full convictions of the enormity of American slavery, and the wickedness of their policy towards the colored people, were fully expressed. At the sitting of the Convention in this year, a number, perhaps all of these gentlemen were present, and those who had denounced the Colonization scheme, and espoused the cause of the elevation of the colored people in this country, or the Anti-Slavery cause, as it was now termed, expressed themselves openly and without reserve.

Sensible of the high-handed injustice done to the colored people in the United States, and the mischief likely to emanate from the unchristian proceedings of the deceptious Colonization scheme, like all honest hearted penitents, with the ardor only known to new converts, they entreated the Convention, whatever they did, not to entertain for a moment, the idea of recommending emigration to their people, nor the establishment of separate institutions of learning. They earnestly contended, and doubtless honestly meaning what they said, that they (the whites) had been our oppressors and injurers, they had obstructed our progress to the high positions of civilization, and now, it was their bounden duty to make full amends for the injuries thus inflicted on an unoffending people. They exhorted the Convention to cease; as they had laid on the burden, they would also take it off; as they had obstructed our pathway, they would remove the hindrance. In a word, as they had oppressed and trampled down the colored people, they would now elevate them. These suggestions and promises, good enough to be sure, after they were made, were accepted by the Convention—though some gentlemen were still in favor of the first project as the best policy, Mr. A. D. Shadd of West Chester, Pa., as we learn from himself, being one among that number—ran through the country like wild-fire, no one thinking, and if he thought, daring to speak above his breath of going any where out of certain prescribed limits, or of sending a child to school, if it should but have the name of "colored" attached to it, without the risk of being termed a "traitor" to the cause of his people, or an enemy to the Anti-Slavery cause.

At this important point in the history of our efforts, the colored men stopped suddenly, and with their hands thrust deep in their breeches-pockets, and their mouths gaping open, stood gazing with astonishment, wonder, and surprise, at the stupendous moral colossal statues of our Anti-Slavery friends and brethren, who in the heat and zeal of honest hearts, from a desire to make atonement for the many wrongs inflicted, promised a great deal more than they have ever been able half to fulfill, in thrice the period in which they expected it. And in this, we have no fault to find with our Anti-Slavery friends, and here wish it to be understood, that we are not laying any thing to their charge as blame, neither do we desire for a moment to reflect on them, because we heartily believe that all that they did at the time, they did with the purest and best of motives, and further believe that they now are, as they then were, the truest friends we have among the whites in this country. And hope, and desire, and request, that our people should always look upon true anti-slavery people, Abolitionists we mean, as their friends, until they have just cause for acting otherwise. It is true, that the Anti-Slavery, like all good causes, has produced some recreants, but the cause itself is no more to be blamed for that, than Christianity is for the malconduct of any professing hypocrite, nor the society of Friends, for the conduct of a broad-brimmed hat and shad-belly coated horsethief, because he spoke *thee* and *thou* before stealing the horse. But what is our condition even amidst our Anti-Slavery friends? And here, as our sole intention is to contribute to the elevation of our people, we must be permitted to express our opinion freely, without being thought uncharitable.

In the first place, we should look at the objects for which the Anti-Slavery cause was commenced, and the promises or inducements it held out at the commencement. It should be borne in mind, that Anti-Slavery took its rise among colored men, just at the time they were introducing their greatest projects for their own elevation, and that our Anti-Slavery brethren were converts of the colored men, in behalf of their elevation. Of course, it would be expected that being baptized into the new doctrines, their faith would induce them to embrace the principles therein contained, with the strictest possible adherence.

The cause of dissatisfaction with our former condition, was, that we were proscribed, debarred, and shut out from every respectable position, occupying the places of inferiors and menials.

It was expected that Anti-Slavery, according to its professions, would extend to colored persons, as far as in the power of its adherents, those advantages nowhere else to be obtained among white men. That colored boys would get situations in their shops and stores, and every other advantage tending to elevate them as far as possible, would be extended to them. At least, it was expected, that in Anti-Slavery establishments, colored men would have the preference. Because, there was no other ostensible object in view, in the commencement of the Anti-Slavery enterprise, than the *elevation of the colored man*, by facilitating his efforts in attaining to equality with the white man. It was urged, and it was true, that the colored people were susceptible of all that the whites were, and all that was required was to give them a fair opportunity, and they would prove their capacity. That it was unjust, wicked, and cruel, the result of an unnatural prejudice, that debarred them from places of respectability, and that public opinion could and should be corrected upon this subject. That it was only necessary to make a sacrifice of feeling, and an innovation on the customs of society, to establish a different order of things,—that as Anti-Slavery men, they were willing to make these sacrifices, and determined to take the colored man by the hand, making common cause with him in affliction, and bear a part of the odium heaped upon him. That his cause was the cause of God—that "In as much as ye did it not unto the least of these my little ones, ye did it not unto me," and that as Anti-Slavery men, they would "do right if the heavens fell." Thus, was the cause espoused, and thus did we expect much. But in all this, we were doomed to disappointment, sad, sad disappointment. Instead of realising what we had hoped for, we find ourselves occupying the very same position in relation to our Anti-Slavery friends, as we do in relation to the pro-slavery part of the community—a mere secondary, underling position, in all our relations to them, and any thing more than this, is not a matter of course affair—it comes not by established anti-slavery custom or right, but like that which emanates from the pro-slavery portion of the community by mere sufferance.

It is true, that the "Liberator" office, in Boston, has got Elijah Smith, a colored youth, at the cases—the "Standard," in New York, a young colored man, and the "Freeman," in Philadelphia, William Still, another, in the publication office, as "packing clerk"; yet these are but three out of the hosts that fill these offices in their various departments, all occupying places that could have been, and as we once thought, would have been, easily enough, occupied by colored men. Indeed, we can have no other idea about anti-slavery in this country, than that the legitimate persons to fill any and every position about an anti-slavery establishment are colored persons. Nor will it do to argue in extenuation, that white men are as justly entitled to them as colored men; because white men do not from necessity become anti-slavery men in order to get situations; they being white men, may occupy any position they are capable of filling—in a word, their chances are endless, every avenue in the country being opened to them. They do not therefore become abolitionists, for the sake of employment—at least, it is not the song that anti-slavery sung, in the first love of the new faith, proclaimed by its disciples.

And if it be urged that colored men are incapable as yet to fill these positions, all that we have to say is, that the cause has fallen far short; almost equivalent to a failure, of a tithe, of what it promised to do in half the period of its existence, to this time, if it have not as yet, now a period of twenty years, raised up colored men enough, to fill the offices within its patronage. We think it is not unkind to say, if it had been half as faithful to itself, as it should have been—its professed principles we mean; it could have reared and tutored from childhood, colored men enough by this time, for its own especial purpose. These we know could have been easily obtained, because colored people in general, are favorable to the anti-slavery cause, and wherever there is an adverse manifestation, it arises from sheer ignorance; and we have now but comparatively few such among us. There is one thing certain, that no colored person, except such as would reject education altogether, would be adverse to putting their child with an anti-slavery person, for educational advantages. This then could have been done. But it has not been done, and let the cause of it be whatever it may, and let whoever may be to blame, we are willing to let all that pass, and extend to our anti-slavery brethren the right-hand of fellowship, bidding them God-speed in the propagation of good and wholesome sentiments—for whether they are practically carried out or not, the profession are in themselves all right and good. Like Christianity, the principles are holy and of divine origin. And we believe, if ever a man started right, with pure and holy motives, Mr. Garrison did; and that, had he the power of making the cause what it should be, it would all be right, and there never would have been any cause for the remarks we have made, though in kindness, and with the purest of motives. We are nevertheless, still occupying a miserable position in the community, wherever we live; and what we most desire is, to draw the attention of our people to this fact, and point out what, in our opinion, we conceive to be a proper remedy.

QUESTIONS

(1) What is some of the evidence presented by Delany that whites cannot accept blacks as equals?
(2) Why is it important for Delany to draw on some of the similarities between the oppression of blacks in America and the oppressed people of Europe?
(3) How did the earlier leaders and the conventions of the 1830s "devise ways and means" to improve the conditions of blacks? What were some of their limitations? And why was a new direction needed?
(4) How did Delany persuade blacks that he was a leader that blacks should imitate?
(5) How does Delany put forward his argument for blacks in America to emigrate?

5 Why Sit Ye Here and Die

MARIA W. STEWART

Maria W. Stewart (1803–1879), an abolitionist and women's rights activist, was born Maria Miller in Hartford, Connecticut. She was orphaned at five years old and was sent to live with a minister and his wife where she worked as a servant until she was fifteen years old. On August 10, 1826, she married James W. Stewart who died three years later. She did not receive any formal education. But her Christian faith had a great impact on her four public lectures, which were published by *The Liberator*. The extract below is one of the lectures, "Why Sit Ye Here and Die," which she gave on September 21, 1832 at the Franklin Hall in Boston, the meeting site of the New England Anti-Slavery Society. In this lecture, she condemns those that failed to come to terms with the horrors of slavery and demands equal education and job advancement for black women. In the end, she points out that the desolate conditions of black men and women are the same because of slavery in the South and the unequal economic structure in the North.

Why sit ye here and die? If we say we will go to a foreign land, the famine and the pestilence are there, and there we shall die. If we sit here, we shall die. Come let us plead our cause before the whites: if they save us alive, we shall live—and if they kill us, we shall but die.

Methinks I heard a spiritual interrogation—'Who shall go forward, and take off the reproach that is cast upon the people of color? Shall it be a woman?' And my heart made this reply —'If it is thy will, be it even so, Lord Jesus!'

I have heard much respecting the horrors of slavery; but may Heaven forbid that the generality of my color throughout these United States should experience any more of its horrors than to be a servant of servants, or hewers of wood and drawers of water! Tell us no more of southern slavery; for with few exceptions, although I may be very erroneous in my opinion, yet I consider our condition but little better than that. Yet, after all, methinks there are no chains so galling as the chains of ignorance—no fetters so binding as those that bind the soul, and exclude it from the vast field of useful and scientific knowledge. O, had I received the advantages of early education, my ideas would, ere now, have expanded far and wide; but, alas! I possess nothing but moral capability—no teachings but the teachings of the Holy spirit.

I have asked several individuals of my sex, who transact business for themselves, if providing our girls were to give them the most satisfactory references, they would not be willing to grant them an equal opportunity with others? Their reply has been—for their own part, they had no objection; but as it was not the custom, were they to take them into their employ, they would be in danger of losing the public patronage.

And such is the powerful force of prejudice. Let our girls possess what amiable qualities of soul they may; let their characters be fair and spotless as innocence itself; let their natural taste and ingenuity be what they may; it is impossible for scarce an individual of them to rise above the condition of servants. Ah! why is this cruel and unfeeling distinction? Is it merely because God has made our complexion to vary? If it be, O shame to soft, relenting humanity! "Tell it not in Gath! publish it not in the streets of Askelon!" Yet, after all, methinks were the American free people of color to turn their attention more assiduously to moral worth and intellectual improvement, this would be the result: prejudice would gradually diminish, and the whites would be compelled to say, unloose those fetters!

Though black their skins as shades of night, Their hearts are pure, their souls are white.

Few white persons of either sex, who are calculated for any thing else, are willing to spend their lives and bury their talents in performing mean, servile labor. And such is the horrible idea that I entertain respecting a life of servitude, that if I conceived of there being no possibility of my rising above the condition of a servant, I would gladly hail death as a welcome messenger. O, horrible idea, indeed! to possess noble souls aspiring after high and honorable acquirements, yet confined by the chains of ignorance and poverty to lives of continual drudgery and toil. Neither do I know of any who have enriched themselves by spending their lives as house-domestics, washing windows, shaking carpets, brushing boots, or tending upon gentlemen's tables. I can but die for expressing my sentiments; and I am as willing to die by the sword as the pestilence; for I am a true born American; your blood flows in my veins, and your spirit fires my breast.

I observed a piece in the *Liberator* a few months since, stating that the colonizationists had published a work respecting us, asserting that we were lazy and idle. I confute them on that point. Take us generally as a people, we are neither lazy nor idle; and considering how little we have to excite or stimulate us, I am almost astonished that there are so many industrious and ambitious ones to be found; although I acknowledge, with extreme sorrow, that there are some who never were and never will be serviceable to society. And have you not a similar class among yourselves?

Again. It was asserted that we were "a ragged set, crying for liberty." I reply to it, the whites have so long and so loudly proclaimed the theme of equal rights and privileges, that our souls have caught the flame also, ragged as we are. As far as our merit deserves, we feel a common desire to rise above the condition of servants and drudges. I have learnt, by bitter experience, that continual hard labor deadens the energies of the soul, and benumbs the faculties of the mind; the ideas become confined, the mind barren, and, like the scorching sands of Arabia, produces nothing; or, like the uncultivated soil, brings forth thorns and thistles.

Again, continual hard labor irritates our tempers and sours our dispositions; the whole system becomes worn out with toil and failure; nature herself becomes almost exhausted, and we care but little whether we live or die. It is true, that the free people of color throughout these United States are neither bought nor sold, nor under the lash of the cruel driver; many obtain a comfortable support; but few, if any, have an opportunity of becoming rich and independent; and the employments we most pursue are as unprofitable to us as the spider's web or the floating bubbles that vanish into air. As servants, we are respected; but let us presume to aspire any higher, our employer regards us no longer. And were it not that the King eternal has declared that Ethiopia shall stretch forth her hands unto God, I should indeed despair.

I do not consider it derogatory, my friends, for persons to live out to service. There are many whose inclination leads them to aspire no higher; and I would highly commend the performance of almost any thing for an honest livelihood; but where constitutional strength is wanting, labor of this kind, in its mildest form, is painful. And doubtless many are the prayers that have ascended to Heaven from Africa's daughters for strength to perform their work. Oh, many are the tears that have been shed for the want of that strength! Most of our color have dragged out a miserable existence of servitude from the cradle to the grave. And what literary acquirements can be made, or useful knowledge derived, from either maps, books or charm, by those who continually drudge from Monday morning until Sunday noon? O, ye fairer sisters, whose hands are never soiled, whose nerves and muscles are never strained, go learn by experience! Had we had the opportunity that you have had, to improve our moral and mental faculties, what would have hindered our intellects from being as bright, and our manners from being as dignified as yours? Had it been our lot to have been nursed in the lap of affluence and ease, and to have basked beneath the smiles and sunshine of fortune, should we not have naturally supposed that we were never made to toil? And why are not our forms as delicate, and our constitutions as slender, as yours? Is not the workmanship as curious and complete? Have pity upon us, have pity upon us, O ye who have hearts to feel for other's woes; for the hand of God has touched us. Owing to the disadvantages under which we labor, there are many flowers among us that are ... born to bloom unseen, And waste their fragrance on the desert air.

My beloved brethren, as Christ has died in vain for those who will not accept of offered mercy, so will it be vain for the advocates of freedom to spend their breath in our behalf, unless with united hearts and souls you make some mighty efforts to raise your sons, and daughters from the horrible state of servitude and degradation in which they are placed. It is upon you that woman depends; she can do but little besides using her influence; and it is for her sake and yours that I have come forward and made myself a hissing and a reproach among the people; for I am also one of the wretched and miserable daughters of the descendants of fallen Africa. Do you ask, why are you wretched and miserable? I reply, look at many of the most worthy and interesting of us doomed to spend our lives in gentlemen's kitchens. Look at our young men, smart, active and energetic, with souls filled with ambitious fire; if they look forward, alas! what are their prospects? They can be nothing but the humblest laborers, on account of their dark complexions; hence many of them lose their ambition, and become worthless. Look at our middle-aged men, clad in their rusty plaids and coats; in winter, every cent they earn goes to buy their wood and pay their rents; their poor wives also toil beyond their strength, to help support their families. Look at our aged sires, whose heads are whitened with the front of seventy winters, with their old wood-saws on their backs. Alas, what keeps us so? Prejudice, ignorance and poverty. But ah! methinks our oppression is soon to come to an end; yes, before the Majesty of heaven, our groans and cries have reached the ears of the Lord of Sabaoth [James 5:4]. As the prayers and tears of Christians will avail the finally impenitent nothing; neither will the prayers and tears of the friends of humanity avail us any thing, unless we possess a spirit of virtuous emulation within our breasts. Did the pilgrims, when they first landed on these shores, quietly compose themselves, and say, "the Britons have all the money and all the power, and we must continue their servants forever?" Did they sluggishly sigh and say, "our lot is hard, the Indians own the soil, and we cannot cultivate it?" No; they first made powerful efforts to raise themselves and then God raised up those illustrious patriots WASHINGTON and LAFAYETTE, to assist and defend them. And, my brethren, have you made a powerful effort? Have you prayed the Legislature for mercy's sake to grant you all the rights and privileges of free citizens, that your daughters may raise to that degree of respectability which true merit deserves, and your sons above the servile situations which most of them fill?

QUESTIONS

(1) Why is Stewart concerned with the poor education and lack of economic advancement for black women and to demand equal rights for them?

(2) Why for Stewart, were slavery in the South and racism in the North equally horrifying for blacks?

(3) Why, for Stewart, were the unequal conditions of black men not so different from those of black women?

(4) Why, at the end of her lecture, did Stewart reference Washington and Lafayette?

(5) According to Stewart, what are the necessary conditions for blacks to be treated more fairly and to be as successful as whites?

PART II
Reconstruction

NIKKI L. M. BROWN

· ·

During the Reconstruction era (1865–1877), it was important for blacks to gain some political power. Exemplifying political liberation, during Reconstruction 1,465 African Americans held office across the United States, and in South Carolina, African Americans were in the majority party for eight years. The era witnessed the passage of the Enforcement Acts of 1870, which empowered the federal government to subject to surveillance and arrest members of white domestic terrorist groups, and the Civil Rights Act of 1875, which outlawed racial segregation in public places. The American Civil War and the Reconstruction era cast its longest and deepest shadow over black political thought in the following decades. Though these essays were written after the end of Reconstruction, their tone is rich with a small glitter of hopefulness for Reconstruction's transformative potential for blacks' unequal status. As Reconstruction progressed, W. E. B. Du Bois, for one, would recognize that "almost every law and method ingenuity could devise was employed by the legislatures to reduce the Negroes to serfdom, – to make them the slaves of the State." And even though, for Du Bois, the Freedmen's Bureau officials were often determined to provide "the freedmen a power and independence which they could not yet use," Du Bois later on, in *Black Reconstruction in America*, would conclude that "Abraham Lincoln himself could not have settled the question of Emancipation, Negro Citizenship and the vote without tremendous difficulty."[1]

As products of their times, the essays from W. E. B. Du Bois, T. Thomas Fortune, and Booker T. Washington reflect a general consensus among historians of African

---

[1] W. E. B. Du Bois, *Black Reconstruction*, with Introduction by Herbert Aptheker (Millwood, NY: Kraus Thomson Organization, 1976), p. 165.

American life and culture about the causes of black poverty and disenfranchisement during the Reconstruction era. Their opinions were in agreement that pervasive racism – the denial of voting rights, employment, and housing rights – in the Southern states, where 95 percent of African Americans lived, were the biggest impediments to black success, which took shape, most disturbingly, in the form of extralegal violence – race riots, lynchings, and intimidation by terrorist groups.[2] W. E. B. Du Bois, T. Thomas Fortune, and Booker T. Washington wrote for the reading public (blacks) who were convinced that their lives and their livelihoods were viscerally threatened by these economic and social disruptions.

It should be noted that all three men were financially well-off and enjoyed their positions of power in their respective fields of journalism (Fortune), organizational protest (Du Bois), and academia and philanthropy (Washington). They were patriarchal and classist. They took a short-sighted and hetero-normative view of black success, in which black men stood at the helm of the family and black women and children followed obediently in tow. However, these writers felt the sting of racial prejudice and discrimination in their lives keenly and they believed that African Americans would be condemned to a century of poverty and disenfranchisement, if immediate action was not taken. Their essays here reflect their sense of urgency, culled from their personal stories from the grassroots and an elite bird's-eye view of race relations across the nation.

W. E. B. Du Bois and the Redemption of Reconstruction

Du Bois wrote for historians, and his vision remains the most far-reaching. His essay, "Of the Dawn of Freedom," offers the most famous pronouncement about racism in modern US history, in which he declares, "The problem of the twentieth century is the problem of the color-line, – the relation of the darker to the lighter races of men in Asia and Africa, in America and the islands of the sea." Du Bois' essay represents the essence of the "Sankofa bird"[3] or "the two-headed Janus,"[4] in which it looks into

---

[2] Indeed, the Reconstruction era was a violent period in America's history. There were hundreds of race riots during this period across the country, some of the most devastating in Southern cities with high concentrations of middle-class African Americans. The Memphis and New Orleans riots of 1866 are widely discussed by many historians. For a more comprehensive discussion of race violence, see Melinda Meek Hennessey, "Racial Violence during Reconstruction: The 1876 Riots in Charleston and Cainhoy," *The South Carolina Historical Magazine* 86, no. 2 (April 1985): 100–112.

[3] For more on the Sankofa bird symbol, see W. E. B. Du Bois Learning Center, www.duboislc.net/SankofaMeaning.html.

[4] In Shakespeare's *The Merchant of Venice*, Janus is the "God of beginnings, transitions, and endings." Janus is portrayed as having two faces, one happy and one sad, signifying the uncertainty of the future. We remember in Act 1, Scene 1, how Salarino refers to Antonio as "the two-headed Janus."

America's racist past and its racist present at the same time so as to derive a good grasp of blacks' uncertain future. The problem of the color-line undergirded the institution of slavery. Du Bois also foresaw that Reconstruction had not resolved the problem of racism, and racism would continue to be a heavy burden on American politics and culture until a second, better Reconstruction was enacted.

He spent most of the essay setting the record straight about Reconstruction and black citizenship. In 1903, when "Of the Dawn of Freedom" was published in *The Souls of Black Folk*, the Civil War was within living memory and there was much debate on the causes and consequences of the war. "Lost Cause" historians dominated the narrative of the Civil War, misconceiving the Confederate cause as a heroic, yet doomed sacrifice. Du Bois cautioned those historians who believed that slavery did not cause the Civil War to reconsider their positions, adding "it is doubly difficult to write of this period calmly, so intense was the telling, so mighty the human passions that swayed and blinded men." Though he concluded that Reconstruction failed African Americans ultimately – "despite compromise, war, and struggle, the Negro is not free" – Du Bois encouraged his audience of historians to throw out the weak "Lost Cause" analyses of Civil War and Reconstruction in favor of more accurate histories, in which African Americans' contributions were included and heralded.

All of Reconstruction was a "splendid failure," he declared in his magnum opus, *Reconstruction in America*, because those in power failed "to grapple with vast problems of race and social condition." Hence, the primary reason for this failure, Du Bois concluded, was "the utter inability of the American mind to grasp its real significance, its national and worldwide implications."[5] Extremist groups, a weak federal government, and outbreaks of violence between Southern whites and blacks were so numerous that they became impossible to solve. There was the Colfax Massacre of 1873 in Louisiana, where 150 blacks and three whites died in a two-day riot, or the Battle of Liberty Place in New Orleans in 1874, where a white supremacist group led a coup d'état over the legally elected black city council. Historian Eric Foner writes that at the time, Du Bois' view of Reconstruction, in both *Souls of Black Folk* and *Black Reconstruction*, was largely ignored or dismissed by white historians.[6] Now, the general consensus is that Du Bois' view is the historically correct one.

And even though Reconstruction was a "splendid failure" in dealing with blacks' inequality, Du Bois' essay retold the history of the Freedmen's Bureau, its successes and failures. Indeed, for Du Bois, the Freedmen's Bureau "stood for a thing in the South which for two centuries and better men had refused even to argue, – that life amid free Negroes was simply unthinkable, the maddest of experiments." Its

---

[5] Du Bois, *Black Reconstruction*, p. 708.
[6] Eric Foner, *Reconstruction: America's Unfinished Revolution, 1863–1877* (New York: HarperCollins, 2011), p. xix.

primary success "lay in the planting of the free school among Negroes, and the idea of free elementary education among all classes in the South," concerning which, Du Bois discusses some vivid examples of white backlash caused by education for Negroes. In the words of Du Bois: "So the Freedmen's Bureau died, and its child was the Fifteenth Amendment," which bestowed upon black men the right to vote.

T. Thomas Fortune and Advocacy Journalism

T. Thomas Fortune wrote that African American men must use their hard-won voting rights to support a strong federal government, reasoning that the federal government would protect African Americans from legal abuses in the states. While Fortune declared his fidelity to the United States on many occasions in his essay when he acknowledged: "In a word, I am an American citizen," he wrote that Reconstruction's most obvious miscarriage was its inability to enforce the rules of citizenship for African Americans "as enunciated by Alexander Hamilton, and maintained by the present Republican party, and the question of the rights and powers of the States, as enunciated by Thomas Jefferson." Also, there was bitter disappointment at the victory of the white backlash that contributed to Reconstruction's end. In the pages of the *New York Globe*, Fortune railed against the failure of federal government to protect African Americans, adding, "this is a government of the people – not white or black people but of the people ... In a commonwealth of equals such as ours claims to be, no race, class or party had the right to claim to be the 'governing class.'"[7] In the essay in this volume, "Political Independence of the Negro," Fortune's most optimistic advice was reserved for entrepreneurs, white and black, who could put aside racism to work with each other. His essay was written in 1884, and it is likely that he directed it at grassroots politics and businessmen, who still held enough political power among African Americans in the South to make another solid run for state and federal seats. While he was disappointed that "The Republican Party has degenerated into an ignoble scramble for place and power [and] has forgotten the principles for which Sumner contended, and for which Lincoln died," Fortune believed in his rights as an American citizen so fiercely that he pledged to defend those rights with his life "should this heritage be attempted to be filched from me by a man or body of men." Instead of traditional political parties, Fortune argued in his essay that "harmony of sentiment between blacks and whites of the country ... is natural and necessary," which is important for the flourishing of a truly democratic government.

The weakness of Fortune's pronouncement was that it did not account for the profoundly deep white backlash against Reconstruction. In 1883, the Supreme

---

[7] Shawn Leigh Alexander, *T. Thomas Fortune, the Afro-American Agitator: A Collection of Writings, 1880 to 1928* (Gainesville, FL: University Press of Florida, 2008), p. xv.

Court had already ruled the 1875 Civil Rights Act unconstitutional, and by 1885 a movement was underway to separate African Americans and whites from each other in all public arenas. The most pivotal and depressing legal event was the *Plessy v. Ferguson* decision of 1896. Writing for the Supreme Court eight to one majority, Justice Henry Billings Brown of Michigan infamously declared that, "If one race be inferior to the other socially, the Constitution of the United States cannot put them on the same plane." The Supreme Court supported the prevailing racist beliefs about African Americans, according to which African Americans and white Americans possessed different characters, worldviews, and lifestyles, and that these differences made African Americans inferior in every way. The Supreme Court's views reflected the libertarian racist ideology that was in vogue at the time, which held that the federal government should not regulate equality among the races which were inherently unequal.

The demise of the Reconstruction era promises and the onset of the Jim Crow South gravely deepened Fortune's dissatisfaction with the South.[8] There was no going back to the high times of Reconstruction. For what it's worth, the *New Orleans Picayune*, the major white paper in the city, argued that the decision "does not create inequality between the citizens of the state," nor does it "discriminate unfairly between citizens of the state, of whatever color or race." The *Picayune* maintained that at its center, the *Plessy* decision was the right one because it granted state legislatures and the police the power to protect lily-white public spaces by preventing race-mixing in the "lives, limbs, health, comfort, morals, and quiet of society, private [i.e. African American] interest being subservient to the public."[9] In 1898, soon after the *Plessy* decision, the state of Louisiana authorized grandfather clauses as a legitimate tool to deny black voting rights and reaffirm white voting rights. The same year that grandfather clauses were declared legal, the Supreme Court decided *Williams v. Mississippi* (1898) and allowed literacy tests, poll taxes, and other forms of voter registration restrictions aimed primarily at African Americans. Nearly every Southern state legislature legalized racial segregation in all public places.

It was a grave mistake for the government to enact discriminatory measures that upheld and reinforced the view that blacks were unequal to whites. For Fortune "the best interests of the race and the best interests of the country will be conserved by building up a bond of union between the white people and the Negroes of the South – advocating the doctrine that the interests of the white and the interests of the colored people are one and the same; that the legislation which affects the one will affect the other." It was clear that Fortune had relied too heavily on the belief that working-class whites would overcome hundreds of years of racial prejudice to unite politically and economically with African Americans.

---

[8] T. Thomas Fortune, *After War Time: An African American Childhood in Reconstruction-Era Florida*, ed. Daniel R. Weinfeld (Tuscaloosa: University of Alabama Press, 2014), p. xi.

[9] "The Supreme Court Decides Three Louisiana Cases," *New Orleans Daily Picayune*, 19 May 1896.

Booker T. Washington and Racial Accommodationism

Booker T. Washington considered himself an energetic optimist, and he was sure that African Americans would grow into economic self-sufficiency. In "The Case of the Negro," Washington's eagerness to direct his public utterances to the ears of white Southerners is on full view. His essay was published in 1899, just four years after his 1895 speech at the Atlanta Cotton Exposition, in which he famously argued that racial segregation and industrial education were the solutions to black poverty. Early in his essay, Washington summarized why all of the progressive and radical ideas for black advancement were wrong and destined for failure. He wrote that emigration to Africa was not a serious or tenable solution, clearly a rebuttal to the growing popularity of the back-to-Africa movement in the late 1800s. He singled out radical black activists as well, saying that they were leading Southern blacks astray with their talk of "armed resistance or the use of the torch in order to secure justice" and concluded that "the Negro is at his best in the Southern states."

Washington took special aim at black newspapers, and likely had Fortune in mind when he added that it was black newspapers and "impatient extremists among the Negroes in the North" who were leading the masses of Southern blacks astray. Washington believed that black newspapers exaggerated the social problems of poverty, lynching, and unemployment that blacks experienced after the end of slavery. And, though he decried how African Americans were disenfranchised by literacy tests and property clauses that were enacted after the passing of the Fifteenth Amendment, he added that "with the help and sympathy and justice from the law," blacks "must begin at the bottom and lay a sure foundation" by using the skills they had learned as slaves, which, he was convinced, would provide them with "the means of earning a living."

Washington's essay reassured white Southerners that African Americans were not planning a widespread revolution. Whites could trust African Americans to follow the rules and pursue a gradual claim for democracy. In short, Washington wrote for conservative white businessmen and philanthropists, subtly drawing their attention to the Tuskegee Institute, Washington's private university and a center of conservative black thought.

Conclusion

The essays of this section are at their most poignant if viewed through the frame of political and economic loss for blacks in America during Reconstruction. When the United States emerged as a world industrial power in the late nineteenth century, its tremendous economic growth in manufacturing also ushered in a restructuring of American politics. Even though the period between 1880 and 1920 witnessed the Gilded Age and, soon after, the Progressive Era when American literary and political audiences were obsessed with Social Darwinism, the Gospel of Wealth, and conspicuous consumption, the financial collapse, first in 1873 and then again in 1893, led to a nationwide populist fervor, which, in turn, fed an early world war between United States and Spain, which was fought in Cuba, Puerto Rico, Guam, and the Philippines. Benjamin Quarles, historian of Reconstruction and the Gilded Age, called this period "the decades of disappointment." Similarly, the historian Rayford W. Logan described this period – starting in 1877, the end of the Reconstruction era – as "the nadir of the Negro,"[10] condemning both Republican and Democratic administrations for abandoning African Americans' civil rights.[11]

All three thinkers, Du Bois, Fortune, and Washington acknowledged that the United States was a meaner, crueler country for African Americans during and after Reconstruction. The National Association for the Advancement of Colored People (NAACP) authored *Thirty Years of Lynching*, a study of extralegal brutality and murder in the United States from 1889 to 1918. It found that 2,522 African Americans were killed by mobs, policemen, political officials, and jailhouse guards. It amounted to two deaths per week, every month, for thirty years. Just one year before Booker T. Washington wrote the essay appearing in this volume, three African American men were lynched in Alabama, when a white mob broke into the jail where the men were awaiting trial for burning a barn. The mob brought the men to a local bridge, tied ropes around the men's necks, and forced the men to jump.[12]

But, their audience at the time, who were black voters and potential power-brokers of the future, played a critical role in the success of their visions for African American advancement. Readers of black political philosophy continue

---

[10] See Rayford Logan, *The Negro in American Life and Thought: The Nadir 1877–1901* (New York: Dial Press, 1954).

[11] Benjamin Quarles, *The Negro in the Making of America* (London: Collier-Macmillian, 1969), p. 126; Rayford Logan, *The Betrayal of the Negro, from Rutherford B. Hayes to Woodrow Wilson* (New York: Collier, 1965), p. 85. There was also the European imperial plundering of the continent of Africa, starting at full speed in 1884 with the Berlin Conference. African Americans and Pan-Africanists witnessed myriad social and economic problems underway and, as a result, multiple approaches of political thought emerged with widely varying levels of success. As historian Nell Irvin Painter surmised, "Between the late nineteenth and early twentieth centuries large numbers of Americans came to realize that economic, social, and demographic changes needed to be taken into account politically, or grave injustices would result." See Nell Irvin Painter, *Standing at Armageddon: The United States, 1877 to 1919* (New York: W. W. Norton, 1987), p. xxxviii. All of these events affected the worldviews of these authors. They shared a resignation that bad times had descended for African Americans, and they saw no end in sight.

[12] National Association for the Advancement of Colored People, *Thirty Years of Lynching in the United States, 1889 to 1918* (New York: Arno Press and the New York Times, 1919), pp. 7, 11.

to carry on the tradition of vigorous debate, interweaving these foundational ideas in current debate. The political visions of Du Bois, Fortune, and Washington contributed greatly to the post-World War II Civil Rights Movement. Fortune's call for black independence from traditional American party politics reverberated in the Mississippi Freedom Democratic Party of 1964 and the National Black Political Assembly in Gary, Indiana in 1972. Washington's conviction in black self-sufficiency is a mainstay of Black Power ideology, apparent in the celebration of Kwanzaa and the principle of Ujamaa, or cooperative economics. Du Bois' declaration about the "problem of the color-line" finds new avenues of thought and discussion with each successive generation. Moreover, Du Bois lived long enough to see much of his work touch a new generation of African American activists and scholars. Together, these thinkers shaped black political thought by presenting three visions of the African American political landscape in ways that continue to evolve.

QUESTIONS

(1) According to the articles presented in this section, was Reconstruction a success or a failure? Discuss.
(2) What was the main purpose of the Freedmen's Bureau, initially referred to as the Freemen's Act Society? Was it a success or a failure? Explain.
(3) The essays in the section provide a socio-historical account of blacks in the United States during the Reconstruction period. Even though slavery ended, blacks continued to be enslaved through customs, laws, and systems. What evidence of this is provided by the authors?
(4) According to Du Bois, Fortune, and Washington, what were some of the socio-political and economic advantages and disadvantages for blacks during the Reconstruction period?
(5) How can the Reconstruction period be compared with slavery?

FURTHER READINGS

- Alrutheus A. Taylor, "The Aftermath of Reconstruction," *The Journal of Negro History* 9, no. 10 (October 1924): 546–553.
- Archibald H. Grimke, *Modern Industrialism and the Negroes of the United States* (Washington, DC: The American Negro Academy, 1908).
- Fannie Barrier Williams, "The Intellectual Progress of the Women of the United States since the Emancipation Proclamation," in *The World Conference of Representative Women*, ed. May Wright Sewall (New York: Rand, McNally & Company, 1894), pp. 711–715. Available at: https://archive.org/stream/worldscongressof00worluoft/worldscongressof00worluoft_djvu.txt.
- Frederick Douglass, "The Future of the Colored Race" (May 1886). Available at: http://teachingamericanhistory.org/library/document/the-future-of-the-colored-race/.

- John Hope Franklin, *Reconstruction after the Civil War* (University of Chicago Press, 1961).
- Julie Saville, *The Work of Reconstruction: From Slavery to Wage Labor in South Carolina, 1860–1870* (New York: Cambridge University Press, 1994).
- Lerone Bennett, *Black Power USA: The Human Side of Reconstruction, 1867–1877* (Chicago, IL: Johnson Publishing Company, 1967).
- Reginald F. Hildebrand, *The Times Were Strange and Stirring: Methodist Preachers and the Crisis of Emancipation* (Durham, NC: Duke University Press, 1995).
- Stephen Middleton, *Black Congressmen during Reconstruction: A Documentary Source Book* (Westport, CT: Greenwood Press, 2002).
- W. E. B. Du Bois, "Reconstruction and Its Benefits," *American Historical Review* 15 (July 1910): 781–799.

6 Of the Dawn of Freedom

W. E. B. DU BOIS

William Edward Burghardt Du Bois (1868–1963), a historian, sociologist, activist, and Pan-Africanist, was born in Great Barrington, Massachusetts, where he grew up. After graduating from high school, he moved to Nashville, Tennessee, to attend Fisk University. In 1888, he graduated with a BA from Fisk. In the same year, Du Bois returned to Massachusetts and attended Harvard University as a junior, took a Bachelor of Arts cum laude in 1890, and was one of the six commencement speakers. He was the first African American to have obtained a doctoral degree from Harvard University. Du Bois was the leader of the Niagara Movement founded in 1905 and one of the co-founders of the National Association for the Advancement of Colored People founded in 1909. He was famous for his book *The Souls of Black Folk*, which was published in 1909. In his essay below, "Of the Dawn of Freedom," Du Bois provides a historical account of blacks in the United States, and points out that, in spite of the "freedom" granted to newly freed slaves, the color-line would continue to bar blacks from attaining such a "freedom."

The problem of the twentieth century is the problem of the color-line, – the relation of the darker to the lighter races of men in Asia and Africa, in America and the islands of the sea. It was a phase of this problem that caused the Civil War; and however much they who marched South and North in 1861 may have fixed on the technical points, of union and local autonomy as a shibboleth, all nevertheless knew, as we know, that the question of Negro slavery was the real cause of the conflict. Curious it was, too, how this deeper question ever forced itself to the surface despite effort and disclaimer. No sooner had Northern armies touched Southern soil than this old question, newly guised, sprang from the earth, – What shall be done with Negroes? Peremptory military commands this way and that, could not answer the query; the Emancipation Proclamation seemed but to broaden and intensify the difficulties; and the War Amendments made the Negro problems of to-day.

It is the aim of this essay to study the period of history from 1861 to 1872 so far as it relates to the American Negro. In effect, this tale of the dawn of Freedom is an account of that government of men called the Freedmen's Bureau, – one of the most singular and interesting of the attempts made by a great nation to grapple with vast problems of race and social condition.

The war has naught to do with slaves, cried Congress, the President, and the Nation; and yet no sooner had the armies, East and West, penetrated Virginia and Tennessee than fugitive slaves appeared within their lines. They came at night, when the flickering camp-fires shone like vast unsteady stars along the black horizon: old men and thin, with gray and tufted hair; women with frightened eyes, dragging whimpering hungry children; men and girls, stalwart and gaunt, – a horde of starving vagabonds, homeless, helpless, and pitiable, in their dark distress. Two methods of treating these newcomers seemed equally logical to opposite sorts of minds. Ben Butler, in Virginia, quickly declared slave property contraband of war, and put the fugitives to work; while Fremont, in Missouri, declared the slaves free under martial law. Butler's action was approved, but Fremont's was hastily countermanded, and his successor, Halleck, saw things differently. "Hereafter," he commanded, "no slaves should be allowed to come into your lines at all; if any come without your knowledge, when owners call for them deliver them." Such a policy was difficult to enforce; some of the black refugees declared themselves freemen, others showed that their masters had deserted them, and still others were captured with forts and plantations. Evidently, too, slaves were a source of strength to the Confederacy, and were being used as laborers and producers. "They constitute a military resource," wrote Secretary Cameron, late in 1861; "and being such, that they should not be turned over to the enemy is too plain to discuss." So gradually the tone of the army chiefs changed; Congress forbade the rendition of fugitives, and Butler's "contrabands" were welcomed as military laborers. This complicated rather than solved the problem, for now the scattering fugitives became a steady stream, which flowed faster as the armies marched.

Then the long-headed man with care-chiselled face who sat in the White House saw the inevitable, and emancipated the slaves of rebels on New Year's, 1863. A month later Congress called earnestly for the Negro soldiers whom the act of July, 1862, had half grudgingly allowed to enlist. Thus the barriers were levelled and the deed was done. The stream of fugitives swelled to a flood, and anxious army officers kept inquiring: "What must be done with slaves, arriving almost daily? Are we to find food and shelter for women and children?"

It was a Pierce of Boston who pointed out the way, and thus became in a sense the founder of the Freedmen's Bureau. He was a firm friend of Secretary Chase; and when, in 1861, the care of slaves and abandoned lands devolved upon the Treasury officials, Pierce was specially detailed from the ranks to study the conditions. First, he cared for the refugees at Fortress Monroe; and then, after Sherman had captured Hilton Head, Pierce was sent there to found his Port Royal experiment of making free workingmen out of slaves. Before his experiment was barely started, however, the problem of the fugitives had assumed such proportions that it was taken from the hands of the over-burdened Treasury Department and given to the army officials. Already centres of massed freedmen were forming at Fortress Monroe, Washington, New Orleans, Vicksburg and Corinth, Columbus, Ky., and Cairo, Ill., as well as at Port Royal. Army chaplains found here new and fruitful fields; "superintendents of contrabands" multiplied, and some attempt at systematic work was made by enlisting the able-bodied men and giving work to the others.

Then came the Freedmen's Aid societies, born of the touching appeals from Pierce and from these other centres of distress. There was the American Missionary Association, sprung from the Amistad, and now full-grown for work; the various church organizations, the National Freedmen's Relief Association, the American Freedmen's Union, the Western Freedmen's Aid Commission, – in all fifty or more active organizations, which sent clothes, money, school-books, and teachers southward. All they did was needed, for the destitution of the freedmen was often reported as "too appalling for belief," and the situation was daily growing worse rather than better.

And daily, too, it seemed more plain that this was no ordinary matter of temporary relief, but a national crisis; for here loomed a labor problem of vast dimensions. Masses of Negroes stood idle, or, if they worked spasmodically, were never sure of pay; and if perchance they received pay, squandered the new thing thoughtlessly. In these and other ways were camp-life and the new liberty demoralizing the freedmen. The broader economic organization thus clearly demanded sprang up here and there as accident and local conditions determined. Here it was that Pierce's Port Royal plan of leased plantations and guided workmen pointed out the rough way. In Washington the military governor, at the urgent appeal of the superintendent, opened confiscated estates to the cultivation of the fugitives, and there in the shadow of the dome gathered black farm villages. General Dix gave over estates to the freedmen of Fortress Monroe, and so on, South and West. The government and benevolent societies furnished the means of cultivation, and the Negro turned again slowly to work. The systems of control, thus started, rapidly grew, here and there, into strange little governments, like that of General Banks in Louisiana, with its ninety thousand black subjects, its fifty thousand guided laborers, and its annual budget of one hundred thousand dollars and more. It made out four thousand pay-rolls a year, registered all freedmen, inquired into grievances and redressed them, laid and collected taxes, and established a system of public schools. So, too, Colonel Eaton, the superintendent of Tennessee and Arkansas, ruled over one hundred thousand freedmen, leased and cultivated seven thousand acres of cotton land, and fed ten thousand paupers a year. In South Carolina was General Saxton, with his deep interest in black folk. He succeeded Pierce and the Treasury officials, and sold forfeited estates, leased abandoned plantations, encouraged schools, and received from Sherman, after that terribly picturesque march to the sea, thousands of the wretched camp followers.

Three characteristic things one might have seen in Sherman's raid through Georgia, which threw the new situation in shadowy relief: the Conqueror, the Conquered, and the Negro. Some see all significance in the grim front of the destroyer, and some in the bitter sufferers of the Lost Cause. But to me neither soldier nor fugitive speaks with so deep a meaning as that dark human cloud that clung like remorse on the rear of those swift columns, swelling at times to half their size, almost engulfing and choking them. In vain were they ordered back, in vain were bridges hewn from beneath their feet; on they trudged and writhed and surged, until they rolled into Savannah, a starved and naked horde of tens of thousands. There too came the characteristic military remedy: "The islands from Charleston south, the abandoned rice-fields along the rivers for thirty miles back from the sea, and the country bordering the St. John's River, Florida, are reserved and set apart for the settlement of Negroes now made free by act of war." So read the celebrated "Field-order Number Fifteen."

All these experiments, orders, and systems were bound to attract and perplex the government and the nation. Directly after the Emancipation Proclamation, Representative Eliot had introduced a bill creating a Bureau of Emancipation; but it was never reported. The following June a committee of inquiry, appointed by the Secretary of War, reported in favor of a temporary bureau for the "improvement, protection, and employment of refugee freedmen," on much the same lines as were afterwards followed. Petitions came in to President Lincoln from distinguished citizens and organizations, strongly urging a comprehensive and unified plan of dealing with the freedmen, under a bureau which should be "charged with the study of plans and execution of measures for easily guiding, and in every way judiciously and humanely aiding, the passage of our emancipated and yet to be emancipated blacks from the old condition of forced labor to their new state of voluntary industry."

Some half-hearted steps were taken to accomplish this, in part, by putting the whole matter again in charge of the special Treasury agents. Laws of 1863 and 1864 directed them to take charge of and lease abandoned lands for periods not exceeding twelve months, and to "provide in such leases, or otherwise, for the employment and general welfare" of the freedmen. Most of the army officers greeted this as a welcome relief from perplexing "Negro affairs," and Secretary Fessenden, July 29, 1864, issued an excellent system of regulations, which were afterward closely followed by General Howard. Under Treasury agents, large quantities of land were leased in the Mississippi Valley, and many Negroes were employed; but in August, 1864, the new regulations were suspended for reasons of "public policy," and the army was again in control.

Meanwhile Congress had turned its attention to the subject; and in March the House passed a bill by a majority of two establishing a Bureau for Freedmen in the War Department. Charles Sumner, who had charge of the bill in the Senate, argued that freedmen and abandoned lands ought to be under the same department, and reported a substitute for the House bill attaching the Bureau to the Treasury Department. This bill passed, but too late for action by the House. The debates wandered over the whole policy of the administration and the general question of slavery, without touching very closely the specific merits of the measure in hand. Then the national election took place; and the administration, with a vote of renewed confidence from the country, addressed itself to the matter more seriously. A conference between the two branches of Congress agreed upon a carefully drawn measure which contained the chief provisions of Sumner's bill, but made the proposed organization a department independent of both the War and the Treasury officials. The bill was conservative, giving the new department "general superintendence of all freedmen." Its purpose was to "establish regulations" for them, protect them, lease them lands, adjust their wages, and appear in civil and military courts as their "next friend." There were many limitations attached to the powers thus granted, and the organization was made permanent. Nevertheless, the Senate defeated the bill, and a new conference committee was appointed. This committee reported a new bill, February 28, which was whirled through just as the session closed, and became the act of 1865 establishing in the War Department a "Bureau of Refugees, Freedmen, and Abandoned Lands."

This last compromise was a hasty bit of legislation, vague and uncertain in outline. A Bureau was created, "to continue during the present War of Rebellion, and for one year thereafter," to which was given "the supervision and management of all abandoned lands and the control of all subjects relating to refugees and freedmen," under "such rules and regulations as may be presented by the head of the Bureau and approved by the President." A Commissioner, appointed by the President and Senate, was to control the Bureau, with an office force not exceeding ten clerks. The President might also appoint assistant commissioners in the seceded States, and to all these offices military officials might be detailed at regular pay. The Secretary of War could issue rations, clothing, and fuel to the destitute, and all abandoned property was placed in the hands of the Bureau for eventual lease and sale to ex-slaves in forty-acre parcels.

Thus did the United States government definitely assume charge of the emancipated Negro as the ward of the nation. It was a tremendous undertaking. Here at a stroke of the pen was erected a government of millions of men, – and not ordinary men either, but black men emasculated by a peculiarly complete system of slavery, centuries old; and now, suddenly, violently, they come into a new birthright, at a time of war and passion, in the midst of the stricken and embittered population of their former masters. Any man might well have hesitated to assume charge of such a work, with vast responsibilities, indefinite powers, and limited resources. Probably no one but a soldier would have answered such a call promptly; and, indeed, no one but a soldier could be called, for Congress had appropriated no money for salaries and expenses.

Less than a month after the weary Emancipator passed to his rest, his successor assigned Major-Gen. Oliver O. Howard to duty as Commissioner of the new Bureau. He was a Maine man, then only thirty-five years of age. He had marched with Sherman to the sea, had fought well at Gettysburg, and but the year before had been assigned to the command of the Department of Tennessee. An honest man, with too much faith in human nature, little aptitude for business and intricate detail, he had had large opportunity of becoming acquainted at first hand with much of the work before him. And of that work it has been truly said that "no approximately correct history of civilization can ever be written which does not throw out in bold relief, as one of the great landmarks of political and social progress, the organization and administration of the Freedmen's Bureau."

On May 12, 1865, Howard was appointed; and he assumed the duties of his office promptly on the 15th, and began examining the field of work. A curious mess he looked upon: little despotisms, communistic experiments, slavery, peonage, business speculations, organized charity, unorganized almsgiving, – all reeling on under the guise of helping the freedmen, and all enshrined in the smoke and blood of the war and the cursing and silence of angry men. On May 19th the new government – for a government it really was – issued its constitution; commissioners were to be appointed in each of the seceded states, who were to take charge of "all subjects relating to refugees and freedmen," and all relief and rations were to be given by their consent alone. The Bureau invited continued cooperation with benevolent societies, and declared: "It will be the object of all commissioners to introduce practicable systems of compensated labor," and to establish schools. Forthwith nine assistant commissioners were appointed. They were to hasten to their fields of work; seek gradually to close relief establishments, and make the destitute self-supporting; act as courts of law where there were no courts, or where Negroes were not recognized in them as free; establish the institution of marriage among ex-slaves, and keep records; see that freedmen were free to choose their employers, and help in making fair contracts for them; and finally, the circular said: "Simple good faith, for which we hope on all hands for those concerned in the passing away of slavery, will especially relieve the assistant commissioners in the discharge of their duties toward the freedmen, as well as promote the general welfare."

No sooner was the work thus started, and the general system and local organization in some measure begun, than two grave difficulties appeared which changed largely the theory and outcome of Bureau work. First, there were the abandoned lands of the South. It had long been the more or less definitely expressed theory of the North that all the chief problems of Emancipation might be settled by establishing the slaves on the forfeited lands of their masters, – a sort of poetic justice, said some. But this poetry done into solemn prose meant either wholesale confiscation of private property in the South, or vast appropriations. Now Congress had not appropriated a cent, and no sooner did the proclamations of general amnesty appear than the eight hundred thousand acres of abandoned lands in the hands of the Freedmen's Bureau melted quickly away. The second difficulty lay in perfecting the local organization of the Bureau throughout the wide field of work. Making a new machine and sending out officials of duly ascertained fitness for a great work of social reform is no child's task; but this task was even harder, for a new central organization had to be fitted on a heterogeneous and confused but already existing system of relief and control of ex-slaves; and the agents available for this work must be sought for in an army still busy with war operations, – men in the very nature of the case ill fitted for delicate social work, – or among the questionable camp followers of an invading host. Thus, after a year's work, vigorously as it was pushed, the problem looked even more difficult to grasp and solve than at the beginning. Nevertheless, three things that year's work did, well worth the doing: it relieved a vast amount of physical suffering; it transported seven thousand fugitives from congested centres back to the farm; and, best of all, it inaugurated the crusade of the New England schoolma'am.

The annals of this Ninth Crusade are yet to be written, – the tale of a mission that seemed to our age far more quixotic than the quest of St. Louis seemed to his. Behind the mists of ruin and rapine waved the calico dresses of women who dared, and after the hoarse mouthings of the field guns rang the rhythm of the alphabet. Rich and poor they were, serious and curious. Bereaved now of a father, now of a brother, now of more than these, they came seeking a life work in planting New England schoolhouses among the white and black of the South. They did their work well. In that first year they taught one hundred thousand souls, and more.

Evidently, Congress must soon legislate again on the hastily organized Bureau, which had so quickly grown into wide significance and vast possibilities. An institution such as that was well-nigh as difficult to end as to begin. Early in 1866 Congress took up the matter, when Senator Trumbull, of Illinois, introduced a bill to extend the Bureau and enlarge its powers. This measure received, at the hands of Congress, far more thorough discussion and attention than its predecessor. The war cloud had thinned enough to allow a clearer conception of the work of Emancipation. The champions of the bill argued that the strengthening of the Freedmen's Bureau was still a military necessity; that it was needed for the proper carrying out of the Thirteenth Amendment, and was a work of sheer justice to the ex-slave, at a trifling cost to the government. The opponents of the measure declared that the war was over, and the necessity for war measures past; that the Bureau, by reason of its extraordinary powers, was clearly unconstitutional in time of peace, and was destined to irritate the South and pauperize the freedmen, at a final cost of possibly hundreds of millions. These two arguments were unanswered, and indeed unanswerable: the one that the extraordinary powers of the Bureau threatened the civil rights of all citizens; and the other that the government must have power to do what manifestly must be done, and that present abandonment of the freedmen meant their practical re-enslavement. The bill which finally passed enlarged and made permanent the Freedmen's Bureau. It was promptly vetoed by President Johnson as "unconstitutional," "unnecessary," and "extrajudicial," and failed of passage over the veto. Meantime, however, the breach between Congress and the President began to broaden, and a modified form of the lost bill was finally passed over the President's second veto, July 16.

The act of 1866 gave the Freedmen's Bureau its final form, – the form by which it will be known to posterity and judged of men. It extended the existence of the Bureau to July, 1868; it authorized additional assistant commissioners, the retention of army officers mustered out of regular service, the sale of certain forfeited lands to freedmen on nominal terms, the sale of Confederate public property for Negro schools, and a wider field of judicial interpretation and cognizance. The government of the unreconstructed South was thus put very largely in the hands of the Freedmen's Bureau, especially as in many cases the departmental military commander was now made also assistant commissioner. It was thus that the Freedmen's Bureau became a full-fledged government of men. It made laws, executed them and interpreted them; it laid and collected taxes, defined and punished crime, maintained and used military force, and dictated such measures as it thought necessary and proper for the accomplishment of its varied ends. Naturally, all these powers were not exercised continuously nor to their fullest extent; and yet, as General Howard has said, "scarcely any subject that has to be legislated upon in civil society failed, at one time or another, to demand the action of this singular Bureau."

To understand and criticize intelligently so vast a work, one must not forget an instant the drift of things in the later sixties. Lee had surrendered, Lincoln was dead, and Johnson and Congress were at loggerheads; the Thirteenth Amendment was adopted, the Fourteenth pending, and the Fifteenth declared in force in 1870. Guerrilla raiding, the ever-present flickering after-flame of war, was spending its forces against the Negroes, and all the Southern land was awakening as from some wild dream to poverty and social revolution. In a time of perfect calm, amid willing neighbors and streaming wealth, the social uplifting of four million slaves to an assured and self-sustaining place in the body politic and economic would have been a herculean task; but when to the inherent difficulties of so delicate and nice a social operation were added the spite and hate of conflict, the hell of war; when suspicion and cruelty were rife, and gaunt Hunger wept beside Bereavement, – in such a case, the work of any instrument of social regeneration was in large part foredoomed to failure. The very name of the Bureau stood for a thing in the South which for two centuries and better men had refused even to argue, – that life amid free Negroes was simply unthinkable, the maddest of experiments.

The agents that the Bureau could command varied all the way from unselfish philanthropists to narrow-minded busybodies and thieves; and even though it be true that the average was far better than the worst, it was the occasional fly that helped spoil the ointment. Then amid all crouched the freed slave, bewildered between friend and foe. He had emerged from slavery, – not the worst slavery in the world, not a slavery that made all life unbearable, rather a slavery that had here and there something of kindliness, fidelity, and happiness, – but withal slavery, which, so far as human aspiration and desert were concerned, classed the black man and the ox together. And the Negro knew full well that, whatever their deeper convictions may have been, Southern men had fought with desperate energy to perpetuate this slavery under which the black masses, with half-articulate thought, had writhed and shivered. They welcomed freedom with a cry. They shrank from the master who still strove for their chains; they fled to the friends that had freed them, even though those friends stood ready to use them as a club for driving the recalcitrant South back into loyalty. So the cleft between the white and black South grew. Idle to say it never should have been; it was as inevitable as its results were pitiable. Curiously incongruous elements were left arrayed against each other, – the North, the government, the carpet-baggers, and the slave, here; and there, all the South that was white, whether gentleman or vagabond, honest man or rascal, lawless murderer or martyr to duty.

Thus it is doubly difficult to write of this period calmly, so intense was the feeling, so mighty the human passions that swayed and blinded men. Amid it all, two figures ever stand to typify that day to coming ages, – the one, a gray-haired gentleman, whose fathers had quit themselves like men, whose sons lay in nameless graves; who bowed to the evil of slavery because its abolition threatened untold ill to all; who stood at last, in the evening of life, a blighted, ruined form, with hate in his eyes; – and the other, a form hovering dark and mother-like, her awful face black with the mists of centuries, had aforetime quailed at that white master's command, had bent in love over the cradles of his sons and daughters, and closed in death the sunken eyes of his wife, – aye, too, at his behest had laid herself low to his lust, and borne a tawny man-child to the world, only to see her dark boy's limbs scattered to the winds by midnight marauders riding after "damned Niggers." These were the saddest sights of that woeful day; and no man clasped the hands of these two passing figures of the present-past; but, hating, they went to their long home, and, hating, their children's children live today.

Here, then, was the field of work for the Freedmen's Bureau; and since, with some hesitation, it was continued by the act of 1868 until 1869, let us look upon four years of its work as a whole. There were, in 1868, nine hundred Bureau officials scattered from Washington to Texas, ruling, directly and indirectly, many millions of men. The deeds of these rulers fall mainly under seven heads: the relief of physical suffering, the overseeing of the beginnings of free labor, the buying and selling of land, the establishment of schools, the paying of bounties, the administration of justice, and the financiering of all these activities.

Up to June, 1869, over half a million patients had been treated by Bureau physicians and surgeons, and sixty hospitals and asylums had been in operation. In fifty months twenty-one million free rations were distributed at a cost of over four million dollars. Next came the difficult question of labor. First, thirty thousand black men were transported from the refuges and relief stations back to the farms, back to the critical trial of a new way of working. Plain instructions went out from Washington: the laborers must be free to choose their employers, no fixed rate of wages was prescribed, and there was to be no peonage or forced labor. So far, so good; but where local agents differed *toto caelo* in capacity and character, where the personnel was continually changing, the outcome was necessarily varied. The largest element of success lay in the fact that the majority of the freedmen were willing, even eager, to work. So labor contracts were written, – fifty thousand in a single State, – laborers advised, wages guaranteed, and employers supplied. In truth, the organization became a vast labor bureau, – not perfect, indeed, notably defective here and there, but on the whole successful beyond the dreams of thoughtful men. The two great obstacles which confronted the officials were the tyrant and the idler, – the slaveholder who was determined to perpetuate slavery under another name; and, the freedman who regarded freedom as perpetual rest, – the Devil and the Deep Sea.

In the work of establishing the Negroes as peasant proprietors, the Bureau was from the first handicapped and at last absolutely checked. Something was done, and larger things were planned; abandoned lands were leased so long as they remained in the hands of the Bureau, and a total revenue of nearly half a million dollars derived from black tenants. Some other lands to which the nation had gained title were sold on easy terms, and public lands were opened for settlement to the very few freedmen who had tools and capital. But the vision of "forty acres and a mule" – the righteous and reasonable ambition to become a landholder, which the nation had all but categorically promised the freedmen – was destined in most cases to bitter disappointment. And those men of marvellous hindsight who are today seeking to preach the Negro back to the present peonage of the soil know well, or ought to know, that the opportunity of binding the Negro peasant willingly to the soil was lost on that day when the Commissioner of the Freedmen's Bureau had to go to South Carolina and tell the weeping freedmen, after their years of toil, that their land was not theirs, that there was a mistake – somewhere. If by 1874 the Georgia Negro alone owned three hundred and fifty thousand acres of land, it was by grace of his thrift rather than by bounty of the government.

The greatest success of the Freedmen's Bureau lay in the planting of the free school among Negroes, and the idea of free elementary education among all classes in the South. It not only called the school-mistresses through the benevolent agencies and built them schoolhouses, but it helped discover and support such apostles of human culture as Edmund Ware, Samuel Armstrong, and Erastus Cravath. The opposition to Negro education in the South was at first bitter, and showed itself in ashes, insult, and blood; for the South believed an educated Negro to be a dangerous Negro. And the South was not wholly wrong; for education among all kinds of men always has had, and always will have, an element of danger and revolution, of dissatisfaction and discontent. Nevertheless, men strive to know. Perhaps some inkling of this paradox, even in the unquiet days of the Bureau, helped the bayonets allay an opposition to human training which still to-day lies smouldering in the South, but not flaming. Fisk, Atlanta, Howard, and Hampton were founded in these days, and six million dollars were expended for educational work, seven hundred and fifty thousand dollars of which the freedmen themselves gave of their poverty.

Such contributions, together with the buying of land and various other enterprises, showed that the ex-slave was handling some free capital already. The chief initial source of this was labor in the army, and his pay and bounty as a soldier. Payments to Negro soldiers were at first complicated by the ignorance of the recipients, and the fact that the quotas of colored regiments from Northern States were largely filled by recruits from the South, unknown to their fellow soldiers. Consequently, payments were accompanied by such frauds that Congress, by joint resolution in 1867, put the whole matter in the hands of the Freedmen's Bureau. In two years six million dollars was thus distributed to five thousand claimants, and in the end the sum exceeded eight million dollars. Even in this system fraud was frequent; but still the work put needed capital in the hands of practical paupers, and some, at least, was well spent.

The most perplexing and least successful part of the Bureau's work lay in the exercise of its judicial functions. The regular Bureau court consisted of one representative of the employer, one of the Negro, and one of the Bureau. If the Bureau could have maintained a perfectly judicial attitude, this arrangement would have been ideal, and must in time have gained confidence; but the nature of its other activities and the character of its personnel prejudiced the Bureau in favor of the black litigants, and led without doubt to much injustice and annoyance. On the other hand, to leave the Negro in the hands of Southern courts was impossible. In a distracted land where slavery had hardly fallen, to keep the strong from wanton abuse of the weak, and the weak from gloating insolently over the half-shorn strength of the strong, was a thankless, hopeless task. The former masters of the land were peremptorily ordered about, seized, and imprisoned, and punished over and again, with scant courtesy from army officers. The former slaves were intimidated, beaten, raped, and butchered by angry and revengeful men. Bureau courts tended to become centres simply for punishing whites, while the regular civil courts tended to become solely institutions for perpetuating the slavery of blacks.

Almost every law and method ingenuity could devise was employed by the legis-latures to reduce the Negroes to serfdom, – to make them the slaves of the State, if not of individual owners; while the Bureau officials too often were found striving to put the "bottom rail on top," and gave the freedmen a power and independence which they could not yet use. It is all well enough for us of another generation to wax wise with advice to those who bore the burden in the heat of the day. It is full easy now to see that the man who lost home, fortune, and family at a stroke, and saw his land ruled by "mules and niggers," was really benefited by the passing of slavery. It is not difficult now to say to the young freedman, cheated and cuffed about who has seen his father's head beaten to a jelly and his own mother name-lessly assaulted, that the meek shall inherit the earth. Above all, nothing is more convenient than to heap on the Freedmen's Bureau all the evils of that evil day, and damn it utterly for every mistake and blunder that was made.

All this is easy, but it is neither sensible nor just. Someone had blundered, but that was long before Oliver Howard was born; there was criminal aggression and heedless neglect, but without some system of control there would have been far more than there was. Had that control been from within, the Negro would have been re-enslaved, to all intents and purposes. Coming as the control did from without, perfect men and methods would have bettered all things; and even with imperfect agents and questionable methods, the work accomplished was not unde-serving of commendation.Such was the dawn of Freedom; such was the work of the Freedmen's Bureau, which, summed up in brief, may be epitomized thus: for some fifteen million dollars, beside the sums spent before 1865, and the dole of benevolent societies, this Bureau set going a system of free labor, established a beginning of peasant proprietorship, secured the recognition of black freedmen before courts of law, and founded the free common school in the South. On the other hand, it failed to begin the establishment of good-will between ex-masters and freedmen, to guard its work wholly from paternalistic methods which dis-couraged self-reliance, and to carry out to any considerable extent its implied promises to furnish the freedmen with land. Its successes were the result of hard work, supplemented by the aid of philanthropists and the eager striving of black men. Its failures were the result of bad local agents, the inherent difficulties of the work, and national neglect.

Such an institution, from its wide powers, great responsibilities, large control of moneys, and generally conspicuous position, was naturally open to repeated and bitter attack. It sustained a searching Congressional investigation at the instance of Fernando Wood in 1870. Its archives and few remaining functions were with blunt discourtesy transferred from Howard's control, in his absence, to the supervision of Secretary of War Belknap in 1872, on the Secretary's recommendation. Finally, in consequence of grave intimations of wrong-doing made by the Secretary and his subordinates, General Howard was court-martialed in 1874. In both of these trials the Commissioner of the Freedmen's Bureau was officially exonerated from any wilful misdoing, and his work commended. Nevertheless, many unpleasant things were brought to light, – the methods of transacting the business of the Bureau were faulty; several cases of defalcation were proved, and other frauds strongly suspected; there were some business transactions which savored of dangerous speculation, if not dishonesty; and around it all lay the smirch of the Freedmen's Bank.

Morally and practically, the Freedmen's Bank was part of the Freedmen's Bureau, although it had no legal connection with it. With the prestige of the government back of it, and a directing board of unusual respectability and national reputation, this banking institution had made a remarkable start in the development of that thrift among black folk which slavery had kept them from knowing. Then in one sad day came the crash, – all the hard-earned dollars of the freedmen disappeared; but that was the least of the loss, – all the faith in saving went too, and much of the faith in men; and that was a loss that a Nation which to-day sneers at Negro shiftlessness has never yet made good. Not even ten additional years of slavery could have done so much to throttle the thrift of the freedmen as the mismanagement and bankruptcy of the series of savings banks chartered by the Nation for their especial aid. Where all the blame should rest, it is hard to say; whether the Bureau and the Bank died chiefly by reason of the blows of its selfish friends or the dark machinations of its foes, perhaps even time will never reveal, for here lies unwritten history.

Of the foes without the Bureau, the bitterest were those who attacked not so much its conduct or policy under the law as the necessity for any such institution at all. Such attacks came primarily from the Border States and the South; and they were summed up by Senator Davis, of Kentucky, when he moved to entitle the act of 1866 a bill "to promote strife and conflict between the white and black races ... by a grant of unconstitutional power." The argument gathered tremendous strength South and North; but its very strength was its weakness. For, argued the plain common-sense of the nation, if it is unconstitutional, unpractical, and futile for the nation to stand guardian over its helpless wards, then there is left but one alternative, – to make those wards their own guardians by arming them with the ballot. Moreover, the path of the practical politician pointed the same way; for, argued this opportunist, if we cannot peacefully reconstruct the South with white votes, we certainly can with black votes. So justice and force joined hands.

The alternative thus offered the nation was not between full and restricted Negro suffrage; else every sensible man, black and white, would easily have chosen the latter. It was rather a choice between suffrage and slavery, after endless blood and gold had flowed to sweep human bondage away. Not a single Southern legislature stood ready to admit a Negro, under any conditions, to the polls; not a single Southern legislature believed free Negro labor was possible without a system of restrictions that took all its freedom away; there was scarcely a white man in the South who did not honestly regard Emancipation as a crime, and its practical nullification as a duty. In such a situation, the granting of the ballot to the black man was a necessity, the very least a guilty nation could grant a wronged race, and the only method of compelling the South to accept the results of the war. Thus Negro suffrage ended a civil war by beginning a race feud. And some felt gratitude toward the race thus sacrificed in its swaddling clothes on the altar of national integrity; and some felt and feel only indifference and contempt.

Had political exigencies been less pressing, the opposition to government guardianship of Negroes less bitter, and the attachment to the slave system less strong, the social seer can well imagine a far better policy, – a permanent Freedmen's Bureau, with a national system of Negro schools; a carefully supervised employment and labor office; a system of impartial protection before the regular courts; and such institutions for social betterment as savings-banks, land and building associations, and social settlements. All this vast expenditure of money and brains might have formed a great school of prospective citizenship, and solved in a way we have not yet solved the most perplexing and persistent of the Negro problems.

That such an institution was unthinkable in 1870 was due in part to certain acts of the Freedmen's Bureau itself. It came to regard its work as merely temporary, and Negro suffrage as a final answer to all present perplexities. The political ambition of many of its agents and protégés led it far afield into questionable activities, until the South, nursing its own deep prejudices, came easily to ignore all the good deeds of the Bureau and hate its very name with perfect hatred. So the Freedmen's Bureau died, and its child was the Fifteenth Amendment.

The passing of a great human institution before its work is done, like the untimely passing of a single soul, but leaves a legacy of striving for other men. The legacy of the Freedmen's Bureau is the heavy heritage of this generation. To-day, when new and vaster problems are destined to strain every fibre of the national mind and soul, would it not be well to count this legacy honestly and carefully? For this much all men know: despite compromise, war, and struggle, the Negro is not free. In the backwoods of the Gulf States, for miles and miles, he may not leave the plantation of his birth; in well-nigh the whole rural South the black farmers are peons, bound by law and custom to an economic slavery, from which the only escape is death or the penitentiary. In the most cultured sections and cities of the South the Negroes are a segregated servile caste, with restricted rights and privileges. Before the courts, both in law and custom, they stand on a different and peculiar basis. Taxation without representation is the rule of their political life. And the result of all this is, and in nature must have been, lawlessness and crime. That is the large legacy of the Freedmen's Bureau, the work it did not do because it could not.

I have seen a land right merry with the sun, where children sing, and rolling hills lie like passioned women wanton with harvest. And there in the King's Highways sat and sits a figure veiled and bowed, by which the traveller's footsteps hasten as they go. On the tainted air broods fear. Three centuries' thought has been the raising and unveiling of that bowed human heart, and now behold a century new for the duty and the deed. The problem of the twentieth century is the problem of the color-line.

QUESTIONS

(1) According to Du Bois, during Reconstruction, what were some of the ways in which the inequalities of the Negro were to be addressed?

(2) What are some of the advantages and the disadvantages of the Freedmen's Bureau?

(3) In spite of laws that granted freedom to Negroes, what were some of the reasons, according to Du Bois, that the Negroes remained enslaved through other measures?

(4) Why is it that for Du Bois, "the problem of the twentieth century is the problem of the color-line"? In the twenty-first century is the color-line still a problem for blacks in the United States?

(5) Why was the American government unable to reach a consensus on how to deal with the newly freed Negroes?

7 Political Independence of the Negro

T. THOMAS FORTUNE

Timothy Thomas Fortune (1856–1928) was born into slavery in Marianna, Jackson County, Florida. He attended the Marianna's school for blacks. Later on, when his family moved to Jacksonville, he attended Stanton High School for Negroes. He was the editor of *The New York Age*, one of the most influential black newspapers that existed from 1887–1953. He was an adviser to Booker T. Washington, the architect of the Atlanta Compromise, and the ghost writer and editor of Washington's autobiography, *The Story of My Life and Work*. He was admitted to Howard University to study Law. He changed his major to Journalism. In 1876, he worked at the *People's Advocate*, a newspaper in Washington DC. In 1879, he moved to New York City and worked as a printer at the *Weekly Witness*, which became the *New York Globe* and came to an end in 1880. In the same year, he became the journalist and editor of *The Rumor*, which, in 1885, changed its name to the *New York Freeman* and then the *New York Age*. In 1884, he published *Black and White: Land, Labor, and Politics in the South*. The excerpt below, "Political Independence of the Negro," is a chapter in the book. His philosophy of militant agitation on behalf of the rights of blacks laid the foundations of the Civil Rights Movement.

In addressing myself to a consideration of the subject: "The colored man as an Independent Force in our Politics," I come at once to one of the vital principles underlying American citizenship and the citizenship of the colored man in a peculiar manner. Upon this question hang all the conditions of man as a free moral agent, as an intelligent reasoning being; as a man thoughtful for the best interests of his country, of his individual interests, and of the interests of those who must take up the work of republican government when the present generation has passed away. When I say that this question is of a most complex and perplexing nature, I only assert what is known of all men.

I would not forget that the arguments for and against independent action on our part are based upon two parties or sets of principles. Principles are inherent in government by the people, and parties are engines created by the people through which to voice the principles they espouse. Parties have divided on one line in this country from the beginning of our national existence to the present time. All other issues merge into two distinct ones – the question of a strong Federal Government, as enunciated by Alexander Hamilton, and maintained by the present Republican party, and the question of the rights and powers of the States, as enunciated by Thomas Jefferson, and as maintained by the present Democratic party, – called the "party of the people," but in fact the party of oligarchy, bloodshed, violence and oppression. The Republican party won its first great victory on the inherent weakness of the Democratic party on the question of Human Rights and the right of the Federal Government to protect itself from the assumption, the aggression, the attempted usurpation, of the States and it has maintained its supremacy for so long a time as to lead to the supposition that it will rule until such time as it shall fall to pieces of itself because of internal decay and exterior cancers. There does not appear to exist sufficient vitality outside of the Republican party to keep its members loyal to the people or honest to the government. The loyal legislation which would be occasioned by dread of loss of power, and the administration of the government in the most economical form, are wanting, because of the absence of an honest, healthy opposing party.

But it is not my purpose to dwell upon the mechanism of parties but rather to show why colored Americans should be independent voters, independent citizens, independent men. To this end I am led to lay it down: (1.) That an independent voter must be intelligent, must comprehend the science of government, and be versed in the history of governments and of men; (2.) That an independent voter must be not only a citizen versed in government, but one loyal to his country, and generous and forbearing with his fellow-citizens, not looking always to the word and the act, but looking sometimes to the undercurrent which actuates these – to the presence of immediate interest, which is always strong in human nature, to the love of race, and to the love of section, which comes next to the love of country.

Our country is great not only in mineral and cereal resources, in numbers, and in accumulated wealth, but great in extent of territory, and in multiplicity of interests, out-growing from peculiarities of locality, race, and education of the people. Thus the people of the North and East and West are given to farming, manufacturing, and speculation, making politics a subordinate, not a leading interest; they are consequently wealthy, thrifty and contented: while the people of the South, still in the shadow of defeat in the bloodiest and most tremendous conflict since the Napoleonic wars, are divided sharply into two classes, and given almost exclusively to the pursuits of agriculture and hatred of one another. The existence of this state of things is most disastrous in its nature, and deplorable in its results. It is a barrier against the progress of that section and alien to the spirit and subversive of the principles of our free institutions.

It is in the South that the largest number of our people live; it is there that they encounter the greatest hardships; it is there the problem of their future usefulness as American citizens must have full and satisfactory, or disastrous and disheartening demonstration. Consequently, the colored statesman and the colored editor must turn their attention to the South and make that field the center of speculation, education and practical application. We all understand the conditions of society in the section and the causes which have produced them, and, while not forgetting the causes, it is a common purpose to alter the existing conditions, so that they may conform to the logic of the great Rebellion and the spirit and letter of the Federal Constitution. It is not surprising, therefore, that, as a humble worker in the interest of my race and the common good, I have decided views as to the course best to be pursued by our people in that section, and the fruits likely to spring from a consistent advocacy of such views.

I may stand alone in the opinion that the best interests of the race and the best interests of the country will be conserved by building up a bond of union between the white people and the Negroes of the South – advocating the doctrine that the interests of the white and the interests of the colored people are one and the same; that the legislation which affects the one will affect the other; that the good which comes to the one should come to the other, and that, as one people, the evils which blight the hopes of the one blight the hopes of the other; I say, I may stand alone among colored men in the belief that harmony of sentiment between the blacks and whites of the country, in so far forth as it tends to honest division and healthy opposition, is natural and necessary, but I speak that which is a conviction as strong as the Stalwart idea of diversity between black and white, which has so crystallized the opinion of the race.

It is not safe in a republican form of government that clannishness should exist, either by compulsory or voluntary reason; it is not good for the government, it is not good for the individual. A government like ours some and natural, but upon the fundamental idea incorporated in the Declaration of Independence and re-affirmed in the Federal Constitution the utmost unanimity should prevail. That all men are born equal, so far as the benefits of government extend; that each and every man is justly entitled to the enjoyment of life, liberty, and the pursuit of happiness, so long as these benign benefits be not forfeited by infraction upon the rights of others; that freedom of thought and unmolested expression of honest conviction and the right to make these effective through the sacred medium of a fair vote and an honest count, are God-given and not to be curtailed – these are the foundations of republican government; these are the foundations of our institutions; these are the birthright of every American citizen; these are the guarantees which make men free and independent and great.

The colored man must rise to a full conception of his citizenship before he can make his citizenship effective. It is a fatality to create or foster clannishness in a government like ours. Assimilation of sentiment must be the property of the German, the Irish, the English, the Anglo-African, and all other racial elements that contribute to the formation of the American type of citizen. The moment you create a caste standard, the moment you recognize the existence of such, that moment republican government stands beneath the sword of Damocles, the vitality of its being becomes vitiated and endangered. If this be true, the American people have grave cause for apprehension. The Anglo-African element of our population is classed off by popular sentiment, and kept so. It is for the thoughtful, the honest, the calm but resolute men of the race to mould the sentiment of the masses, lift them up into the broad sunlight of freedom. Ignorance, superstition, prejudice, and intolerance are elements in our nature born of the malign institution of servitude. No fiat of government can eradicate these. As they were the slow growth, the gradual development of long years of inhuman conditions. Let us recognize these facts as facts, and labor honestly to supplant them with more wholesome, more cheering realities. The Independent colored man, like the Independent white man, is an American citizen who does his own thinking. When someone else thinks for him he ceases to be an intelligent citizen and becomes a dangerous dupe – dangerous to himself, dangerous to the State.

It is not to be expected now that the colored voters will continue to maintain that unanimity of idea and action characteristic of them when the legislative halls of States resounded with the clamor of law-makers of their creation, and when their breath flooded or depleted State treasuries. The conditions are different now. They find themselves citizens without a voice in the shapement of legislation; tax-payers without representation; men without leadership masterful enough to force respect from inferior numbers in some States, or to hold the balance of power in others. They find themselves at the mercy of a relentless public opinion which tolerates but does not respect their existence as a voting force; but which, on the contrary, while recognizing their right to the free exercise of the suffrage, forbids such exercise at the point of the shotgun of the assassin, whom it not only nerves but shields in the perpetration of his lawless and infamous crimes. And why is this? Why is it that the one hundred and twenty thousand black voters of South Carolina allow the eight thousand white voters of that State to grind the life out of them by laws more odious, more infamous, more tyrannical and subversive of manhood than any which depopulate the governments of the old world? Is it because the white man is the created viceregent of government? The Scriptures affirm that all are sprung from one parental stem. Is it because he is the constitutionally invested oligarch of government? The magna charta of our liberties affirms that "all men are created equal." Is it because the law of the land reserves unto him the dominance of power? The preamble of the Federal Constitution declares that "We" and not "I," constituted "the people of the United States." If the law of God and the law of man agree in the equality of right of man, explain to me the cause which keeps a superior force in subjection to a minority. Look to the misgovernment of the Reconstruction period for the answer – misgovernment by white men and black men who were lifted into a "little brief authority" by a mighty but unwieldy voting force. That black man who connived at and shared in the corruption in the South which resulted in the subversion of the majority rule, is a traitor to his race and his country, wherever he may now be eking out a precarious and inglorious existence, and I have nothing to heap upon his head but the curses, the execrations of an injured people. Like Benedict Arnold he should seek a garret in the desert of population, living unnoticed, and without respect, where he might die without arousing the contempt of his people.

The love of Liberty carries with it the courage to preserve it from encroachments from without and from contempt from within. A people in whom the love of Liberty is in-born cannot be enslaved, though they may be exterminated by superior force and intelligence, as in the case of the poor Indian of our own land – a people who, two hundred years ago, spread their untamed hordes from the icebergs of Main to the balmy sunland of Florida. But today where are they? Their love of freedom and valorous defense of priority of ownership of our domain have caused them to be swept from the face of the earth. Had they possessed intelligence with their more than Spartan courage, the wave of extermination could never have rolled over them forever. As a man I admire the unconquerable heroism and fortitude of the Indian. So brave a race of people were worthy a nobler and a happier destiny. As an American citizen, I feel it born in my nature to share the fullest measure all that is American. I sympathize in all the hopes, aspirations and fruitations of my country. There is no pulsation in the animated frame of my native land which does not thrill my nature. There is no height of glory we may reach as a government in which I should not feel myself individually lifted; and there is no depth of degradation to which we may fall to which I should not feel myself individually dragged. In a word, I am an American citizen. I have a heritage in each and every provision incorporated in the Constitution of my country, and should this heritage be attempted to be filched from me by any man or body of men, I should deem the provocation sufficiently grievous to stake even life in defense of it. I would plant every colored man in this country on a platform of this nature – to think for himself, to speak for himself, to act for himself. This is the ideal citizen of an ideal government such as ours is modeled to become. This is my conception of the colored man as an independent force in our politics. To aid in lifting our people to this standard, is one of the missions which I have mapped out for my life-work. I may be sowing the seed that will ripen into disastrous results, but I don't think so. My conception of republican government does not lead me to a conclusion so inconsistent with my hopes, my love of my country and of my race.

I look upon my race in the South and I see that they are helplessly at the mercy of a popular prejudice outgrowing from a previous condition of servitude; I find them clothed in the garments of citizenship by the Federal Government and opposed in the enjoyment of it by their equals, not their superiors, in the benefits of government; I find that the government which conferred the right of citizenship is powerless, or indisposed, to force respect for its own enactments; I find that these people, left to the mercy of their enemies, alone and defenseless, and without judicious leadership, are urged to preserve themselves loyal to the men and to the party which have shown themselves unable to extend to them substantial protection; I find that these people, alone in their struggles of doubt and of prejudice, are surrounded by a public opinion powerful to create and powerful to destroy; I find them poor in culture and poor in worldly substance, and dependent for the bread they eat upon those they antagonize politically. As a consequence, though having magnificent majorities, they have no voice in shaping the legislation which is too often made an engine to oppress them; though performing the greatest amount of labor, they suffer from overwork and insufficient remuneration; though having the greater number of children, the facilities of education are not as ample or as good as those provided for the whites out of the common fund, nor have they means to supply from private avenues the benefits of education denied them by the State. Now, what is the solution of this manifold and grievous state of things? Will it come by standing solidly opposed to the sentiment, the culture, the statesmanship, and the possession of the soil and wealth of the South? Let the history of the past be spread before the eyes of a candid and thoughtful people; let the bulky roll of misgovernment, incompetence, and blind folly be enrolled on the one hand, and then turn to the terrors of the midnight assassin and the lawless deeds which desecrate the sunlight of noontide, walking abroad as a phantom armed with the desperation of the damned!

I maintain the idea that the preservation of our liberties, the consummation of our citizenship, must be conserved and matured, not by standing alone and apart, sullen as the melancholy Dane, but by imbibing all that is American, entering into the life and spirit of our institutions, spreading abroad in sentiment, feeling the full force of the fact that while we are classed as Africans, just as the Germans are classed as Germans, we are in all things American citizens, American freemen. Since we have tried the idea of political unanimity let us now try other ideas, ideas more in consonance with the spirit of our institution. There is no strength in a union that enfeebles. Assimilation, a melting into the corporate body, having no distinction from others, equally the recipients of government – this it is to be the independent man, be his skin tanned by the torrid heat of Africa, or bleached by the eternal snows of the Caucasus. To preach the independence of the colored man is to preach his Americanization. The shackles of slavery have been torn from his limbs by the stern arbitrament of arms; the shackles of political enslavement, of ignorance, and of popular prejudice must be broken on the wheels of ceaseless study and the facility with which he becomes absorbed into the body of the people. To aid himself is his first duty if he believes that he is here to stay, and not a probationer for the land of his forefathers – a land upon which he has no other claim than one of sentiment.

What vital principle affecting our citizenship is championed by the National Republican party of today? Is it fair vote and an honest count? Measure our strength in the South and gaze upon the solitary expression of our citizenship in the halls of the National Legislature. The fair vote which we cast for Rutherford B. Hayes seemed to have incurred the enmity of that chief Executive, and he and his advisers turned the colored voters of the South over to the bloodthirsty minority of that section.

The Republican party has degenerated into an ignoble scramble for place and power. It has forgotten the principles for which Sumner contended, and for which Lincoln died. It betrayed the cause for which Douglass, Garrison and others labored, in the blind policy it pursued in reconstructing the rebellious States. It made slaves freemen and freemen slaves in the same breath by conferring the franchise and withholding the guarantees to insure its exercise; it betrayed its trust in permitting thousands of innocent men to be slaughtered without declaring the South in rebellion, and in pardoning murderers, whom tardy justice had consigned to a felon's dungeon. It is even now powerless to insure an honest expression of the vote of the colored citizen. For these things, I do not deem it binding upon colored men further to support the Republican party when other more advantageous affiliations can be formed. And what of the Bourbon Democratic party? There has not been, there is not now, nor will there ever be, any good thing in it for the colored man. Bourbon Democracy is a curse to our land. Any party is a curse which arrays itself in opposition to human freedom, to the universal brotherhood of man. No colored man can ever claim truthfully to be a Bourbon Democrat. It is a fundamental impossibility. But he can be an independent, a progressive Democrat.

The hour has arrived when thoughtful colored men should cease to put their faith upon broken straws; when they should cease to be the willing tools of a treacherous and corrupt party; when they should cease to support men and measures which do not benefit them or the race; when they should cease to be duped by one faction and shot by the other. The time has fully arrived when they should have their position in parties more fully defined, and when, by the ballot which they hold, they should force more respect for the rights of life and property.

To do this, they must adjust themselves to the altered condition which surrounds them. They must make for themselves a place to stand. In the politics of the country the colored vote must be made as uncertain a quantity as the German and Irish vote. The color of their skin must cease to be an index to their political creed. They must think less of "the party" and more of themselves; give less heed to a name and more heed to principles.

The black men and white men of the South have a common destiny. Circumstances have brought them together and so interwoven their interests that nothing but a miracle can dissolve the link that binds them. It is, therefore, to their mutual disadvantage that anything but sympathy and good will should prevail. A reign of terror means a stagnation of all the energies of the people and a corruption of the fountains of law and justice.

The colored men of the South must cultivate more cordial relations with the white men of the South. They must, by a wise policy, hasten the day when politics shall cease to be the shibboleth that creates perpetual warfare. The citizen of a State is far more sovereign than the citizen of the United States. The State is real, tangible reality; a thing of life and power; while the United States is, purely, an abstraction – a thing that no man has successfully defined, although many, wise in their way and in their own conceit, have philosophized upon it to their own satisfaction. The metaphysical polemics of men learned in the science of republican government, covering volume upon volume of "debates," the legislation of ignoramuses, styled statesmen and the "strict" and "liberal" construction placed upon their work by the judicial *magi,* together with a long and disastrous rebellion, to the cruel arbitrament of which the question had been, as finally hoped, in the last resort, submitted, have failed, all and each, to define that visionary thing that so-called Federal government, and its just rights and powers. As Alexander Hamilton and Thomas Jefferson left it, so it is today, a bone of contention, a red flag in the hands of the political matadors of one party to infuriate those of the other parties.

No: it is time that the colored voter learned to leave his powerless "protectors" and take care of himself. Let every one read, listen, think, reform his own ideas of affairs in his own locality; let him be less interested in the continual wars of national politics than in the interests of his own town and county and state; let him make friends of the mammon of unrighteousness of his own neighborhood, so far as to take an intelligent part among his neighbors, white and black, and vote for the men and for the party that will do the best for him and his race, and best conserve the interest of his vicinity. Let there be no aim of *solidifying* the colored vote; the missing of black means the massing of white by contrast. Individual colored men – and many of them – have done wonders in self-evaluation; but there can be no general elevation of the colored men of the South until they use their voting power in independent local affairs with some discrimination more reasonable that an obstinate clinging to a party name. When the colored voters differ among themselves and are to be found on *both sides* of local political contests, they will begin to find themselves of some political importance; their votes will be sought, cast, and *counted.*

And this is the key to the whole situation; let them make themselves a part of the people. It will take time, patience, intelligence, courage; but it can be done: and until it is done their path will lie in darkness and perhaps in blood.

QUESTIONS

(1) Why, according to Fortune, was it important for blacks to have the right to vote and to be an "influential force" in American politics?

(2) Why was it impossible for a black person to be a Bourbon democrat?

(3) Given that during Reconstruction the political interests of blacks and whites were not the same, what was the common destiny of blacks and whites in the South?

(4) Why, for Fortune, is it important for blacks to put their own interests above the party's interests?

(5) Why did Fortune think that the union between whites and the Negroes of the South would preserve the best interests of the race and the American society as a whole?

8 The Case of the Negro

BOOKER T. WASHINGTON

Booker Taliaferro Washington (1856–1915) was born in Franklin County, Virginia as a slave. With the Emancipation Proclamation, after the Civil War, Washington and his family were freed from slavery. He moved with his mother to Malden, West Virginia, to join his stepfather Washington Ferguson who had escaped from slavery during the War. In 1875, Washington graduated from Hampton Institute. Later on, he was offered a job as a teacher at Hampton. He then moved on to become the principal of the Tuskegee Normal and Industrial Institute now known as the Tuskegee University. In 1885, Washington delivered a speech, the "Atlanta Compromise." In 1901, President Theodore Roosevelt invited Washington to the White House, making him the first black American to be so honored. In 1889, in *The Atlantic Monthly*, Washington published "The Case of the Negro" provided below.

All attempts to settle the question of the Negro in the South by his removal from this country have so far failed, and I think that they are likely to fail. The next census will probably show that we have nearly ten million black people in the United States, about eight million of whom are in the Southern states. In fact we have almost a nation within a nation. The Negro population in the United States lacks but two millions of being as large as the whole population Mexico, and is nearly twice as large as that of Canada. Our black people equal in number the combined populations of Switzerland, Greece, Honduras, Nicaragua, Uruguay, Santo Domingo, Paraguay, and Costa Rica. When we consider, in connection with these facts that the race has doubled itself since its freedom, and is still increasing, it hardly seems possible for anyone to take seriously any scheme of emigration from America as a method of solution. At most, even if the government were to provide the means, but a few hundred thousand could be transported each year. The yearly increase in population would more than likely overbalance the number transported. Even if it did not, the time required to get rid of the Negro by this method would perhaps be fifty or seventy-five years.

Some have advised that the Negro leave the South, and take up his residence in the Northern states. I question whether this would make him any better off than he is in the South, when all things are considered. It has been my privilege to study the condition of our people in nearly every part of America; and I say without hesitation that, with some exceptional cases, the Negro is at his best in the Southern states. While he enjoys certain privileges in the North that he does not have in the South, when it comes to the matter of securing property, enjoying business advantages and employment, the South presents a far better opportunity than the North. Few colored men from the South are as yet able to stand up against the severe and increasing competition that exists in the North, to say nothing of the unfriendly influence of labor organizations, which in some way prevents black men in the North, as a rule, from securing occupation in the line of skilled labor.

Another point of great danger for the colored man who goes North is the matter of morals, owing to the numerous temptations by which he finds himself surrounded. More ways offer in which he can spend money than in the South, but fewer avenues of employment for earning money are open to him. The fact that at the North the Negro is almost confined to one line of occupation often tends to discourage and demoralize the strongest who go from the South, and makes them an easy prey for temptation. A few years ago, I made an examination into the condition of a settlement of Negroes who left the South and went into Kansas about twenty years since, when there was a good deal of excitement in the South concerning emigration from the West, and found it much below the standard of that of similar communities in the South. The only conclusion which any one can reach, from this and like instances, is that the Negroes are to remain in the Southern states. As a race they do not want to leave the South, and the Southern white people do not want them to leave. We must therefore find some basis of settlement that will be constitutional, just, manly; that will be fair to both races in the South and to the whole country. This cannot be done in a day, a year, or any short period of time. We can, however, with the present light, decide upon a reasonably safe method of solving the problem, and turn our strength and effort in that direction. In doing this, I would not have the Negro deprived of any privilege guaranteed to him by the Constitution of the United States. It is not best for the Negro that he relinquish any of his constitutional rights; it is not best for the Southern white man that he should, as I shall attempt to show in this article.

In order that we may concentrate our forces upon a wise object, without loss of time or effort, I want to suggest what seems to me and many others the wisest policy to be pursued. I have reached these conclusions not only by reason of my own observations and experience, but after eighteen years of direct contact with leading and influential colored and white men in most parts of our country. But I wish first to mention some elements of danger in the present situation, which all who desire the permanent welfare of both races in the South should carefully take into account.

First. There is danger that a certain class of impatient extremists among the Negroes in the North, who have little knowledge of the actual conditions in the

South, may do the entire race injury by attempting to advise their brethren in the South to resort to armed resistance or the use of the torch, in order to secure justice. All intelligent and well-considered discussion of any important question, or condemnation of any wrong, whether in the North or the South, from the public platform and through the press, is to be commended and encouraged; but ill-considered and incendiary utterances from black men in the North will tend to add to the burdens of our people in the South rather than to relieve them. We must not fall into the temptation of believing that we can raise ourselves by abusing some one else.

Second. Another danger in the South which should be guarded against is that the whole white South, including the wise, conservative, law-abiding element may find itself represented before the bar of public opinion by the mob or lawless element, which gives expression to its feelings and tendency in a manner that advertises the South through world; while too often those who have no sympathy with such disregard of law are either silent, or fail to speak in a sufficiently emphatic manner to offset in any large degree the unfortunate representation which the lawless have made for many portions of the South.

Third. No race or people ever get upon its feet without severe and constant struggle, often in the face of the greatest discouragement. While passing through the present trying period of its history, there is danger that a large and valuable element of the Negro race may become discouraged in the effort to better its condition. Every possible influence should be exerted to prevent this.

Fourth. There is a possibility that harm may be done to the South and the Negro by exaggerated newspaper articles which are written near the scene or in the midst of specially aggravating occurrences. Often these reports are written by newspaper men, who give the impression that there is a race conflict throughout the South, and that all Southern white people are opposed to the Negro's progress; overlooking the fact that though in some sections there is trouble, in most parts of the South, if matters are not yet in all respects as we would have them, there is nevertheless a very large measure of peace, good will, and mutual helpfulness. In the same relation, much can be done to retard the progress of the Negro by a certain class of Southern white people, who in the midst of excitement speak or write in a manner that gives the impression that all Negroes are lawless, untrustworthy, and shiftless. For example, a Southern writer said, not long ago, in a communication in the *New York Independent*: "Even in small towns the husband cannot venture to leave his wife alone for an hour at night. At no time, in no place, is the Roman safe from the insults and assaults of these creatures." These statements, I presume, represented the feelings and the conditions that existed, at the time of the writing, in one community or county in the South; but thousands of Southern white men and women would be ready to testify that this is not the condition throughout the South, nor throughout any Southern state.

Fifth. Owing to the lack of school opportunities for the Negro in the rural districts of the South, there is danger that ignorance and idleness may increase to the extent of giving the Negro race a reputation for crime, and that immorality may eat its way into the fibre of the race so as to retard its progress for many years. In judging the Negro we must not be too harsh. We must remember that it has been only within the last thirty-four years that the black father and mother have had the responsibility, and consequently the experience, of training their own children. That perfection has not been reached in one generation, with the obstacles that the parents have been compelled to overcome, is not to be wondered at.

Sixth. Finally, I would mention my fear that some of the white people of the South may be led to feel that the way to settle the race problem is to repress the aspirations of the Negro by legislation of a kind that confers certain legal or political privileges upon an ignorant and poor white man, and withholds the same privileges from a black man in a similar condition. Such legislation injures and retards the progress of both races. It is an injustice to the poor white man, because it takes from him incentive to secure education and property as prerequisites for voting. He feels that because he is a white man, regardless of his possessions, a way will be found for him to vote. I would label all such measures "laws to keep the poor white man in ignorance and poverty."

The *Talladega News Reporter*, a Democratic newspaper of Alabama, recently said: "But it is a weak cry when the white man asks odds on intelligence over the Negro. When nature has already so handicapped the African in the race for knowledge, the cry of the boasted Anglo-Saxon for still further odds seems babyish. What wonder that the world looks on in surprise, if not disgust? It cannot help but say, if our contention be true that the Negro is an inferior race, then the odds ought to be on the other side, if any are to be given. And why not? No; the thing to do – the only thing that will stand the test of time – is to do right, exactly right, let come what will. And that right thing, as it seems to us, is to place a fair educational qualification before every citizen, – one that is self-testing, and not dependent on the wishes of weak men, – letting all who pass the test stand in the proud ranks of American voters, whose votes shall be counted as cast, and whose sovereign will shall be maintained as law by all the powers that be. Nothing short of this will do. Every exemption, on whatsoever ground, is an outrage that can only rob some legitimate voter of his rights."

Such laws as have been made, – in Mississippi, for example, – with the "understanding" clause, hold out a temptation for the election officer to perjure and degrade himself by too often deciding that the ignorant white man does understand the Constitution when it is read to him, and that the ignorant black man does not. By such a law, the state not only commits a wrong against its black citizens; it injures the morals of its white citizens by conferring such a power upon any white man who may happen to be a judge of elections.

Such laws are hurtful, again, because they keep alive in the heart of the black man the feeling that the white man means to oppress him. The only safe way out is to set a high standard as a test of citizenship, and require blacks and whites alike to come up to it. When this is done, both will have a higher respect for the election laws, and for those who make them. I do not believe that, with his centuries of advantage over the Negro in the opportunity to acquire property and education as prerequisites for voting, the average white man in the South desires that any special law be passed to give him further advantage over one who has had but a little more than thirty years in which to prepare himself for citizenship. In this relation, another point of danger is that the Negro has been made to feel that it is his duty continually to oppose the Southern white man in politics, even in matters where no principle is involved; and that he is only loyal to his own race and acting in a manly way in thus opposing the white man. Such a policy has proved very hurtful to both races. Where it is a matter of principle, where a question of right or wrong is involved, I would advise the Negro to stand by principle at all hazards. A Southern white man has no respect for or confidence in a Negro who acts merely for policy's sake; but there are many cases, and the number is growing, where the Negro has nothing to gain, and much to lose, by opposing the Southern white man in matters that relate to government.

Under the foregoing six heads I believe I have stated some of the main points which, all high-minded white men and black men, North and South, will agree need our most earnest and thoughtful consideration, if we would hasten, and not hinder, the progress of our country.

Now as to the policy that should be pursued. On this subject I claim to possess no superior wisdom or unusual insight. I may be wrong; I may be in some degree right.

In the future we want to impress upon the Negro, more than we have done in the past, the importance of identifying himself more closely with the interests of the South: of making himself part of the South, and at home in it. Heretofore, for reasons which were natural, and for which no one is especially to blame, the colored people have been too much like a foreign nation residing in the midst of another nation. If William Lloyd Garrison, Wendell Phillips, or Geoff Stearns were alive to-day, I feel sure that he would advise the Negroes to identify their interests as closely as possible with those of their white neighbors, – all understanding that no question of right and wrong is involved. In no other way, it seems to me, can we get a foundation for peace and progress. He who advises against this policy will advise the Negro to do that which no people in history, who have succeeded, have done. The white man, North or South, who advises the Negro against it advises him to do that which he himself has not done. The bed rock upon which every individual rests his chances for success in life is the friendship, the confidence, the respect of his next-door neighbor in the little community in which he lives. The problem of the Negro in the South turns on whether he can make himself of such indispensable service to his neighbor in the community that no one can fill his place better in the body politic. There is at present no other safe course for the black man to pursue. If the Negro in the South has a friend in his white neighbor, and a still larger number of friends in his own community, he has a protection and a guarantee of his rights that will be more potent and more lasting than any our Federal Congress or any outside power can confer.

The London Times, in a recent edition discussing affairs in the Transvaal, where Englishmen have been denied certain privileges by the Boers, says: "England is too sagacious not to prefer a gradual reform from within, even should it be less rapid than most of us might wish, to the most sweeping redress of grievances imposed from without. Our object is to obtain fair play for the Outlanders, but the best way to do it is to enable them to help themselves." This policy, I think, is equally safe when applied to conditions in the South. The foreigner who comes to America identifies himself as soon as possible, in business, education, and politics, with the community in which he settles. We have a conspicuous example of this in the case of the Jews, who in the South, as well as in other parts of our country, have not always been justly treated; but the Jews have so woven themselves into the business and patriotic interests of the communities in which they live, have made themselves so valuable as citizens, that they have won a place in the South which they could have obtained in no other way. The Negro in Cuba has practically settled the race question there, because he has made himself a part of Cuba in thought and action.

What I have tried to indicate cannot be accomplished by any sudden revolution of methods, but it does seem that the tendency should be more and more in this direction. Let me emphasize this by a practical example. The North sends thousands of dollars into the South every year for the education of the Negro. The teachers in most of the Southern schools supported by the North are Northern men and women of the highest Christian culture and most unselfish devotion. The Negro owes them a debt of gratitude which can never be paid. The various missionary societies in the North have done a work which to a large degree has proved the salvation of the South, and the results of it will appear more in future generations than in this. We have now reached the point, in the South, where, I believe, great good could be accomplished in changing the attitude of the white people toward the Negro, and of the Negro toward the whites, if a few Southern white teachers, of high character, would take an active interest in the work of our higher schools. Can this be done? Yes. The medical school connected with Shaw University at Raleigh, North Carolina, has from the first had as instructors and professors almost exclusively Southern white doctors who reside in Raleigh, and they have given the highest satisfaction. This gives the people of Raleigh the feeling that the school is theirs, and not something located in, but not a part of, the South. In Augusta, Georgia, the Payne Institute, one of the best colleges for our people, is officered and taught almost wholly by Southern white men and women. The Presbyterian Theological School at Tuscaloosa, Alabama, has only Southern white men as instructors. Some time ago, at the Calhoun School in Alabama, one of the leading white men in the county was given an important position; since then the feeling of the white people in the county has greatly changed toward the school.

We must admit the stern fact that at present the Negro, through no choice of his own, is living in the midst of another race, which is far ahead of him in education, property, and experience: and further, that the Negro's present condition makes him dependent upon the white people for most of the things necessary to sustain life, as well as, in a large measure, for his education. In all history, those who have possessed the property and intelligence have exercised the greatest control in government, regardless of color, race, or geographical location. This being the case, how can the black man in the South improve his estate? And does the Southern white man want him to improve it? The latter part of this question I shall attempt to answer later in this article.

The Negro in the South has it within his power, if he properly utilizes the forces at hand, to make of himself such a valuable factor in the life of the South that for the most part he need not seek privileges, but they will be conferred upon him. To bring this about, the Negro must begin at the bottom and lay a sure foundation, and not be lured by any temptation into trying to rise on a false footing. While the Negro is laying this foundation, he will need help and sympathy and justice from the law. Progress by any other method will be but temporary and superficial, and the end of it will be worse than the beginning. American slavery was a great curse to both races and I should be the last to apologize for it; but in the providence of God I believe that slavery laid the foundation for the solution of the problem that is now before us in the South. Under slavery, the Negro was taught every trade, every industry, that furnishes the means of earning a living. Now if on this foundation, laid in a rather crude way, it is true, but a foundation nevertheless, we can gradually grow and improve, the future for us is bright. Let me be more specific. Agriculture is or has been the basic industry of nearly every race or nation that has succeeded. The Negro got a knowledge of this under slavery: hence in a large measure he is in possession of this industry in the South to-day. Taking the whole South, I should say that eighty per cent of the Negroes live by agriculture in some form, though it is often a very primitive and crude form. The Negro can buy land in the South, as a rule, wherever the white man can buy it, and at very low prices. Now, since the bulk of our people already have a foundation in agriculture, are at their best when living in the country engaged in agricultural pursuits, plainly, the best thing, the logical thing, is to turn the larger part of our strength in a direction that will put the Negroes among the most skilled agriculture people in the world. The man who has learned to do something better than any one else, has learned to do a common thing in an uncommon manner, has power and influence which no adverse surroundings can take from him. It is better to show a man how to make a place for himself than to put him in one that some one else has made for him. The Negro who can make himself so conspicuous as a successful farmer, a large tax-payer, a wise helper of his fellow men, as to be placed in a position of trust and honor by natural selection, whether the position be political or not, is a hundred-fold more secure in that position than one placed there by mere outside force or pressure. I know a Negro, Hon. Isaiah T. Montgomery, in Mississippi, who is mayor of a town; it is true that the town is composed almost wholly of Negroes. Mr. Montgomery is mayor of this town because his genius, thrift, and foresight have created it; and he is held and supported in his office by a charter granted by the state of Mississippi, and by the vote and public sentiment of the community in which he lives.

Let us help the Negro by every means possible to acquire such an education in farming, dairying, stock-raising, horticulture, etc., as will place him near the top in these industries, and the race problem will in a large part be settled or at least stripped of many of its most perplexing elements. This policy would also tend to keep the Negro in the country and smaller towns, where he succeeds best, and stop the influx into the large cities, where he does not succeed so well. The race, like the individual which produces something of superior worth that has a common human interest, wins a permanent place, and is bound to be recognized.

At a county fair in the South, not long ago I saw a Negro awarded the first prize, by a jury of white men, over white competitors for the production of the best specimen of Indian corn. Every white man at the fair seemed to be proud of the achievement of the Negro, because it was apparent that he had done something that would add to wealth and comfort of the people both races in that county. At the Tuskegee Normal and Industrial Institute, in Alabama, we have a department devoted to training men along the lines of agriculture that I have named; but what we are doing is small when compared with what should be done in Tuskegee, and at other educational centers. In a material sense the South is still an undeveloped country. While in some other affairs race prejudice is strongly marked, in the matter of business, of commercial and industrial development, there are few obstacles in the Negro's way. A Negro who produces or has for sale something that the community wants finds customers among white people as well as black. Upon equal security, a Negro can borrow money at a bank as readily as a white man can. A bank in Birmingham, Alabama, which has existed ten years is officered and controlled wholly by Negroes. This bank has white borrowers and white depositors. A graduate of the Tuskegee Institute keeps a well-appointed grocery store in Tuskegee, and he tells me that he sells about as many goods to one race as to the other. What I have said of the opening that awaits the Negro in the business of agriculture is almost equally true of mechanics, manufacturing, and all the domestic arts. The field is before him and right about him. Will he seize upon it? Will he "cast down his bucket where he is"? Will his friends, North and South, encourage him and prepare him to occupy it? Every city in the South, for example, would give support to a first-class architect or housebuilder or contractor of our race. The architect or contractor would not only receive support, but through his example numbers of young colored men would learn such trades as carpentry, brickmasonry, plastering, painting, etc., and the race would be put into a position to hold on to many of the industries which it is now in danger of losing, because in too many cases brain, skill, and dignity are not imparted to the common occupations. Any individual or race that does not fit itself to occupy in the best manner the field or service that is right about it will sooner or later be asked to move on and let another take it.

But I may be asked, would you confine the Negro to agriculture, mechanics, the domestic arts, etc.? Not at all; but just now and for a number of years the stress should be laid along the lines that I have mentioned. We shall need and must have many teachers and ministers, some doctors and lawyers and statesmen, but these professional men will have a constituency or a foundation from which to draw support just in proportion as the race prospers along the economic lines that I have pointed out. During the first fifty or one hundred years of the life of any people, are not the economic occupations always given the greater attention? This is not only the historic, but, I think, the common-sense view. If this generation will lay the material foundation, it will be the quickest and surest way for enabling later generations to succeed in the cultivation of the fine arts, and to surround themselves with some of the luxuries of life, if desired. What the race most needs now, in my opinion, is a whole army of men and women well trained to lead, and at the same time devote themselves to agriculture, mechanics, domestic employment, and business. As to the mental training that these educated leaders should be equipped with, I should say, give them all the mental training and culture that the circumstances of individuals will allow, – the more the better. No race can permanently succeed until its mind is awakened and strengthened by the ripest thought. But I would constantly have it kept in the minds of those who are educated in books that a large proportion of those who are educated should be so trained in hand that they can bring this mental strength and knowledge to bear upon the physical conditions in the South, which I have tried to emphasize.

Frederick Douglass, of sainted memory, once, in addressing his race, used these words: "We are to prove that we can better our own condition. One way to do this is to accumulate property. This may sound to you like a new gospel. You have been accustomed to hear that money is the root of all evil, etc.; on the other hand, property, money, if you please, will purchase for us the only condition by which any people can rise to the dignity of genuine manhood; for without property there can be no leisure, without leisure there can be no thought, without thought there can be no invention, without invention there can be no progress."

The Negro should be taught that material development is not an end but merely a means to an end. As Professor W. E. B. Du Bois puts it, the idea should not be simply to make men carpenters, but to make carpenters men. The Negro has a highly religious temperament; but what he needs more and more is to be convinced of the importance of weaving his religion and morality into the practical affairs of daily life. Equally does he need to be taught to put so much intelligence into his labor that he will see dignity and beauty in the occupation and love it for its own sake. The Negro needs to be taught to apply more of the religion that manifests itself in his happiness in prayer meeting to the performance of his daily task. The man who owns a home, and is in the possession of the elements by which he is sure of a daily living, has a great aid to a moral and religious life. What bearing will all this have upon the Negro's place in the South, as a citizen and in the enjoyment of the privileges which our government confers?

To state in detail just what place the black man will occupy in the South as a citizen, when he has developed in the direction named, is beyond the wisdom of any one. Much will depend upon the sense of justice which can be kept alive in the breast of the American people almost as much will depend upon the good sense of the Negro himself. That question, I confess, does not give me the most concern just now. The important and pressing question is, Will the Negro, with his own help and that of his friends take advantage of the opportunities that surround him? When he has done this, I believe, speaking of his future in general terms, that he will be treated with justice, be given the protection of the law and the recognition which his usefulness and ability warrant. If, fifty years ago, one had predicted that the Negro would receive the recognition and honor which individuals have already received, he would have been laughed at as an idle dreamer. Time, patience, and constant achievement are great factors in the rise of a race.

I do not believe that the world ever takes a race seriously, in its desire to share in the government of a nation, until a large number of individual members of that race have demonstrated beyond question their ability to control and develop their own business enterprises. Once a number of Negroes rise to point where they own and operate the most successful farms, are among the largest taxpayers in their county, are moral and intelligent, I do not believe that in many portions of the South such men need long be denied the right of saying by their votes how they prefer their property to be taxed, and who are to make and administer the laws.

I was walking the street of a certain town in the South lately in company with the most prominent Negro there. While we were together, the mayor of the town sought out the black man and said, "Next week we are going to vote on the question of issuing bonds to secure water works; you must be sure to vote on the day of election." The mayor did not suggest whether he should vote yes or no; but he knew that the very fact of this Negro's owning nearly a block of the most valuable property in the town was a guarantee that he would cast a safe, wise vote on this important proposition. The white man knew that because of this Negro's property interests he would cast his vote the way he thought would benefit every white and black citizen in the town and not be controlled by influences a thousand miles away. But a short time ago I read letters from nearly every prominent white man in Birmingham, Alabama, asking that the Rev. W. R. Pettiford, a Negro, be appointed to a certain important federal office. What is the explanation of this? For nine years Mr. Pettiford has been the president the Negro bank in Birmingham, to which I have alluded. During these nine years, the white citizens have had the opportunity of seeing that Mr. Pettiford can manage successfully a private business, and that he has proved himself a conservative, thoughtful citizen, and they are willing to trust him in a public office. Such individual examples will have to be multiplied, till they become more nearly the rule than the exception they now are. While we are multiplying these examples, the Negro must keep a strong and courageous heart. He cannot improve his condition by any short-cut course or by artificial methods. Above all, he must not be deluded into believing that his condition can be permanently bettered by a mere battledoor and shuttlecock of words, or by any process of mere mental gymnastics or oratory. What is desired along with a logical defense of his cause are deeds, results, – continued results, in the direction of building himself up, so as to leave no doubt in the mind of any one of his ability to succeed.

An important question often asked is, Does the white man in the South want the Negro to improve his present condition? I say yes. From the *Montgomery (Alabama) Daily Advertiser* I clip the following in reference to the closing of a colored school in a town in Alabama: –

EUFAULA, May 25, 1899. The closing exercises of the city colored public school were held at St. Luke's A. M. E. Church last night, and were witnessed by a large gathering, including many whites. The recitations by the pupils were excellent, and the music was also an interesting feature. Rev. R. T. Pollard delivered the address, which was quite an able one, and the certificates were presented by Professor T. L. McCoy, white, of the Sanford Street School. The success of the exercises reflects great credit on Professor S. M. Murphy, the principal, who enjoys a deserved good reputation as a capable and efficient educator.

I quote this report, not because it is the exception, but because such marks of interest in the education of the Negro on the part of the Southern white people may be seen almost every day in the local papers. Why should white people, by their presence, words, and actions, encourage the black man to get education, if they do not desire him to improve his condition?

The Payne Institute, an excellent college, to which I have already referred, is supported almost wholly by the Southern white Methodist church. The Southern white Presbyterians support a theological school for Negroes at Tuscaloosa. For a number of years the Southern white Baptists have contributed toward Negro education. Other denominations have done the same. If these people do not want the Negro educated to a higher standard, there is no reason why they should pretend they do.

Though some of the lynchings in the South have indicated a barbarous feeling toward Negroes, Southern white men here and there, as well as newspapers, have spoken out strongly against lynching. I quote from the address of the Rev. Mr. Vance, of Nashville, Tennessee, delivered before the National Sunday School Union, in Atlanta, not long since, as an example: –

> And yet, as I stand here to-night, a Southerner speaking for my section and addressing an audience from all sections, there is one foul blot upon the fair fame of the South, at the bare mention of which the heart turns sick and the cheek is crimsoned with shame. I want to lift my voice to-night in loud and long and indignant protest against the awful horror of mob violence, which the other day reached the climax of its madness and infamy in a deed as black and brutal and barbarous as can be found in the annals of human crime.
>
> I have a right to speak on the subject, and I propose to be heard. The time has come for every lover of the South to set the might of an angered and resolute manhood against the shame and peril of the lynch demon. These people whose fiendish glee taunts their victim as his flesh crackles in the flames do not represent the South. I have not a syllable of apology for the sickening crime they meant to avenge. But it is high time we were learning that lawlessness is no remedy for crime. For one I dare to believe that the people of my section are able to cope with crime, however treacherous and defiant, through their courts of justice; and I plead for the masterful sway of a righteous and exalted public sentiment that shall class lynch law in the category with crime.

It is a notable and encouraging fact that no Negro educated in any of our larger institutions of learning in the South has been charged with any of the recent crimes connected with assault upon women.

If we go on making progress in the directions that I have tried to indicate, more and more the South will be drawn to one course. As I have already said, it is not to the best interests of the white race of the South that the Negro be deprived of any privilege guaranteed him by the Constitution of the United States. This would put upon the South a burden under which no government could stand and prosper. Every article in our Federal Constitution was placed there with a view of stimulating and encouraging the highest type of citizenship. To continue to tax the Negro without giving him the right to vote, as fast as he qualifies himself in education and property for voting, would insure the alienation of the affections of the Negro from the state in which he lives, and would be the reversal of the fundamental principles of government for which our states have stood. In other ways than this the injury would be as great to the white man as to the Negro.

Taxation without the hope of becoming voters would take away from one of the citizens of the Gulf states their interest in government, and a stimulus to become taxpayers or to secure education, and thus be able and willing to bear their share of the cost of education and government, which now rests so heavily upon the white taxpayers of the South. The more the Negro is stimulated and encouraged, the sooner will he be able to bear a larger share of the burdens of the South. We have recently had before us an example, in the case of Spain, of a government that left a large portion of its citizens in ignorance, and neglected their highest interests.

> As I have said elsewhere:
> There is no escape, through law of man or God, from the inevitable.
> The laws of changeless justice bind
> Oppressor with oppressed;
> And close as sin and suffering joined
> We march to fate abreast.
>
> Nearly sixteen millions of hands will aid you in pulling the load upwards, or they will pull the load downwards against you. We shall constitute one third and more of the ignorance and crime of the South, or one third of its intelligence and progress; we shall contribute one third to the business and industrial prosperity of the South, or we shall prove a veritable body of death, stagnating, depressing, retarding every effort to advance the body politic.

My own feeling is that the South will gradually reach the point where it will see the wisdom and the justice of enacting an educational or property qualification, or both, for voting, that shall be made to apply honestly to both races. The industrial development of the Negro in connection with education and Christian character will help to hasten this end. When this is done, we shall have a foundation, in my opinion, upon which to build a government that is honest, and that will be in a high degree satisfactory to both races.

I do not suffer myself to take too optimistic a view of the conditions in the South. The problem is a large and serious one, and will require the patient help, sympathy, and advice of our most patriotic citizens, North and South, for years to come. But I believe that if the principles which I have tried to indicate are followed, a solution of the question will come. So long as the Negro is permitted to get education, acquire property, and secure employment, and is treated with respect in the business world, as is now true in the greater part of the South, I shall have the greatest faith in his working out his own destiny in our Southern states. The education and preparation for citizenship of nearly eight millions of people is a tremendous task, and every lover of humanity should count it a privilege to help in the solution of a problem for which our whole country is responsible.

QUESTIONS

(1) Why, for Booker T. Washington, were blacks better off in the South?

(2) During Reconstruction, how for some whites could the race problem in the South be addressed?

(3) Why, for Washington, must the Negro start at the very bottom in order to be successful?

(4) According to Washington, why, in the end, was it not in the interests of whites to deprive blacks of their constitutional rights?

(5) Why is it important for blacks to determine their own destiny?

PART III
Black Nationalism

BABACAR M'BAYE

. . . .

One of the gravest errors in contemporary interdisciplinary and literary studies is the conception of Black Nationalism as an intellectual tradition that is completely detached from black cosmopolitanism. This perception has led to intellectual climates in which the contributions of black intellectuals to cosmopolitanism are largely neglected and to an atmosphere in which black radicalism is perceived as an irrational and reactionary response to oppression rather than as an intellectual and legitimate answer to tyranny. Viewing Black Nationalism and black radicalism as movements that are unrelated to cosmopolitanism is ahistorical since the three concepts are not antithetical to one another. These movements are founded on the centrality of Pan-Africanism in a context in which black identities have been constantly influenced by the cosmos (understood here as world cultures and civilizations) and vice versa.

Black Nationalism is a theory founded on the shared struggle against historical forces that have prevented many black communities from establishing either a collective entity such as a country, a meta-nation, or another geographic political and economic entity for themselves. William L. Van Deburg provides a fitting definition of Black Nationalism among African Americans when he writes: "Bound together by ties of history, culture, and kinship, they conceptualize themselves as being differentiated and (at least potentially) separated from competing social and ethnic groups. At various times and under certain conditions, these deep-rooted feelings of racial consanguinity may be manifested in overt political movements arguing for the creation of an autonomous nation-state or a transnational union of states grounded in shared experiences."[1] Therefore, the

---

[1] William L. Van Deburg (ed.), *Modern Black Nationalism: From Marcus Garvey to Louis Farrakhan* (New York University Press, 1997), pp. 4–5.

origins of Pan-Africanism are found in Black Nationalism from where the desire and urgency for oppressed blacks to have their own sense of racial, communal, and cultural solidarity against subjugation stemmed. As a theory, Pan-Africanism makes official and strengthens Black Nationalism by expanding it into a transnational or global movement and scope through which black experiences are studied and understood. In this sense, Pan-Africanism, Black Nationalism, black radicalism, and their corollaries cannot be disassociated from black cosmopolitanism. The latter concept describes how blacks have historically viewed themselves as world citizens who must have enjoyed the same benefits of civilizations which any other people also deserve. Having been historically enslaved, colonized, forcibly migrated, and fragmented into different parts of the world, blacks have attempted to rebuild their communities and traditions and gain social, political, and economic power while emphasizing the importance of their cosmopolitanism. The latter concept refers to these blacks' human rights to share in the benefits of progress and modernity to which they have greatly contributed. The struggle to claim, safeguard, and expand those rights for blacks and all humanity is the bedrock of black cosmopolitanism. The following discussion aims to show the ways in which such rights are emphasized to varying degrees in James Theodore Holly's, Marcus Garvey's, and Stokely Carmichael's black nationalist texts: a vibrant black nationalism is salient in these texts despite the context in which each was written. Holly, Garvey, and Carmichael were all imbued with a staunch will to secure the civil rights of not just blacks of the United States, but also of those from other parts of the black diaspora.

James Theodore Holly: A Quintessential Cosmopolitan

In a 2008 article for *Cultures Sud* magazine the Martiniquan scholar Édouard Glissant describes Haiti as "le point focal de la Caraïbe" (the focal point of the Caribbean) because of "les capacités de fédération" (the federation potentials) that it gives to "Caribéens créolophones, anglophones, francophones, hispanophones et les autres" (Creolophone, Anglophone, Francophone, and Hispanophone Caribbeans as well as others) by allowing them to "nous retrouver en Haïti dans tous les sens du terme" (find ourselves in Haiti in every sense of the word).[2] Holly recognized the transnational significance of Haiti more than a century before Glissant, and before scholar Aimé Césaire did. Holly seems to be one of the first black intellectuals who understood Haiti's primary significance not only in the Caribbean, or the regions that Glissant calls "les archipels" ("the

---

[2] Édouard Glissant, "Haïti, point focal de la Caraïbe," *Cultures Sud, Caraïbes: un monde à partager* 168 (2008), p. 28.

archipelagos"), but also in the history of the black world. Glissant's representation of Haiti as the "focal point of the Caribbean" suggests this island's major role in the history of transnational Black Nationalist resistance against colonialism and other forms of domination. Holly's lecture is crucial in the history of Black Nationalism since it was a seminal part of the transnational interests in the plight of Haitians that African Americans have historically pioneered. Holly paved the ways for not only Frederick Douglass, but also James Weldon Johnson and Mercer Cook, who, like their predecessor, made it their personal responsibility to make Americans aware of Haiti's importance in modern and global black history and stress their duty to support the island's population.[3] Holly's reasons for backing that support stemmed not from paternalism, but from a deep belief in Haiti's enduring status as an emblem of republican principles such as liberty, fraternity, equality, and democracy upon which the United States was founded. Holly was one of the first black intellectuals to show that Haiti demonstrated through its status as the first black republic in the Western hemisphere its ability to govern itself under democratic principles, taking its place among great nations. He writes:

> Notwithstanding the remarkable progress of philanthropic ideas and humanitarian feelings, during the last half century, among almost every nation and people throughout the habitable globe; yet the great mass of the Caucasian race still deem the Negro as entirely destitute of those qualities, on which they selfishly predicate their own superiority.

The elements to which Holly alludes as the things on which "Caucasians" "predicate their own superiority" are contradicted by the blend of republican and democratic principles that he identifies in a previous paragraph as "the inherent capabilities of the Negro race, for self-government and civilized progress." Going beyond a mere recognition of such facts, Holly then challenges the colonialist and non-cosmopolitan American attitudes towards Haiti which consist of refusing to perceive this island as an equal partner and a contributor to the core democratic principles on which the American republic was founded. Holly shows how Americans failed to respect Haiti despite its pivotal role in resistance against colonial tyranny. Consequently, Holly laments how the Christian missionaries who sponsored his mission to Haiti supported the condescending Western view of the island and its populations as dependents rather than equals of whites and

---

[3] See Louis Martin Sears, "Frederick Douglass and the Mission to Haiti, 1889–1891," *The Hispanic American Historical Review* 21, no. 2 (May 1941): 222–238; James Weldon Johnson, "Self-Determining Haiti: What the United States Has Accomplished," Pt. 2, *The Nation 111.2879* (September 4, 1920): 265–267; and Mercer Cook, *Education in Haiti* (Federal Security Agency, Office of Education, 1948).

Europeans. Challenging this racism and the stereotypes of the American clergy as bigotry which belied the philanthropic claims of the missionaries, Holly states:

> Yes, I say, we may add a large number of the noisy agitators of the present day, who would persuade themselves and the world, that they are really Christian philanthropists, to that overwhelming crowd who openly traduce the Negro; because too many of those pseudo-humanitarians have lurking in their heart of hearts, a secret infidelity in regard to the real equality of the black man, which is ever ready to manifest its concealed sting, when the full and unequivocal recognition of the Negro, in all respects, is pressed home upon their hearts.

Here, Holly aims a heavy blow at two things. First, he challenges the Western (and mostly white Western) conception of cosmopolitanism as a philosophy based on perceptions of human beings as individuals who are naturally inclined to develop mutual and reciprocal love, care, respect, equality, and other virtues.[4] Holly refutes this abstract and self-congratulatory view of cosmopolitanism by suggesting that it is limited when people of color, such as blacks, are written out of it. As Holly's above statement suggests, Europeans did not count Haitians as human beings let alone view them as people who deserved equality. This treatment of Haitians has endured to this day, as was recently noticed in declarations of US President Donald Trump towards these populations who founded the first independent black republic and became the prime defenders of human rights in the Western hemisphere. Trump's representation of Haitians, Africans, and other people as coming from "shithole countries" demonstrates the persistence of the racism and ignorance which render Western cosmopolitanism futile.[5] In their introduction to *The Cosmopolitan Reader*, Garrett Wallace Brown and David Held define cosmopolitanism as "the idea that we have universal duties to all human beings" and rightly argue that this philosophy that has been given "contemporary relevance" by "the forces of globalization" is "not a particularly new way of thinking."[6] Yet, it is quite strange that most Westerners, including intellectuals, have written Africa out of the history of cosmopolitanism by representing it as a history traceable mainly to Hellenic and Indo-European traditions that are perceived as having nothing to do with Africa and black people. Holly's lecture will help to correct this mistaken attitude and help readers learn how a very brave and caring nineteenth-century African American reverend intellectually challenged whites who refused to treat Haitians as equals.

---

[4] For such a generic Western definition of cosmopolitanism, see Garrett Wallace Brown and David Held, "Editors' Introduction," *The Cosmopolitanism Reader* (Cambridge: Polity Press, 2010), pp. 1–2.

[5] See Julie Hirschfeld Davis, Sheryl Gay Stolberg, and Thomas Kaplan, "Trump Alarms Lawmakers With Disparaging Words for Haiti and Africa," https://www.nytimes.com/192018/01/11/us/politics/trump-shithole-countries.html, accessed January 18, 2018.

[6] Brown and Held, "Editors' Introduction," p. 3.

Holly and the Question of Colonization

In *American Intellectuals and African Nationalists, 1955–1970*, Martin Staniland wonders if the experiences of blacks in the United States and in Africa could be regarded as comparable when scholars continue to perceive African Americans as victims of "domestic colonialism" and not of global "colonialism."[7] As Staniland argues, unlike Harold Cruse and John Henrik Clarke, most African American intellectuals of the 1960s and 1970s were reluctant to perceive themselves as "US colonials" or to trace black struggle in the United States to "the same kind of soil as the nationalism of the African colonies proper."[8] The critics of global injustice find the analogy of slavery and segregation with colonialism as loosely drawn and inapplicable to the United States where blacks were, unlike in a true colony, a minority population that was scattered across regions and was unable to expulse the white majority that subjugated them.[9]

Holly's lecture helps to put to rest the controversy as to whether African Americans have been historically treated as "colonized." Although his lecture focuses on the laborious and ingenious work that Haitian blacks did to organize their revolutions against French imperialism during the late eighteenth century and the succeeding decades, its narration of how this nationalist resistance unfolded suggests his criticisms of the prejudices that white Americans had towards African Americans during that time. Holly perceived white colonialists of both late eighteenth-century France and the United States as imperialists who were hypocritical since they refused to extend to the blacks of Haiti and the United States whom they subjugated the same principles and rights of liberty, equality, fraternity, and justice that they demanded from their monarch oppressors. Holly says: "The white colonists of St. Domingo, like our liberty loving and democratic fellow citizens of the United States, never meant to include this despised race, in their glowing dreams of 'Liberty, Equality, and Fraternity'." Next, he asserts: "Like our *model Republicans*, they looked upon this hated race of beings, as placed so far down the scale of humanity, that when the 'Rights of man' were spoken of, they did not imagine that the most distant reference was thereby made to the Negro; or any one through whose veins his tainted blood sent its crimsoned tide." Thus, Holly reveals the ways in which, in the mid-nineteenth century, Black Nationalism's main goal was not only to achieve liberation for people of African descent but also to dispel an enduring myth. This is the inherent belief of white colonists in Europe, the

---

[7] Martin Staniland, *American Intellectuals and African Nationalists, 1955–1970* (New Haven: Yale University Press, 1991), p. 189.

[8] Ibid., p. 190.

[9] Ibid., pp. 190–191.

United States, and Haiti about black people's inability to govern themselves. Holly dispels this myth that Europeans used to justify colonization of blacks and other people of color around the world. He declares: "The exceptional part which the blacks played in the moving drama that was then being enacted in St. Domingo, by their stern self-possession amid the furious excitement of the whites, is one of the strongest proofs that can be adduced to substantiate the capabilities of the Negro race for self-government." In this passage, Holly shows that he was a pioneer in the representation of the nationalist ideas of black self-rule and self-determination and sovereignty as foundations of social, political, economic, and cultural liberation that Garvey and Carmichael inherited in the twentieth century.

Marcus Garvey and Self-Determination

Garvey's approach to Black Nationalism is particularly significant because it was not focused solely on the United States but also on Africa, specifically Senegal, Liberia, and Kenya, where the Jamaicans attempted to counter the colonial dominations that France, the United States, and England attempted to impose on blacks of these territories. But the catalyst of his nationalism was the United States where his political prominence began. Garvey's political fame in the United States arose during the early twentieth century when blacks in the United States faced vitriolic racism, violence, and disenfranchisement in northern cities as well as in the South. Following their massive migration from the South to the North during the 1910s and 1920s, African Americans were confronted with increasing hostility in metropolitan areas where they were segregated, mostly unemployed, and kept in poor living conditions. From these circumstances emerged racial violence such as the deadly riot which erupted in East St. Louis on July 2, 1917. That day, angry white mobs attacked defenseless black migrants whom they accused of taking their jobs in the city's industrial plants. The riot ended after thirty-nine blacks and nine whites were killed. As Lawrence Levine points out, in *The Unpredictable Past: Explorations in American Cultural History*, Garvey intervened promptly by denouncing the massacre as part of "America's continuous round of oppression of black people who for three hundred years had given their life blood to help build the republic."[10]

By denouncing and promising to end the killing of black people through resistance, Garvey created a popular base and appeal for himself and his organization, outwitting the progressive and liberal integrationism of Du Bois and the NAACP. Garvey was able to appeal to disenfranchised African Americans and calibrate their

---

[10] Lawrence Levine, *The Unpredictable Past: Explorations in American Cultural History* (Oxford University Press, 1993), pp. 118–119.

frustration towards racial injustice, thereby beginning a movement of liberation and uplift that has left indelible marks on Black Nationalist movements around the world. As Houston Baker argues in *Modernism and the Harlem Renaissance*, Garvey was one of the first "modern" black intellectuals who were able to convert "*marronage*," the idea of banding black people together, into an art of resistance and liberation.[11] Baker refers to Richard Price's definition of *marronage* as "the banding together [of individual fugitives] to create independent communities of their own, [communities] that struck directly at the foundations of the plantation system, presenting military and economic threats that often taxed the colonists to their limits."[12] Using *marronage*, Garvey was able to calibrate the discontent that African Americans had felt toward whites' racism and violence and use it as the basis for his nationalist campaign.

Moreover, Garvey's nationalism was not chimeric or selfless because it was founded on a cosmopolitan view of the world. Cosmopolitanism was integral to Garvey's liberation ideology which was based on the refrain "Africa for Africans, those at home and those abroad" and the call "to embrace the purpose of all black humanity" which, as Ngũgĩ wa Thiong'o argues in *Something Torn and New: An African Renaissance*, are two axioms that were meant to make blacks "be free and equal members of the community of nations and peoples."[13] Ngũgĩ writes:

> For behind the rhetoric of blackness was also the universalist-humanist vision of using the Universal Negro Improvement Association to inspire African peoples 'with pride in self and with the determination of going ahead in the creation of those ideals that will lift them to the unprejudiced company of races and nations. There is no desire for hate or malice, but every wish to see all mankind linked into a common fraternity of progress and achievement that will wipe away the odor of prejudice, and elevate the human race to the height of real godly love and satisfaction.' Garvey's detractors ignored this aspect of his thought.[14]

Garvey's radicalism partly stemmed from his realization of the Western world's betrayals of the cosmopolitan principles founded on the common and collective uplift of the world from poverty, inequity, and misery. These words have equivalents in the terms that Garvey uses in his address "The True Solution of the Negro Problem" to draw attention to the unfair treatment of blacks in the early twentieth century in the West. In unapologetic and unequivocal ways, Garvey laments, in

---

[11] Houston A. Baker, *Modernism and the Harlem Renaissance* (University of Chicago Press, 1987), p. 95.

[12] Ibid., p. 76. See Richard Price (ed.) *Maroon Societies: Rebel Slave Communities in the Americas* (Baltimore, MD: Johns Hopkins University Press, 1979), p. 3.

[13] Ngũgĩ wa Thiong'o, *Something Torn and New: An African Renaissance* (New York: Civitas Books, 2009), p. 36.

[14] Ibid.

his address, the ways in which lynching, "peonage," "slavery," "political monopoly," and other forms of violence and inequalities assailed the blacks of the United States, the West Indies, South and Central America, and Africa during the early twentieth century. By denouncing such injustices, Garvey was a visionary since his assessments of the plight of people of African descent resonates with the plight of these populations' descendants during current times. Whether one talks about Haiti, the United States, Brazil, Columbia, Africa and other parts of the world where blacks live, dire conditions connected to racism and systemic social and political inequalities prevail. Such conditions contradict cosmopolitan, republican, and democratic ideals, severely hampering the lives of people of African descent and other victimized populations. Their lives are marked not just by oppressions such as police brutality, racism, poor healthcare, limited socio-economic facilities, and joblessness, but also by the Western world's obdurate refusal to cooperate with and compensate the toiling masses of the world for the sake of the common good and prosperity.

Stokely Carmichael: The Younger Race Rebel

Stokely Carmichael's nationalism was also foundational even if it occurred during the mid-twentieth century. His revolution occurred about 190 years after Phyllis Wheatley began her nationalist uprising in her 1773 book, *Poems on Various Subjects, Religious and Moral.* Like his contemporary Amiri Baraka, aka Leroy Jones, Carmichael was part of a generation of African American intellectuals who had lost faith in the main institutions of the United States due to the inhumane ways in which blacks were being treated in that country and abroad. These black intellectuals were also severely disheartened because of the lingering effects of Jim Crow racism and segregation which worsened the experiences of unemployment, family breakdown, lack of self-esteem, uprootedness, and other predicaments of African Americans. While previous nationalisms, notably Garvey's, often perceived repatriation to Africa as the best way to address such injustices, Carmichael and Baraka's generation believed that the struggle must start in the United States where equality must be achieved "by any means necessary," as Malcolm X stated most clearly in his own movement. Thus, Carmichael's nationalism predicates the liberation of blacks on radical resistance rather than on the amiable rhetoric of non-violence that has been historically ascribed to Martin Luther King, Jr. According to James H. Cone, in the 1960s, the Black Church in America was confronted with a dilemma in deciding who, between King and Carmichael, to support after the divide between these two leaders: "black theologians and preachers felt themselves caught in a terrible predicament of wanting to express their continued respect for and solidarity with King, but disagreeing with his rejection of Black Power."[15] These black theologians' willingness to veer away from a part of King's non-violence rhetoric stemmed from their recognition of Carmichael's radicalism as a legitimate resistance justified by centuries of mistreatment of blacks in the United States and abroad.

Another quality that makes Carmichael's chapter important is its enduring significance in a modern history in which blacks and other people of color remain largely ghettoized, colonized, and disenfranchised in the United States despite the absence of legal slavery. The situation is so grave that the adjective "colonized" can unquestionably and rightfully be used to describe the plight of African Americans due to massive imprisonment of black men and women that Michelle Alexander examines in her book, *The New Jim Crow: Mass Incarceration in the Age of Colorblindness.* Alexander asserts: "The superlative nature of individual black achievement today in formerly white domains is a good indicator that the old Jim Crow is dead, but it does not necessarily mean the end of racial caste."[16] By the term, "racial caste," Alexander alludes to the process in which racial privilege is always maintained in the United States with a process of "preservation through transformation." She states: "The rules and reasons the political system employs to enforce status relations of any kind, including racial hierarchy, evolve and change as they are challenged."[17] In order to better understand this process of reification of racist structures, one may revert to Paul Gilroy, who, drawing from Amiri Baraka (Leroy Jones) theorized the concept of the "changing same" to describe how "we are more or less what we used to be."[18] For Gilroy, the "changing same" is also an alert to the dangers of essentialism, be it cultural, racial, or ethnic, and a call for a search for negotiation of meaning in collective struggles or tradition. Encapsulating Gilroy's concept, one scholar writes:

> The changing same seizes the ways in which the tension between having been, being and becoming is negotiated, conjugated or resolved. Though some collective recollections may be lived as enduring traditions, they result, rather, from the processing and reprocessing of cultural forms.

[15] James H. Cone, "Black Theology and the Black Church: Where Do We Go from Here?," in *Modern Black Nationalism: From Marcus Garvey to Louis Farrakhan*, ed. William L. Van Deburg (New York University Press, 1997), p. 305.

[16] Michelle Alexander, *The New Jim Crow: Mass Incarceration in the Age of Colorblindness* (New York: New Press, 2010), p. 21.

[17] Ibid.

[18] Paul Gilroy, "Roots and Routes: Black Identity as an Outernational Project," in *Racial and Ethnic Identity: Psychological Development and Creative Expression*, ed.H. W. Harris, H. C. Blue, and E. E. M. Griffith (London and New York: Routledge, 1994), p. 30.

The changing same not only defeats the idea that the homeland is the constant and sole principle of collective mobilization, it also questions linear conceptions of history, continuity and progress. The changing same is part of the communal project of recovery; or the 'rediscovery' of a past, of a place, a *grounding*, which, as Stuart Hall points out, is grasped through reconstruction.[19]

It would be interesting to see how the concept of the "changing same" is reconstructed in Black Nationalist literature in which it has been written out. Certainly, as one can see in the writings of Holly, Garvey, and Carmichael, Black Nationalists were not locked into essentialist notions of culture, race, or place. Nevertheless, they were non-hesitant in claiming absolute racial or diasporan identities constructed out of the disjointed and frustrating experiences of the "changing same." The more they witnessed history, the further dejected these Black Nationalists became about the process in which white supremacy reinvented the pillars of racial hierarchy in terms that compromised the foundations of the American republic. These intellectuals were nationalists because they believed that the marginalization to which they were subjected in the United States from the time of slavery to the 1950s contradicted America's self-representation as a cosmopolitan nation that is founded on republicanism and democracy. Being one of the last bearers of Black Nationalism, Carmichael, who later changed his name to Kwame Touré, expressed African Americans' state of being oppressed more clearly than anybody else in the American republic. In his address, Carmichael asserts:

The vast majority of Negroes in this country live in these captive communities and must endure these conditions of oppression because, and only because, *they are black and powerless.* I do not suppose that at any point the men who control the power and resources of this country ever sat down and designed these black enclaves, and formally articulated the terms of their colonial and dependent status, as was done, for example, by the Apartheid government of South Africa. Yet, one cannot distinguish between one ghetto and another. As one moves from city to city it is as though some malignant racist planning-unit had done precisely this—designed each one from the same master blueprint. And indeed, if the ghetto had been formally and deliberately planned, instead of growing spontaneously and inevitably from the racist functioning of the various institutions that combine to make the society, it would be somehow less frightening.

Carmichael's statement is relevant for many reasons. First, it suggests the systemic injustices and inequalities that prompted the radical Black Nationalism of the 1960s to resist oppression. Such inequities are apparent in Carmichael's representations

---

[19] Anne-Marie Fortier, "Diaspora," in *Cultural Geography: A Critical Dictionary of Key Ideas*, ed. David Atkinson, Peter Jackson, David Sibley, and Neil Washbourne (London and New York: I. B. Tauris, 2007), p. 184.

of blacks in the 1960s as people who were sequestered in "enclaves" and were therefore treated like colonized populations. To prove his point, Carmichael notes the parallels between the ways in which segregation in the United States and apartheid in South Africa were identical racist systems in that they orchestrated the ghettoization of blacks in geographical fringes of a society in which they were feared and treated as less than second-class citizens. Carmichael's analogy is also relevant since it touches on the issue of the colonial status of African Americans that most scholars have been hesitant to recognize. As discussed earlier, the hesitation is apparent in the popular belief that the experiences of black Americans cannot be termed "colonial" or "anti-colonial" in the ways in which the histories of Africans are often interpreted.

QUESTIONS

(1) Did Black Nationalism promote self-sufficiency for blacks? If not, how can self-sufficiency be achieved?
(2) The authors in this section, in different ways, draw on Black Nationalism as a response to the unequal position of blacks in the United States. How do the authors approach the issue of blacks' inequality? What are some of the similarities and differences in their approaches?
(3) What were some of the problems that Black Nationalism sought to address? Was it successful?
(4) What was the role of Black Nationalism in addressing blacks' second-class status in the United States?
(5) What are the political, economic, social, and cultural ideologies of Black Nationalism? Why does Black Nationalism reject blacks' integration into American society?

FURTHER READINGS

- E. Frances White, "Africa on My Mind: Gender, Counterdiscourse, and African American Nationalism," *Journal of Women's History* 2, no. 1 (1990): 73–97.
- Henry McNeal Turner. *A Speech on the Present Duties and Future Destiny of the Negro Race* [Delivered September 2, 1872] (Charlestown, NC: Nabu Press, 2014).
- Hollis Lynch, "Pan Negro Nationalism in the New World, Before 1862," *Boston University Papers on Africa, Volume II: African History* (1966): 149–179.
- Leonord W. Levy and Alfred F. Young (eds.), *Black Nationalism in America* (New York: Bobbs-Merrill, 1970).
- Malcolm X, "Prospects for Freedom in 1965" [January 7, 1965]. Available at: http://malcolmxfiles.blogspot.com/2013/07/prospects-for-freedom-in-1965-january-7.html.
- Marin R. Delany. *The Condition, Elevation, Emigration, and Destiny of the Colored People of the United States, Politically Considered*, with an introduction by Toyin Falola (Amherst, NY: Humanity Books, 2004).

- Maulana Karenga, "Which Road to Revolution: Nationalism, Pan-Africanism, or Socialism?," *Black Scholar* 6 no. 2 (October 1974): 21–31.
- Molefi Kete Asante, *The Afrocentric Idea* (Philadelphia, PA: Temple University Press, 1998).
- Stokley Carmichael and Charles V. Hamilton, *Black Power: The Politics of Liberation in America* (New York: Vintage, 1967).
- Tunde Adeleke, "Who Are We? Africa and the Problem of Black American Identity," *Canadian Review of American Studies* 29 (1999): 49–88.

9 A Vindication of the Capacity of the Negro Race for Self-Government, and Civilized Progress

JAMES THEODORE HOLLY

James Theodore Holly (1829–1911), an emigrationist, missionary, and bishop, was born in Washington, DC. When he was fourteen, his parents who were freed slaves moved to Brooklyn, New York. In New York, he met many important abolitionists and worked with the abolitionist Lewis Tappan. Holly was married in 1851 in New York. Before moving to Windsor, Ontario, Canada, with his family, Holly joined the Protestant Episcopal Church. When he returned to the United States, in 1854, he attended the first National Emigration Convention held in Cleveland, Ohio and became the Commissioner of the National Emigration Board. From 1856 to 1861, he served as a rector in St. Luke's Church, New Haven, Connecticut. He continued his religious activities but was drawn to the idea of black emigration because he saw no future for blacks in the United States. Holly was aware of the American Colonization Society that aided blacks' emigration to Haiti beginning in 1824. Partly for this reason, he travelled to Haiti to explore emigration options for free blacks in the United States. In 1862, he became a Haitian citizen but returned to the United States hoping for financial support to establish a mission station, which was denied by the Board of Mission of the Protestant Episcopal Church. It was not until 1865, three years later, that the Board of Mission accepted sponsorship of Holly's mission in Haiti. Holly's well-known lecture, "A Vindication of the Capacity of the Negro Race for Self-Government, and Civilized Progress," is reproduced, in part, below.

DEDICATION
To REV. WILLIAM C. MUNROE,
RECTOR OF ST. MATTHEW'S CHURCH, DETROIT, MICHIGAN

Permit me the honor of inscribing this work to you. It is a lecture that I prepared and delivered before a Literary Society of Colored Young Men, in the City of New Haven, Ct., after my return from Hayti, in the autumn of 1855; and subsequently repeated in Ohio, Michigan, and Canada West, during the summer of 1856.

I have permitted it to be published at the request of the Afric-American Printing Company, an association for the publication of Negro literature, organized in connection with the Board of Publication, which forms a constituent part of the

National Emigration Convention, over which you so ably presided, at its sessions, held in Cleveland, Ohio, in the years 1854–56.

I dedicate this work to you, in token of my appreciation of the life-long services you have so sacredly devoted to the cause of our oppressed race; the ardor of which devotion has not yet abated, although the evening of your life has far advanced in the deepening shadows of the approaching night of physical death. And as the ground-work of this skeleton treatise is based in the events of Haytian History, it becomes peculiarly appropriate that I should thus dedicate it to one who has spent three of the most valuable years of his life as a missionary of the cross in that island; who there deposited the slumbering ashes of his own bosom companion a willing sacrifice to her constancy and devotion; and who yet desires to consume the remainder of his own flickering lamp of life by the resumption of those labors in that island, under more favorable and better auspices, in the service of Christ and his church.

Finally, I dedicate this work to you as a filial token of gratitude, for that guidance which under God, I have received from your fatherly teachings; by which I have been awakened to higher inspirations, of our most holy religion; aroused to deeper emotions of human liberty and quicker pulsations of the universal brotherhood of man; and thereby animated with a more consecrated devotion to the service of my suffering race than might otherwise have fallen to my lot.

Deign, therefore, I beseech you, to accept this dedication as the spontaneous offering of a grateful and dutiful heart.

Lecture

The task that I propose to myself in the present lecture, is an earnest attempt to defend the inherent capabilities of the Negro race, for self-government and civilized progress. For this purpose, I will examine the events of Haytian History, from the commencement of their revolution down to the present period, so far as the same may contribute to illustrate the points I propose to prove and defend. Permit me, however, to add, in extenuation of this last comprehensive proposition, that I must, necessarily, review these events hastily, in order to crowd them within the compass of an ordinary lecture.

Reasons for Assuming Such a Task

Notwithstanding the remarkable progress of philanthropic ideas and humanitarian feelings, during the last half century, among almost every nation and people throughout the habitable globe; yet the great mass of the Caucasian race still deem the Negro as entirely destitute of those qualities, on which they selfishly predicate their own superiority.

And we may add to this overwhelming class that cherish such self-complacent ideas of themselves, to the great prejudice of the Negro, a large quota also of that small portion of the white race, who profess to believe the truths, "That God is no respecter of persons;" and that "He has made of one blood, all the nations that dwell upon the face of the earth." Yes, I say, we may add a large number of the noisy agitators of the present day, who would persuade themselves and the world, that they are really Christian philanthropists, to that overwhelming crowd who openly traduce the Negro; because too many of those pseudo-humanitarians have lurking in their heart of hearts, a secret infidelity in regard to the real equality of the black man, which is ever ready to manifest its concealed sting, when the full and unequivocal recognition of the Negro, in all respects, is pressed home upon their hearts.

Hence, between this downright prejudice against this long abused race, which is flauntingly maintained by myriads of their oppressors on the one hand; and this woeful distrust of his natural equality, among those who claim to be his friends, on the other; no earnest and fearless efforts are put forth to vindicate their character, by even the few who may really acknowledge this equality of the races. They are overawed by the overpowering influence of the contrary sentiment. This sentiment unnerves their hands and palsies their tongue; and no pen is wielded or voice heard, among that race of men, which fearlessly and boldly places the Negro side by side with the white man, as his equal in all respects. But to the contrary, every thing is done by the enemies of the Negro race to vilify and debase them. And the result is, that many of the race themselves, are almost persuaded that they are a brood of inferior beings.

It is then, to attempt a fearless but truthful vindication of this race, with which I am identified – however feeble and immature that effort may be – that I now proceed to set forth the following address:

I wish, by the undoubted facts of history, to cast back the vile aspersions and foul calumnies that have been heaped upon my race for the last four centuries, by our unprincipled oppressors; whose base interest, at the expense of our blood and our bones, have made them reiterate, from generation to generation, during the long march of ages, everything that would prop up the impious dogma of our natural and inherent inferiority.

An Additional Reason for the Present Talk

But this is not all. I wish hereby to contribute my influence – however small that influence – to effect a grandeur and dearer object to our race than even this truthful vindication of them before the world. I wish to do all in my power to inflame the latent embers of self-respect, that the cruelty and injustice of our oppressors, have nearly extinguished in our bosoms, during the midnight chill of centuries, that we have clanked the galling chains of slavery. To this end, I wish to remind my oppressed brethren, that dark and dismal as this horrid night has been, and sorrow-ful as the general reflections are, in regard to our race; yet, notwithstanding these discouraging considerations, there are still some proud historic recollections, linked indissolubly with the most important events of the past and present century, which break the general monotony, and remove some of the gloom that hang over the dark historic period of African slavery, and the accursed traffic in which it was cradled.

The Revolutionary History of Hayti

The Basis of This Argument

These recollections are to be found in the history of the heroic events of the Revolution of Hayti.

This revolution is one of the noblest, grandest, and most justifiable outbursts against tyrannical oppression that is recorded on the pages of the world's history.

A race of almost dehumanized men – made so by an oppressive slavery of three centuries – arose from their slumber of ages, and redressed their own unparalleled wrongs with a terrible hand in the name of God and humanity.

In this terrible struggle for liberty, the Lord of Hosts directed their arms to be the instruments of His judgment on their oppressors, as the recompense of His violated law of love between man and his fellow, which these tyrants of the new world had been guilty of, in the centuries of blood, wrong, and oppression, which they had perpetrated on the Negro race in that isle of the Carribean Sea.

But aside from this great providential and religious view of this great movement, that we are always bound to seek for, in all human affairs, to see how they square with the mind of God, more especially if they relate to the destinies of nations and people; – the Haytian Revolution is also the grandest political event of this or any other age. In weighty causes, and wondrous and momentous features, it surpasses the American revolution, in an incomparable degree. The revolution of this country was only the revolt of a people already comparatively free, independent, and highly enlightened. Their greatest grievance was the imposition of three pence per pound tax on tea, by the mother country, without their consent. But the Haytian revolution was a revolt of an uneducated and menial class of slaves, against their tyrannical oppressors, who not only imposed an absolute tax on their unrequited labor, but also usurped their very bodies; and who would have been prompted by the brazen infidelity of the age then rampant, to dispute with the Almighty, the possession of the souls of these poor creatures, could such brazen effrontery have been of any avail, to have wrung more ill-gotten gain out of their victims to add to their worldly goods.

These oppressors, against whom the Negro insurgents of Hayti had to contend, were not only the government of a far distant mother country, as in the case of the American revolution; but unlike and more fearful than this revolt, the colonial government of Hayti was also thrown in the balance against the Negro revolters. The American revolters had their colonial government in their own hands, as well as their individual liberty at the commencement of the revolution. The black insurgents of Hayti had yet to grasp both their personal liberty and the control of their colonial government, by the might of their own right hands, when their heroic struggle began.

The obstacles to surmount, and the difficulties to contend against, in the American revolution, when compared to those of the Haytian, were, (to use a homely but classic phrase,) but a "tempest in a teapot," compared to the dark and lurid thunder storm of the dissolving heavens.

Never before, in all the annals of the world's history, did a nation of abject and chattel slaves arise in the terrific might of their resuscitated manhood, and regenerate, redeem, and disenthrall themselves: by taking their station at one gigantic bound, as an independent nation, among the sovereignties of the world.

It is, therefore, the unparalleled incidents that led to this wonderful event, that I now intend to review rapidly, in order to demonstrate thereby, the capacity of the Negro race for self-government and civilized progress, to the fullest extent and in the highest sense of these terms.

Preliminary Incidents of the Revolution

I shall proceed to develop the first evidence of the competency of the Negro race for self-government, amid the historical incidents that preceded their terrible and bloody revolution; and in the events of that heroic struggle itself.

When the cosmopolitan ideas of "Liberty, Fraternity, and Equality," which swayed the mighty minds of France, toward the close of the 18th century, reached the colony of St. Domingo, through the Massaic club, composed of wealthy colonial planters, organized in the French capital; all classes in that island, except the black slave and the free colored man, were instantly wrought up to the greatest effervescence, and swayed with the deepest emotions, by the startling doctrines of the equal political rights of all men, which were then so boldly enunciated in the face of the tyrannical despotisms and the immemorial assumptions of the feudal aristocracies of the old world.

The colonial dignitaries, the military officers, and other agents of the government of France, then resident in St. Domingo, the rich planters and the poor whites, (these latter called in the parlance of that colony *Les petits blancs*,) were all from first to last, swayed with the intensest and the most indescribable feelings, at the promulgation of these bold and radical theories.

All were in a perfect fever to realize and enjoy the priceless boon of political and social privileges that these revolutionary ideas held out before them. And in their impatience to grasp these precious prerogatives, they momentarily forgot their colonial dependance on France, and spontaneously came together in a general assembly, at a small town of St. Domingo, called St. Marc; and proceeded to deliberate seriously about taking upon themselves all the attributes of national sovereignty and independence.

And when they had deliberately matured plans to suit themselves, they did not hesitate to send representatives to propose them to the national government of France, for its acknowledgment and acquiescence in their desires.

Such was the radical consequence to which the various classes of white colonists in St. Domingo seized upon, and carried the cosmopolitan theories of the French philosophers and political agitators of the last century.

But from all this excitement and enthusiasm, I have already excepted the black and colored inhabitants of that island.

The white colonists of St. Domingo, like our liberty loving and democratic fellow citizens of the United States, never meant to include this despised race, in their glowing dreams of "Liberty, Equality, and Fraternity."

Like our *model Republicans*, they looked upon this hated race of beings, as placed so far down the scale of humanity, that when the "Rights of man" were spoken of, they did not imagine that the most distant reference was thereby made to the Negro; or any one through whose veins his tainted blood sent its crimsoned tide.

And so blind were they to the fact that the "Rights of Man" could be so construed as to recognise the humanity of that oppressed race; that when the National assembly of France, swayed by the just representations of the "Friends of the Blacks" was led to extend equal political rights to the free men of color in St. Domingo, at the same time that this National body ratified the doings of the General Colonial assembly of St. Marc: these same colonists who had been so loud in their hurrahs for the "Rights of Man," now ceased their clamors for liberty in the face of this just national decree, and sullenly resolved "To die rather than share equal political rights with a bastard race." Such was the insulting term that this colonial assembly then applied to the free men of color, in whose veins coursed the blood of the proud planter, commingled with that of the lowly Negress.

The Self-Possession of the Black

An Evidence of Their Capacity for Self-Government

The exceptional part which the blacks played in the moving drama that was then being enacted in St. Domingo, by their stern self-possession amid the furious excitement of the whites, is one of the strongest proofs that can be adduced to substantiate the capabilities of the Negro race for self-government.

The *careless reserve* of the seemingly dehumanized black slave, who continued to toil and delve on, in the monotonous round of plantation labor, under a cruel task master, in a manner so entirely heedless of the furious hurrahs for freedom and independence; the planting of Liberty poles, surmounted by the cap of Liberty; and the erection of statues to the goddess of Liberty, which was going on around him: this apparent indifference and carelessness to the surging waves of freedom that were then awakening the despotisms of earth from their slumber of ages, showed that the slave understood and appreciated the difficulties of his position. He felt that the hour of destiny, appointed by the Almighty, had not yet tolled its summons for him to arise, and avenge the wrong of ages.

He therefore remained heedless of the effervescence of liberty that bubbled over in the bosom of the white man; and continued at his sullen labors, biding his time for deliverance. And in this judicious reserve on the part of the blacks, we have one of the strongest traits of self-government.

When we look upon this characteristic of cool, self-possession, we cannot but regard it as almost a miracle under the circumstances. We cannot see what magic power could keep such a warm blooded race of men in such an ice bound spell of cold indifference, when every other class of men in that colony was flush with the excitement of liberty; and the whole island was rocked to its center, with the deafening surges of Equality, that echoed from ten thousand throats.

One would have supposed, that at the very first sound of freedom, the 500,000 bondmen in that island, whose ancestry for three centuries had worn the yoke of slavery; would have raised up, at once, in their overwhelming numerical power and physical stalwartness, and cried out LIBERTY! with a voice so powerful as to have cleft asunder the bowels of the earth, and buried slavery and every Negro hater and oppressor who might dare oppose their just rights, in one common grave.

But as I have said, they did no such thing; they had a conscious faith in the ultimate designs of God; and they silently waited, trusting to the workings of His over-ruling Providence to bring about the final day of their deliverance. In doing so, I claim they have given an evidence of their ability to govern themselves, that ought to silence all pro-slavery calumniators of my race at once, and forever, by its powerful and undying refutation of their slanders.

And let no one dare to rob them of this glorious trait of character, either by alleging that they remained thus indifferent, because they were too ignorant to appreciate the blessings of liberty; or by saying, that if they understood the import of these clamors for the "Rights of Man," they were thus quiet, because they were too cowardly to strike for their disenthralment.

The charge that they were thus ignorant of the priceless boon of freedom, is refuted by the antecedent history of the servile insurrections, which never ceased to rack that island from 1522 down to the era of negro independence. The Negro insurgents, Polydore, Macandel, and Padrejan, who had at various times, led on their enslaved brethren to daring deeds, in order to regain their God-given liberty, brand that assertion as a libel on the Negro character, that says, he was too cowardly to strike for the inheritance of its precious boon.

And the desperate resolution to be free, that the Maroon Negroes of the island maintained for 85 years, by their valorous struggles, in their wild mountain fastnesses, against the concentrated and combined operations of the French and Spanish authorities then in that colony; and which finally compelled these authorities to conclude a treaty with the intrepid Maroon chief, Santiago, and thereby acknowledge their freedom forever thereafter: this fact I say, proves him to be a base calumniator, who shall dare to say that a keen appreciation of liberty existed not in the bosom of the Negroes of St. Domingo.

But again, as to the plea of cowardice, in order to account for the fact of their cool self-possession amidst the first convulsive throes of Revolutionary liberty, permit me to add in refutation of this fallacy, that if the daring incidents of antecedent insurrections do not sufficiently refute this correlative charge also; then the daring deeds of dreadless heroism performed by a Toussaint, a Dessalines, a Rigaud, and a Christophe, in the subsequent terrible, but necessary revolution of the Negroes; in which black troops gathered from the plantations of slavery, met the best appointed armies of France, and at various times, those of England and Spain also: and proved their equal valor and prowess with these best disciplined armies of Europe – this dreadless heroism, evinced by the blacks, I say, is sufficient to nail the infamous imputation of cowardice to the wall, at once and forever.

Hence nothing shall rob them of the immaculate glory of exhibiting a stern self-possession, in that feverish hour of excitement, when every body around them were crying out Liberty. And in this judicious self-control at this critical juncture, when their destiny hung on the decision of the hour, we have a brilliant illustration of the capacity of the race for self-government.

Similar Evidence on the Part of the Free Men of Color

But additional and still stronger evidence of this fact crowd upon us, when we see that the free men of color remained entirely passive during the first stage of this revolutionary effervescence. This class of men, as a general thing, was educated and wealthy; and they were burthened with duties by the State, without being invested with corresponding political privileges. From such unjust exactions they had every reason to seek a speedy deliverance. And this great tumult that now swept over the island, offered them a propitious opportunity to agitate with the rest of the free men of the colony for the removal of their political disabilities.

They had greater cause to agitate than the whites, because they suffered under heavier burdens than that class. Nevertheless, in the first great outbreak of the water-floods of liberty – tempting as the occasion was, and difficult as restraint must have been; yet the free men of color also possessed their souls in patience, and awaited a more propitious opportunity. Certainly no one will attempt to stigmatise the calm judgment of these men in this awful crisis of suspense, as the result of ignorance of the blessings of freedom, when it is known that many of this class were educated in the seminaries of France, under her most brilliant professors; and that they were also patrons of that prodigy of literature, the Encyclopedia of France.

Neither can they stigmatize this class of men as cowards, as it is also known that they were the voluntary compeers of the Revolutionary heroes of the United

States; and who, under the banners of France, mingled their sable blood with the Saxon and the French in the heroic battle of Savannah.

Then this calm indifference of the men of color in this crisis, notwithstanding the blood of three excitable races mingled in their veins with that of the African, viz: that of the French, the Spanish, and the Indian; and notwithstanding, they had glorious recollections of their services in the cause of American Independence, inciting them on – this calm indifference, on their part, I say, notwithstanding these exciting causes, is another grand and striking illustration of the conservative characteristics of the Negro race, that demonstrate their capacity for self-government.

The Opportune Movement of the Free Colored Men

The tumultuous events of this excitement among the white colonists rolled onward, and brought the auspicious hour of Negro destiny in that island nearer and nearer, when Providence designed that he should play his part in the great drama of freedom that was then being enacted. Of course the propitious moment for the free men of color to begin to move would present itself prior to that for the movement of the Negro slaves.

The opportunity for the men of color presented itself when the general colonial assembly of St. Marc's (already referred to) sent deputies to France, to present the result of its deliberations to the National Assembly; and to ask that august body to confer on the colony the right of self-government.

At this time, therefore, when the affairs of the colony were about to undergo examination in the supreme legislature of the mother country, the free men of color seized upon the occasion to send deputies to France also, men of their own caste, to represent their grievances and make their wishes known to the National Assembly. This discreet discernment of such an opportune moment to make such a movement divested of every other consideration, shows a people who understand themselves, what they want, and how to seek it. But when we proceed to consider the most approved manner in which the representations were made to the National Assembly, by the colored delegates on behalf of their caste, in the colony of St. Domingo, and the influences they brought to bear upon that body, as exhibited hereafter: we shall perceive thereby that they showed such an intimate acquaintance with the secret springs of governmental machinery, as demonstrated at once their capacity to govern themselves.

This deputation first drew up a statement on behalf of their caste in the colony, of such a stirring nature as would be certain to command the national sympathy in their cause, when presented to the National Assembly. But previously to presenting it to that assembly, they took the wise precaution to wait upon the honorable president of that august body, in order to enlist and commit him in their favor, as the first stepping stone to secure the success of their object before the Supreme Legislature.

They prevailed in their mission to the President of the Assembly; and succeeded in obtaining this very emphatic assurance from him: "No part of the nation shall vainly reclaim their rights before the assembly of the representatives of the French people."

Having accomplished this important step, the colored deputies next began to operate through the Abolition Society of Paris, called "*Les Amis des Noirs*," upon such of the members of the assembly as were affiliated with this society, and thus already indirectly pledged to favor such a project as theirs, asking simple justice for their race. They were again successful, and Charles De Lameth, one of the zealous patrons of that society, and an active member of the National Assembly, was engaged to argue their cause before the Supreme Legislature of the nation, although strange to say, he was himself a colonial slaveholder at that time.

And at the appointed moment in the National Assembly, this remarkable man felt prompted to utter these astounding words in behalf of this oppressed and disfranchised class of the colony: "I am one of the greatest proprietors of St. Domingo; yet I declare to you, that sooner than lose sight of principles so sacred to justice and humanity, I would prefer to lose all that I possess. I declare myself in favor of admitting: the men of color to the rights of citizenship; and in favor of the freedom of the blacks."

Now let us for a moment stop and reflect on the measures resorted to by the colored deputies of St. Domingo, in Paris, who, by their wise stratagems, had brought their cause step by step to such an eventful and auspicious crisis as this.

Could there have been surer measures concocted for the success of their plans, than thus committing the president of the assembly to their cause in the first place; and afterwards pressing a liberty-loving slaveholder into their service, to thunder their measures through the National Assembly, by such a bold declaration?

Who among the old fogies of Tammany Hall – that junta of scheming politicians who govern this country by pulling the wires of party, and thereby making every official of the nation, from the President of the United States down to the Commissioners for Street Sweeping in the City of New York, dance as so many puppets at their bidding – I repeat it – who among these all powerful but venal politicians of old Tammany, could have surpassed these tactics of those much abused men of color, who thus swayed the secret springs of the National Assembly of France? And who, after this convincing proof to the contrary, shall dare to say that the Negro race is not capable of self-government?

But to return to the thread of our narrative. When the secret springs had been thus secured in their behalf, they had nothing to fear from the popular heart of the nation, already keenly alive to the sentiments of Liberty, Equality, and Fraternity; because the simple justice of their demands would commend them to the people as soon as they were publicly made known in France.

In order to make the very best impression on the popular heart of the nation, their petition demanding simple justice to their caste was accompanied with a statement very carefully drawn up.

In this statement they showed that their caste in the colony of St. Domingo possessed one-third of the real estate, and one-fourth of the personal effects of the island. They also set forth the advantages of their position in the political and social affairs of St. Domingo, as a balance of power in the hand of the imperial government of France, against the high pretensions of the haughty planters on the one hand, and the seditious spirit of the poor whites on the other. And, as an additional consideration, by way of capping the climax, they offered in the name, and on behalf of the free men of color in the colony, six millions of francs as a loyal contribution to the wants and financial exigencies of the National Treasury, to be employed in liquidating the debt of their common country.

Thus, if neither their wire-working maneuvers, the justice of their cause, or the conservative influence which their position gave them in the colony, had not been enough to secure the end which they sought; then the tempting glitter of so much cash, could not be resisted, when its ponderous weight was also thrown in the scale of justice. They succeeded, as a matter of course, in accomplishing their purpose; and the National Assembly of France promulgated a decree on the 8th of March, 1790, securing equal political rights to the men of color.

The very success of this movement, and the means by which its success was effected, the opportune moment when it was commenced, and the immense odds that were against those that sought its accomplishment – all these things must hereafter be emblazoned on the historic page as an everlasting tribute to the genius of the negro race, and remain an ineffaceable evidence of their capacity for self-government; that may be triumphantly adduced and proudly pointed at in this and every succeeding generation of the world, until the latest syllable of recorded time.

The Crisis Produced in the Colony by This Decree
The Men of Color on the Side of Liberty, Law, and Order

It was when this decree was made known in the colony of St. Domingo, that the General Assembly of the colony, then sitting at St. Marc's, expressed the malignant sentiments of the white colonists, in a resolution that I have already quoted, viz: they resolved that they would "Rather die, than share equal political rights with a bastard race."

Vincent Oje, a man of color, and one of the delegates to Paris, on behalf of his caste, anticipated a venomous feeling of this kind against his race, on the part of the white colonists, when these decrees should be made known to them. He however, resolved to do whatever was within his power, to allay this rancorous feeling. He did not therefore hasten home to the colony immediately after the decree was promulgated. He delayed, in order to allow time for their momentary excitement as expressed in the resolution above, to cool off, by a more calm reflection on their sober second thought. He also tarried in France, to secure a higher political end, by which he would be personally prepared to return to St. Domingo, to make the most favorable impression on behalf of his race, and the objects of that decree, on the minds of the white colonists.

To this end he succeeds in getting the appointment of Commissioner of France, from the French government, to superintend the execution of the decree of the 8th of March, 1790, in the island of St. Domingo.

Certainly, he might hope, that being invested with the sacred dignity of France, his person, his race, (thus honored through him by that imperial government,) and the National decree itself, with which he was charged, would now be respected.

But not content with accumulating the national honors of France; fearing lest the pro-Slavery colonists would disregard these high prerogatives, by looking upon them as having been obtained through the fanatical "Friends of the Blacks" at Paris, by those partisans exerting an undue influence on the National Government: he further proceeds to gather additional honors, by ingratiating himself into the favor of a potentate of Holland – the Prince of Limbourg; from whom he received the rank of Lieutenant Colonel, and the order of the Lion. Thus he wished to demonstrate to the infatuated colonists, who regarded his race as beneath their consideration, that he could not only obtain titles and reputation in France, by means of ardent friends, but that over and above these, and beyond the boundaries of France, he could also command an European celebrity.

This was indeed a splendid course of conduct on his part; and by thus gathering around him and centering within himself these commanding prestiges of respect, he demonstrated his thorough knowledge of one of the most important secrets in the art of governing; and so far made another noble vindication of the capacity of the Negro race for self-government.

But as we proceed to consider the manner that he afterwards undertook to prosecute his high National Commission in promulgating in St. Domingo, the decree of the 8th of March, 1790, we shall see additional evidence of the same master skill crowd upon us.

He had now delayed his return from Europe in order to allow time for the allaying of hasty excitement, and for the purpose of making the most favorable advent to the island.

He comes a commissioned envoy of the French nation, and an honored chevalier of Europe. Nevertheless, with that prudent foresight which anticipates all possible emergencies, he landed in St. Domingo in a cautious and unostentatious manner, so as not to provoke any forcible demonstration against him. Having landed, he gathered around him a suite of 200 men for his personal escort, which his station justified him in having as his cortege; and which might also serve the very convenient

purpose of a body guard to defend him against any attempt at a cowardly assassination from any lawless or ruthless desperadoes of oppression in the colony.

At the head of this body of men, he at once proceeded to place himself in communication with the Colonial Assembly, then in session; to inform it officially of
his commission and the national decree which he bore; and to require that assembly, as the legislative authority of the island, to enforce its observance, by enacting
an ordinance in accordance with the same.

In this communication of Oje, being aware of their proslavery prejudices, he
endeavored to conciliate them by a peace offering. That peace offering was the
sanctioning of Negro Slavery; for he stated to the assembly that the decree did
not refer to the blacks in servitude; neither did the men of color, said he, desire to
acknowledge their equality.

This specific assurance on the part of Oje, although it does not speak much for
his high sense of justice, when abstractly considered; yet it shows as much wisdom
and tact in the science of government, as is evinced by the sapient or sap headed
legislators of this country, who make similar compromises as a peace offering to
the prejudice and injustice of the oligarchic despots of this nation.

Oje, however, failed to make the desired impression on the infatuated colonists,
either by his National and European dignities, or by his peace offering of 500,000
of his blacker brethren. He fell beneath the malignant hate of the slaveholding colonists, after defending himself with his little band of followers, against the overwhelming odds of these sanguinary tigers, with a manly heroism, only equalled by
the Spartans at the pass of Thermopylse, and thus has cut for himself an enduring
niche among the heroes in the temple of fame.

He was captured; and after, a mock trial, illustrative of pro-slavery justice; something similar, for instance, to our Fugitive Slave Law trials in Boston, Philadelphia,
and Cincinnati – (though more merciful in its penalty than these) – this mock court
of St. Domingo condemned Vincent Oje and his brave lieutenant, Jean Chevanne,
with their surviving compatriots, to be broken alive on the wheel.

We forget the error of the head committed by this right hearted, noble, and
generous man, towards his more unfortunate brethren, in order to weep over his
ignoble and unworthy fate, received at the hands of those monsters of cruelty in
St. Domingo.

I cannot better close this notice of Oje, than by repeating the concluding lines
from a Poem dedicated to him, by that distinguished man of color, our own fellow
countryman, Prof. George B. Vashon, of McGrawville College:

Sad was your fate, heroic band,
Yet mourn we not, for yours the stand
Which will secure to you a fame,
That never dieth, and a name
That will, in coming ages be

A signal word for Liberty.
Upon the Slave's o'erclouded sky,
Your gallant actions traced the bow.
Which whispered of deliverance nigh —
The need of one decisive blow.
Thy coming fame, Oje! is sure;
Thy name with that of L'Ouverture,
And the noble souls that stood
With both of you, in times of blood,
Will live to be the tyrant's fear —
Will live, the sinking soul to cheer!

The Hour of Destiny for the Blacks

This untimely death of the great leader of the men of color, served only to develop how plentifully the race was supplied with sagacious characters, capable of performing daring deeds – it served to show how well the race was supplied with the material out of which great leaders are made, at any moment, and for any exigency.

Now came the hour for the patient, delving black slave to begin to move. He has manfully bided his time, whilst the white colonists were rampant in pursuit of high political prerogatives; and he has remained quiet, whilst his brother – the freed man of color, has carried his cause demanding equal political rights, triumphantly through the National Assembly of France.

But most intolerable of all, he has been perfectly still, whilst his more fortunate brethren have offered even to strike hands with the vile oppressor in keeping the iron yoke on his neck.

Nevertheless, he has lived to see both of these classes foiled by the over-ruling hand of Providence, from interpreting the words "Liberty, Equality, and Fraternity," to suit their own selfish and narrow notions. He finds these two parties now at open hostilities with one another. He sees, on one hand, the despicable colonists inviting foreign aid into the island, to resist the execution of the National decree and to prop up their unhallowed cause by the dread alternative of treason and rebellion. Whilst on the other hand, he beholds the men of color fighting on the side of the nation, law, and order, against the white colonists. Amid this general commotion his pulsations grow quick, and he feels that the hour of destiny is coming for even him to strike.

Yet he still possesses his soul in patience until the destined moment. At last he hears that France now vacillates in carrying out the tardy measure of justice that her National Legislature had enacted. The mother country, that had so nobly commenced the work of justice, by the national decree, enfranchising the free men of color, now begins to recede from the high position she had assumed, in order to favor the frenzied prejudice of the infatuated colonists. The Negro slave had hoped that by this national act of justice to the free man of color, that a permanent step had been taken towards universal emancipation, and consequently his own eventual disenthralment. With this hope he was willing to continue quietly to wear his galling chains, rejoicing in the newly acquired boon of his more fortunate brethren, as the earnest and pledge of his own future deliverance, by a similar act of national justice. Thus the way seemed already paved for a peaceful termination of his servitude.

But, I repeat it again, the toiling black slave at last hears that the National Government of France vacillates in her judgment, quails before the storm of pro-slavery invectives, hurled by the insensate bigots of St. Domingo against the men of color, and finally, she recedes from her high position by the National Assembly repealing the decree of the 8th of March, 1790. Thus the slaves dawning ray of hope and liberty is extinguished, and there is nothing ahead but the impenetrable gloom of eternal slavery.

This, then, is the ominous moment reserved for the chained bondmen to strike; and he rises now from his slumber of degradation in the terrific power of brute force. Bouckman, (called by a Haytian historian the Spartacus of his race,) was raised up as the leader of the insurgents, who directed their fury in the desperate struggle for liberty and revenge, until the work of devastation and death was spread throughout the island to the most frightful extent. He continued to ride on the storm of revolution in its hurricane march, with a fury that became intensified as it progressed, until the colonists, by some fortuitous circumstances, were enabled to wreak their vengeance on this Negro hero.

But when this first hero of the slaves was captured and executed by their oppressors, like Oje, the first hero of the free men of color; the capacity of the race to furnish leaders equal to any emergency, was again demonstrated.

A triumvirate of Negro and mulatto chieftains now succeeded these two martyred heroes.

Jean Francois, Biassou, and Jeannot, now appeared upon the stage of action, and directed the arms of the exasperated insurgents against a faithless nation, the cruel colonists and their English allies, whose aid these colonists had invited, in their treasonable resistance to the National decree, which Oje came from France to promulgate in the name of the nation.

In order to contend against such overwhelming odds effectually, and for the purpose of obtaining the necessary supply of arms and ammunition, the insurgents went over, for a time, to the service of Spain. This government had always regarded the French as usurpers in the island; and the Spaniards were therefore glad of any prospect of expelling the French colonists entirely from St. Domingo. Hence they gladly accepted the proffered service of the blacks as a means to effect this end.

However, we have no reason to regard the Spanish government as being more favorably disposed towards the blacks than that of France. We may rather conclude that Spain was willing to use the blacks to subserve her end, and afterwards would doubtless have endeavored to reduce them to a state of slavery again.

Nevertheless the black slaves and free men of color went over to the cause of Spain, and used her to subserve their purpose in driving France not only to re-enact her previous decree in relation to the men of color; but also to proclaim the immediate emancipation of the blacks, and to invest them with equal political rights. For this purpose, three National Commissioners of France were sent to the island, bearing these decrees of the Supreme Government.

When this glorious result was thus triumphantly effected, they left the service of Spain and returned to the cause of France again.

During the struggles that took place while the insurgents were in the cause of Spain, the three leaders who headed them when they united with the Spaniards, were shifted, by the fortunes of war, from their chieftainship, and replaced by Toussaint and Rigaud – one a black, and the other a mulatto, when they returned to the service of France.

These two leaders, at the head of their respective castes in the service of France, fighting on the side of liberty, law, and order, compelled the turbulent and treasonable colonists to respect these last national decrees; drove their English allies from the colony, and extinguished the Spanish dominion therein, and thus reduced the whole island to the subjection of France.

When we duly consider this shrewd movement of the blacks in thus pressing Spain in their service at that critical moment, when every thing depended upon the decision of the hour, by which they were enabled to accomplish such a glorious result, we have thereby presented another strong and convincing proof of the capacity of the Negro to adopt suitable means to accomplish great ends; and it therefore demonstrates in the most powerful manner, his ability for self-government.

The Auspicious Dawn of Negro Rule

Toussaint, by his acute genius and daring prowess, made himself the most efficient instrument in accomplishing these important results, contemplated by the three French Commissioners, who brought the last decrees of the National Assembly of France, proclaiming liberty throughout the island to all the inhabitants thereof; and thus, like another Washington, proved himself the regenerator and savior of his country.

On this account, therefore, he was solemnly invested with the executive authority of the colony; and their labors having been thus brought to such a satisfactory and auspicious result, two of the Commissioners returned home to France.

No man was more competent to sway the civil destinies of these enfranchised bondmen than he who had preserved such an unbounded control over them as their military chieftain, and led them on to glorious deeds amid the fortunes of warfare recently waged in that island. And no one else could hold that responsible position of an official mediator between them and the government of France, with so great a surety and pledge of their continued freedom, as Toussaint L'Ouverture. And there was no other man, in fine, that these rightfully jealous freemen would have permitted to carry out such stringent measures in the island, so nearly verging, to serfdom, which were so necessary at that time in order to restore industry, but one of their own caste whose unreserved devotion to the cause of their freedom, placed him beyond the suspicion of any treacherous design to re-enslave them.

Hence, by these eminent characteristics possessed by Toussaint in a super excellent degree, he was the very man for the hour; and the only one fitted for the governorship of the colony calculated to preserve the interests of all concerned.

The leading Commissioners of France, then in the island, duly recognized this fact, and did not dispute with him the claim to this responsible position. Thus had the genius of Toussaint developed itself to meet an emergency that no other man in the world was so peculiarly prepared to fulfill; and thereby he has added another inextinguishable proof of the capacity of the Negro for self-government.

But if the combination of causes, which thus pointed him out as the only man that could safely undertake the fulfillment of the gubernatorial duties, are such manifest proofs of Negro capacity; then the manner in which we shall see that he afterwards discharged the duties of that official station, goes still further to magnify the self-evident fact of Negro capability.

The means that he adapted to heal the internecine dissensions that threatened civil turmoil; and the manner that he successfully counteracted the machinations of the ambitious General Hedouville, a French Commissioner that remained in the colony, who desired to overthrow Toussaint, showed that the Negro chieftain was no tyro in the secret of government.

He also established commercial relations between that island and foreign nations; and he is said to be the first states-man of modern times, who promulgated the doctrine of free trade and reduced it to practice. He also desired to secure a constitutional government to St. Domingo, and for this purpose he assembled around him a select council of the most eminent men in the colony, who drew up a form of constitution under his supervision and approval, and which he transmitted, with a commendatory letter to Napoleon Bonaparte, then First Consul of France, in order to obtain the sanction of the imperial government.

But that great bad man did not even acknowledge its receipt to Toussaint; but in his mad ambition he silently meditated when he should safely dislodge the Negro chief from his responsible position, as the necessary prelude to the re-enslavement of his sable brethren, whose freedom was secure against his nefarious designs, so long as Toussaint stood at the helm of affairs in the colony.

But decidedly the crowning act of Toussaint L'Ouverture's statesmanship, was the enactment of the Rural Code, by the operation of which, he was successful in restoring industrial prosperity to the island, which had been sadly ruined by the late events of sanguinary warfare. He effectually solved the problem of immediate emancipation and unimpaired industry by having the emancipated slaves produce thereafter, as much of the usual staple productions of the country, as was produced under the horrible regime of slavery; nevertheless, the lash was entirely abolished, and a system of wages adopted, instead of the uncompensated toil of the lacerated and delving bondman.

In fact, the island reached the highest degree of prosperity that it ever attained, under the Negro governorship of Toussaint.

The rural code, by which so much was accomplished, instead of being the horrible nightmare of despotism – worse than slavery, that some of the pro-slavery calumniators of Negro freedom and rule would have us believe; was, in fact, nothing more than a prudent government regulation of labor – a regulation which made labor the first necessity of a people in a state of freedom, – a regulation which struck a death blow at idleness, the parent of poverty and all the vices – a regulation, in fine, which might be adopted with advantage in every civilized country in the world, and thereby extinguish two-thirds of the pauperism, vagrancy, and crime, that curse these nations of the earth; and thus lessen the need for poor-houses, police officers, and prisons, that are now sustained at such an enormous expense, for the relief of the poor and the correction of felons.

This Haytian Code compelled every vagabond or loafer about the towns and cities, who had no visible means of an honest livelihood, to find an employer and work to do in the rural districts. And if no private employer could be found, then the government employed such on its rural estates, until they had found a private employer. The hours and days of labor were prescribed by this code, and the terms of agreement and compensation between employer and employed were also determined by its provisions. Thus, there could be no private imposition on the laborers; and, as a further security against such a spirit, the government maintained rural magistrates and a rural police, whose duty it was to see to the faithful execution of the law on both sides.

By the arrangement of this excellent and celebrated code, every body in the commonwealth was sure of work and compensation for the same, either from private employers or from the government. No body need fear being starved for want of work to support themselves, as is often the case among the laborers of Europe, and is fast coming to pass in the densely populated communities of this country, where labor is left to take care of itself under the private exploitation of mercenary capitalists. Under this code nobody need fear being exploited on by such unprincipled and usurious men, who willingly take advantage of the poor to pay them starvation prices for their labor; because, against such, the law of Toussaint secured to each laborer a living compensation.

By the operation of this code, towns and cities were cleared of all those idle persons who calculate to live by their wits, and who commit nine-tenths of all the crimes that afflict civilized society. All such were compelled to be engaged at active industrial labors, and thus rendered a help to themselves and a blessing to the community at large.

By this industrial regulation, every thing flourished in the island in an unprecedented degree; and the Negro genius of Toussaint, by a bold and straight-forward provision for the regulation and protection of his emancipated brethren, affected that high degree of prosperity in Hayti, which all the wisdom of the British nation has not been able to accomplish in her emancipated West India colonies, in consequence of her miserable shuffling in establishing Coolie and Chinese apprenticeship – that semi-system of slavery – in order to gratify the prejudices of her pro-slavery colonial planters; and because of the baneful influence of absentee landlordism, which seems to be an inseparable incident of the British system of property.

Thus did the Negro government of St. Domingo, show more paternal solicitude for the well being of her free citizens, than they ever could have enjoyed under the capricious despotism of individual masters who might pretend to care for them; and thus did it more truly subserve the purposes of a government than any or all of the similar organizations of civilization, whose only care and object seem to be the protection of the feudal rights of property in the hands of the wealthy few; leaving the honest labor of the many unprotected, and the poor laborer left to starve, or to become a criminal, to be punished either by incarceration in the jails, prisons and dungeons provided for common felons; or executed on the gallows as the greatest of malefactors.

The genius of Toussaint by towering so far above the common ideas of this age in relation to the true purposes of government; and by carrying out his bold problem with such eminent success, has thereby emblazoned on the historic page of the world's statesmanship a fame more enduring than Pitt, who laid the foundation of a perpetual fund to liquidate the national debt of England.

I say Toussaint has carved for himself a more enduring fame, because his scheme was more useful to mankind. The Negro statesman devised a plan that comprehended in its scope the well being of the masses of humanity. But Pitt only laid a scheme whereby the few hereditary paupers pensioned on a whole nation, with the absurd right to govern it, might still continue to plunge their country deeper and deeper into debt, to subserve their own extravagant purposes; and then provide for the payment of the same out of the blood and sweat, and bones of the delving operatives and colliers of Great Britain. Thus, then Toussaint by the evident superiority of his statesmanship, has left on the pages of the world's statute book, an enduring and irrefutable testimony of the capacity of the Negro for self-government, and the loftiest achievements in national statesmanship.

And Toussaint showed that he had not mistaken his position by proving himself equal to that trying emergency when that demigod of the historian Abbott, Napoleon Bonaparte, first Consul of France, conceived the infernal design of reenslaving the heroic blacks of St. Domingo; and who for the execution of this nefarious purpose sent the flower of the French Army, and a naval fleet of fifty-six vessels under command of General Leclerc, the husband of Pauline, the voluptuous and abandoned sister of Napoleon.

When this formidable expedition arrived on the coast of St. Domingo, the Commander found Toussaint and his heroic compeers ready to defend their God given liberty against even the terrors of the godless First Consul of France. Wheresoever these minions of slavery and despotism made their sacrilegious advances, devastation and death reigned under the exasperated genius of Toussaint.

He made that bold resolution and unalterable determination, which, in ancient times, would have entitled him to be deified among the gods; that resolution was to reduce the fair eden-like Isle of Hispaniola to a desolate waste like Sahara; and suffer every black to be immolated in a manly defense of his liberty, rather than the infernal and accursed system of Negro slavery should again be established on that soil. He considered it far better, that his sable countrymen should be DEAD FREEMEN than LIVING SLAVES.

The French veterans grew pale at the terrible manner that the blacks set to work to execute this resolution. Leclerc found it impossible to execute his design by force; and he was only able to win the reconciliation of the exasperated blacks to the government of France, by abandoning his hostilities and pledging himself to respect their freedom thereafter. It was then that the brave Negro Generals of Toussaint went over in the service of Leclerc; and it was then, that the Negro Chieftain himself, resigned his post to the Governor General appointed by Napoleon, and went into the shades of domestic retirement, at his home in Ennery.

Thus did Toussaint, by his firm resolution to execute his purpose, by his devotion to liberty and the cause of his race, so consistently maintained under all circumstances, more than deify himself; he proved himself more than a patriot; he showed himself to be the unswerving friend and servant of God and humanity.

Now, with the illustrious traits of character of this brilliant Negro before us, who will dare to say that the race who can thus produce such a noble specimen of a hero and statesman, is incapable of self-government. Let such a vile slanderer, if there any longer remains such, hide his diminutive head in the presence of his illustrious Negro superior!

I know it may be said that, after all Toussaint was found wanting in the necessary qualities to meet, and triumph in, the last emergency, when he was finally beguiled, and sent to perish in the dungeons of France, a victim of the perfidious machinations of the heartless Napoleon.

On this point I will frankly own that Toussaint was deficient in those qualities by which his antagonist finally succeeded in getting him in his power.

So long as manly skill and shrewdness – so long as bold and open tactics and honorable stratagems were resorted to, the black had proved himself, in every respect, the equal of the white man. But the negro's heart had not yet descended to that infamous depth of subtle depravity, that could justify him in solemnly and publicly taking an oath, with the concealed, Jesuitical purpose, of thereby gaining an opportunity to deliberately violate the same. He had no conception, therefore, that the white man from whom he had learned all that he knew of true – religion I repeat it – he had no conception that the white man, bad as he was, slaveholder as he was – that even he was really so debased, vile, and depraved, as to be capable of such a double-dyed act of villainy, as breaking an oath solemnly sealed by invoking the name of the Eternal God of Ages.

Hence, when the Captain General, Leclerc, said to Toussaint, in presence of the French and Black Generals, uplifting his hand and jewelled sword to heaven: "I swear before the face of the Supreme Being, to respect the liberty of the people of St. Domingo." Toussaint believed in the sincerity of this solemn oath of the white man. He threw down his arms, and went to end the remainder of his days in the bosom of his family. This was, indeed, a sad mistake for him, to place so much confidence in the word of the white man. As the result of this first error, he easily fell into another equally treacherous. He was invited by General Brunet, another minion of Napoleon, in St. Domingo, to partake of the social hospitalities of his home; but, Toussaint, instead of finding the domestic civilities that he expected, was bound in chains, sent on board the Hero, a vessel already held in readiness for the consummation of the vile deed, in which he was carried a prisoner to France.

That magnanimous man bitterly repented at his leisure, his too great confidence in the word of the white man, in the cold dark dungeons of the castle of Joux. And the depth of this repentance was intensified by a compulsory fast ordered by that would-be great and magnanimous man, Napoleon Bonaparte, who denied him food, and starved him to death.

Great God! how the blood runs chill, in contemplating the ignoble end of the illustrious negro chieftain and statesman, by such base and perfidious means!

A Bloody Interlude Finally Establishes Negro Sovereignty

But if the godlike Toussaint had thus proved himself deficient in those mean and unhallowed qualities that proved his sad overthrow, nevertheless, the race again proved itself equal to the emergency, by producing other leaders to fill up the gap now left open.

The Negro generals, who had gone over to the service of France, on the solemn assurances and protestations of Leclerc, soon learned to imitate this new lesson of treachery, and accordingly deserted his cause, and took up arms against France again.

And, if afterwards, the heroic but sanguinary black chief, Dessalines, who had previously massacred 500 innocent whites (if any of these treacherous colonists can be called innocent) at Mirebalais; 700 more at Verettes, and several hundred others at La Riviere – I say again, if we now see him resume his work of slaughter and death, and hang 500 French prisoners on gibbets erected in sight of the very camp of General Rochambeau, we may see in this the bitter fruit of the treachery of the whites, in this dreadful reaction of the blacks.* These were the roots springing up, which Toussaint spoke of so sorrowfully on the ship's deck, as he was borne away a prisoner to France, from the coast of St. Domingo. The captive hero, on this occasion, compared himself to a tree, saying: "They have cut down in me the trunk of the tree; but the roots are many and deep." The furious Dessalines was, therefore, one of the foremost and firmest of these roots left in St. Domingo by the fallen chief, Toussaint, who soon sprung up into a verdant and luxurious growth of sanguinary deeds, by which the independence of his Island home was baptized in a Sea of Blood.

Finally, if we see Dessalines with red hot shot, prepared to sink the squadron of general Rochambeau, as it departed from France, although the Negro chief had solemnly stipulated to allow it to sail from the harbor unmolested, we find in this determination of the blood-thirsty man, how well he had learned the lesson of treachery and perfidy from the example of the white man.

Thus, if shocking depravity in perfidiousness and covenant breaking, is needed as another evidence of the Negro's equality with the white man, in order to prove his ability to govern himself, then the implacable black chief, Dessalines, furnishes us with that proof.

I think, however, we may thank God, that the last act of destruction contemplated by Dessalines was not consummated, in consequence of an English fleet taking Rochambeau and his squadron as prisoners of war in the harbor of Port-au-Prince; and thus, by this providential interposition, saved the race from a stigma on the pages of history, as foul as that which darkens the moral character of their antagonists.

Having now arrived at the epoch when the banners of Negro independence waved triumphantly over the Queen of the Antilles; if we look back at the trials and tribulations through which they came up to this point of National regeneration, we have presented to us, in the hardy endurance and perseverance manifested

---

* General Leclerc had now fallen a victim to the ravages of yellow fever, and Rochambeau had succeeded to the supreme command of the invading forces.

by them, in the steady pursuit of Liberty and Independence, the overwhelming evidence of their ability to govern themselves. For fourteen long and soul-trying years – twice the period of the revolutionary struggle of this country – they battled manfully for freedom. It was on the 8th of March, 1790, as we have seen, that the immortal man of color, Vincent Oje, obtained a decree from the National Assembly guaranteeing equal political privileges to the free men of color in the island. And, after a continued sanguinary struggle dating from that time, the never-to-be-forgotten self-emancipated black slave, Jean Jacque Dessalines, on the 1st of January, 1804, proclaimed negro freedom and independence throughout the island of St. Domingo.

That freedom and independence are written in the world's history in the ineffaceable characters of blood; and its crimsoned letters will ever testify of the determination and of the ability of the negro to be free, throughout the everlasting succession of ages.

Evidences of Self-Government Since 1804

I will now proceed to give a hasty synopsis of the evidences that the Haytians have continued to manifest since their independence in demonstration of the Negroes' ability to govern themselves.

Dessalines the Liberator of his country was chosen as a matter of course the first Ruler of Hayti. During his administration, the efficient organization of an army of 60,000 men to defend the country against invaders – the erection of immense fortifications, and the effort to unite and consolidate the Spanish part of the Island in one government with the French portion over which he presided, showed that he understood the precautionary measures necessary to preserve the freedom and independence of his country; and so far he kept up the character of the race for capacity in self-government.

In the succeeding administrations of the rival chiefs, Christophe and Petion, we have indeed the sorrowful evidence of division, between the blacks and the men of color or mulatoes, the seeds of which was planted in the days of slavery. Nevertheless in that mutual good understanding that existed between them by which it was agreed to unite together whenever a foreign foe invaded the island; and in the contemptuous manner that both chiefs rejected the perfidious overtures of Bonaparte, we have still the evidence of that conservative good sense which fully exhibits the negroes ability to take care of himself.

In the next administration of Boyer where we find these divisions in the French part of the island happily healed; and the Spanish colony also united in one government with the French, as Dessalines ardently desired in his time; we have the most astonishing evidence of the perfection the Black race could make in the art of self-government, during the short period of twenty years independence.

After Boyer's administration there were some slight manifestations of disorder, arising from the smouldering feud between the blacks and men of color that the ancient regime of slavery had created among them; the baneful influence of which the work of freedom and independence has not yet had time to entirely efface. In this disorder we find the Spanish part of the island secede and set up a separate nationality. – But we find everything in the French part soon settling down into order again, under the vigorous sceptre of the present ruler, Faustin I.

And in his known sentiments to harmonize all classes of his people, and to unite the whole island under one strong government, to secure which end he has exerted every influence within his power, we have the continued evidence of those large and extended views of national policy among the rulers of Hayti, that proves their ability to govern themselves in a manner that will compare favorably with the statesmanship of any existing government of modern civilization.

Here we shall rest the evidence in proof of the competency of the negro race for self-government which we have drawn out to rather a protracted length for the space assigned to a single Lecture; and turn our attention now to some of the evidences of civilized progress evinced by that people. We shall be brief in the elucidation of this point, because as their ample competency to govern themselves, has now been firmly established from the highest point of view, this fact of itself demonstrates that the soundest elements of civilized progress are inherent among such a people. Nevertheless it will be well to particularize some of the proofs on this point also.

Evidences of a Civilized Progress

National Enterprise

Under the administration of Dessalines aside from the Military preparations we have noticed; he continued the Code Rural of Toussaint as the law of the land, thereby demonstrating that the Negro in independence could carry forward measures of industry for his own benefit as well as for the whites when he governed for and in the name of France; for such was the case during the Governor Generalship of Toussaint. He also established schools in nearly every district of his dominions, and the people seeing what advantage was possessed by those who had received instruction, attached great importance to its acquisition; and as the result in a short time there were but few who did not learn to read and write.

In the constitution that he promulgated, it was declared that he who was not a good father, a good husband, and above all a good soldier, was unworthy to be called a Haytian citizen. It was not permitted fathers to disinherit their children; and every person was required by law to exercise some mechanical art or handicraft.

Thus fundamental measures were taken to make education, well regulated families and the mechanic arts, those three pillars of civilization, the basis of Haytian Society. – And in this fact where such high necessities were recognized and appreciated, we have the most undoubted evidence of civilized progress.

The overthrow of the government of Dessalines, by the spontaneous uprising of the people in their majesty, when it had become a merciless and tyrannical despotism, may also be noted here as another evidence of progress in political freedom of thought that made the race scorn to be tyrannized over by an oppressive master, whether that master was a cruel white tyrant, or a merciless negro despot.

Passing on to the two-fold government of Petion and Christophe, we not only discover the same military vigilance kept up by the construction of the tremendous fortification called the Citadel Henry that was erected by Christophe, under the direction of European Engineers, mounting 300 cannons; – but we also find both of these chiefs introducing teachers from Europe in their respective dominions; and establishing the Lancasterian system of schools.

We discover also during their administration, Protestant Missionaries availing themselves of the tolerant provision in regard to religious worship that had been maintained in the fundamental laws of the country since the days of Dessalines. These Missionaries commenced their work of evangelization with the approbation of the negro and mulatto chieftains; – and Christophe went so far as to import a cargo of Bibles for gratuitous distribution among his people. Thus do we find that progress continued to make its steady steps of advancement among these people, notwithstanding the political divisions that had now taken place among them. The succeeding administration of General Jean Pierre Boyer, under whom these divisions were happily healed, was fraught with stupendous projects of advancement.

The whole of the laws of the island were codified and made simple, under six different heads, viz: The Code Rural, the Civil Code, the Commercial Code, the Criminal Code, and the Code of Civil and Criminal procedure, regulating the practice in the several courts of the island. Thus, by this codification of her laws, did Hayti execute over thirty years ago, that which the States of this Union are just arousing to the necessity of doing. Boyer also set on foot a project of emigration, for the purpose of inducing the colored people of the United States to remove to Hayti, in order to replenish and accelerate the growth of the Haytian population. This project resulted in the removal of 6,000 colored people to that island from this country.

In addition to this important movement, various enterprises were undertaken by men of public spirit, during this administration, to promote industry among the people of Hayti. A company was formed to carry on a mahogany saw mill, which expended $20,000 in the purchase of the necessary machinery from France. The mill was erected at St. Marc's. Judge Lespinasse, chief justice of the Court of Cassation, was President of the Company; and it was under the special patronage of General Boyer, the President of the Republic.

Another company was also formed, under the presidency of Senator Jorge, for tanning purposes, and expended $10,000 in preparations for carrying on the business. A saw mill was also erected at Port-au-Prince, by a private individual, at the cost of $15,000.

Thus were the most vigorous efforts of progress manifested during the administration of Boyer.

In the subsequent administration of Guerrier, Pierrot, and Riviere, which followed each other in quick and rather chaotic succession, the work of industrial progress did not abate. Two steamers were purchased by the government, a model agricultural farm was established under a scientific director from France; and English architects, carpenters, and stone masons were hired to come in the country to improve the style of building.

Finally, we also discover the same evidences of gradual progress, when we come down to the present administration of Faustin I. A navy of about twenty armed vessels has been created. Thirteen steam sugar mills have been erected. The system of education improved and extended. And a house of industry erected at Port-au-Prince, for the purpose of instructing boys in the mechanic arts. And here let me add, that during the whole period of these successive administrations, that we have thus summarily passed under review, a thrifty commercial trade has been maintained between that island and the maritime nations of Europe and America, amounting in the aggregate, to several millions of dollars per annum. Hence, these evidences of educational and industrial development, expanding continually as years roll onward, we regard as the most irrefragable proof of true civilized progress on the part of the Haytian people.

Stability of the Government

But in addition to these facts, we may adduce the general stability of the government they have maintained, as another evidence of civilized progress. There have been but eight rulers in Hayti since 1804, counting separately, Christophe and Petion, who ruled contemporaneously. This is a period of fifty-three years down to the present time. And in the United States, since 1809, there have been ten different chief magistrates – a period of forty-eight years. Thus, this country has had two more rulers than Hayti, within a period five years less than the Haytian sovereignty.

The fact is, there is no nation in North America, but the United States, nor any in South America, except Brazil, that can pretend to compare with Hayti, in respect to general stability of government. The Spanish Republics of America will have as many different rulers in eight years as Hayti has had in a half century.

And the colonial dependencies of European nations change governors at least three times as often as that negro nation has done. This political stability, therefore, on the part of the Haytians, indicates a vast remove from Barbarism. It is far ahead of the anarchy of some so-called civilized nations. And it therefore indicates a high degree of civilization and progress.

Some exceptions might be taken, by the over scrupulous partizan of popular institutions, at the tendency manifested to vacillate between a Republican and Monarchial form of government, that has constantly been exhibited in Hayti, since the days of Dessalines.

The desire for Republican institutions has its rise in the Cosmopolitan ideas and example of France, at the time of the Haytian Revolution. The proximate example of the United States may also influence this desire for republicanism to some extent.

On the other hand, Monarchy is an ancient traditionary predilection of the race derived from Africa, which ancient continent maintains that form of government in common with the rest of the old world. The gorgeous splendor and august prestige of aristocratic rank and title, always attendant on this form of government, hold an imperious sway over the minds of this race of men who have such a keen appreciation of the beautiful. With these monarchical instincts on the one hand, and those powerful republican influences on the other, Hayti has continually oscillated between a republican and a monarchial form of government. But be it ever remembered to her credit, this oscillation has not unsettled the permanent stability of her national administration, as the facts previously adduced, abundantly prove.

Permit me, however, to urge with due deference to the republican ideas which surround me, that it matters not in the eternal principles of morality, what the form of government may be, so long as the ruling powers of a nation maintain the inviolability of personal liberty, exact justice and political equality among all of its honest citizens and subjects. If these things are not so maintained, a republic is as great, nay a greater despotism that an autocracy.

If there is but one despot to oppress the people, then there is but one neck to be severed in order to rid the earth of such a loathesome pest. But if the petty despots are numbered by the millions; then woe to that prescribed class that may fall under their tyranny, for it will need more axes and more executioners than can be supplied, in order to get this countless brood out of the way.

A popular despotism therefore, whose rulers are composed of political gamblers for the spoils of office and burglarious plunderers of the public treasury that tyrannizes over any class of its citizens and subject, is less tolerable than a monarchical or an aristocratic despotism, even though its rulers are a hereditary class of blood-titled paupers pensioned from generation to generation, on the public bounty of the nation. Among this latter class of rulers there is not to be found such a desperate and reckless set of lawless adventurers as will be found among the former. And should such monsters present themselves, they are in a more tangible shape to be got at and disposed of in a government of the few, than in that of the many. Hence the sacred purposes of government in securing the welfare of the whole people will always be more nearly arrived at in the one than in the other.

The Haytian people when governed by the crowned and imperial Dessalines testified their love of liberty, by destroying the tyrant when he violated the constitution and overstepped the laws of his country.

The American people under a republican form of government manifest their want of a love of true liberty, when they permit a vagabond set of politicians, whose character for rowdyism disgraces the nation, to enact such an odious law as the Fugitive Slave bill, violating the writ of *Habeas Corpus*, and other sacred guarantees of the Constitution; – and then tamely submit to this high handed outrage, because such unprincipled scoundrels voted in their insane revelry, that it must be the Supreme law of the land.

If there was one-half of the real love of liberty among even the people of the professedly free northern states, as there is among the Negroes of Hayti, every one of their national representatives who voted for that infamous bill, or who would not vote instantaneously for its repeal, would be tried for his life, condemned and publicly executed as accessory to man stealing. Thus would a free people, determined to preserve their liberties, rid themselves of a brood of petty tyrants who seek to impose their unhallowed partizan caprices upon the country, as the supreme law of the land, over-riding even the Higher Law of God. And thus in time would they exhibit an equally jealous regard for their rights, as the Haytians did, when they rid themselves of the tyrant Dessalines.

If such was the real love of liberty among the northern people of this vainglorious Republic, we should soon annihilate that morally spineless class of politicians, who need decision of character, when they get to Washington, to legislate for freedom. All such as were thus morally destitute of spinal vertebrae to resist the aggressions of the slave power, in the National Halls of legislation, would also soon be physically deficient in their cervical vertebrae, when they returned home, to meet the extreme penalty of an outraged and indignant constituency.

But such a determined spirit of liberty does not exist here, and honest men must submit therefore with lamb-like patience to this republican despotism of irresponsible political partizans who violate every just principle of law, because these unrighteous decrees are perpetrated in the name of the sovereign people. Hence there is far more security for personal liberty and the general welfare of the governed, among the monarchical negroes of Hayti where the rulers are held individually responsible for their public acts, than exists in this bastard democracy.

The single necked despot is soon reached by the keen avenging axe of liberty, for any acts of despotism among the Haytian blacks; but here its dull and blunted edge lays useless; for it might be hurled in vain and fall powerless among a nameless crowd of millions.

Conclusion

But our historical investigations are at an end, and we must hasten to bring our reflections to a conclusion. I have now fulfilled my design in vindicating the capacity of the negro race for self-government and civilized progress against the unjust aspersions of our unprincipled oppressors, by boldly examining the facts of Haytian history and deducing legitimate conclusions therefrom. I have summoned the sable heroes and statesmen of that independent isle of the Caribbean Sea, and tried them by the high standard of modern civilization, fearlessly comparing them with the most illustrious men of the most enlightened nations of the earth; – and in this examination and comparison the negro race has not fell one whit behind their contemporaries. And in this investigation I have made no allowance for the negroes just emerging from a barbarous condition and out of the brutish ignorance of West Indian slavery. I have been careful not to make such an allowance, for fear that instead of proving negro equality only, I should prove negro superiority. I shun the point of making this allowance to the negro, as it might reverse the case of the question entirely, that I have been combatting and instead of disproving his alleged inferiority only, would on the other hand, go farther, and establish his superiority. Therefore as it is my design to banish the words "superiority" and "inferiority" from the vocabulary of the world, when applied to the natural capacity of races of men, I claim no allowance for them on the score of their condition and circumstances.

Having now presented the preceding array of facts and arguments to establish, before the world, the negro's equality with the white man in carrying forward the great principles of self-government and civilized progress; I would now have these facts exert their legitimate influence over the minds of my race, in this country, in producing that most desirable object of arousing them to a full consciousness of their own inherent dignity; and thereby increasing among them that self-respect which shall urge them on to the performance of those great deeds which the age and the race now demand at their hands.

Our brethren of Hayti, who stand in the vanguard of the race, have already made a name, and a fame for us, that is as imperishable as the world's history. They exercise sovereign authority over an island, that in natural advantages, is the Eden of America, and the garden spot of the world. Her rich resources invite the capacity of 10,000,000 human beings to adequately use them. It becomes then an important question for the negro race in America to well consider the weighty responsibility that the present exigency devolves upon them, to contribute to the continued advancement of this negro nationality of the New World until its glory and renown shall overspread and cover the whole earth, and redeem and regenerate by its influence in the future, the benighted Fatherland of the race in Africa.

Here in this black nationality of the "New World," erected under such glorious auspices, is the stand point that must be occupied, and the lever that must be exerted, to regenerate and disenthrall the oppression and ignorance of the race, throughout the world. We must not overlook this practical vantage ground which Providence has raised up for us out of the depths of the sea, for any man-made and Utopian scheme that is prematurely forced upon us, to send us across the ocean, to rummage the graves of our ancestors, in fruitless, and ill-directed efforts at the wrong end of human progress. Civilization and Christianity is passing from the East to the West; and its pristine splendor will only be rekindled in the ancient nations of the Old World, after it has belted the globe in its westward course, and revisited the Orient again. The Serpentine trial of civilization and Christianity, like the ancient philosophic symbol of eternity, must coil backward to its fountain head. God, therefore in permitting the accursed slave traffic to transplant so many millions of the race, to the New World, and educing therefrom such a negro nationality as Hayti, indicates thereby, that we have a work now to do here in the Western World, which in his own good time shall shed its orient beams upon the Fatherland of the race. Let us see to it, that we meet the exigency now imposed upon us, as nobly on our part at this time as the Haytians met theirs at the opening of the present century. And in seeking to perform this duty, it may well be a question with us, whether it is not our duty, to go and identify our destiny with our heroic brethren in that independent isle of the Carribean Sea, carrying with us such of the arts, sciences and genius of modern civilization, as we may gain from this hardy and enterprising Anglo-American race, in order to add to Haytian advancement; rather than to indolently remain here, asking for political rights, which, if granted a social proscription stronger than conventional legislation will ever render nugatory and of no avail for the manly elevation and general well-being of the race. If one powerful and civilized negro sovereignty can be developed to the summit of national grandeur in the West Indies, where the keys to the commerce of both hemispheres can be held; this fact will solve all questions respecting the negro, whether they be those of slavery, prejudice or proscription, and wheresoever on the face of the globe such questions shall present themselves for a satisfactory solution.

A concentration and combination of the negro race, of the Western Hemisphere in Hayti, can produce just such a national development. The duty to do so, is therefore incumbent on them. And the responsibility of leading off in this gigantic enterprise. Providence seems to have made our peculiar task by the eligibility of our situation in this country, as a point for gaining an easy access to that island. Then let us boldly enlist in this high pathway of duty, while the watchwords that shall cheer and inspire us in our noble and glorious undertaking, shall be the soul-stirring anthem of GOD and HUMANITY.

QUESTIONS

(1) Why is Holly increasingly drawn to the emigration of blacks in the United States to Hayti (Haiti)?

(2) What evidence points to Negroes' capability to govern themselves?

(3) Was the emigration of blacks to Haiti successful?

(4) Slaves in Haiti had led a successful revolt against the white colonists in Haiti. How was this possible?

(5) After Haiti gained independence, what were some of the fundamental changes in Haiti to reflect that Negroes were equal to whites?

10 The True Solution of the Negro Problem

MARCUS GARVEY

Marcus Garvey (1887–1940), a Black Nationalist, was born in St. Ann's Bay, Jamaica. He was the leader of the Pan-Africanist movement and, in 1914, he founded the Universal Negro Improvement Association and African Communities League as a movement of redemption, which, later on, inspired other movements including the Nation of Islam and the Rastafari movement. In 1916, he moved to Harlem, New York, where his movement grew enormously. In 1919, he also found the Black Star Line, a shipping and passenger line, which promoted the return of blacks to Africa. Eventually, the Black Star Line was bankrupted. Garvey sold the stocks and was jailed for mail fraud. He was then deported back to Jamaica. In 1935, he moved to London, England, and lived there until his death on June 10, 1940. Garvey wrote and spoke of the racism that blacks experience in the African diasporas. The solution for Garvey was a movement of blacks to Africa. The selection below, "The True Solution of the Negro Problem" is a speech he delivered in 1922, in which he encouraged blacks to emigrate to Africa.

As far as Negroes are concerned, in America we have the problem of lynching, peonage and disfranchisement.

In the West Indies, South and Central America we have the problem of peonage, serfdom, industrial and political governmental inequality.

In Africa we have, not only peonage and serfdom, but outright slavery, racial exploitation and alien political monopoly.

We cannot allow a continuation of these crimes against our race. As four hundred million men, women and children, worthy of the existence given us by the Divine Creator, we are determined to solve our own problem, by redeeming our Motherland Africa from the hands of alien exploiters and found there a government, a nation of our own, strong enough to lend protection to the members of our race scattered all over the world, and to compel the respect of the nations and races of the earth.

Do they lynch Englishmen, Frenchmen, Germans or Japanese? No. And Why? Because these people are represented by great governments, mighty nations and empires, strongly organized. Yes, and ever ready to shed the last drop of blood and spend the last penny in the national treasury to protect the honor and integrity of a citizen outraged anywhere.

Until the Negro reaches this point of national independence, all he does as a race will count for naught, because the prejudice that will stand out against him even with his ballot in his hand, with his industrial progress to show, will be of such an overwhelming nature as to perpetuate mob violence and mob rule, from which he will suffer, and which he will not be able to stop with his industrial wealth and with his ballot.

If the Negro were to live in this Western Hemisphere for another five hundred years he would still be outnumbered by other races who are prejudiced against him. He cannot resort to the government for protection for government will be in the hands of the majority of the people who are prejudiced against him, hence for the Negro to depend on the ballot and his industrial progress alone, will be hopeless as it does not help him when he is lynched, burned, jim-crowed and segregated. The future of the Negro therefore, outside of Africa, spells ruin and disaster.

QUESTIONS

(1) What were some of the problems that blacks faced in Africa, the West Indies, South and Central America, and the United States? And, according to Garvey, how could these problems be solved?
(2) According to Garvey, why did the future of blacks lie outside of the United States?
(3) In the United States, why did blacks continue to be treated as second-class citizens?
(4) How can race relations be addressed and solved in the United States?
(5) According to Garvey, why was it important for blacks to look to Africa for independence and self-realization?

11 Toward Black Liberation

STOKELY CARMICHAEL

Stokely Carmichael (1941–1998), a significant figure in the Civil Rights Movement and the global Pan-African movement, was born in Port of Spain, Trinidad and Tobago. At the age of eleven, he rejoined his parents who had already emigrated to the United States, and lived with them in Harlem, New York, until the family moved to Van Nest, East Bronx. In 1960, he enrolled at Howard University, where his activism started. In 1961, Carmichael participated in the Freedom Rides initiated by the Congress of Racial Equality (CORE). Along with the other Freedom Riders, Carmichael was arrested, jailed, and later on transferred to the notorious Parchman Farm in Sunflower County, Mississippi, where he served forty-nine days. After graduating in 1964 with a BA in philosophy, two years later, in 1966, he became the Chairman of the Student Non-violence Coordinating Committee (SNCC). He was arrested during the March Against Fear and released, which inspired him to give his first "Black Power" speech. In 1966, he published "Toward Black Liberation" in the *Massachusetts Review*. The article is reproduced below. Carmichael outlines what he sees as some of the products of "Black Power."

One of the most pointed illustrations of the need for Black Power, as a positive and redemptive force in a society degenerating into a form of totalitarianism, is to be made by examining the history of distortion that the concept has received in national media of publicity. In this "debate," as in everything else that affects our lives, Negroes are dependent on, and at the discretion of, forces and institutions within the white society which have little interest in representing us honestly. Our experience with the national press has been that where they have managed to escape a meretricious special interest in "Git Whitey" sensationalism and race-war mongering, individual reporters and commentators have been conditioned by the enveloping racism of the society to the point where they are incapable even of objective observation and reporting of racial *incidents* much less the analysis of *ideas*. But this limitation of vision and perceptions is an inevitable consequence of the dictatorship of definition, interpretation and consciousness, along with the censorship of history that the society has inflicted upon the Negro—and itself.

Our concern for black power addresses itself directly to this problem, the necessity to reclaim our history and our identity from the cultural terrorism and depredation of self-justifying white guilt.

To do this we shall have to struggle for the right to create our own terms through which to define ourselves and our relationship to the society, and to have these terms recognized. This is the first necessity of a free people, and the first right that any oppressor must suspend. The white fathers of American racism knew this—instinctively it seems—as is indicated by the continuous record of the distortion and omission in their dealings with the red and black men. In the same way that southern apologists for the "Jim Crow" society have so obscured, muddied and misrepresented the record of the reconstruction period, until it is almost impossible to tell what really happened, their contemporary counterparts are busy doing the same thing with the recent history of the civil rights movement.

In 1964, for example, the National Democratic Party, led by L. B. Johnson and Hubert H. Humphrey, cynically undermined the efforts of Mississippi's Black population to achieve some degree of political representation. Yet, whenever the events of that convention are recalled by the press, one sees only that version fabricated by the press agents of the Democratic Party. A year later the House of Representatives in an even more vulgar display of political racism made a mockery of the political rights of Mississippi's Negroes when it failed to unseat the Mississippi Delegation to the House which had been elected through a process which methodically and systematically excluded over 450,000 voting-age Negroes, almost one half of the total electorate of the state. Whenever this event is mentioned in print it is in terms which leaves one with the rather curious impression that somehow the oppressed Negro people of Mississippi are at fault for confronting the Congress with a situation in which they had no alternative but to endorse Mississippi's racist political practices.

I mention these two examples because, having been directly involved in them, I can see very clearly the discrepancies between what happened, and the versions that are finding their way into general acceptance as a kind of popular mythology. Thus the victimization of the Negro takes place in two phases—first it occurs in fact and deed, then, and this is equally sinister, in the official recording of those facts.

The "Black Power" program and concept which is being articulated by SNCC, CORE, and a host of community organizations in the ghettoes of the North and South has not escaped that process. The white press has been busy articulating their own analyses, their own interpretations, and criticisms of their own creations. For example, while the press had given wide and sensational dissemination to attacks made by figures in the Civil Rights movement—foremost among which are Roy Wilkins of the NACCP and Whitney Young of the Urban League—and to the hysterical ranting about black racism made by the political chameleon that now serves as Vice-President, it has generally failed to give accounts of the reasonable and productive dialogue which is taking place in the Negro community, and in certain important areas in the white religious and intellectual community. A national committee of influential Negro Churchmen affiliated with the National Council of Churches, despite their obvious respectability and responsibility, had to resort to a paid advertisement to articulate their position, while anyone shouting the hysterical yappings of "Black Racism" got ample space. Thus the American people have gotten at best a superficial and misleading account of the very terms and tenor of this debate. I wish to quote briefly from the statement by the national committee of Churchmen which I suspect that the majority of Americans will not have seen. This statement appeared in the *New York Times* of July 31, 1966.

> *We an informal group of Negro Churchmen in America are deeply disturbed about the crisis brought upon our country by historic distortions of important human realities in the controversy about "Black Power". What we see shining through the variety of rhetoric is not anything new but the same old problem of power and race which has faced our beloved country since 1619.*
>
> *... The conscience of black men is corrupted because having no power to implement the demands of conscience, the concern for justice in the absence of justice becomes a chaotic self-surrender. Powerlessness breeds a race of beggars. We are faced now with a situation where powerless conscience meets conscience-less power, threatening the very foundations of our Nation.*
>
> *... We deplore the overt violence of riots, but we feel it is more important to focus on the real sources of these eruptions. These sources may be abetted inside the Ghetto, but their basic cause lies in the silent and covert violence which white middleclass America inflicts upon the victims of the inner city.*
>
> *... In short; the failure of American leaders to use American power to create equal opportunity* in life *as well as* law, *this is the real problem and not the anguished cry for black power.*
>
> *... Without the capacity to* participate with power, i.e., *to have some organized political and economic strength to really influence people with whom one interacts— integration is not meaningful.*
>
> *... America has asked its Negro citizens to fight for opportunity as individuals, whereas at certain points in our history what we have needed most has been opportunity for the* whole group, *not just for selected and approved Negroes.*
>
> *... We must not apologize for the existence of this form of group power, for we have been oppressed as a group and not as individuals. We will not find our way out of that oppression until both we and America accept the need for Negro Americans, as well as for Jews, Italians, Poles, and white Anglosaxon Protestants, among others to have and to wield group power.*

Traditionally, for each new ethnic group, the route to social and political integration into America's pluralistic society, has been through the organization of their own institutions with which to represent their communal needs within the larger society. This is simply stating what the advocates of black power are saying. The strident outcry, *particularly* from the liberal community, that has been evoked by this proposal can only be understood by examining the historic relationship between Negro and White power in this country.

Negroes are defined by two forces, their blackness and their powerlessness. There have been traditionally two communities in America. The White community, which controlled and defined the forms that all institutions within the society would take, and the Negro community which has been excluded from participation in the power decisions that shaped the society, and has traditionally been dependent upon, and subservient to the White community.

This has not been accidental. The history of every institution of this society indicates that a major concern in the ordering and structuring of the society has been the maintaining of the Negro community in its condition of dependence and oppression. This has not been on the level of individual acts of discrimination between individual whites against individual Negroes, but as total acts by the White community against the Negro community. This fact cannot be too strongly emphasized—that racist assumptions of white superiority have been so deeply ingrained in the structure of the society that it infuses its entire functioning, and is so much a part of the national subconscious that it is taken for granted and is frequently not even recognized.

Let me give an example of the difference between individual racism and institutionalized racism, and the society's response to both. When unidentified white terrorists bomb a Negro Church and kill five children, that is an act of individual racism, widely deplored by most segments of the society. But when in that same city, Birmingham, Alabama, not five but 500 Negro babies die each year because of a lack of proper food, shelter and medical facilities, and thousands more are destroyed and maimed physically, emotionally and intellectually because of conditions of poverty and deprivation in the ghetto, that is a function of institutionalized racism. But the society either pretends it doesn't know of this situation, or is incapable of doing anything meaningful about it. And this resistance to doing anything meaningful about conditions in that ghetto comes from the fact that the ghetto is itself a product of a combination of forces and special interests in the white community, and the groups that have access to the resources and power to change that situation benefit, politically and economically, from the existence of that ghetto.

It is more than a figure of speech to say that the Negro community in America is the victim of white imperialism and colonial exploitation. This is in practical economic and political terms true. There are over 20 million black people comprising ten percent of this nation. They for the most part live in well defined areas of the country—in the shanty-towns and rural black belt areas of the South, and increasingly in the slums of northern and western industrial cities. If one goes into any Negro community, whether it be in Jackson, Miss., Cambridge, Md. or Harlem, N. Y., one will find that the same combination of political, economic, and social forces are at work. The people in the Negro community do not control the resources of that community, its political decisions, its law enforcement, its housing standards; and even the physical ownership of the land, houses, and stores *lie outside that community.*

It is white power that makes the laws, and it is violent white power in the form of armed white cops that enforces those laws with guns and nightsticks. The vast majority of Negroes in this country live in these captive communities and must endure these conditions of oppression because, and only because, *they are black and powerless.* I do not suppose that at any point the men who control the power and resources of this country ever sat down and designed these black enclaves, and formally articulated the terms of their colonial and dependent status, as was done, for example, by the Apartheid government of South Africa. Yet, one cannot distinguish between one ghetto and another. As one moves from city to city it is as though some malignant racist planning-unit had done precisely this—designed each one from the same master blueprint. And indeed, if the ghetto had been formally and deliberately planned, instead of growing spontaneously and inevitably from the racist functioning of the various institutions that combine to make the society, it would be somehow less frightening. The situation would be less frightening because, if these ghettoes were the result of design and conspiracy, one could understand their similarity as being artificial and consciously imposed, rather than the result of identical patterns of white racism which repeat themselves in cities as distant as Boston and Birmingham. Without bothering to list the historic factors which contribute to this pattern—economic exploitation, political impotence, discrimination in employment and education—one can see that to correct this pattern will require far-reaching changes in the basic power-relationships and the ingrained social patterns within the society. The question is, of course, what kinds of changes are necessary, and how is it possible to bring them about?

In recent years the answer to these questions which has been given by most articulate groups of Negroes and their white allies, the "liberals" of all stripes, has been in terms of something called "integration." According to the advocates of integration, social justice will be accomplished by "integrating the Negro into the mainstream institutions of the society from which he has been traditionally excluded." It is very significant that each time I have heard this formulation it has been in terms of "the Negro," the individual Negro, rather than in terms of the community.

This concept of integration had to be based on the assumption that there was nothing of value in the Negro community and that little of value could be created among Negroes, so the thing to do was to siphon off the "acceptable" Negroes into the surrounding middle-class white community. Thus the goal of the movement for integration was simply to loosen up the restrictions barring the entry of Negroes into the white community. Goals around which the struggle took place, such as public accommodation, open housing, job opportunity on the executive level (which is easier to deal with than the problem of semi-skilled and blue collar jobs which involve more far reaching economic adjustments), are quite simply middle class goals, articulated by a tiny group of Negroes who had middleclass aspirations. It is true that the student demonstrations in the South during the early sixties, out of which SNCC came, had a similar orientation. But while it is hardly a concern of a black sharecropper, dishwasher, or welfare recipient whether a certain fifteen-dollar-a-day motel offers accommodations to Negroes, the overt symbols of white superiority and the imposed limitations on the Negro community had to be destroyed. Now, black people must look beyond these goals, to the issue of collective power.

Such a limited class orientation was reflected not only in the program and goals of the civil rights movement, but in its tactics and organization. It is very significant that the two oldest and most "respectable" civil rights organizations have constitutions which *specifically* prohibit partisan political activity. CORE once did, but changed that clause when it changed its orientation toward black power. But this is perfectly understandable in terms of the strategy and goals of the older organizations. The civil rights movement saw its role as a kind of liaison between the powerful white community and the dependent Negro one. The dependent status of the black community apparently was unimportant since—if the movement were successful—it was going to blend into the white community anyway. We made no pretense of organizing and developing institutions of community power in the Negro community, but appealed to the conscience of white institutions of power. The posture of the civil rights movement was that of the dependent, the suppliant. The theory was that without attempting to create any organized base of political strength itself, the civil rights movement could, by forming coalitions with various "liberal" pressure organizations in the white community—liberal reform clubs, labor unions, church groups, progressive civic groups—and at times one or other of the major political parties—influence national legislation and national social patterns.

I think we all have seen the limitations of this approach. We have repeatedly seen that political alliances based on appeals to conscience and decency are chancy things, simply because institutions and political organizations have no consciences outside their own special interests. The political and social rights of Negroes have been and always will be negotiable and expendable the moment they conflict with the interests of our "allies." If we do not learn from history, we are doomed to repeat it, and that is precisely the lesson of the Reconstruction. Black people were allowed to register, vote and participate in politics because it was to the advantage of powerful white allies to promote this. But this was the result of white decision, and it was ended by other white men's decision before any political base powerful enough to challenge that decision could be established in the southern Negro community. (Thus at this point in the struggle Negroes have no assurance—save a kind of idiot optimism and faith in a society whose history is one of racism—that if it were to become necessary, even the painfully limited gains thrown to the civil rights movement by the Congress will not be revoked as soon as a shift in political sentiments should occur.)

The major limitation of this approach was that it tended to maintain the traditional dependence of Negroes, and of the movement. We depended upon the good-will and support of various groups within the white community whose interests were not always compatible with ours. To the extent that we depended on the financial support of other groups, we were vulnerable to their influence and domination.

Also the program that evolved out of this coalition was really limited and inadequate in the long term and one which affected only a small select group of Negroes. Its goal was to make the white community accessible to "qualified" Negroes and presumably each year a few more Negroes armed with their passport—a couple of university degrees—would escape into middle-class America and adopt the attitudes and life styles of that group; and one day the Harlems and the Watts would stand empty, a tribute to the success of integration. This is simply neither realistic nor particularly desirable. You can integrate communities, but you assimilate individuals. Even if such a program were possible its result would be, not to develop the black community as a functional and honorable segment of the total society, with its own cultural identity, life patterns, and institutions, but to abolish it—the final solution to the Negro problem. Marx said that the working class is the first class in history that ever wanted to abolish itself. If one listens to some of our "moderate" Negro leaders it appears that the American Negro is the first race that ever wished to abolish itself. The fact is that what must be abolished is not the black community, but the dependent colonial status that has been inflicted upon it. The racial and cultural personality of the black community must be preserved and the community must win its freedom while preserving its cultural integrity. This is the essential difference between integration as it is currently practised and the concept of black power.

What has the movement for integration accomplished to date? The Negro graduating from M.I.T. with a doctorate will have better job opportunities available to him than to Lynda Bird Johnson. But the rate of unemployment in the Negro community is steadily increasing, while that in the white community decreases. More educated Negroes hold executive jobs in major corporations and federal agencies than ever before, but the gap between white income and Negro income has almost doubled in the last twenty years. More suburban housing is available to Negroes, but housing conditions in the ghetto are steadily declining. While the infant mortality rate of New York City is at its lowest rate ever in the city's history, the infant mortality rate of Harlem is steadily climbing. There has been an organized national resistance to the Supreme Court's order to integrate the schools, and the federal government has not acted to enforce that order. Less than fifteen percent of black children in the South attend integrated schools; and Negro schools, which the vast majority of black children still attend, are increasingly decrepit, over crowded, under-staffed, inadequately equipped and funded.

This explains why the rate of school dropouts is increasing among Negro teenagers, who then express their bitterness, hopelessness, and alienation by the only means they have—rebellion. As long as people in the ghettoes of our large cities feel that they are victims of the misuse of white power without any way to have their needs represented—and these are frequently simple needs: to get the welfare inspectors to stop kicking down your doors in the middle of the night, the cops from beating your children, the landlord to exterminate the vermin in your home, the city to collect your garbage—we will continue to have riots. These are not the products of "black power," but of the absence of any organization capable of giving the community the power, the black power, to deal with its problems.

SNCC proposes that it is now time for the black freedom movement to stop pandering to the fears and anxieties of the white middle class in the attempt to earn its "good-will," and to return to the ghetto to organize these communities to control themselves. This organization must be attempted in northern and southern urban areas as well as in the rural black belt counties of the South. The chief antagonist to this organization is, in the South, the overtly racist Democratic party, and in the North the equally corrupt big city machines.

The standard argument presented against independent political organization is "But you are only 10%." I cannot see the relevance of this observation, since no one is talking about taking over the country, but taking control over our own communities.

The fact is that the Negro population, 10% or not, is very strategically placed because—ironically—of segregation. What is also true is that Negroes have never been able to utilize the full voting potential of our numbers. Where we could vote, the case has always been that the white political machine stacks and gerrymanders the political subdivisions in Negro neighborhoods so the true voting strength is never reflected in political strength. Would anyone looking at the distribution of political power in Manhattan, ever think that Negroes represented 60% of the population there?

Just as often the effective political organization in Negro communities is absorbed by tokenism and patronage—the time honored practice of "giving" certain offices to selected Negroes. The machine thus creates a "little machine," which is subordinate and responsive to it, in the Negro community. These Negro political "leaders" are really vote deliverers, more responsible to the white machine and the white power structure, than to the community they allegedly represent. Thus the white community is able to substitute patronage control for audacious black power in the Negro community. This is precisely what Johnson tried to do even before the Voting Rights Act of 1966 was passed. The National Democrats made it very clear that the measure was intended to register Democrats, not Negroes. The President and top officials of the Democratic Party called in almost 100 selected Negro "leaders" from the Deep South. Nothing was said about changing the policies of the racist state parties, nothing was said about repudiating such leadership figures as Eastland and Ross Barnett in Mississippi or George Wallace in Alabama. What was said was simply "Go home and organize your people into the local Democratic Party—*then* we'll see about poverty money and appointments." (Incidentally, for the most part the War on Poverty in the South is controlled by local Democratic ward heelers—and outspoken racists who have used the program to change the form of the Negroes' dependence. People who were afraid to register for fear of being thrown off the farm are now afraid to register for fear of losing their Head-Start jobs.)

We must organize black community power to end these abuses, and to give the Negro community a chance to have its needs expressed. A leadership which is truly "responsible" —not to the white press and power structure, but to the community—must be developed. Such leadership will recognize that its power lies in the unified and collective strength of that community. This will make it difficult for the white leadership group to conduct its dialogue with individuals in terms of patronage and prestige, and will force them to talk to the community's representatives in terms of real power.

The single aspect of the black power program that has encountered most criticism is this concept of independent organization. This is presented as third-partyism which has never worked, or a withdrawal into black nationalism and isolationism. If such a program is developed it will not have the effect of isolating the Negro community but the reverse. When the Negro community is able to control local office, and negotiate with other groups from a position of organized strength, the possibility of meaningful political alliances on specific issues will be increased. That is a rule of politics and there is no reason why it should not operate here. The only difference is that we will have the power to define the terms of these alliances.

The next question usually is, "So—can it work, can the ghettoes in fact be organized?" The answer is that this organization must be successful, because there are no viable alternatives—not the War on Poverty, which was at its inception limited to dealing with effects rather than causes, and has become simply another source of machine patronage. And "Integration" is meaningful only to a small chosen class within the community.

The revolution in agricultural technology in the South is displacing the rural Negro community into northern urban areas. Both Washington, D.C. and Newark, N.J. have Negro majorities. One third of Philadelphia's population of two million people is black. "Inner city" in most major urban areas is already predominantly Negro, and with the white rush to suburbia, Negroes will in the next three decades control the heart of our great cities. These areas can become either concentration camps with a bitter and volatile population whose only power is the power to destroy, or organized and powerful communities able to make constructive contributions to the total society. Without the power to control their lives and their communities, without effective political institutions through which to relate to the total society, these communities will exist in a constant state of insurrection. This is a choice that the country will have to make.

QUESTIONS

(1) According to Carmichael, what are some of the accomplishments of the Civil Rights Movement for integration?
(2) What are some of the products of "black power"?
(3) Is integration the final solution to the "Negro problem"?
(4) According to Carmichael, Negroes are defined by "two forces." Outline and explain these forces.
(5) What are some of the issues facing black communities and how can these issues be dealt with?

PART IV
Race and Racism

CHARISSE BURDEN-STELLY

In mainstream political historiography, the period spanning 1890–1920 is known as both the Progressive Era and the Woman's Era. Yet, in African American history, this same epoch is deemed "the Nadir" of race relations because of its brutality and injustice. Blacks were forced to rely upon themselves for survival, defense against white supremacist barbarism, and the cultivation of community in the face of betrayal and abandonment by the federal government. The entrenchment of "separate-but-equal," anti-black public opinion, and daily indignity called into question the meaning of "progress" in US racial policy, politics, and practice.[1] The explosion of black print media at the end of the nineteenth century allowed for the dissemination of black political thought that offered analyses of racial oppression, segregation, and diminishing rights, and proposed programs for progress and race regeneration. Journals and newspapers, magazines and manifestos, pamphlets and periodicals were packed with careful examinations of, thoughtful mediations on, and vehement polemics about the dialectics of race and racism.

Moreover, these dubious citizens took full advantage of their recently acquired freedom of assembly, gathering in newly independent institutions – churches, conventions, civic organizations, lodges, social clubs – to discuss and debate the problems and prospects of what came to be known as "the Negro problem." Alexander Crummell, William Edward Burghardt Du Bois, and Ida Bell Wells were instrumental in shaping the "careful

---

[1] See e.g., Rayford Logan, *The Negro in American Life and Thought: The Nadir, 1877–1901* (New York: Dial Press, 1974); Rayford Logan, *The Betrayal of the Negro: From Rutherford B. Hayes to Woodrow Wilson* (New York: Collier Books, 1965); and Joel Williamson, *A Rage for Order: Black/White Relations in the American South since Emancipation* (Oxford University Press, 1986).

organization and long conference" taking place among elite and educated blacks in the United States. Their political thought, articulated through evangelical, ethnological, racial uplift, and republican discourse, confronted the contradictions between idealized notions of American progress and the realities of the racial Nadir. The chapters in this section vivify the tensions between strivings for socio-economic development and self-determination, on the one hand, and the deterioration of race relations into ritualized acts of gratuitous violence and the negation of basic rights, on the other.

Alexander Crummell, Race, and Evangelicalism

In "The Race-Problem in America," a paper read at the Protestant Episcopal Church Congress in Buffalo, New York on November 20, 1888, Alexander Crummell argued for the permanence of race as a means of organizing human groups, and for the central role of Christian morals, ideas, and ethics in the resolution of the "race-problem" and the "caste-spirit." For Crummell, race was an historical "destiny," a hereditary fact, and a persistent structural feature that, unlike nations, families, and clans, could not be destroyed. Though race was a matter of blood, ancestry, and lineage, the *race problem* was not a "carnal" one, hence the lack of historical indication or precedent for US racial antagonism. Such a problem stemmed entirely from ideas, and therefore could not be resolved through extinction, assimilation, or miscegenation (the "gross and violent intermingling" of blood). Nor should "whining and crying" about social interaction distract from agitation for liberty, civil rights, and political prerogative – the essential elements of equality. Crummell believed that the democratic spirit could only be preserved through strict adherence to Christian principles. These included education, civil freedom, and the elimination of barriers to access and opportunity that precluded the development of "the 'Sambos' and 'Pompeys'" into "the Toussaints and Christophes, the Wards and the Garnets."

According to Cedric Robinson, during the post-Civil War era, black Christianity permeated the political, social, and moral philosophy of free blacks and freedmen alike. It provided the conceptual framework for understanding collective racial identity, the black historical past, and socio-political destiny. It shaped the ways that blacks engaged with and participated in political formations of the era, especially radical republicanism.[2] Indeed, it is no coincidence that by 1890 over one-third of US blacks were church members, and many more belonged to institutions developed by black religious denominations.[3]

---

[2] Cedric Robinson, *Black Movements in America* (New York: Routledge, 1997), p. 98.

[3] Albert J. Raboteau, *Canaan Land: A Religious History of African Americans* (Oxford University Press, 1999), p. 79.

While the writings of Crummell, Du Bois, and Wells articulate "Christian ideal-ism" and "theological racialism,"[4] Crummell's work in particular conveys the belief that the improvement of the race and the development of black people into citi-zens represented the will of God and the truest application of Christian principles on earth. He enjoined that the convergence of Christian values and secular mor-alism, including thrift, industriousness, self-sufficiency, honesty, and discipline, represented the swiftest means of acclimatizing black folks to American civil life. This political "Mission of the Darker Races"[5] linked virtuousness, equal treatment among the races, the right to vote, an end to lynching, and a fair chance for autonomous race development. It was through the church and the secularization of Christian morality that black women and men of this era learned organizational skills, developed political programs for progress, and agitated for legal protection.

Separate black worship, which took off with the formation of the African Methodist Episcopal Church in 1816 and the National Black Baptist Convention, USA in 1895, allowed for a modicum of black independence and self-assertion that transcended religion. Black independent religious institutions provided a public sphere and intellectual commons for black communities. Additionally, as Bishop Daniel A. Payne explained, black churches were crucibles for the development of political thought, political action, and "heaven-created manhood." Here, manhood was the aspiration for "freedom and the fullest liberty."[6] As an articulation of courage, leadership, self-sacrifice, and protest against racism, exploitation, and inequality, it was an essential feature of black political thought. For Crummell, manhood deserved and demanded honor and recognition; as such, black leaders had the divine responsibility and mission to develop manhood among the masses and to uphold God's word in their manly demands for equality, self-improve-ment, and autonomy. Moreover, Christian manhood required blacks to overcome contempt for their race, to reject doctrines of white supremacy and black inferi-ority, and to affirm their blackness. This was the only way, as Du Bois wrote in "The Conservation of the Races," that the "mission of the Negro people [could be] accomplished, and the ideal of human brotherhood [could] become a practical possibility."

Black evangelicalism also articulated a vision of black womanhood. For Wells, despite the rhetoric of lynching, it was *black womanhood* that needed to be defended against white men's lies, violence, and racial fantasies. White women were not the standard of morality and chastity; in fact, she warned,

---

[4] Wilson J. Moses, "'The Conservation of the Races' in Context: Idealism, Conservatism, and Hero Worship," *The Massachusetts Review* 43 (1993), p. 285.

[5] Raboteau, *Canaan Land*, p. 76.

[6] William H. Becker, "The Black Church: Manhood and Mission," in *African-American Religion: Interpretive Essays in History and Culture*, ed. Timothy E. Fulop and Albert H. Raboteau (New York: Routledge, 1997), pp. 182–184, p. 190.

if Southern white men continued to promulgate the lie of the black male rapist, "A conclusion [would] be reached which [would] be very damaging to the moral reputation of their women." The constant physical and sexual threat black women faced undoubtedly shaped the puritanical gender standards to which they were expected to ascribe in the name of race development. Du Bois claimed that it was pure and noble-minded black womanhood that embodied godliness and grace; a "vast army of black prostitutes" – of "devils" whose sexual impurity dishonored and shamed the race – could only lead blacks to hell. Black women, too, believed that respectable behavior, refined manners, and Victorian sexual mores would garner esteem from the dominant society. Nonetheless, a tradition of empowered and resistant black womanhood also emanated from the black church. Through, *inter alia*, fundraising that provided the basis for a multitude of outreach programs; earnest anti-lynching campaigns; the formation of public sentiment through church-centered civic engagement; and the creation of separate spheres of women's influence, like the Woman's Convention (formed in 1900), black women were able to assert, define, and shape black womanhood. They encouraged temperance, modesty, hard work, and bourgeois ideals, at the same time that they struggled for educational opportunity, suffrage, and equality with black men in the church.[7]

Of course, these values largely represented the morality and method of worship – and therefore the political and social aims – of the black elite. Crummell believed that the religion of the masses was escapist, irresponsible, emotionalist, and licentious; by contrast, his evangelical political discourse emphasized that struggle and hard work were akin to godliness.[8] As servants of God, Crummell offered, an elite cadre of blacks would lead the masses in affirming their dedication to the race, in connecting hard work to salvation, and in aspiring to culture, refinement, and chastity to lift blacks to "the grand plane of civilization."[9] Importantly, the imbrication of evangelicalism and black political thought constructed racism as both a violation of the laws of the land codified in the United States Constitution, and the Scriptures of God that dictated the principles and morals of society.

---

[7] Evelyn Brooks Higginbotham, "The Black Church: A Gender Perspective," in *African-American Religion*, ed. Fulop and Raboteau, pp. 205–215. For comprehensive treatments of US black women's activism on behalf of black womanhood during this time period, see e.g., Deborah Gray White, *Too Heavy a Load: Black Women in Defense of Themselves 1894–1994* (New York: W. W. Norton, 1999) and Darlene Clark Hine, Wilma King, and Linda Reed (eds.), *"We Specialize in the Wholly Impossible": A Reader in Black Women's History* (Brooklyn: Carlson Publishing, Inc., 1995), pp. 3–56, pp. 237–406.

[8] Moses, "'The Conservation of the Races' in Context," pp. 279–280.

[9] Alexander Crummell, *Civilization: The Primal Need of the Race*, American Negro Academy Occasional Paper Number 3 (Washington: The American Negro Academy, 1898).

W. E. B. Du Bois, Racism, and Ethnology

Evangelical discourse that posited "the God ordained, intelligent self-sufficiency of modern man to work out his own way in his common sense, his analytical reason, and his specific moral sense"[10] was linked to black ethnological political thought through the sociology of progress. "The Conservation of the Races," presented by W. E. B. Du Bois at the inaugural meeting of the American Negro Academy in 1897, emphasized the importance of race unity, race solidarity, and moral correction to the settlement of the Negro problem. Like Crummell, Du Bois believed that race was a sociological fact in world history; as such, attempting to overcome or move beyond it was futile. Instead, the goal was to come up with a set of principles that made possible racial coexistence and the ability of each group to contribute its unique message and spirit of civilization to human brotherhood. Shifting focus away from adherence to Christian principles to achieve racial equality and progress, and from the responsibility of the federal government to protect black people against racist violence, "Conservation" offered the cultural-ethnological argument that as an historical race, blacks must work doggedly and collectively for their own uplift. Du Bois maintained that black "Americanism" was limited to politics, language, and religion; beyond that, black folk constituted a separate group that must cultivate autonomous institutions, ideals, and identity. It was only through a "general expression of policy," sustained striving, and race responsibility that black people could develop, advance, and assert influence.

By the end of the nineteenth century, ethnology – the comparative study of the development and culture of social man that prefigured cultural anthropology[11] – had become one of the most significant social scientific fields of study. Ethnological concepts of race and social evolution were grounded in a belief in progress, capacity for elevation, and the perfectibility of man. Ethnologists linked the transcendence of "nature" and "savagery" to a drive toward democracy and discernible contributions to civilization. Apropos the times, Du Bois understood race as a naturally occurring law of development; but, unlike racist ethnologists like Herbert Spencer and Lewis Henry Morgan, their approaches centered on cultural, moral, and ethical development – not natural selection, craniometrical findings, the cephalic index, "cheirization," phrenology, or other pseudoscientific measures – in theories of racial progress. Du Bois held that race was a spirit, an idea, and an ideal that produced psychic and identitarian differences constituted by, *inter alia*, common blood, history, habits of thought, and conscious striving

---

[10] Roy Harvey Pearce, *The Savages of America: A Study of the Indian and the Idea of Civilization* (Baltimore: Johns Hopkins University Press, 1956), p. 82.

[11] See e.g., Franz Boas, "Some Recent Criticism of Physical Anthropology," *American Anthropology* 1 (1899): 98–106; and Robert F. Spencer (ed.), *Method and Perspective in Anthropology* (Minneapolis: University of Minnesota Press).

toward a particular conception of life. Each race, he believed, possessed a different articulation of civilization that contributed to the progress of humanity as a whole.

Black political thought between Reconstruction and the Great War repudiated ideas that connected black physical features and characteristics to low intelligence and inability for race improvement. John H. Van Evrie, for example, argued that the coarse, blunt, clumsy fingers of black people reflected their limited intellect, their subordination to the white race, and their fit for only the lower trades that required little more than muscular strength.[12] In contradistinction to these racist arguments, black ethnological scholars insisted that while race had cultural, historical, and sociological significance, it had little explanatory value in terms of biology. They also rejected the contention that "blood intermixture" would get rid of the "lower races" and their "primitive" cultures. Du Bois held that losing one's race and cultural identity – through miscegenation or aping Anglo-Saxon culture – to become American was the gravest of follies that would inevitably result in self-obliteration. Relatedly, Crummell maintained that such commingling of blood required a level of affinity that the races in the United States did not have, and that as black women gained possession of their bodies against the barbaric sexual attacks of white men, forced miscegenation would be relegated to the past.

Du Bois in particular was representative of the idealist wing of ethnology at the end of the late nineteenth century. His emphasis on the development of mind was a direct critique not only of somatic approaches to ethnology, but also of materialism, whose main proponent at the time was Booker T. Washington. Materialism linked racial progress to practical labor, entrepreneurship, economic prosperity, and property ownership, along with more abstract principles like thrift, delayed gratification, and prudence.[13] Idealists, on the other hand, proffered improvement in conduct and conscience, alongside imagination and inventiveness, as the keys to full equality. They linked racial progress not to brute toil, accumulation, and commercialism, but to racial integrity, collective identity, and cultural reform.

Ida B. Wells, Republicanism, and the Challenge to Racial Uplift

Ida B. Wells' February 13, 1893 speech "Lynch Laws in all its Phases," delivered at Tremont Temple in Boston, MA and published that same year in *Our Day* magazine, revealed the true motivations for anti-black mob violence in the South. Wells

---

[12] John H. Van Evrie, *White Supremacy and Negro Subordination* (New York: Van Evrie, Horton & Co., 1870), p. 121.

[13] See e.g., W. E. B. Du Bois, *The Souls of Black Folk* (Chicago: Dover Thrift Publications, 1994 [1903]), pp. 25–36; Booker T. Washington, *The Future of the American Negro* (Boston: Small, Maynard & Co., 1899), pp. 67–105, pp. 157–199; and Booker T. Washington, *Working with the Hands* (New York: Doubleday, 1904).

contended that, contrary to racial uplift narratives that emphasized the moral development of black folk as foundational to citizenship, white supremacy ensured that black folk would perpetually be foreclosed from exercising their full rights. Racial uplift became a leading force in black political thought between 1880 and 1920. The following statement by Nannie Helen Burroughs sums up this political project: "the race that fails to do all within its powers to help itself will never rise ... God does not do for us what we can do for ourselves."[14] Through a combination of self-help, moral reform, socio-political organization, institution building, and community development, blacks struggled to radically improve their living conditions, ensure group survival, and challenge racist structures that circumscribed their life-chances.

Civic and political activism, programs for literary, institutional, and social reform, and the formation of clubs and organizations flourished.[15] Racial self-help doctrine required black bourgeois women to engage in philanthropic, welfare, educational, and mutual aid activities to remedy the problems of the black community. In turn, poor black folk were instructed to pool their meager resources, save their earnings, sacrifice for the good of the community, and patronize and support black-owned businesses. As Wells noted about blacks in Memphis, honest convictions, cooperation, hard labor, and patience "bore fruit" in the form of nice homes, black presence in most branches of business and the professions, urbane social life, and vibrant black enterprises. Thus, the black masses must strive to support black bourgeois institutions and aims, while the educated class was obligated to model the values, ethics, and self-reformation that would save the race from degradation and vice.

Thinkers of this generation, including Anna Julia Cooper, admonished that racial esteem and sincere service were the sources of advancement and change. This socio-political program inhered in a "politics of respectability" directed at managing the behavior and lifestyles of the uncultured, the uneducated, and the unassimilated.[16] Such politics reflected the belief that equality and justice could best be achieved through the adaptation of liberal bourgeois standards of decency, civility, and refinement; public displays of unbecoming behavior helped to rationalize racial barriers against black people. That black bourgeois values were superior to – and should therefore replace – those of the masses went

---

[14] Quoted in Karen A. Johnson, *Uplifting the Women and the Race: The Educational Philosophies of Anna Julia Cooper and Nannie Helen Burroughs* (New York: Routledge, 2000), p. 131.

[15] See e.g., Kevin Gaines, *Uplifting the Race: Black Middle-Class Ideology in the Era of the "New Negro," 1890–1935* (Chapel Hill: University of North Carolina Press, 1996).

[16] Evelyn Brooks Higginbotham, *Righteous Discontent: The Women's Movement in the Black Baptist Church, 1880–1920* (Cambridge, MA: Harvard University Press, 1993), pp. 185–229. For a critique of black bourgeois politics and sociality, see E. Franklin Frazier, *Black Bourgeoisie* (New York: Macmillan, 1957).

unquestioned. The combination of ethnological ideas of cultural perfectibility, Protestant evangelicalism, and racial uplift infused notions of racial unity and self-determination with elements of conservatism, paternalism, and aversion to "folk" culture.

Even as blacks worked to prove that they were worthy of citizenship by casting off the vestiges of depravity, immorality, idleness, and illiteracy, Wells argued, the pervasiveness of the white supremacist backlash, economic subjection, disenfranchisement, and lynching called into question the effectiveness of racial uplift and the utility of respectability politics. The rule of lynch law continued to strip black people of their First Amendment right to assemble, their Second Amendment right to bear arms, their Fourteenth Amendment right to equal protection of the law, and most significantly, their Fifth Amendment right to due process. She explained that the threat of black economic independence and political assertion – not the protection of white womanhood from black rapists – incited the thousands of lynchings that usurped constitutional and federal law through the rabid lawlessness of the mob. White supremacy was so entrenched and pervasive that lynch mob "justice" was condoned and rationalized even as blacks were victimized by the formal legal system, convicted, by dint of race, of virtually all crimes of which they were accused and making up the overwhelming majority within jails, penitentiaries, and convict farms. "Lynch Laws" convincingly demonstrated that as long as capital, public sentiment, and the federal government refused to condemn white supremacist barbarism, the entire society was complicit in the routinized racist violence against black people, and Southern whites would continue their drive to rule black people irrespective of "age, sex, or decency"; to reduce them to slaves and peons; and to disrespect and disregard the authority of the national government.

Prior to March 9, 1892, Wells believed that racial uplift and striving would eradicate racism. She agreed with Crummell and Du Bois that it was the battle for truth, ethics, and common principles – not political intervention – that would ultimately resolve the "Negro problem." Racial self-help, moral uplift, hard work, and "manly striving," they argued, would do more for race relations than any civil rights bill. Du Bois in particular was highly critical of the role of black political participation in "disgracing" religion and degrading the morality of the race; he argued that merely protesting, passing resolutions, and gaining political "spoils" did nothing to advance the project of black ethical and spiritual development. While a secondary step in settling the "Negro problem" was greater respect for personal liberty and worth, a more equitable integration of blacks into political, economic, and intellectual life on a meritocratic basis, the most important and substantial step toward improved race relations was the expunging of the social legacies of slavery: immorality, criminality, and shiftlessness.

Wells' position shifted drastically after the economically motivated lynching of her close friend Thomas Moss, along with Cal McDowell and Will Stewart. She then realized that "maintenance of character, money getting, and education" would *not* resolve race antagonism, and that blacks had little power to determine when such a solution would be reached. The development of the black community along economic and cultural lines would continue to be disrupted by white supremacist assault. To be sure, respectability politics were no match for the tearing asunder of black flesh as a form of amusement and control, the collection of mutilated body parts as souvenirs, the selling of charred organs for profit, and the elation experienced by witnessing the suspended black body.[17] After the lynching of these upstanding Negroes, Wells understood that only the federal government could contravene white extralegal racial terrorism masquerading as Southern "chivalry" and racial "custom."

In arguing that systematic and vitriolic attacks on black people – especially black men – were attacks on American institutions, Wells was appealing to republicanism, not sentimentalism or morality, in her defense of black citizenship. Akin to T. Thomas Fortune, who wrote that a republican form of government must serve all of its citizens and uphold the fundamental ideas of the Declaration of Independence and the Constitution, she insisted that it was incumbent upon the national government to ensure racial justice for the country's black inhabitants. Wells resolved that racism was an American problem, not a black problem, and that the subjection of blacks in the South fundamentally threatened and endangered the government's legitimacy. Without the vote, equal protection, and due process, blacks were left to the whim of public opinion that neither valued their existence nor respected the sanctity of their personhood. Thus, the federal government, which conferred citizenship upon black people, had the obligation to enforce this status against those who were committed to stealing the rights, property, wages, and lives of black people.

Contrary to Du Bois' counsel that social equilibrium could be achieved through the fair evaluation of black "culture, ability, and moral worth," Wells argued that the realities of white supremacy were such that "no matter what the attainments, character or standing of an Afro-American, the laws of the South will not protect him against a white man." Likewise, Crummell's idealist appeal to respect for the "democratic spirit" against the "barriers of caste" so that "the lowest of kind" could realize their ambitions was absolutely immaterial to the realities of anti-black lawlessness that was "like unto that which prevailed in slavery." Because moral and ethical arguments required decency, sympathy, and rationality – none of which

---

[17] Edward W. Blyden, "The Negro in the United States," *A.M.E. Church Review* 7 (1890), p. 59.

white supremacist brutes possessed – such pleas fell on deaf ears as the color line hardened around the curtailment of black political and civil rights and violent black death. In the final analysis, Wells contended, the rule of the lynch mob, construed as "state's rights," required federal intervention to uphold the Constitutional rights of aggrieved black citizens.

Conclusion

The political thought of Alexander Crummell, W. E. B. Du Bois, and Ida B. Wells presented in the following pages represent the evangelical, ethnological, racial uplift, and republican intellectual approaches prevalent at the dawn of the twentieth century. Traversing the divide between notions of American progress and lived experiences of racism and dispossession, these chapters present programs for the cultivation of a vibrant black community: economic development, moral uplift, social organization, political protection, self-determination, race unity, cultural pride. Equally important, these writings conceptualize a more responsible, representative, equitable, and ethical American society.

QUESTIONS

(1) What is the crucial test of the "race-problem" in the United States? And why has the "race-problem" not been settled in the United States?
(2) The existential question that daily confronts blacks in America is addressed in different ways by Crummell, Du Bois, and Wells. How does each author address this question?
(3) What are some of the ways presented by Crummell, Du Bois, and Wells that the "race-problem" can be settled in America?
(4) In spite of America's democratic ideals, why was it that blacks continued to experience unequal treatment, socially, economically, and politically?
(5) In order for blacks to secure their equal status in the United States certain actions must be taken. Outline and explain the different actions that are expressed by Crummell, Du Bois, and Wells?

FURTHER READINGS

- Anthony K. Appiah, "The Uncompleted Argument: Du Bois and the Illusion of Race," *Critical Inquiry* 12, no. 1 (1985): 21–37.
- Beverly Daniel Tatum, "Talking About Race, Learning About Racism: The Application of Racial Identity Development Theory in the Classroom," *Harvard Educational Review* 62, no. 1 (1992): 1–24.

- Charles Mills, *The Racial Contract* (Ithaca, NY: Cornell University Press, 1999).
- Cornel West, *Race Matters* (New York: Vintage, 1994).
- John Hope Franklin, "The Two Worlds of Race: An Historical View," *The Negro American* 94, no. 4 (1965): 899–920.
- Mary Church Terrell, "The Duty of the National Association of Colored Women to the Race," *AME Church Review* (January 1900): 340–354.
- Oliver C. Cox, "Race Relations: Its Meaning, Beginning and Progress," in *Theories of Race and Racism: A Reader*, ed. Les Back and John Solomos (New York: Routledge, 2000), pp. 75–82.
- Patricia Williams, *Alchemy of Race and Rights: Diary of A Law Professor* (Cambridge, MA: Harvard University Press, 1992).
- Randall Kennedy, *Race, Crime, and the Law* (New York: Vintage Books, 1998).
- Robert F. Williams, *Negroes With Guns* (Chicago, IL: Third World Press, 1962 and 1973).

12 | The Race-Problem in America

ALEXANDER CRUMMELL

Alexander Crummell (1819–1898) was born in New York City, and later trained to become an Episcopal priest. He was refused admission to the Diocese of Pennsylvania because he was black. He wanted to raise money for his church. So, in 1848, he traveled to England to lecture on slavery in the United States. He enrolled in Queen's College, Cambridge University, and graduated in 1853. Later on, Crummell moved to Liberia where he lived for almost two decades. He was appointed as a professor at Liberia College in 1861. In 1873, he returned to the United States and founded and pastored St. Luke's Episcopal Church. Crummell taught at Howard University from 1895 to 1897. One of his major achievements was the establishment of the American Negro Academy in 1897, which was the first society of black scholars in the United States. He authored several books on issues pertaining to blacks in the United States and in Africa that include *The Future of Africa* and *America: Addresses and Discourses*. The selection "The Race-Problem in America" is a paper that Crummell presented at the Church Congress (Protestant Episcopal Church) in Buffalo, New York, on November 20, 1888. In this lecture, Crummell pointed out that the probable resolution of the race problem in America is for all people, especially blacks, to participate equally in America's democracy, which, in theory, recognizes human rights for all people and should be extended to practice.

The residence of various races of men in the same national community, is a fact which has occurred in every period of time and in every quarter of the globe. So well known is this fact of history that the mention of a few special instances will be sufficient for this occasion.

It took place in earliest times on the plains of Babylon. It was seen on the banks of the Nile, in the land of the Pharaohs. The same fact occurred again when the barbarian hosts of the North fell upon effete Roman society, and changed the fate of Europe. Once more we witness the like fact when the Moors swept along the banks of the Mediterranean, and seated themselves in might and majesty on the hills of Granada and along the fertile slopes of Arragon and Castile. And now, in the 19th century, we have the largest illustration of the same fact in our own Republic, where we are gathered together, in one national community, sixty millions of people of every race and kindred under the sun. It might be supposed that an historical fact so large and multiform would furnish a solution of the great race-problem, which now invites attention in American society. We read the future by the past. And without doubt there are certain principles of population which are invariable in their working and universal in their results. Such principles are inductions from definite conditions, and may be called the laws of population. They are, too, both historical and predictive. One cannot only ascertain through them the past condition of States and peoples, but they give a light which opens up with clearness the future of great commonwealths.

But, singular as it may seem, there is no fixed law of history by which to determine the probabilities of the race-problem in the United States. We can find nowhere such invariability of result as to set a principle or determine what may be called an historical axiom.

Observe just here the inevitable confusion which is sure to follow the aim after historical precedent in this problem. The descendants of Nimrod and Assur, people of two different stocks, settled in Babylon; and the result was amalgamation. The Jews and the Egyptians under the Pharaohs inhabited the same country 400 years; but antagonism was the result, and expulsion the final issue. The Tartars overran China in the tenth century, and the result has been amalgamation. The Goths and Vandals poured into Italy like a flood, and the result has been absorption. The Celts and Scandinavians clustered like bees from the fourth to the sixth centuries in the British Isles, and the result has been absorption. The Northmen and Gauls have lived side by side in Normandy since the tenth century, and the result has been absorption. The Moors and Spaniards came into the closest contact in the sixth century, and it resulted in constant antagonism and in final expulsion. The Caucasian and the Indian have lived in close neighborhood on this continent since 1492, and the result has been the extinction of the Indian. The Papuan and the Malay have lived side by side for ages in the tropical regions of the Pacific, and have maintained every possible divergence of tribal life, of blood, government, and religion, down to the present, and yet have remained perpetually and yet peacefully separate and distinct.

These facts, circling deep historic ages, show that we can find no definite historical precedent or principle applicable to the race-problem in America. Nevertheless we are not entirely at sea with regard to this problem. There are certain tendencies, seen for over 200 years in our population, which indicate settled, determinate proclivities, and which show, if I mistake not, the destiny of races.

What, then, are the probabilities of the future? Do the indications point to amalgamation or to absorption as the outcome of race-life in America? Are we to have the intermingling of our peoples into one common blood or the perpetuity of our diverse stocks, with the abiding integrity of race, blood, and character? I might meet the theory which anticipates amalgamation by the great principle manifested in every sphere, viz: "That nature is constantly departing from the simple to the complex; starting off in new lines from the homogeneous to the heterogeneous;" striking out in divers ways into variety; and hence we are hedged in, in the aim after blood-unity, by a law of nature which is universal, and which excludes the notion of amalgamation.

But I turn from the abstract to history. It is now about 268 years since the tides of immigration began to beat upon our shores. This may be called a brief period, but 268 years is long enough to fix a new type of man. Has such a new type sprung up here to life? Has a new commingled race, the result of our diverse elements, come forth from the crucible of our heterogeneous nationality?

We will indulge in no speculation upon this subject. We will exclude even the faintest tinge of the imagination. The facts alone shall speak for themselves.

First of all is the history of the Anglo-Saxon race in America. In many respects it has been the foremost element in the American population; in largeness of numbers, in civil polity and power, in educational impress, and in religious influence. What has become of this element of our population? Has it been lost in the current of the divergent streams of life which have been spreading abroad throughout the land? Why, every one knows that in New England, in Virginia, in the Far West, along the Atlantic Seaboard, that fully three-fifths of the whole American population are the offspring of this same hardy, plodding, common sense people that they were centuries ago, when their fathers pressed through the forests of Jamestown or planted their feet upon the sterile soil of Plymouth.

Some of you may remember the remark of Mr. Lowell, on his return in 1885 from his mission to England. He said that when English people spoke to him of Americans as a people different from themselves, he always told them that in blood he was just as much an Englishman as they were; and Mr. Lowell in this remark was the spokesman of not less than thirty-six millions of men of as direct Anglo-Saxon descent as the men of Kent or the people of Yorkshire.

The Celtic element came to America in two separate columns. The French entered Canada in 1607. They came with all that glow, fervor, gallantry, social aptitudes, and religious loyalty which, for centuries, have characterized the Gallic blood, and which are still conspicuous features on both sides of the Atlantic. The other section of the Celtic family began their immigration about 1640; and they have almost depopulated Ireland to populate America; and their numbers now are millions. One or two facts are observable concerning the French and Irish, viz: (1) That, although kindred in blood, temperament, and religion, they have avoided both neighborhood of locality and marital alliance; and (2) so great has been the increase of the Hibernian family that in Church life and political importance they form a vast solidarity in the nation.

The German, like the Celtic family, came over in two sections. The Batavian stock came first from Holland in 1608, and made New York, New Jersey, and Pennsylvania their habitat. The Germans proper, or High Germans, have been streaming into the Republic since 1680, bringing with them that steadiness and sturdiness, that thrift and acquisitiveness, that art and learning, that genius and acumen, which have given an elastic spring to American culture, depth to philosophy, and inspiration to music and to art.

And here they are in great colonies in the Middle and Western States, and in vast sections of our great cities. And yet where can one discover any decline in the purity of German blood, or the likelihood of its ultimate loss in the veins of alien people?

The Negro contingent was one of the earliest contributions to the American population. The black man came quickly on the heel of the Cavalier at Jamestown, and before the arrival of the Puritan in the east. "That fatal, that perfidious bark" of Sir John Hawkins, that "ferried the slave captive o'er the sea" from Africa, preceded the Mayflower one year and five months. From that small cargo and its after arrivals have arisen the large black population, variously estimated from 8 to 10,000,000. It is mostly, especially in the wide rural areas of the South, a purely Negro population. In the large cities there is a wide intermixture of blood. This, by some writers, is taken as the indication of ultimate and entire amalgamation. But the past in this incident is no sign of the future. The gross and violent intermingling of the blood of the southern white man cannot be taken as an index of the future of the black race.

Amalgamation in its exact sense means the approach of affinities. The word applied to human beings implies will, and the consent of two parties. In this sense there has been no amalgamation of the two races; for the Negro in this land has ever been the truest of men, in marital allegiance, to his own race.

Intermixture of blood there has been – not by the amalgamation, which implies consent, but through the victimizing of the helpless black woman. But even this has been limited in extent. Out of 4,500,000 of this race in the census of 1861, 400,000 were set down as of mixed blood. Thousands of these were the legitimate offspring of colored parents; and the probability is that not more than 150,000 had white fathers. Since emancipation the black woman has gained possession of her own person, and it is the testimony of Dr. Haygood and other eminent Southerners that the base process of intermixture has had a wide and sudden decline, and that the likelihood of the so-called amalgamation of the future is fast dying out.

And now, after this survey of race tides and race life during 268 years, I repeat the question: "Has a *new* race, the product of our diverse elements, sprung up here in America? Or, is there any such a probability for the future?" Let me answer this question by a recent and striking reference.

Dr. Strong, in his able, startling, striking Tractate, entitled *Our Country*, speaks, in ch. 4, p. 44, of the Helvetian settlement in southern Wisconsin. He deprecates the preservation of its race, its language, its worship, and its customs in their integrity. In this, you see, he forgets the old Roman adage that "though men cross the seas they do not change their nature." He then protests (and rightly, too) against the perpetuation of race antipathies, and closes his criticism with the suggestion, similar to that of Canon Rawlinson, of Oxford, viz., that the American people should seek the solution of the race-problem by universal assimilation of blood.

Dr. Strong evidently forgets that the principle of race is one of the most persistent of all things in the constitution of man. It is one of those structural facts in our nature which abide with a fixed, vital, and reproductive power. Races, like families, are the organisms and the ordinance of God; and race feeling, like the family feeling, is of divine origin. The extinction of race feeling is just as possible as the extinction of family feeling. Indeed, a race is a family. The principle of continuity is as masterful in races as it is in families – as it is in nations. History is filled with the attempts of kings and mighty generals and great statesmen to extinguish this instinct. But their failures are as numerous as their futile attempts; for this sentiment, alike subtle and spontaneous, has both pervaded and stimulated society in every quarter. Indeed, as Lord Beaconsfield says, "race is the key to history." When once the race-type gets fixed as a new variety, then it acts precisely as the family life; for, 1st, it propagates itself by that divine instinct of reproduction, vital in all living creatures, and next, 2nd, it has a growth as a "seed after its own kind and in itself," whereby the race-type becomes a perpetuity, with its own distinctive form, constitution, features, and structure. Heredity is just as true a fact in races as in families, as it is in individuals.

Nay, we see, not seldom, a special persistency in the race life. We see families and tribes and clans swept out of existence, while race "goes on forever." Yea, even nations suffer the same fate. Take, for instance, the unification of States now constantly occurring. One small nation after another is swallowed up by another to magnify its strength and importance, and thus the great empires of the world become colossal powers. But it is observable that the process of unification leaves untouched the vitality and the persistency of race. You have only to turn to Great Britain and to Austria to verify this statement. In both nations we see the intensity of race cohesion, and at the same time the process of unification. Indeed, on all sides, in Europe, we see the consolidation of States; and at the same time the integration of race: Nature and Providence thus developing that principle of unity which binds the universe, and yet at the same time manifesting that conserving power which tends everywhere to fixity of type. And this reminds us of the lines of Tennyson:

> That nature lends such evil dreams?
> Are God and nature, then, at strife,
> So careful of the type she seems,
> So careless of the single life.

Hence, when a race once seats itself permanently in a land it is almost as impossible to get rid of it as it is to extirpate a plant that is indigenous to its soil. You can drive out a family from a community. You can rid yourself of a clan or a single tribe by expulsion. You can swallow up by amalgamation a simple emigrant people.

But when a RACE, *i.e.*, a compact, homogeneous population of one blood, ancestry, and lineage – numbering, perchance, some eight or ten millions – once enters a land and settles therein as its home and heritage, then occurs an event as fixed and abiding as the rooting of the Pyrenees in Spain or the Alps in Italy.

The race-problem, it will thus be seen, cannot be settled by extinction of race. No amalgamating process can eliminate it. It is not a carnal question – a problem of breeds, or blood, or lineage. And even if it were, amalgamation would be an impossibility. How can any one persuade seven or eight millions of people to forget the ties of race? No one could force them into the arms of another race. And even then it would take generations upon generations to make the American people homogeneous in blood and essential qualities. Thus take one single case: There are thirty millions of Negroes on the American continent (eight or more millions in the United States of America), and constantly increasing at an immense ratio. Nothing but the sheerest, haziest imagination can anticipate the future dissolution of this race and its final loss; and so, too, of the other races of men in America.

Indeed, the race-problem is a moral one. It is a question entirely of ideas. Its solution will come especially from the domain of principles. Like all the other great battles of humanity, it is to be fought out with the weapons of truth. The race-problem is a question of organic life, and it must be dealt with as an ethical matter by the laws of the Christian system. "As diseases of the mind are invisible, so must their remedies be."

And this brings me to the one vast question that still lingers, *i.e.*, the question of AMITY. Race-life is a permanent element in our system. Can it be maintained in peace? Can these races give the world the show of brotherhood and fraternity? Is there a moral remedy in this problem? Such a state of concord is, we must admit, a rare sight, even in christendom. There is great friction between Celt and Saxon in Britain. We see the violence of both Russ and German against the Jew. The bitterness is a mutual one between Russia on the one hand and Bulgaria and the neighboring dependent principalities on the other, and France and Germany stand facing one another like great fighting cocks. All this is by no means assuring, and hence we cannot dismiss this question in an off-hand and careless manner. The current, however, does not set all one way. There is another aspect to this question. Thus, the Norman and the Frank have lived together harmoniously for centuries; the Welsh, English, and Scotch in England; the Indian, the Spaniard, and Negro in Brazil, and people of very divergent lineage in Spain. And now the question arises: What are the probabilities of amity in a land where exists such wide divergence of race as the Saxon on the one hand and the Negro on the other?

First of all, let me say that the social idea is to be entirely excluded from consideration. It is absolutely a personal matter, regulated by taste, condition, or either by racial or family affinities; and there it must remain undisturbed forever. The Jews in this land are sufficient for themselves. So are the Germans, the Italians, the Irish, and so are the Negroes. Civil and political freedom trench in no way upon the domestic state or social relations. Besides, there is something ignoble in any man, any class, any race of men whining and crying because they cannot move in spheres where they are not wanted.

But, beyond the social range there should be no compromise; and this country should be agitated and even convulsed till the battle of liberty is won, and every man in the land is guaranteed fully every civil and political right and prerogative. The question of equality pertains entirely to the two domains of civil and political life and prerogative.

Now, I wish to show that the probabilities tend toward the complete and entire civil and political equality of all the peoples of this land.

1st. Observe that this is the age of civil freedom. It has not as yet gained its fullest triumphs; neither yet has Christianity. But it is to be observed in the history of man that, in due time, certain principles get their set in human society, and there is no such thing as successfully resisting them. Their rise is not a matter of chance or haphazard. It is God's hand in history. It is the providence of the Almighty, and no earthly power can stay it. Such, pre-eminently, was the entrance of Christianity in the centre of the world's civilization, and the planting of the idea of human brotherhood amid the ideas in the laws and legislation of great nations. That was the seed from which have sprung all the great revolutions in thought and governmental policies during the Christian era. Its work has been slow, but it has been certain and unfailing. I cannot pause to narrate all its early victories. We will take a limited period. We will begin at the dawn of modern civilization, and note the grand achievements of the idea of Christian brotherhood. It struck at the doctrine of the Divine Right of Kings, and mortally wounded it. It demanded the extinction of Feudalism, and it got it. It demanded the abolition of the Slave Trade, and it got it. It demanded the abolition of Russian Serfage, and it got it. It demanded the education of the masses, and it got it.

In the early part of the eighteenth century this principle of brotherhood sprouted forth into a grander and more consummate growth, and generated the spirit of democracy. When I speak of the spirit of democracy I have no reference to that spurious, blustering, self-sufficient spirit which derides God and authority on the one hand, and crushes the weak and helpless on the other. The democratic spirit I am speaking of is that which upholds the doctrine of human rights; which demands honor to all men; which recognizes manhood in all conditions; which uses the State as the means and agency for the unlimited progress of humanity. This principle has its root in the Scriptures of God, and it has come forth in political society to stay! In the hands of man it has indeed suffered harm. It has been both distorted and exaggerated, and without doubt it needs to be chastised, regulated, and sanctified. But the democratic principle in its essence is of God, and in its normal state it is the consummate flower of Christianity, and is irresistible because it is the mighty breath of God. It is democracy which has demanded the people's participation in government and the extension of suffrage, and it got it. It has demanded a higher wage for labor, and it has got it, and will get more. It has demanded the abolition of Negro slavery, and it has got it. Its present demand is the equality of man in the State, irrespective of race, condition, or lineage. The answer to this demand is the solution of the race-problem.

In this land the crucial test in the race-problem is the civil and political rights of the black man. The only question now remaining among us for the full triumph of Christian democracy is the equality of the Negro. Nay, I take back my own words. It is NOT the case of the Negro in this land. It is the nation which is on trial. The Negro is only the touch-stone. By this black man she stands or falls. If the black man cannot be free in this land, if he cannot tread with firmness every pathway to preferment and superiority, neither can the white man. "A bridge is never stronger than its weakest point." In nature's chain, whatever link you strike, Tenth or ten-thousandth, breaks the chain alike. So compact a thing is humanity that the despoiling of an individual is an injury to society.

This nation has staked her existence on this principle of democracy in her every fundamental political dogma, and in every organic State document. The democratic idea is neither Anglo-Saxonism, nor Germanism, nor Hibernianism, but HUMANITY, and humanity can live when Anglo-Saxonism or any class of the race of man has perished. Humanity anticipated all human varieties by thousands of years, and rides above them all, and outlives them all, and swallows up them all! If this nation is not truly democratic then she must die! Nothing is more destructive to a nation than an organic falsehood! This nation cannot live – this nation does not deserve to live – on the basis of a lie! Her fundamental idea is democracy; and if this nation will not submit herself to the domination of this idea – if she refuses to live in the spirit of this creed – then she is already doomed, and she will certainly be damned. But neither calamity, I ween, is her destiny.

The democratic spirit is of itself a prophecy of its own fulfillment. Its disasters are trivialities; its repulses only temporary. In this nation the Negro has been the test for over 200 years. But see how far the Negro has traveled this time. In less than the lifetime of such a man as the great George Bancroft, observe the transformation in the status of the Negro in this land. When he was a child the Negro was a marketable commodity, a beast of the field, a chattel in the shambles, outside of the pale of the law, and ignorant as a pagan.

Nay, when I was a boy of 13, I heard the utterance fresh from the lips of the great J. C. Calhoun, to wit, that if he could find a Negro who knew the Greek syntax he would then believe that the Negro was a human being and should be treated as a man. If he were living to-day he would come across scores of Negroes, not only versed in the Greek syntax, but doctors, lawyers, college students, clergymen, some learned professors, and one author of a new Greek Grammar.

But just here the caste spirit interferes in this race-problem and declares: "You Negroes may get learning; you may get property; you may have churches and religion; but this is your limit! This is a white man's Government! No matter how many millions you may number, we Anglo-Saxons are to rule!" This is the edict constantly hissed in the Negro's ear, in one vast section of the land.

Let me tell you of a similar edict in another land:

Some sixty years ago there was a young nobleman, an undergraduate at Oxford University, a youth of much talent, learning, and political ambition; but, at the same time, he was *then* a foolish youth! His patrician spirit rose in bitter protest against the Reform Bill of that day, which lessened the power of the British aristocracy and increased the suffrages of the Commons. He was a clever young fellow, and he wrote a brilliant poem in defense of his order, notable, as you will see, for its rhythm, melody, and withal for its – silliness! Here are two lines from it:

Let Laws and Letters, Arts and Learning die;
But give us still our old Nobility.

Yes, let everything go to smash! Let civilization itself go to the dogs, if only an oligarchy may rule, flourish, and dominate! We have a blatant provincialism in our own country, whose only solution of the race-problem is the eternal subjection of the Negro, and the endless domination of a lawless and self created aristocracy. Such men forget that the democratic spirit rejects the factious barriers of caste, and stimulates the lowest of the kind to the very noblest ambitions of life. They forget that nations are no longer governed by races, but by ideas. They forget that the triumphant spirit of democracy has bred an individualism which brooks not the restraints of classes and aristocracies. They forget that, regardless of "Pope, Consul, King," or oligarchy, this same spirit of democracy lifts up to place and power her own agents for the rule of the world; and brings to the front, now a Dane as King of Greece, and now a Frenchman as King of Sweden; now a Jewish D'Israeli as Prime Minister of England, and now a Gallatin and a Schurz as cabinet ministers in America. They forget that a Wamba and a Gurth in one generation, whispering angry discontent in secret places, become, by the inspiration of democracy, the outspoken Hampdens and Sydneys of another. They forget that, as letters ripen and education spreads, the "Sambos" and "Pompeys" of to-day will surely develop into the Touissants and the Christophes, the Wards and the Garnets of the morrow, champions of their race and vindicators of their rights. They forget that democracy, to use the words of De Tocqueville, "has severed every link of the chain" by which aristocracy had fixed every member of the community, "from the peasant to the king." They forget that the Church of God is in the world; that her mission is, by the Holy Ghost, "to take the weak things of the world to confound the mighty," "to put down the mighty from their seats, and to exalt them of low degree"; that now, as in all the ages, she will, by the Gospel, break up tyrannies and useless dynasties, and lift up the masses to nobleness of life, and exalt the humblest of men to excellence and superiority.

Above all things, they forget that "the King invisible, immortal, eternal" is upon the throne of the universe; that thither caste, and bigotry, and race-hate can never reach; that He is everlastingly committed to the interests of the oppressed; that He is constantly sending forth succors and assistances for the rescue of the wronged and injured; that He brings all the forces of the universe to grind to powder all the enormities of earth, and to rectify all the ills of humanity, and so hasten on the day of universal brotherhood. By the presence and the power of that Divine Being all the alienations and disseverances of men shall be healed; all the race-problems of this land easily be solved; and love and peace prevail among men.

QUESTIONS

(1) What, for Crummell, is the "race-problem" and how would the equal participation of all people in American democracy provide a solution to the "race-problem" in America?

(2) What does Crummell mean by "the democratic spirit" and how can the "democratic spirit" prevail in the United States?

(3) How did blacks and whites come to be in the United States? Is it true that blacks were in the United States before the arrival of the Puritans? And what were some of the main reasons for the antagonisms between blacks and whites?

(4) Why is Crummell comparing race with families? And what are some of the differences between these two categories?

(5) According to Crummell, what is race? And why is the "race-problem" in the United States a moral issue?

13 | The Conservation of the Races

W. E. B. DU BOIS

We have earlier encountered W. E. B. Du Bois' writing in the section on Reconstruction (biographical details can be found in Chapter 6). The extract reproduced here is also concerned with certain assumptions about blacks as an inferior race. Initially, "The Conservation of the Races" was an address that Du Bois gave to the American Negro Academy. He draws our attention to race as a sociological fact. However, the view that races are biologically determined does not take into account the spiritual and psychical distinctiveness of the races, which for him is one of the aspects of the "Negro problem" in the United States. This is one of the reasons, at least for Du Bois, that races must be conserved because each race has a contribution to make to American society. Nonetheless, some principles must be developed whereby blacks and whites can coexist in the United States. The equal integration of blacks into the political, economic, and intellectual life of the United States is important. Blacks must work hard to uplift all blacks and be self-sufficient.

The American Negro has always felt an intense personal interest in discussions as to the origins and destinies of races: primarily because back of most discussions of race with which he is familiar, have lurked certain assumptions as to his natural abilities, as to his political, intellectual and moral status, which he felt were wrong. He has, consequently, been led to deprecate and minimize race distinctions, to believe intensely that out of one blood God created all nations, and to speak of human brotherhood as though it were the possibility of an already dawning tomorrow.

Nevertheless, in our calmer moments we must acknowledge that human beings are divided into races; that in this country the two most extreme types of the world's races have met, and the resulting problem as to the future relations of these types is not only of intense and living interest to us, but forms an epoch in the history of mankind.

It is necessary, therefore, in planning our movements, in guiding our future development, that at times we rise above the pressing, but smaller questions of separate schools and cars, wage-discrimination and lynch law, to survey the whole questions of race in human philosophy and to lay, on a basis of broad knowledge and careful insight, those large lines of policy and higher ideals which may form our guiding lines and boundaries in the practical difficulties of every day. For it is certain that all human striving must recognize the hard limits of natural law, and that any striving, no matter how intense and earnest, which is against the constitution of the world, is vain. The question, then, which we must seriously consider is this: What is the real meaning of Race; what has, in the past, been the law of race development, and what lessons has the past history of race development to teach the rising Negro people?

When we thus come to inquire into the essential difference of races we find it hard to come at once to any definite conclusion. Many criteria of race differences have in the past been proposed, as color, hair, cranial measurements and language. And manifestly, in each of these respects, human beings differ widely. They vary in color, for instance, from the marble-like pallor of the Scandinavian to the rich, dark brown of the Zulu, passing by the creamy Slav, the yellow Chinese, the light brown Sicilian and the brown Egyptian. Men vary, too, in the texture of hair from the obstinately straight hair of the Chinese to the obstinately tufted and frizzled hair of the Bushman. In measurement of heads, again, men vary; from the broad-headed Tartar to the medium-headed European and the narrow-headed Hottentot; or, again in language, from the highly-inflected Roman tongue to the monosyllabic Chinese. All these physical characteristics are patent enough, and if they agreed with each other it would be very easy to classify mankind. Unfortunately for scientists, however, these criteria of race are most exasperatingly intermingled. Color does not agree with texture of hair, for many of the dark races have straight hair; nor does color agree with the breadth of the head, for the yellow Tartar has a broader head than the German; nor, again, has the science of language as yet succeeded in clearing up the relative authority of these various and contradictory criteria. The final word of science, so far, is that we have at least two, perhaps three, great families of human beings—the whites and Negroes, possibly the yellow race. That other races have arisen from the intermingling of the blood of these two. This broad division of the world's races which men like Huxley and Raetzel have introduced as more nearly true than the old five-race scheme of Blumenbach, is nothing more than an acknowledgment that, so far as purely physical characteristics are concerned, the differences between men do not explain all the differences of their history. It declares, as Darwin himself said, that great as is the physical unlikeness of the various races of men their likenesses are greater, and upon this rests the whole scientific doctrine of Human Brotherhood.

Although the wonderful developments of human history teach that the grosser physical differences of color, hair and bone go but a short way toward explaining the different roles which groups of men have played in Human Progress, yet there are differences—subtle, delicate and elusive, though they may be—which have silently but definitely separated men into groups. While these subtle forces have generally followed the natural cleavage of common blood, descent and physical peculiarities, they have at other times swept across and ignored these. At all times, however, they have divided human beings into races, which, while they perhaps transcend scientific definition, nevertheless, are clearly defined to the eye of the Historian and Sociologist.

If this be true, then the history of the world is the history, not of individuals, but of groups, not of nations, but of races, and he who ignores or seeks to override the race idea in human history ignores and overrides the central thought of all history. What, then, is a race? It is a vast family of human beings, generally of common blood and language, always of common history, traditions and impulses, who are both voluntarily and involuntarily striving together for the accomplishment of certain more or less vividly conceived ideals of life.

Turning to real history, there can be no doubt, first, as to the widespread, nay, universal, prevalence of the race idea, the race spirit, the race ideal, and as to its efficiency as the vastest and most ingenious invention of human progress. We, who have been reared and trained under the individualistic philosophy of the Declaration of Independence and the laisser-faire philosophy of Adam Smith, are loath to see and loath to acknowledge this patent fact of human history. We see the Pharaohs, Caesars, Toussaints and Napoleons of history and forget the vast races of which they were but epitomized expressions. We are apt to think in our American impatience, that while it may have been true in the past that closed race groups made history, that here in conglomerate America NOUS AVONS CHANGER TOUT CELA—we have changed all that, and have no need of this ancient instrument of progress. This assumption of which the Negro people are especially fond, cannot be established by a careful consideration of history.

We find upon the world's stage today eight distinctly differentiated races, in the sense in which History tells us the word must be used. They are, the Slavs of eastern Europe, the Teutons of middle Europe, the English of Great Britain and America, the Romance nations of Southern and Western Europe, the Negroes of Africa and America, the Semitic people of Western Asia and Northern Africa, the Hindoos of Central Asia and the Mongolians of Eastern Asia. There are, of course, other minor race groups, as the American Indians, the Esquimaux and the South Sea Islanders; these larger races, too, are far from homogeneous; the Slav includes the Czech, the Magyar, the Pole and the Russian; the Teuton includes the German, the Scandinavian and the Dutch; the English include the Scotch, the Irish and the conglomerate American. Under Romance nations the widely-differing Frenchman, Italian, Sicilian and Spaniard are comprehended. The term Negro is, perhaps, the most indefinite of all, combining the Mulattoes and Zamboes of America and the Egyptians, Bantus and Bushmen of Africa. Among the Hindoos are traces of widely differing nations, while the great Chinese, Tartar, Corean and Japanese families fall under the one designation—Mongolian.

The question now is: What is the real distinction between these nations? Is it the physical differences of blood, color and cranial measurements? Certainly we must all acknowledge that physical differences play a great part, and that, with wide exceptions and qualifications, these eight great races of to-day follow the cleavage of physical race distinctions; the English and Teuton represent the white variety of mankind; the Mongolian, the yellow; the Negroes, the black. Between these are many crosses and mixtures, where Mongolian and Teuton have blended into the Slav, and other mixtures have produced the Romance nations and the Semites. But while race differences have followed mainly physical race lines, yet no mere physical distinctions would really define or explain the deeper differences—the cohesiveness and continuity of these groups. The deeper differences are spiritual, psychical, differences—undoubtedly based on the physical, but infinitely transcending them. The forces that bind together the Teuton nations are, then, first, their race identity and common blood; secondly, and more important, a common history, common laws and religion, similar habits of thought and a conscious striving together for certain ideals of life. The whole process which has brought about these race differentiations has been a growth, and the great characteristic of this growth has been the differentiation of spiritual and mental differences between great races of mankind and the integration of physical differences.

The age of nomadic tribes of closely related individuals represents the maximum of physical differences. They were practically vast families, and there were as many groups as families. As the families came together to form cities the physical differences lessened, purity of blood was replaced by the requirement of domicile, and all who lived within the city bounds became gradually to be regarded as members of the group; i.e., there was a slight and slow breaking down of physical barriers. This, however, was accompanied by an increase of the spiritual and social differences between cities. This city became husbandmen, this, merchants, another warriors, and so on. The IDEALS OF LIFE for which the different cities struggled were different. When at last cities began to coalesce into nations there was another breaking down of barriers which separated groups of men. The larger and broader differences of color, hair and physical proportions were not by any means ignored, but myriads of minor differences disappeared, and the sociological and historical races of men began to approximate the present division of races as indicated by physical researches. At the same time the spiritual and physical differences of race groups which constituted the nations became deep and decisive. The English nation stood for constitutional liberty and commercial freedom; the German nation for science and philosophy; the Romance nations stood for literature and art, and the other race groups are striving, each in its own way, to develop for civilization its particular message, it particular ideal, which shall help to guide the world nearer and nearer that perfection of human life for which we all long, that "one far off Divine event."

This has been the function of race differences up to the present time. What shall be its function in the future? Manifestly some of the great races of today—particularly the Negro race—have not as yet given to civilization the full spiritual message which they are capable of giving. I will not say that the Negro race has yet given no message to the world, for it is still a mooted question among scientists as to just how far Egyptian civilization was Negro in its origin; if it was not wholly Negro, it was certainly very closely allied. Be that as it may, however, the fact still remains that the full, complete Negro message of the whole Negro race has not as yet been given to the world: that the messages and ideal of the yellow race have not been completed, and that the striving of the mighty Slavs has but begun. The question is, then: How shall this message be delivered; how shall these various ideals be realized? The answer is plain: By the development of these race groups, not as individuals, but as races. For the development of Japanese genius, Japanese literature and art, Japanese spirit, only Japanese, bound and welded together, Japanese inspired by one vast ideal, can work out in its fullness the wonderful message which Japan has for the nations of the earth. For the development of Negro genius, of Negro literature and art, of Negro spirit, only Negroes bound and welded together, Negroes inspired by one vast ideal, can work out in its fullness that great message we have for humanity. We cannot reverse history; we are subject to the same natural laws as other races, and if the Negro is ever to be a factor in the world's history—if among the gaily-colored banners that deck the broad ramparts of civilizations is to hang one uncompromising black, then it must be placed there by black hands, fashioned by black heads and hallowed by the travail of 200,000,000 black hearts beating in one glad song of jubilee.

For this reason, the advance guard of the Negro people—the 8,000,000 people of Negro blood in the United States of America—must soon come to realize that if they are to take their just place in the van of Pan-Negroism, then their destiny is NOT absorption by the white Americans. That if in America it is to be proven for the first time in the modern world that not only Negroes are capable of evolving individual men like Toussaint, the Saviour, but are a nation stored with wonderful possibilities of culture, then their destiny is not a servile imitation of Anglo-Saxon culture, but a stalwart originality which shall unswervingly follow Negro ideals.

It may, however, be objected here that the situation of our race in America renders this attitude impossible; that our sole hope of salvation lies in our being able to lose our race identity in the commingled blood of the nation; and that any other course would merely increase the friction of races which we call race prejudice, and against which we have so long and so earnestly fought.

Here, then, is the dilemma, and it is a puzzling one, I admit. No Negro who has given earnest thought to the situation of his people in America has failed, at some time in life, to find himself at these cross-roads; has failed to ask himself at some time: What, after all, am I? Am I an American or am I a Negro? Can I be both? Or is it my duty to cease to be a Negro as soon as possible and be an American? If I strive as a Negro, am I not perpetuating the very cleft that threatens and separates Black and White America? Is not my only possible practical aim the subduction of all that is Negro in me to the American? Does my black blood place upon me any more obligation to assert my nationality than German, or Irish or Italian blood would?

It is such incessant self-questioning and the hesitation that arises from it, that is making the present period a time of vacillation and contradiction for the American Negro; combined race action is stifled, race responsibility is shirked, race enterprises languish, and the best blood, the best talent, the best energy of the Negro people cannot be marshalled to do the bidding of the race. They stand back to make room for every rascal and demagogue who chooses to cloak his selfish deviltry under the veil of race pride.

Is this right? Is it rational? Is it good policy? Have we in America a distinct mission as a race—a distinct sphere of action and an opportunity for race development, or is self-obliteration the highest end to which Negro blood dare aspire?

If we carefully consider what race prejudice really is, we find it, historically, to be nothing but the friction between different groups of people; it is the difference in aim, in feeling, in ideals of two different races; if, now, this difference exists touching territory, laws, language, or even religion, it is manifest that these people cannot live in the same territory without fatal collision; but if, on the other hand, there is substantial agreement in laws, language and religion; if there is a satisfactory adjustment of economic life, then there is no reason why, in the same country and on the same street, two or three great national ideals might not thrive and develop, that men of different races might not strive together for their race ideals as well, perhaps even better, than in isolation. Here, it seems to me, is the reading of the riddle that puzzles so many of us. We are Americans, not only by birth and by citizenship, but by our political ideals, our language, our religion. Farther than that, our Americanism does not go. At that point, we are Negroes, members of a vast historic race that from the very dawn of creation has slept, but half awakening in the dark forests of its African fatherland. We are the first fruits of this new nation, the harbinger of that black to-morrow which is yet destined to soften the whiteness of the Teutonic to-day. We are that people whose subtle sense of song has given America its only American music, its only American fairy tales, its only touch of pathos and humor amid its mad money-getting plutocracy. As such, it is our duty to conserve our physical powers, our intellectual endowments, our spiritual ideals; as a race we must strive by race organization, by race solidarity, by race unity to the realization of that broader humanity which freely recognizes differences in men, but sternly deprecates inequality in their opportunities of development.

For the accomplishment of these ends we need race organizations: Negro colleges, Negro newspapers, Negro business organizations, a Negro school of literature and art, and an intellectual clearing house, for all these products of the Negro mind, which we may call a Negro Academy. Not only is all this necessary for positive advance, it is absolutely imperative for negative defense. Let us not deceive ourselves at our situation in this country. Weighted with a heritage of moral iniquity from our past history, hard pressed in the economic world by foreign immigrants and native prejudice, hated here, despised there and pitied everywhere; our one haven of refuge is ourselves, and but one means of advance, our own belief in our great destiny, our own implicit trust in our ability and worth. There is no power under God's high heaven that can stop the advance of eight thousand thousand honest, earnest, inspired and united people. But—and here is the rub—they MUST be honest, fearlessly criticizing their own faults, zealously correcting them; they must be EARNEST. No people that laughs at itself, and ridicules itself, and wishes to God it was anything but itself ever wrote its name in history; it MUST be inspired with the Divine faith of our black mothers, that out of the blood and dust of battle will march a victorious host, a mighty nation, a peculiar people, to speak to the nations of earth a Divine truth that shall make them free. And such a people must be united; not merely united for the organized theft of political spoils, not united to disgrace religion with whoremongers and ward-heelers; not united merely to protest and pass resolutions, but united to stop the ravages of consumption among the Negro people, united to keep black boys from loafing, gambling and crime; united to guard the purity of black women and to reduce the vast army of black prostitutes that is today marching to hell; and united in serious organizations, to determine by careful conference and thoughtful interchange of opinion the broad lines of policy and action for the American Negro.

This, is the reason for being which the American Negro Academy has. It aims at once to be the epitome and expression of the intellect of the black-blooded people of America, the exponent of the race ideals of one of the world's great races. As such, the Academy must, if successful, be

(a) Representative in character.
(b) Impartial in conduct.
(c) Firm in leadership.

It must be representative in character; not in that it represents all interests or all factions, but in that it seeks to comprise something of the BEST thought, the most unselfish striving and the highest ideals. There are scattered in forgotten nooks and corners throughout the land, Negroes of some considerable training, of high minds, and high motives, who are unknown to their fellows, who exert far too little influence. These the Negro Academy should strive to bring into touch with each other and to give them a common mouthpiece.

The Academy should be impartial in conduct; while it aims to exalt the people it should aim to do so by truth—not by lies, by honesty—not by flattery. It should continually impress the fact upon the Negro people that they must not expect to have things done for them—they MUST DO FOR THEMSELVES; that they have on their hands a vast work of self-reformation to do, and that a little less complaint and whining, and a little more dogged work and manly striving would do us more credit and benefit than a thousand Force or Civil Rights bills.

Finally, the American Negro Academy must point out a practical path of advance to the Negro people; there lie before every Negro today hundreds of questions of policy and right which must be settled and which each one settles now, not in accordance with any rule, but by impulse or individual preference; for instance: What should be the attitude of Negroes toward the educational qualification for voters? What should be our attitude toward separate schools? How should we meet discriminations on railways and in hotels? Such questions need not so much specific answers for each part as a general expression of policy, and nobody should be better fitted to announce such a policy than a representative honest Negro Academy.

All this, however, must come in time after careful organization and long conference. The immediate work before us should be practical and have direct bearing upon the situation of the Negro. The historical work of collecting the laws of the United States and of the various States of the Union with regard to the Negro is a work of such magnitude and importance that no body but one like this could think of undertaking it. If we could accomplish that one task we would justify our existence.

In the field of Sociology an appalling work lies before us. First, we must unflinchingly and bravely face the truth, not with apologies, but with solemn earnestness. The Negro Academy ought to sound a note of warning that would echo in every black cabin in the land: UNLESS WE CONQUER OUR PRESENT VICES THEY WILL CONQUER US; we are diseased, we are developing criminal tendencies, and an alarmingly large percentage of our men and women are sexually impure. The Negro Academy should stand and proclaim this over the housetops, crying with Garrison: I WILL NOT EQUIVOCATE, I WILL NOT RETREAT A SINGLE INCH, AND I WILL BE HEARD. The Academy should seek to gather about it the talented, unselfish men, the pure and noble-minded women, to fight an army of devils that disgraces our manhood and our womanhood. There does not stand today upon God's earth a race more capable in muscle, in intellect, in morals, than the American Negro, if he will bend his energies in the right direction; if he will Burst his birth's invidious bar And grasp the skirts of happy chance, And breast the blow of circumstance, And grapple with his evil star.

In science and morals, I have indicated two fields of work for the Academy. Finally, in practical policy, I wish to suggest the following ACADEMY CREED:

1. We believe that the Negro people, as a race, have a contribution to make to civilization and humanity, which no other race can make.

2. We believe it is the duty of the Americans of Negro descent, as a body, to maintain their race identity until this mission of the Negro people is accomplished, and the ideal of human brotherhood has become a practical possibility.

3. We believe that, unless modern civilization is a failure, it is entirely feasible and practicable for two races in such essential political, economic and religious harmony as the white and colored people in America, to develop side by side in peace and mutual happiness, the peculiar contribution which each has to make to the culture of their common country.

4. As a means to this end we advocate, not such social equality between these races as would disregard human likes and dislikes, but such a social equilibrium as would, throughout all the complicated relations of life, give due and just consideration to culture, ability, and moral worth, whether they be found under white or black skins.

5. We believe that the first and greatest step toward the settlement of the present friction between the races commonly called the Negro Problem lies in the correction of the immorality, crime and laziness among the Negroes themselves, which still remains as a heritage from slavery. We believe that only earnest and long continued efforts on our own part can cure these social ills.

6. We believe that the second great step toward a better adjustment of the relations between races, should be a more impartial selection of ability in the economic and intellectual world, and a greater respect for personal liberty and worth, regardless of race. We believe that only earnest efforts on the part of the white people of this country will bring much needed reform in these matters.

7. On the basis of the foregoing declaration, and firmly believing in our high destiny, we, as American Negroes, are resolved to strive in every honorable way for the realization of the best and highest aims, for the development of strong manhood and pure womanhood, and for the rearing of a race ideal in America and Africa, to the glory of God and the uplifting of the Negro people.

QUESTIONS

(1) In examining the development of the race concept, what is the real meaning of race?

(2) How did the American Negro Academy help blacks to tap in to their true potentials, which would contribute to the American society as a whole?

(3) According to Du Bois, why is the conservation of the black race important?

(4) What is some of the evidence that Du Bois provides to show that social and historical facts of race transcend the scientific definition of race?

(5) Why are blacks, according to Du Bois, distinguished from other races?

14 | Lynch Laws in all its Phases

IDA B. WELLS

Ida B. Wells (1862–1931), a journalist, newspaper editor, and an activist for women's rights, was born into slavery in Holly Springs, Mississippi. She completed her studies at Rust College and became a teacher. In the 1880s, she moved to Memphis, Tennessee. Her activism started when she was traveling from her work to Memphis with a first-class train ticket that she had purchased and was ordered to move to the train's smoking car. She refused and the conductor and other passengers tried to physically remove her from the train. She successfully sued the railroad company and was awarded $500. The company appealed the decision and, in 1887, the Supreme Court of Tennessee reversed the decision and ordered Wells to pay court fees. Wells, under a pseudonym (Iola), began to challenge Jim Crow South laws with her editorials published in black newspapers. Later on, she bought a share in the *Free Speech and Headline*. In 1882, after the lynching of three of her friends, she launched an intensive investigation on lynching and brought international attention to the lynching of blacks. Wells was a founding member of the National Association for the Advancement of Colored People. Through her lectures, editorials, and books, she countered the "rape myth" that was used by whites to justify the murder of black men. In 1892, Wells published *Southern Horrors: Lynch Law in all its Phases*, in which, in great detail, she narrated the lynching of blacks. The excerpt "Lynch Laws in all its Phases," reproduced below, draws on the horrors of America's racism, which was exemplified in the lynching of blacks.

I am before the American people today through no inclination of my own, but because of a deep seated conviction that the country at large does not know the extent to which lynch law prevails in parts of the Republic nor the conditions which force into exile those who speak the truth. I cannot believe that the apathy and indifference which so largely obtains regarding mob rule is other than the result of ignorance of the true situation. And yet, the observing and thoughtful must know that in one section, at least, of our common country, a government of the people, by the people, and for the people, means a government by the mob; where the land of the free and home of the brave means a land of lawlessness, murder and outrage; and where liberty of speech means the license of might to destroy the business and drive from home those who exercise this privilege contrary to the will of the mob. Repeated attacks on the life, liberty and happiness of any citizen or class of citizens are attacks on distinctive American institutions; such attacks imperiling as they do the foundation of government, law and order, merit the thoughtful consideration of far sighted Americans; not from a standpoint of sentiment, not even so much from a standpoint of justice to a weak race, as from a desire to preserve our institutions.

The race problem or Negro question, as it has been called, has been omnipresent and all pervading since long before the Afro American was raised from the degradation of the slave to the dignity of the citizen. It has never been settled because the right methods have not been employed in the solution. It is the Banquo's ghost of politics, religion, and sociology which will not down at the bidding of those who are tormented with its ubiquitous appearance on every occasion. Times without number, since invested with citizenship, the race has been indicted for ignorance, immorality and general worthlessness—declared guilty and executed by its self constituted judges. The operations of law do not dispose of Negroes fast enough, and lynching bees have become the favorite pastime of the South. As excuse for the same, a new cry, as false as it is foul, is raised in an effort to blast race character, a cry which has proclaimed to the world that virtue and innocence are violated by Afro-Americans who must be killed like wild beasts to protect womanhood and childhood.

Born and reared in the South, I had never expected to live elsewhere. Until this past year I was one among those who believed the condition of masses gave large excuse for the humiliations and proscriptions under which we labored; that when wealth, education and character became more feral among us, the cause being removed the effect would cease, and justice being accorded to all alike. I shared the general belief that good newspapers entering regularly the homes of our people in every state could do more to bring about this result than any agency. Preaching the doctrine of self help, thrift and economy every week, they would be the teachers to those who had been deprived of school advantages, yet were making history every day and train to think for themselves our mental children of a larger growth. And so, three years ago last June, I became editor and part owner of the *Memphis Free Speech.* As editor, I had occasion to criticize the city School Board's employment of inefficient teachers and poor school buildings for Afro-American children. I was in the employ of that board at the time, and at the close of that school term one year ago, was not reelected to a position I had held in the city schools for seven years. Accepting the decision of the Board of Education, I set out to make a race newspaper pay—a thing which older and wiser heads said could not be done. But there were enough of our people in Memphis and surrounding territory to support a paper, and I believed they would do so. With nine months hard work the circulation increased from 1,500 to 3,500; in twelve months it was on a good paying basis. Throughout the Mississippi Valley in Arkansas, Tennessee and Mississippi on plantations and in towns, the demand for and interest in the paper increased among the masses. The newsboys who would not sell it on the trains, voluntarily testified that they had never known colored people to demand a paper so eagerly.

To make the paper a paying business I became advertising agent, solicitor, as well as editor, and was continually on the go. Wherever I went among the people, I gave them in church, school, public gatherings, and home, the benefit of my honest conviction that maintenance of character, money getting and education would finally solve our problem and that it depended on us to say how soon this would be brought about. This sentiment bore good fruit in Memphis. We had nice homes, representatives in almost every branch of business and profession, and refined society. We had learned helping each other helped all, and every well conducted business by Afro-Americans prospered. With all our proscription in theatres, hotels and railroads, we had never had a lynching and did not believe we could have one. There had been lynchings and brutal outrages of all sorts in our state and those adjoining us, but we had confidence and pride in our city and the majesty of its laws. So far in advance of other Southern cities was ours, we were content to endure the evils we had, to labor and to wait.

But there was a rude awakening. On the morning of March 9, the bodies of three of our best young men were found in an old field horribly shot to pieces. These young men had owned and operated the "People's Grocery," situated at what was known as the Curve a suburb made up almost entirely of colored people about a mile from city limits. Thomas Moss, one of the oldest letter carriers in the city, was president of the company, Cal McDowell was manager and Will Stewart was a clerk. There were about ten other stockholders, all colored men. The young men were well known and popular and their business flourished, and that of Barrett, a white grocer who kept store there before the "People's Grocery" was established, went down. One day an officer came to the "People's Grocery" and inquired for a colored man who lived in the neighborhood, and for whom the officer had a warrant. Barrett was with him and when McDowell said he knew nothing as to the whereabouts of the man for whom they were searching, Barrett, not the officer, then accused McDowell of harboring the man, and McDowell gave the lie. Barrett drew his pistol and struck McDowell with it; thereupon McDowell who was a tall, fine looking six footer, took Barrett's pistol from him, knocked him down and gave him a good thrashing, while Will Stewart, the clerk, kept the special officer at bay. Barrett went to town, swore out a warrant for their arrest on a charge of assault and battery. McDowell went before the Criminal Court, immediately gave bond and returned to his store. Barrett then threatened (to use his own words) that he was going to clean out the whole store. Knowing how anxious he was to destroy their business, these young men consulted a lawyer who told them they were justified in defending themselves if attacked, as they were a mile beyond city limits and police protection. They accordingly armed several of their friends–not to assail, but to resist the threatened Saturday night attack.

When they saw Barrett enter the front door and a half dozen men at the rear door at 11 o'clock that night, they supposed the attack was on and immediately fired into the crowd, wounding three men. These men, dressed in citizen's clothes, turned out to be deputies who claimed to be hunting for another man for whom they had a warrant, and whom any one of them could have arrested without trouble. When these men found they had fired upon officers of the law, they threw away their firearms and submitted to arrest, confident they should establish their innocence of intent to fire upon officers of the law. The daily papers in flaming headlines roused the evil passions of whites, denounced these poor boys in unmeasured terms, nor permitted a word in their own defense.

The neighborhood of the Curve was searched next day, and about thirty persons were thrown into jail, charged with conspiracy. No communication was to be had with friends any of the three days these men were in jail; bail was refused and Thomas Moss was not allowed to eat the food his wife prepared for him. The judge is reported to have said, "Any one can see them after three days." They were seen after three days, but they were no longer able to respond to the greetings of friends. On Tuesday following the shootings at the grocery, the papers which had made much of the sufferings of the wounded deputies, and promised it would go hard with those who did the shooting, if they died, announced that the officers were all out of danger, and would recover. The friends of the prisoners breathed more easily and relaxed their vigilance. They felt that as the officers would not die, there was no danger that in the heat of passion the prisoners would meet violent death at hands of the mob. Besides, we had such confidence in the law. But the law did not provide capital punishment for shooting which did not kill. So the mob did what the law could not be made to do, as a lesson to the Afro-American that he must not shoot a white man, no matter what the provocation. The same night after the announcement was made in the papers that the officers would get well, the mob, in obedience to a plan known to every eminent white man in the city, went to the jail between two and three in the morning, dragged out these young men, hatless and shoeless, put them on the yard engine of the railroad which was in waiting just behind the jail, carried them a mile north of the city limits and horribly shot them to death while the locomotive at a given signal let off steam and blew the whistle to deaden the sound of the firing.

"It was done by unknown men," said the jury, yet the *Appeal Avalanche* which goes to press at 3 a.m., had a two column account of the lynching. The papers also told how McDowell got hold of the guns of the mob and as his grasp could not be loosened, his hand was shattered with a pistol ball and all the lower part of his face was torn away. There were four pools of blood found and only three bodies. It was whispered that he, McDowell killed one of the lynchers with his gun, and it is well known that a police man who was seen on the street a few days previous to the lynching, died very suddenly the next day after.

"It was done by unknown parties," said the jury, yet the papers told how Tom Moss begged for his life, for the sake of his wife, his little daughter and his unborn infant. They also told us that his last words were, "If you will kill us, turn our faces to the West."

All this we learned too late to save these men, even if the law had not be in the hands of their murderers. When the colored people realized that the flower of our young manhood had been stolen away at night and murdered there was a rush for firearms to avenge the wrong, but no house would sell a colored man a gun; the armory of the Tennessee Rifles, our only colored military company, and of which McDowell was a member, was broken into by order of the Criminal Court judge, and its guns taken. One hundred men and irresponsible boys from fifteen years and up were armed by order of authorities and rushed out to the Curve, where it was reported that the colored people were massing, and at point of the bayonet dispersed these men who could do nothing but talk. The cigars, wines, etc., of the grocery stock were freely used by the mob, who possessed the place on pretence of dispersing the conspiracy. The money drawer was broken into and contents taken. The trunk of Calvin McDowell, who had a room in the store, was broken open, and his clothing, which was not good enough to take away, was throw out and trampled on the floor.

These men were murdered, their stock was attached by creditors and sold for less than one eighth of its cost to that same man Barrett, who is to-day running his grocery in the same place. He had indeed kept his word, and by aid of the authorities destroyed the People's Grocery Company root and branch. The relatives of Will Stewart and Calvin McDowell are bereft of their protectors. The baby daughter of Tom Moss, too young to express how she misses her father, toddles to the wardrobe, seizes the legs of the trousers of his letter carrier uniform, hugs and kisses them with evident delight and stretches up her little hands to be taken up into the arms which will nevermore clasp his daughter's form. His wife holds Thomas Moss, Jr., in her arms, upon whose unconscious baby face the tears fall thick and fast when she is thinking of the sad fate of the father he will never see, and of the two helpless children who cling to her for the support she cannot give. Although these men were peaceable, law abiding citizens of this country, we are told there can be no punishment for their murderers nor indemnity for relatives.

I have no power to describe the feeling of horror that possessed every member of the race in Memphis when the truth dawned upon us that the protection of the law which we had so long enjoyed was no longer ours; all had been destroyed in a night, and the barriers of the law had been down, and the guardians of the public peace and confidence scoffed into the shadows, and all authority given into the hands of the mob, and innocent men cut down as if they were brutes – the first feeling was one of utter dismay, then intense indignation. Vengeance was whispered from ear to ear, but sober reflection brought the conviction that it would be extreme folly to seek vengeance when such action meant certain death for the men, and horrible slaughter for the women and children, as one of the evening papers took care to remind us. The power of the State, country and city, and civil authorities and the strong arm of the military power were all on the side of the mob and of lawlessness. Few of our men possessed firearms, our only company's guns were confiscated, and the only white man who sell a colored man a gun, was himself jailed, and his store closed. We were helpless in our great strength. It was our first object lesson in the doctrine of white supremacy; an illustration of the South's cardinal principle no matter what the attainments, character or standing of an Afro-American, the laws of the South will not protect him against a white man.

There was only one thing we could do, and a great determination seized the people to follow the advice of the martyred Moss, and "turn our faces to the West," whose laws protect all alike. The *Free Speech* supported ministers and leading business men advised the people to leave a community whose laws did not protect them. Hundreds left on foot to walk four hundred miles between Memphis and Oklahoma. A Baptist minister went to the territory, built a church, and took his entire congregation out in less than a month. Another minister sold his church and took his flock to California, and still another has settled in Kansas. In two months, six thousand persons had left the city and every branch of business began to feel this silent resentment of the outrage, and failure of the authorities to punish lynchers. There were a number of business failures and blocks of houses for rent. The superintendent and treasurer of the street railway company called at the office of the *Free Speech*, to have us urge the colored people again on the street cars. A real estate dealer said to a colored man who returned some property he had been buying on the installment plan: "I see what you 'niggers' are cutting up about. You got off light. We first intend to kill every one of those thirty one 'niggers' in jail, but concluded to let all go but the 'leaders.'" They did let all go to the penitentiary. These so-called rioters have since been tried in the Criminal Court for the conspiracy of defending their property, and are now serving terms of three, eight, and fifteen years each in the Tennessee State prison.

To restore the equilibrium and put a stop to the great financial loss, the next move was to get rid of the *Free Speech*, the disturbing element which kept the waters troubled; which would not let the people forget, and in obedience to whose advice nearly six thousand persons had left the city. In casting about for an excuse, the mob found it in the following editorial which appeared in the *Memphis Free Speech*, May 21, 1892: "Eight negroes lynched at Little Rock, Ark., where the citizens broke into the penitentiary and got their man; three near Anniston, Ala., and one in New Orleans, all on the same charge, the new alarm of assaulting white women and near Clarksville, Ga., for killing a white man. The same program of hanging then shooting bullets into the lifeless bodies was carried out to the letter. Nobody in this section of the country believes the old threadbare lie that negro men rape white women. If Southern white men are not careful they will overreach themselves, and public sentiment will have a reaction. A conclusion will then be reached which will be very damaging to the moral reputation of their women." Commenting on this, *The Daily Commercial* of Wednesday following said: "Those negroes who are attempting to make lynching of individuals of their race a means for arousing the worst passions of their kind, are playing with a dangerous sentiment. The negroes well understand that there is no mercy for the negro rapist, and little patience with his defenders. A negro organ printed in this city in a recent issue published the following atrocious paragraph: 'Nobody in this section believes the old threadbare lie that negro men rape white women. If Southern men are not careful they will overreach themselves and public will have a reaction. A conclusion will be reached which will be very damaging to the moral reputation of their women.' The fact that a black scoundrel is allowed to live and utter such loathsome and repulsive calumnies is a volume of evidence as to the wonderful patience of Southern whites. There are some things the Southern white man will not tolerate, and the intimidation of the foregoing has brought the writer to the very uttermost limit of public patience. We hope we have said enough."

The Evening Scimitar of the same day copied this leading editorial and added this comment: "Patience under such circumstances is not a virtue. If the negroes themselves do not apply the remedy without delay, it will be the duty of those he has attacked, to tie the wretch who utters these calumnies to a stake at the intersection of Main and Madison streets, brand him in the forehead with a hot iron."

Such open suggestions by the leading daily papers of the progressive city of Memphis were acted upon by the leading citizens and a meeting was held at the Cotton Exchange that evening. *The Commercial* two days later had the following account of it:

ATROCIOUS BLACKGUARDISM
There will be no Lynching and no Repetition of the Offense

In its issue of Wednesday *The Commercial* reproduced and commented upon an editorial which appeared a day or two before a negro organ known as the *Free Speech*. The article was so insufferably and indecently slanderous that the whole city awoke to a feeling of intense resentment which came within an ace of culminating in one of those occurrences whose details are so eagerly seized and so prominently published by Northern newspapers. Conservative counsels, however, prevailed, and no extreme measures were resorted to. On Wednesday afternoon a meeting of citizens was held. It was not an assemblage of hoodlums or irresponsible fire eaters, but solid, substantial business men who knew exactly what they were doing and who were far more indignant at the villainous insult to the women of the south than they would have been at any injury done themselves. This meeting appointed a committee to seek the author of the infamous editorial and warn him quietly that upon repetition of the offense, he would find some other part of the country a good deal safer and pleasanter place of residence than this.

The committee called a negro named Nightingale, but he disclaimed responsibility and convinced the gentlemen that he had really sold out his paper to a woman named Wells. This woman is not in Memphis at present. It was finally learned that one Fleming, a negro who was driven out of Crittenden Co. during the trouble there a few years ago, wrote the paragraph. He had, however, heard of the meeting, and fled from a fate he feared was in store for him, and which he knew he deserved. His whereabouts could not be ascertained, and the committee so reported. Later on, a communication from Fleming to a prominent Republican politician, and that politician's reply were shown to one or two gentlemen. The former was an inquiry as to whether the writer might safely return to Memphis, the latter was an emphatic answer in negative, and Fleming is still in hiding. Nothing further will be done in the matter. There will be no lynching, and it is very certain that there will be no repetition of the outrage. If there should be–Friday, May 25.

The only reason there was no lynching of Mr. Fleming who was business manager and half owner of the *Free Speech*, and who did not write the editorials himself because this same white Republican told him the committee was coming and warned him not to trust them, but get out of the way. The committee scoured the city hunting him, and had to be content with Mr. Nightingale who was dragged to the meeting, shamefully abused (although it was known he had sold out his interest in the paper six months before). He was struck in the face and forced at the pistol's point to sign a letter which was written by them, in which he denied all knowledge of the editorial, denounced it and condemned it as slander on white women. I do not censure Mr. Nightingale for his action because, having never been at the pistol's point myself, I do not feel that I am competent to sit in judgment on him, or say what I would do under such circumstances.

I had written that editorial with other matter for the week's paper before leaving home the Friday previous for the General Conference of the A.M.E. Church in Philadelphia. The conference adjourned Tuesday, and Thursday, May 25, at 3 p.m., I landed in New York City for a few days' stay before returning home, and there learned from the papers that my business manager had been driven away and the paper suspended. Telegraphing for news, I received telegrams and letters in return informing me that the trains were being watched, that I was to be dumped into the river and beaten, if not killed; it had been learned that I wrote the editorial and I was to be hanged in front of the court house and my face bled if I returned, and I was implored by my friends to remain away. The creditors attached the office in the meantime and the outfit was sold without more ado, thus destroying effectually that which it had taken years to build. One prominent insurance agent publicly declares he will make it his business to shoot me down on sight if I return to Memphis in twenty years, while a leading white lady had remarked she was opposed to the lynching of those three men in March, but she wished there was some way by which I could be gotten back and lynched.

I have been censured for writing that editorial, but when I think of five men who were lynched that week for assault on white women and that not a week passes but some poor soul is violently ushered into eternity on this trumped up charge, knowing the many things I do, and part of which tried to tell in the *New York Age* of June 25, (and in the pamphlets I have with me) seeing that the whole race in the South was injured in the estimation of the world because of these false reports, I could no longer hold my peace, and I feel, yes, I am sure, that if it had to be done over again (provided no one else was the loser save myself) I would do and say the very same again.

The lawlessness here described is not confined to one locality. In the past ten years over a thousand colored men, women and children have been butchered, murdered and burnt in all parts of the South. The details of these terrible outrages seldom reach beyond the narrow world where they occur. Those who commit the murders write the reports, and hence these blots upon the honor of a nation cause but a faint ripple on the outside world. They arouse no great indignation and call forth no adequate demand for justice. The victims were black, and the reports are so written as to make it appear that the helpless creatures deserved the fate which overtook them.

Not so with the Italian lynching of 1891. They were not black men, and three of them were not citizens of the Republic, but subjects of the King of Italy. The chief of police of New Orleans was shot and eleven Italians arrested and charged with the murder; they were tried and the jury disagreed; the good, law abiding citizens of New Orleans thereupon took them from the jail and lynched them at high noon. A feeling of horror ran through the nation at this outrage. All Europe was amazed. The Italian government demanded thorough investigation and redress, and the Federal Government promised to give the matter the consideration which was its due. The diplomatic relations between the two countries became very much strained and for a while war talk was freely indulged. Here was a case where the power of the Federal Government to protect its own citizens and redeem its pledges to a friendly power was put to the test. When our State Department called upon the authorities of Louisiana for investigation of the crime and punishment of the criminals, the United States government was told that the crime was strictly within the authority of the State of Louisiana, and Louisiana would attend to it. After a farcical investigation, the usual verdict in such cases was rendered: "Death at the hand of parties unknown to the jury," the same verdict which had been pronounced over the bodies of over 1,000 colored persons! Our federal government has thus admitted that it has no jurisdiction over the crimes committed at New Orleans upon citizens of the country, nor upon those citizens of a friendly power to whom the general government and not the State government has pledged protection. Not only has our general government made the confession that one of the states is greater than the Union, but the general government has paid $25,000 of the people's money to the King of Italy for the lynching of those three subjects, the evil doing of one State, over which it has no control, but for whose lawlessness the whole country must pay. The principle involved in the treaty power of the government has not yet been settled to the satisfaction of foreign powers; but the principle involved in the right of State jurisdiction in such matters, was settled long ago by the decision of the United States Supreme Court.

I beg your patience while we look at another phase of the lynching mania. We have turned heretofore to the pages of ancient and medieval history, roman tyranny, the Jesuitical Inquisition of Spain for the spectacle of a human being burnt to death. In the past ten years three instances, at least, have been furnished where men have literally been roasted to death to appease the fury of Southern mobs. The Texarkana instance of last year and Paris, Texas, case of this month are the most recent as they are the most shocking and repulsive. Both were charged with crimes from which the laws provide adequate punishment. The Texarkana man, Ed Coy, was charged with assaulting a white woman. A mob pronounced him guilty, strapped him to a tree, chipped the flesh from his body, poured coal oil over him and the woman in the case set fire to him. The country looked on and in many cases applauded, because it was published that this man had violated the honor of the white woman, although he protested his innocence to the last. Judge Tourjee in the *Chicago Inter Ocean* of recent date says investigation has shown that Ed Coy had supported this woman (who was known to be a bad character) and her drunken husband for over a year previous to the burning.

The Paris, Texas, burning of Henry Smith, February 1st, has exceeded the others in its horrible details. The man was drawn through the streets on a float, as the Roman generals used to parade their trophies of war, while scaffold ten feet high, was being built, and irons were heated in the fire. He was bound on it, and red-hot irons began at his feet and slowly branded his body while the mob howled with delight at his shrieks. Red hot irons were run down his throat and cooked his tongue; his eyes were burned out, when he was at last unconscious, cotton seed hulls were placed under him, coal oil poured all over him, and a torch applied to the mass. When the flames burned away the ropes which bound Smith and scorched his flesh he was brought back to sensibility and burned and maimed and as he was, he rolled off the platform and away from the fire. His half-cooked body was seized and trampled and thrown back into the flames while a mob of twenty thousand persons who came from all over the country howled with delight, and gathered up some buttons and ashes after all was over to preserve for relics. The man was charged with outraging and murdering a four year old white child, covering her body with brush, sleeping beside the body through the night, then making his escape. If true, it was the deed of a mad-man, and should have been clearly proven so. The fact that no time for verification of the newspaper reports was given, is suspicious, especially when I remember that a negro was lynched in Indianola, Sharkey Co., Miss. last summer. The dispatches said it was because he had assaulted the sheriff's eight year old daughter. The girl was more than eighteen years old and was found by her father in this man's room, who was a servant on the place.

These incidents have been made the basis of this terrible story, they overshadow all others of a like nature in cruelty and represent the legal phases of the whole question. They could be multiplied without number and each outrival the other in the fiendish cruelty exercised, and the frequent awful lawlessness exhibited. The following table shows the number of men lynched from January 1, 1882, to January 1, 1892: In 1882, 52; 1883, 39; 1884, 53; 1885, 77; 1886, 73; 1887, 70; 1888, 72; 1889, 95; 1890, 100; 1891, 169. Of these 728 black men who were murdered, 269 were charged with rape, 253 with murder, 44 with robbery, 37 with incendiarism, 32 with reasons unstated (it was not necessary to have a reason), 27 with race prejudice, 13 with quarreling with white men, 10 with making threats, 7 with rioting, 5 with miscegenation, 4 with burglary. One of the men lynched in 1891 was Will Lewis, who was lynched because "he was drunk and saucy to white folks." A woman who was one of the 73 victims in 1886, was hung in Jackson, Tenn., because the white woman for whom she cooked, died suddenly of poisoning. An examination showed arsenical poisoning. A search in the cook's room found rat poison. She was thrown into jail, and when the mob had worked itself up to the lynching pitch, she was dragged out, every stitch of clothing torn from her body, and was hung in the public court house square in sight of everybody. That white woman's husband has since died in the insane asylum, a raving maniac, and his ravings have led to the conclusion that he and not the cook, was the poisoner of his wife. A fifteen year old colored girl was lynched last spring, at Rayville, La., on the same charge of poisoning. A woman was also lynched at Hollendale, Miss. last spring, charged with being an accomplice in the murder of her paramour who had abused her. These were only two of the 159 persons lynched in the South from January 1, 1892, to January 1, 1893. Over a dozen black men have been lynched already since this new year set in, not yet two months old.

It will thus be seen that neither age, sex nor decency are spared. Although the impression has gone abroad that most of the lynchings take place because of assaults on white women only one third of the number lynched in the past ten years have been charged with that offense, to say nothing of those who were not guilty of the charge. And according to law none of them until proven so. But the unsupported word of any white person for any cause is sufficient to cause a lynching. So bold have the lynchers become masks are laid aside, the temples of justice and strongholds of law are invaded in broad daylight and prisoners taken out and lynched, while governors of states and officers of law stand by and see the work well done.

And yet this Christian nation, the flower of the nineteenth century civilization says it can do nothing to stop this inhuman slaughter. The general government is willingly powerless to send troops to protect the lives of its black citizens, but the state governments are free to use state troops to shoot them down like cattle, when in desperation the black men attempt to defend themselves, and then tell the world that it was necessary to put down a "race war."

Persons unfamiliar with the condition of affairs in the Southern States do not credit the truth when it is told them. They cannot conceive how such a condition of affairs prevails so near them with steam power, telegraph wires, and printing presses in daily and hourly touch with the localities where such disorder reigns. In a former generation the ancestors of these same people refused to believe that slavery was the "league with death and the covenant with hell." William Lloyd Garrison declared it to be, until he was thrown into a dungeon in Baltimore, until the signal lights of Nat Turner's lit the dull skies of Northampton County, and until sturdy old John Brown made his attack on Harper's Ferry. When freedom of speech was martyred in the person of Elijah Lovejoy at Alton, when the liberty of free discussion in Senate in the Nation's Congress was struck down in the person of the fearless Charles Sumner, the Nation was at last convinced that slavery was not only a monster by a tyrant. That same tyrant is at work under a new name and guise. The lawlessness which has been here described is like unto that which prevailed under slavery. *The very same forces are at work now as then.*

The attempt is being made to subject to a condition of civil and industrial independence, those whom the Constitution declares to be free men. The events which have led up to the present wide spread lawlessness in the South can be traced to the very first year Lee's conquered veterans marched from Appomattox to their homes in the Southland. They were conquered in war, but not in spirit. They believed as firmly as ever that it was their right to rule black men and dictate to the National Government. The Knights of White Liners, and the Ku Klux Klan were composed of veterans of the army who were determined to destroy the effect of all the slave had gained by the war. They finally accomplished their purpose in 1876. The right of the Afro-American to vote and hold office remains in the Federal Constitution, but is destroyed in the constitution of the Southern states. Having destroyed the citizenship of the man, they are now trying to destroy the manhood of the citizen. All their laws are shaped to this end,—school laws railroad car regulations, those governing labor liens on crops, every device is adopted to make slaves of free men and rob them of their wages. Whenever a malicious law is violated in any of its parts, any farmer, any railroad conductor, or merchant can call together a posse of his neighbors and punish even with death the black man who resists and the legal authorities sanction what is done by failing to prosecute and punish the murders. The Repeal of the Civil Rights Law removed their last barrier and the black man's last bulwark and refuge. The rule of the mob is absolute.

Those who know this recital to be true, say there is nothing they can do, they cannot interfere and vainly hope by further concession to placate the imperious and dominating part of our country in which this lawlessness prevails. Because this country has been almost rent in twain by internal dissension, the other sections seem virtually to have agreed that the best way to heal the breach is to permit the taking away of civil, political, and even human rights, to stand by in silence and utter indifference while the South continues to wreak fiendish vengeance on the irresponsible cause. They pretend to believe that with all the machinery of law and government in its hands; with the jails and penitentiaries and convict farms filled with pretty race criminals; with the well-known fact that no negro has ever been known to escape conviction and punishment for any crime in the South—still there are those who try to justify and condone the lynching of over a thousand black men in less than ten years an average of one hundred a year. The public sentiment of the country, by its silence in press, pulpit and in public meetings has encouraged this state of affairs, and public sentiment is stronger than law. With all this country's disposition to condone and temporize with the South and its methods; with its many instances of sacrificing principles to prejudice for the sake of making friends and healing the breach made by the late war; of going into the lawless country with capital to build up its waste places and remaining silent in the presence of outrage and wrong, the South is as vindictive and bitter as ever. She is willing to make friends as long as she is permitted to pursue unmolested and uncensored, her course of proscription, injustice, outrage and vituperation. The malignant misrepresentation of General Butler, the uniformly indecent and abusive assault of this dead man whose only crime was a defence of his country, is a recent proof that the South has lost none of its bitterness. The *Nashville American*, one of the leading papers of one of the leading southern cities, gleefully announced editorially that "'The Beast is dead.' Early yesterday morning, acting under the devil's orders, the angel of Death took Ben Butler and landed him in the lowest depths of hell, and we pity even the devil the possession has secured." The men who wrote these editorials are without exception young men who know nothing of slavery and scarcely anything of the war. The bitterness and hatred have been instilled in and taught them by their parents, and they are men who make and reflect the sentiment of their section. The South spares nobody else's feelings, and it seems a queer logic that when it comes to a question of right, involving lives of citizens and the honor of the government, the South's feelings must be respected and spared.

Do you ask the remedy? A public sentiment strong against lawlessness must be aroused. Every individual can contribute to this awakening. When a sentiment against lynch law as strong, deep and mighty as that roused by slavery prevails, I have no fear of the result. It should be already established as a fact and not as a theory, that every human being must have a fair trial for his life and liberty, no matter what the charge against him. When a demand goes up from fearless and persistent reformers from press and pulpit, from industrial and moral associations that this shall be so from Maine to Texas and from ocean to ocean, a way will be found to make it so.

In deference to the few words of condemnation uttered at the M.E. General conference last year, and by other organizations, Governors Hogg of Texas, Northern of Georgia, and Tillman of South Carolina, have issued proclamations offering rewards for the apprehension of lynchers. These rewards have never been claimed, and these governors knew they would not be when offered. In many cases they knew the ringleaders of the mobs. The prosecuting attorney of Shelby County, Tenn., wrote Governor Buchanan to offer a reward for the arrest of the lynchers of three young men murdered in Memphis. Everybody in that city and state knew well that the letter was written for the sake of effect and the governor did not even offer the reward. But the country at large deluded itself with the belief that the officials of the South and the leading citizens condemned lynching. The lynchings go on in spite of offered rewards, and in face of Governor Hogg's vigorous talk, the second man was burnt alive in his state with the utmost deliberation and publicity. Since he sent a message to the legislature the mob found and hung Henry Smith's stepson, because he refused to tell where Smith was when they were hunting for him. Public sentiment which shall denounce these crimes in season and out; public sentiment which turns capital and immigration from a section given over to lawlessness; public sentiment which insists on the punishment of criminals and lynchers by law must be aroused.

It is no wonder in my mind that the party which stood for their years as the champion of human liberty and human rights, the part of great moral ideas should suffer overwhelming defeat when it has proven recreant to its professions and abandoned a position it created; when although its followers were being outraged in every sense, it was afraid to stand for the right, and appeal to the American people to sustain them in it. It put aside the question of a free ballot and fair count of every citizen and give its voice and influence for the protection of the coat instead of the man who wore it, for the product of labor instead of the laborer; for the seal of citizenship rather than the citizen, and insisted upon the evils of free trade instead of the sacredness of speech. I am no politician but I believe if the Republican party had met issues squarely for human rights instead of the tariff it would have occupied a different position today. The voice of the people is the voice of God, I long with all the intensity of my soul for the Garrison, Douglass,

Sumner, Whittier, and Phillips who shall rouse this nation to a demand that from Greenland's icy mountains to the coral reefs of the Southern seas, mob rule shall be put down and equal and exact justice be accorded to every citizen of whatever race, who finds a home within the borders of the land of the free and the home of the brave.

Then no longer will our national hymn be sounding brass and a tinkling cymbal, but every member of this great composite nation will be a living, harmonious illustration of the words, and all can honestly and gladly join in singing:

> *My country! 'tis of thee,*
> *Sweet land of liberty*
> *Of thee I sing.*
> *Land where our fathers died,*
> *Land of the Pilgrim's pride,*
> *From every mountain side*
> *Freedom does ring.*

QUESTIONS

(1) What were some of the actions that blacks needed to take so as to address the lynching of blacks in the South?

(2) Among the examples of blacks that were lynched, several lynchings involved black women? What were some of the reasons that black women were lynched?

(3) Wells compares the Italian lynching of 1881 in New Orleans and the numerous lynching of blacks. Why?

(4) There were rarely any whites that were horrified by the lynching of blacks. Why was this the case?

(5) Why was the lynching of blacks not considered a crime? Was lynching another form that racism took?

PART V
Feminism and Difference

SHERROW O. PINDER

. . . .

Feminism has a long history of challenging the unequal position of women in society. Some feminists have focused on ending sexism at the expense of other systems of oppression such as classism and racism. Others have focused more specifically on the definition of the category "woman" arguing that the naturalized concept of "woman" in fact means "white woman." As Audre Lorde in *Sister Outsider* tells us, black women "stand outside the circle of this society definition of acceptable women" and are "forged into the crucible of difference."[1] Black feminists have thus reimagined the category "women" in order to include black women and draw attention to the fact that the lived experience of black women can only be analyzed within an epistemological framework that takes into account black women's daily lives as racialized women subject to unjust treatment. As Lorde perfectly sums it up, for black women "survival is not an academic skill. It is learning how to take our differences and make them strengths."[2] Following Lorde's suggestion, "to take our differences and make them strengths," this section, "Feminism and Difference" focuses on the writings of Mary Church Terrell, Patricia Hill Collins, and Gary L. Lemons. These scholars address in various ways the "woman question" from a black feminist perspective, which destabilizes and undermines a feminist analysis that focuses primarily on gender oppression. They recognize the necessity to promote a black feminist framework as a reasonable project for the advancement of greater equality between the sexes and justice for all people. In the face of global challenges such as the internationalization of the state and the international division of

---

[1] Audre Lorde, *Sister Outsider: Essays and Speeches* (New York: Crossing Press, 2007), p. 112.
[2] Ibid.

labor that are impacting black women in the United States, the need for a black feminist global agenda is more urgent than ever.

Mary Church Terrell and Black Women's Struggles

It is important to recognize why and how black feminists entered the debate of "acceptable woman." Mary Church Terrell, an 1884 Oberlin college graduate, wrote insightfully and revealingly in her article "The Progress of Colored Women," first delivered at the American National Women's Suffrage Association convention on February 18, 1898, by offering some precise ways in which black women, through radical emancipatory praxis, tried hard to gain some recognition as women. She stresses black women's never-ending process of self-improvement and their targeted actions on working to educate and elevate all blacks. Terrell, perhaps more so than any other black feminist then or now, has helped to rethink and problematize black women's fight for the rights to be accepted as women, with "little hope to escape" what Terrell calls the "race of womanhood." Being a black woman, where race is an overdetermined factor of gender positioning, reopens the existential question: "Ain't I a Woman?"[3] that perpetually confronts black women. Indeed, ambitious black women who are marked off as different and are trying to make a difference "with ambition and aspiration," in Terrell's words, must undergo the hardship of race and gender amalgamation. Indeed, for black women, gender does not exist on its own "other than grammatically in language."[4] And since there is a reference to language, one of the concerns, then, is whether an alternative language can be developed to discuss and work through the complexity of black women's positioning as outside of acceptable womanhood.[5] More importantly, the multifaceted situation of a black woman is that she is not only the "other" of

---

[3] "Ain't I a Woman" is a famous speech given by the slave Sojourner Truth at the Women's Convention in Akron, Ohio, on May 29, 1851. It was transcribed by a white abolitionist. For a different interpretation of Truth's speech, see Nell Irvin Painter, *Sojourner Truth: A Life, A Symbol* (New York: W. W. Norton, 1997). The *Feminist Review* in the autumn of 1984, devoted an issue, "Many Voices, One Chant: Black Feminist Perspectives," to the question of who is a woman in the likelihood of inciting future discussions and debates on black women's experiences through the intersectionality of race, gender, class, and sexuality. Black and other feminists of color have indeed focused on intersectionality. See Avtar Brah and Ann Phoenix, "Ain't I a Woman? Revisiting Intersectionality," *Journal of International Women's Studies* 5 no. 3 (2004): 75–86; and bell hooks, *Ain't I a Woman: Black Women and Feminism* (Boston: South End, 1981).

[4] Sherrow O. Pinder, *Colorblindness, Post-Raciality, and Whiteness in the United States* (New York: Palgrave Macmillan, 2015), p. 101.

[5] For a more comprehensive reading on the detriments of true womanhood and its consequences for black women, see Hazel Carby, *Reconstructing Womanhood: The Emergence of the Afro-American Woman Novelist* (Oxford University Press, 1987).

the same (woman), but when placed outside of the same, she is the other of the "other."[6]

Terrell analyzes black women's position in history by drawing on the racialized functionality of gender as that which excludes and makes invisible their concerns. The historical-political discourse of recognizable women according to which black women stand nowhere, somewhere as nothing, everything, and anything outside of the reach of the historical determination of who a woman is, highlights an unjust picture of the ills of being a black woman that she had to and continues to endure. It is often forgotten that even though many black women have sacrificed their lives to their race, "amid surroundings and in the face of privations which only martyrs can tolerate and bear," as Terrell contends, the actions of these women are not recorded in history. Nonetheless, Terrell reminds us that black women's ontological vocation to be fully constituted women subject has left its mark in the fields of medicine, business, the arts, and literature, a fact which singlehandedly refuses and destroys the myth of black women's inferiority.

In addition, it would come as no surprise the many ways in which black women, according to Terrell, "knock[ed] at the bar of justice, asking an equal chance," in a world where liberal values of social justice, democracy, and equality were, from the start, allotted only to white men equipped with autonomy to *will* their own desires and enjoy the full benefits of the American creed of "life, liberty, and the pursuits of happiness." There is something to this. White men were allowed to exercise their rights of citizenship by, for example, entering into a social contract with other men of their class and race. Carol Pateman's *Sexual Contract* draws our attention to the hidden male alliance on which the apparent gender-neutrality of the social contract in fact relies. Pateman further extends the sexual contract to the marriage contract. It cannot be missed that within the marriage contract, the contractual agents (men and women) are unequal subjects from the start.[7] In a word, women are subordinate to men and relegated to the private sphere of domestic labor where their autonomy, for the most part, is tied to being wives and mothers.

It is no wonder that historically white women's continuous fight to be equal to white men propelled them to establish and build many women's organizations. However, black women, because of their race, were excluded from these organizations. It meant that black women had to form their own organizations, looking for no favors because of their race, nor "patronage because of their needs," according to Terrell. Black women became members of the newly formed National Association of Colored Women in which, as Terrell points out, black women were

---

[6] Pinder, *Colorblindness*, p. 101.

[7] Carol Pateman, *The Sexual Contract* (Stanford University Press, 1988). Also, see Sherrow O. Pinder, *Black Women, Work, and Welfare in the Age of Globalization* (Lexington Books, 2018), p. 124.

a medium for the improvement of the conditions of black women and all blacks. To be sure, black women motivated the black communities in the struggle for race equality. Given the naturalizing and totalizing of white supremacy that took on a differentiation of gender norms, situating black women as this inessential "other thing," aggressive, unrestrained, promiscuous, hypersexual, immoral, barbaric, abnormal, and uncivilized regardless of other identity markers such as class, sexuality, and disability, Terrell provides us with an account of black women's history of invisibility and exclusion from the category "woman."

White women were positioned as "natural" women, with an innate nature, and easily recognizable. Although problematic as this naturalness was, black women were and continue to be denaturalized. An account of the history of the United States points to the fact that black women such as Anna J. Cooper, Harriet Ann Jacobs, Marie Stewart, Mary Church Terrell, and Ida B. Wells were very much concerned with the "woman" question of acceptable womanhood and this is still a prevailing concern for black women today. In fact, more recently, in 2015, when the queen of soul, Aretha Franklin, sang at the Kennedy Center Honors, "you make me feel like a natural woman,"[8] she took to task the notion of "natural woman" and drew attention to the denaturalization of black women. Terrell, in many important ways, accounts for black women's positioning outside of "natural womanhood." And while the "race of womanhood" is indeed important for a black feminist analysis, according to Patricia Hill Collins, "the basic challenge of accommodating diversity among black women," which, for the most part, is unacknowledged within feminist discourse, is also paramount. Nonetheless, how to account for black women's inequality remains important for black feminists.

Patricia Hill Collins and Black Feminist Thought

Given the history of race in the United States, the fact of being a white woman means that she is positioned inside normalized whiteness. Hence, white women, for the most part, have accepted America's longstanding racist discourse, epistemology, ethic, and ideology that uphold whiteness as the norm. Patricia Hill Collins, in her article "WHAT's In A NAME? Womanism, Black Feminism and Beyond," is concerned with how to account for black women's unequal positions in society and whether Black Feminism or womanism is a useful framework for such an analysis. And while this is essential, Collins helps us to see that there are certain practices that discursively and nondiscursively constitute, reconstitute, deconstitute, and enable black women's situatedness. Collins, in part, takes to task the racism of

---

[8] "You Make Me Feel Like a Natural Woman," is the title of a song that was co-written by Carole King and Gerry Goffin and released on Aretha Franklin's 1967 album, *Lady Soul*.

white women. Indeed, a closer look at Collins' ubiquitous concern points to the fact that segregated institutions of all types, including feminist organizations, did not worry white women. For sure, many feminist organizations have worked hard to exclude black women's issues such as racism and classism from their struggles for the equality of the sexes. Collins draws our attention to the limited feminist agenda that considered gender oppression as the overarching issue put forward by white women, which prevailed in the early 1970s. And since black women's issues continued to be disregarded within feminist discourses and the women's movement, it is no wonder that many black women became displeased with feminism. As Collins suggests, some black women distanced themselves from feminism and openly challenged the racism within white feminist organizations. There remains, however, in the United States the assumption, as Gary L. Lemons succinctly puts it, that feminism "is a white woman's thing" and, as Collins acknowledges, "the cultural property of white women."

In order to reconfigure the many ways in which black women's oppression is a part of race, gender, and class intersectionality, a term that has been recently introduced into the hermeneutics of black women's experience of discrimination, it is not surprising, then, as the 1977 Combahee River Collective Statement composed by black lesbian writers Cheryl Clarke, Audre Lorde, Barbara Smith, and Beverly Smith would make clear, that black feminist politics has "an obvious connection to movements for black liberation"[9] and would incorporate, for example, some of the ideologies of the Civil Rights Movement, the Black Panther Party, and, as Collins acknowledges, Black Nationalism into its discourse. And even though Collins limits her definition of Black Nationalism as a philosophy that is "organized around the centrality of racial solidarity for black survival" from a system that promotes and upholds white supremacy, she reckons that most whites have a vested interest in sustaining white supremacy. Precisely, for this reason, Black Nationalists would see "little use for black integration or assimilation into a system predicated on black subjugation." Given that white women are a part of the dominant group, black feminists influenced by Black Nationalist philosophy would logically see white women as a part of the problem and express little interest in working with them.

Collins shows how using the term "Black Feminism" dislocates the racism inherent in feminism as "a for-whites-only ideology and political movement." "Inserting the adjective 'black,'" Collins concludes, contests the implicit whiteness of feminism and unsettles the universalism of this term for both white and black women. Partly for this reason, for Collins, Black Feminism "must come to terms with a white feminist agenda incapable of seeing its own racism as well as a black

---

[9] Combahee River Collective, "Combahee River Collective Statement," in *Home Girls: A Black Feminist Anthology*, ed. Barbara Smith (New York: Kitchen Table, Women of Color Press, 1983), p. 273.

nationalist one resistant to grappling with its own sexism." In fact, Collins' antecedent, the Combahee River Collective, points to "a need to develop a politics that was anti-racist unlike those of white women, and anti-sexist, unlike those of black and white men."[10] That said, black feminist criticisms of sexism and misogyny in black communities conjure up ideas that black women are against black men, an expression of *The Color Purple* syndrome that has its roots in many black men's thinking that the book has done nothing but to reinforce negative stereotypes of black men. In fact, Black Feminism is not about "black male bashing," as Collins discusses and explains. It is about black women challenging the reality of a patriarchy "acted out by black men," she insists.

For black feminists, "black" and "feminist," in their somewhat dialectical disunity, incite the existential question: "Are you 'black' first or 'feminist'?" Black feminists, according to Collins, thus find themselves "walking a race/gender tightrope always having to negotiate a position of split allegiance." While this tension between "black" and "feminist" cannot be resolved easily, in most black communities, Black Feminism has been mistakenly equated with a betrayal of race solidarity. No one would argue against the importance for blacks to "act together" through a network of solidarity to fight racism and its multidimensional forms of discriminatory epistemology and practices. However, it is also important for the analytics of blacks' oppression to take into consideration how black women are positioned as racialized gendered bodies. In addition, black feminist discourse, as Collins warns us, unsettles an established and fundamentally accepted support for black racial solidarity "as a deep tap root in black political philosophies," especially Black Nationalism that is nonetheless important for shaping black political thought.

It is this kind of discursive analysis that inspired us to recognize that black women "stand at a different historical moment," as Collins explains it, in which it is paramount to talk about the injustices that black women experience and how this can allow "differences among black women structured along axes of sexuality, social class, nationality, religion, and region to emerge," which, nonetheless, are fashioned into "a dynamic black women's self-defined standpoint" and whether it should be named womanism or Black Feminism.

Given that womanism is a complex concept that accounts for the multiplicities of black women's positioning, this would explain, in part, why some black women prefer the term womanism to feminism. According to Collins, Alice Walker proposes that black women's distinct history of marginality based on race, gender, and class amalgamation upholds a womanist worldview reachable predominantly and possibly only by black women. In other words, black women's location equips them with an "other" kind of black feminist epistemology, a "second sight," an additional way of seeing that "re-sees"—that is, sees again otherwise, and represents

---

[10] Ibid.

an unusual privilege of the underprivileged (black women) that is inaccessible to white women.

Encountering Walker's text on womanism, in its seemingly benign context, is somewhat unsettling for Collins and induces a disquieting reaction because womanism, for Collins, incorporates some of the ideologies of Black Nationalism, which Collins is, somewhat, sensitive to. Furthermore, for Collins, womanism circumnavigates an issue essential to many white feminists, specifically, "finding ways to foster interracial cooperation among women." In other words, Collins postulates that womanism avoids issues fundamental to many white feminists. In this sense, she insists on the necessity for gender plurality and finding ways to foster fundamental ground rules for black women and white women to relate across gender, class, ethnic, sexuality, disability, and other differences; especially at a time when there is an acceleration of women's global poverty, lack of educational opportunities for poor women, environmental racism, Islamophobia, xenophobia, and industrial development that enhance the goals of the rich and powerful. Interestingly, these concerns have brought together feminists of various schools of thought. Suffice to say, nonetheless, that Collins draws our attention to the fact that womanism is different from feminism. However, by analyzing womanism, she opens up another possibility and other ways for black women's issues to be at the forefront of a black feminist analysis. Indeed, any progressive feminist perspective has to take into account the intricate and synchronizing effects of racism with other modes of discrimination—sexism, classism, sexual orientation, disability, and speech and language impairments impacting black women and black communities as a whole, which have shaped and continue to inform Black Feminism. For Gary L. Lemons, Black Feminism should not be limited to black women. It is important for black men to take on black feminists' goals of justice and equality for all people.

Gary L. Lemons: Womanist Consciousness

The evolution of Gary L. Lemons' work, "To Be Black, Male, and 'Feminist' – Making Womanist Space for Black Men," is illustrative of the inevitability of a black feminist analysis of why and how black women are positioned as unequal citizens in society and points to the necessity for Black Feminism not to be restricted to black women. Indeed, if black men are to resist "racist and sexist mythology of their manhood and masculinity," it is important for black feminists to craft what Lemons refers to as a "womanist space" where black men can oppose sexism and act to end the oppression of women.

In relation to black women's situatedness, we cannot simplify that which history has made complex. Indeed, the topographical claim of womanism has its own genealogy. It is rooted in black women's concrete history of marginalization. Black women's lived experience, as feminist and critical race theorist Gary L. Lemons puts it, is "a political (inter)relation of racism and sexism," a form of racism and sexism that attentively interlock and combine under certain conditions into one hybrid phenomenal exercise, a paradigm for forging a "womanist" solidarity that includes black men, which, for Lemons, would take into consideration "black male commitment to a liberatory movement rooted in struggle against racism and sexism" and other forms of oppressive practices. Lemons distinguishes between black women's historical responses to the amalgamation of race, gender, and class oppression as being womanist, and using womanism "as a visionary term delineating an ethical or ideal vision of humanity for all people" that would embrace a posthuman discourse, which, in spite of this discourse producing, to borrow from the feminist Rosi Braidotti's *The Posthuman* "its own form of inhumanity"[11] is, however, another way to rethink and reconceive the category of the human in a field of arbitrary power in the Foucauldian sense. Given that the human was conceptualized as white and male, the "man" of reason with access to rights and entitlement in Western modernity, blacks, from the start, were and continued to be outside of the category of the human. More recently, the Black Lives Matter movement surfaced to protest state-sanctioned violence perpetrated against blacks because blackness is viewed as a liability.

Walker's much cited work, together with Lemons' discussion of a womanist consciousness used to craft a feminist space that includes black men, and Collins' black feminist thought that helps us unpack the hegemonic discourse of first- and second-wave feminism, provide us with tools to think differently about gender inequality. While the textual kinship of Collins and Lemons is clear, Lemons draws on Walker's "womanist" insight, and like Collins, shows that womanism and Black Feminism proliferate and overlap on issues that are important to black women and should be of importance to all members of a democratic polity. In fact, "the womanism/Black Feminism debate" that situates the historicity of black women's unequal position can carve out a feminist space that would focus on constructing and building a community to think differences and be in opposition to sameness or to operate, in Collins' words, "via heterogeneity and not sameness." In the face of neoliberal austerity measures that continue to accelerate and make precarious the human condition for poor people, especially poor black women, this is more significant than ever.

The womanist continuum, as Lemons sees it, is "committed to survival and wholeness of entire people, male and female" notwithstanding their sexual orientation; as Collins points out, a womanist is also "a woman who loves other women, sexually and/or nonsexually." In arenas of institutionalized power, womanism is the starting point for a womanist epistemology to expand and recognize the claims

---

[11] Rosi Braidotti, *The Posthuman* (Cambridge: Polity Press, 2013), p. 2.

of all marginalized groups – blacks and other racialized ethnic groups, women, the disabled, the LGBTQ community, the poor, people who are speech and language impaired, immigrants both documented and undocumented, and refugees. While as Collins says, black women may "define themselves as black feminists, as womanists, as both, or, in some cases, as neither," in the end, womanism provides varied ways for black women to address the synchronicity of race, gender, class, and sexual discriminatory practice and to include black men in the struggle.

Lemons sees womanism as providing a space where black men "can work to empower themselves in feminist solidarity—working in the tradition and spirit of their womanist legacy, and to go beyond such traditions," which would be "a liberatory location for remaking black manhood toward a male identity that transgresses the boundaries of patriarchy." In fact, black men taking on a feminist consciousness indicates an essential withdrawal from "the racist/sexist ideology of black manhood/masculinity" that has held sway among many black men. Lemons' reminder of some black men's historical relations to feminist issues – men such as Frederick Douglass and W. E. B. Du Bois – is valuable. Lemons' emphasis of the need for a continuous "political space for black men 'in' feminism grounded in the history of the fight African-Americans waged for race and gender rights" is welcome in this context.

Both womanists and black feminists have served well in helping us conceptualize how race as a signifier is pegged to other markers such as gender, sexuality, disability, and class in determining black women's marginalized relationships within any feminist discourse that privileges a certain kind of experience and makes invisible and marginalized other experiences and concerns that are important to black women. To correct this, a move toward reestablishing a pedagogical space, which would take into consideration what Lemons defines as a "pedagogical strategy rooted in the politics of progressive feminist movement against all forms of domination, where teachers committed to coalition building cross race, gender, class, and sexual borders teach students ways to oppose the dehumanization of all people," is a good starting point. It would draw on a "liberatory vision of education" put forward by bell hooks, as Lemons recognizes, that would seek out, in Collins' words, "varying expressions in different regions of the world and among diverse populations," which would include migrant workers, refugees, the homeless, the dispossessed, and the LGBTQ community.

Conclusion

Difference within the category of woman continues to be at the forefront of feminist discourse. In fact, today's identity category "woman" is also extended to that of transwomen. However, whiteness has bestowed upon white women many unearned privileges that gives their experience a privileged ontological status and a guarantee of power to define and shape what feminist concerns should be and guide the development of feminist goals. In the face of an accelerating neoliberal governmental agenda and the rise of illiberal governance, if progressive feminist social bonds amongst black and white women are to be conceptualized, feminism itself must be continuously opened to resignification so that the category of woman can be expanded to include black women's experience of inequality. As a starting point, white women would have to unlearn their white privilege and, following Lorde's words, "seek a world in which we can all flourish."[12] But "we," this provisional "we," are not one in the same feminist struggle for a just society. In fact, embracing difference is not about reducing differences amongst women to an absolute indifference. We as feminists may have to learn how "to take our differences and make them our strengths"[13]—perhaps an impossible task. Ultimately, we would have to redefine the category of the woman in a way that does not privilege white women.

QUESTIONS

(1) What are some of the ways in which Terrell, Collins, and Lemons address the lived experience of black women?

(2) Why is it important to make use of an intersectionality framework to analyze the lived experience of black women?

(3) What are some of the ways in which issues that are important to black women can be addressed?

(4) In thinking about feminism, why did the first- and second-wave feminists focus on gender oppression?

(5) What are some of the great challenges for feminism today?

FURTHER READINGS

- Angela Davis, *Women, Race, & Class* (New York: Random House, 1983).
- Anna Julia Cooper, "Women's Cause Is One and Universal." Speech delivered at the World's Congress of Representative Women, 1893. Available at: www.blackpast .org/1893-anna-julia-cooper-womens-cause-one-and-universal.
- Barbara Smith (ed.), *Home Girls: A Black Feminist Anthology* (New Brunswick, NJ: Rutgers University Press, 2002).
- bell hooks, *Black Looks: Race and Representation* (New York: Routledge, 2014).
- Cheryl I. Harris, "Finding Sojourner's Truth: Race, Gender, and the Institution of Property," *Cardozo Law Review* 18, no. 2 (1996): 309–410.
- Elsa Barkley Brown, "'What Happened Here?': The Politics of Difference in Women's History and Feminist Politics," *Feminist Studies* 18 (1992): 295–312.

---

[12] Lorde, *Sister Outsider*, p. 112.
[13] Ibid.

- Evelynn Hammonds, "Black (W)holes and the Geometry of Black Female Sexuality," *Differences: A Journal of Feminist Cultural Studies* 6, no. 2–3 (1994): 126–145.
- Jacquelyn Grant, "Black Theology and the Black Woman," in *Words of Fire: An Anthology of African American Feminist Thought*, ed. Beverly Guy-Sheftal (New York: New Press, 1995), pp. 320–336.
- Kimberlé Crenshaw, "Demarginalizing the Intersection of Race and Sex: A Black Feminist Critique of Antidiscrimination Doctrine, Feminist Theory and Antiracist Politics," *University of Chicago Law Forum* 140 (1989): 139–167.
- Stanlie M. James and Abena P. A. Busia, *Theorizing Black Feminisms: The Visionary Pragmatism of Black Women* (New York: Routledge, 1993).

15 The Progress of Colored Women

MARY CHURCH TERRELL

Mary Church Terrell (1863–1954), a writer, educator, and activist, was born in Memphis, Tennessee. She attended Oberlin College and earned her BA in 1884 and MA in 1888. She was the first African American woman to earn a degree. Terrell started her career as a teacher at a black secondary school in Washington, DC and then at Wilberforce College. She went on to study in Europe for two years and became fluent in French, German, and Italian. She returned to teaching at the M Street High School and later on became the principal. In 1896, she was the president of the National Association of Colored Women and was also an active member of the National American Woman Suffrage Association. With Josephine St. Pierre Ruffin, she formed the Federation of Afro-American Women. She published several articles stressing the need for blacks' and black women's equality. In 1909, Terrell was invited to speak at the International Congress of Women held in Berlin, Germany. The article, "The Progress of Colored Women," reproduced below, was presented at the American National Women's Suffrage Association convention held at the Columbia Theatre in Washington, DC on February 18, 1898. Terrell, in her talk, points to the many challenges that black women face, which can, in part, be dealt with through education and religious faith.

Fifty years ago a meeting such as this, planned, conducted and addressed by women would have been an impossibility. Less than forty years ago, few sane men would have predicted that either a slave or one of his descendants would in this century at least, address such an audience in the Nation's Capital at the invitation of women representing the highest, broadest, best type of womanhood, that can be found anywhere in the world.

Thus to me this semi-centennial of the National American Woman Suffrage Association is a double jubilee, rejoicing as I do, not only in the prospective enfranchisement of my sex but in the emancipation of my race. When Ernestine Rose, Lucretia Mott, Elizabeth Cady Stanton, Lucy Stone and Susan B. Anthony began that agitation by which colleges were opened to women and the numerous reforms inaugurated for the amelioration of their condition along all lines, their sisters who groaned in bondage had little reason to hope that these blessings would ever brighten their crushed and blighted lives, for during those days of oppression and despair, colored women were not only refused admittance to institutions of learning, but the law of the States in which the majority lived made it a crime to teach them to read. Not only could they possess no property, but even their bodies were not their own. Nothing, in short, that could degrade or brutalize the womanhood of the race was lacking in that system from which colored women then had little hope of escape. So gloomy were their prospects, so fatal the laws, so pernicious the customs, only fifty years ago.

But, from the day their fetters were broken and their minds released from the darkness of ignorance to which for more than two hundred years they had been doomed, from the day they could stand erect in the dignity of womanhood, no longer bond but free, till tonight, colored women have forged steadily ahead in the acquisition of knowledge and in the cultivation of those virtues which make for good. To use a thought of the illustrious Frederick Douglass, if judged by the depths from which they have come, rather than by the heights to which those blessed with centuries of opportunities have attained, colored women need not hang their heads in shame.

Consider if you will, the almost insurmountable obstacles which have confronted colored women in their efforts to educate and cultivate themselves since their emancipation, and I dare assert, not boastfully, but with pardonable pride, I hope, that the progress they have made and the work they have accomplished, will bear a favorable comparison at least with that of their more fortunate sisters, from whom the opportunity of acquiring knowledge and the means of self-culture have never been entirely withheld. For, not only are colored women with ambition and aspiration handicapped on account of their sex, but they are everywhere baffled and mocked on account of their race. Desperately and continuously they are forced to fight that opposition, born of a cruel, unreasonable prejudice which neither their merit nor their necessity seems able to subdue. Not only because they are women, but because they are colored women, are discouragement and disappointment meeting them at every turn.

Avocations opened and opportunities offered to their more favored sisters have been and are tonight closed and barred against them. While those of the dominant race have a variety of trades and pursuits from which they may choose, the woman through whose veins one drop of African blood is known to flow is limited to a pitiful few. So overcrowded are the avocations in which colored women may engage and so poor is the pay in consequence, that only the barest livelihood can be eked out by the rank and file. And yet, in spite of the opposition encountered, the obstacles opposed to their acquisition of knowledge and their accumulation of property, the progress made by colored women along these lines has never been surpassed by that of any people in the history of the world.

Though the slaves were liberated less than forty years ago, penniless, and ignorant, with neither shelter nor food, so great was their thirst for knowledge and so herculean were their efforts to secure it, that there are today hundreds of negroes, many of them women, who are graduates, some of them having taken degrees from the best institutions of the land. From Oberlin, that friend of the oppressed, Oberlin, my dear alma mater, whose name will always be loved and whose praise will ever be sung as the first college in the country which was just, broad and benevolent enough to open its doors to negroes and to women on an equal footing with men; from Wellesley and Vassar, from Cornell and Ann Arbor, from the best high schools throughout the North, East and West, colored girls have been graduated with honors, and have thus forever settled the question of their capacity and worth.

But a few years ago in an examination in which a large number of young women and men competed for a scholarship, entitling the successful competitor to an entire course through the Chicago University, the only colored girl among them stood first and captured this great prize. And so, wherever colored girls have studied, their instructors bear testimony to their intelligence, diligence and success.

With this increase of wisdom there has sprung up in the hearts of colored women an ardent desire to do good in the world. No sooner had the favored few availed themselves of such advantages as they could secure than they hastened to dispense these blessings to the less fortunate of their race. With tireless energy and eager zeal, colored women have, since their emancipation, been continuously prosecuting the work of educating and elevating their race, as though upon themselves alone devolved the accomplishment of this great task.

Of the teachers engaged in instructing colored youth, it is perhaps no exaggeration to say that fully ninety percent are women. In the backwoods, remote from the civilization and comforts of the city and town, on the plantations reeking with ignorance and vice, our colored women may be found battling with evils which such conditions always entail. Many a heroine, of whom the world will never hear, has thus sacrificed her life to her race, amid surroundings and in the face of privations which only martyrs can tolerate and bear. Shirking responsibility has never been a fault with which colored women might be truthfully charged. Indefatigably and conscientiously, in public work of all kinds they engage, that they may benefit and elevate their race.

The result of this labor has been prodigious indeed. By banding themselves together in the interest of education and morality, by adopting the most practical and useful means to this end, colored women have in thirty short years become a great power for good. Through the National Association of Colored Women, which was formed by the union of two large organizations in July, 1896, and which is now the only national body among colored women, much good has been done in the past, and more will be accomplished in the future, we hope. Believing that it is only through the home that a people can become really good and truly great, the National Association of Colored Women has entered that sacred domain.

Homes, more homes, better homes, purer homes is the text upon which our sermons have been and will be preached. Through mothers' meetings, which are a special feature of the work planned by the Association, much useful information in everything pertaining to the home will be disseminated. We would have heart-to-heart talks with our women, that we may strike at the root of evils, many of which lie, alas, at the fireside. If the women of the dominant race with all the centuries of education, culture and refinement back of them, with all their wealth of opportunity ever present with them—if these women feel the need of a Mothers' Congress that they may be enlightened as to the best methods of rearing children and conducting their homes, how much more do our women, from whom shackles have but yesterday fallen, need information on the same vital subjects? And so throughout the country we are working vigorously and conscientiously to establish Mothers' Congresses in every community in which our women may be found.

Under the direction of the Tuskegee, Alabama branch of the National Association, the work of bringing the light of knowledge and the gospel of cleanliness to their benighted sisters on the plantations has been conducted with signal success. Their efforts have thus far been confined to four estates, comprising thousands of acres of land, on which live hundreds of colored people, yet in the darkness of ignorance and the grip of sin, miles away from churches and schools. Under the evil influences of plantation owners, and through no fault of their own, the condition of the colored people is, in some sections today no better than it was at the close of the war. Feeling the great responsibility resting upon them, therefore, colored women, both in organizations under the National Association, and as individuals are working with might and main to afford their unfortunate sisters opportunities of civilization and education, which without them, they would be unable to secure.

By the Tuskegee club and many others all over the country, object lessons are given in the best way to sweep, dust, cook, wash and iron, together with other information concerning household affairs. Talks on social purity and the proper method of rearing children are made for the benefit of those mothers, who in many instances fall short of their duty, not because they are vicious and depraved, but because they are ignorant and poor. Against the one-room cabin so common in the rural settlements in the South, we have inaugurated a vigorous crusade. When families of eight or ten, consisting of men, women and children, are all huddled together in a single apartment, a condition of things found not only in the South, but among our poor all over the land, there is little hope of inculcating morality or modesty. And yet, in spite of these environments which are so destructive of virtue, and though the safeguards usually thrown around maidenly youth and innocence are in some sections withheld from colored girls, statistics compiled by men, not inclined to falsify in favor of my race, show that immorality among colored women is not so great as among women in countries like Austria, Italy, Germany, Sweden and France.

In New York City a mission has been established and is entirely supported by colored women under supervision of the New York City Board. It has in operation a kindergarten, classes in cooking and sewing, mothers' meetings, men's meetings, a reading circle and a manual training school for boys. Much the same kind of work is done by the Colored Woman's League and the Ladies Auxiliary of this city, the Kansas City League of Missouri, the Woman's Era Club of Boston, the Woman's Loyal Union of New York, and other organizations representing almost every State in the Union.

The Phyllis Wheatley Club of New Orleans, another daughter of the National Association, has in two short years succeeded in establishing a Sanatorium and a Training School for nurses. The conditions which caused the colored women of New Orleans to choose this special field in which to operate are such as exist in many other sections of our land. From the city hospitals colored doctors are excluded altogether, not even being allowed to practice in the colored wards and colored patients—no matter how wealthy they are—are not received at all, unless they are willing to go into the charity wards. Thus the establishment of a Sanatorium answers a variety of purposes. It affords colored medical students an opportunity of gaining a practical knowledge of their profession, and it furnishes a well-equipped establishment for colored patients who do not care to go into the charity wards of the public hospitals.

The daily clinics have been a great blessing to the colored poor. In the operating department, supplied with all the modern appliances, two hundred operations have been performed, all of which have resulted successfully under the colored surgeon-in-chief. Of the eight nurses who have registered, one has already passed an examination before the State Medical Board of Louisiana, and is now practicing her profession. During the yellow fever epidemic in New Orleans last summer, there was a constant demand for Phyllis Wheatley nurses. By indefatigable energy and heroic sacrifice of both money and time, these noble women raised nearly one thousand dollars, with which to defray the expenses of the Sanatorium for the first eight months of its existence. They have recently succeeded in securing from the city of New Orleans an annual appropriation of two hundred and forty dollars, which they hope will soon be increased. Dotted all over the country are charitable organizations for the aged, orphaned and poor, which have been established by colored women; just how many, it is difficult to state. Since there is such an imperative need of statistics, bearing on the progress, possessions, and prowess of colored women, the National Association has undertaken to secure this data of such value and importance to the race. Among the charitable institutions, either founded, conducted or supported by colored women, may be mentioned the Hale Infirmary of Montgomery, Alabama; the Carrie Steel Orphanage of Atlanta; the Reed Orphan Home of Covington; the Haines Industrial School of Augusta in the State of Georgia; a Home for the Aged of both races at New Bedford and St. Monica's Home of Boston in Massachusetts; Old Folks' Home of Memphis, Tenn; colored Orphan's Home, Lexington, Ky., together with others of which time forbids me to speak.

Mt. Meigs Institute is an excellent example of a work originated and carried into successful execution by a colored woman. The school was established for the benefit of colored people on the plantations in the black belt of Alabama, because of the 700,000 negroes living in that State, probably 90 percent are outside of the cities; and Waugh was selected because in the township of Mt. Meigs, the population is practically all colored. Instruction given in this school is of the kind best suited to the needs of those people for whom it was established. Along with their scholastic training, girls are taught everything pertaining to the management of a home, while boys learn practical farming, carpentering, wheel-wrighting, blacksmithing, and have some military training. Having started with almost nothing, only eight years ago, the trustees of the school now own nine acres of land, and five buildings, in which two thousand pupils have received instruction—all through the courage the industry and sacrifice of one good woman. The Chicago clubs and several others engage in rescue work among fallen women and tempted girls.

Questions affecting our legal status as a race are also constantly agitated by our women. In Louisiana and Tennessee, colored women have several times petitioned the legislatures of their respective States to repeal the obnoxious "Jim Crow Car" laws, nor will any stone be left unturned until this iniquitous and unjust enactment against respectable American citizens be forever wiped from the statutes of the South. Against the barbarous Convict Lease System of Georgia, of which negroes, especially the female prisoners, are the principal victims, colored women are waging a ceaseless war. By two lecturers, each of whom, under the Woman's Christian Temperance Union has been National Superintendent of work among colored people, the cause of temperance has for many years been eloquently espoused.

In business, colored women have had signal success. There is in Alabama a large milling and cotton business belonging to and controlled entirely by a colored woman who has sometimes as many as seventy-five men in her employ. In Halifax, Nova Scotia, the principal ice plant of the city is owned and managed by one of our women. In the professions we have dentists and doctors, whose practice is lucrative and large. Ever since the publication, in 1773, of a book entitled "Poems on Various Subjects, Religious and Moral," by Phyllis Wheatley, a negro servant of Mr. John Wheatley of Boston, colored women have from time to time given abundant evidence of literary ability. In sculpture we are represented by a woman upon whose chisel Italy has set her seal of approval; in painting, by Bougerean's pupil, whose work was exhibited in the last Paris Salon, and in Music by young women holding diplomas from the first conservatories in the land.

And, finally, as an organization of women nothing lies nearer the heart of the National Association than the children, many of whose lives, so sad and dark, we might brighten and bless. It is the kindergarten we need. Free kindergartens in every city and hamlet of this broad land we must have, if the children are to receive from us what it is our duty to give. Already during the past year kindergartens have been established and successfully maintained by several organizations, from which most encouraging reports have come. May their worthy example be emulated, till in no branch of the Association shall the children of the poor, at least, be deprived of the blessings which flow from the kindergarten alone.

The more unfavorable the environments of children, the more necessary is it that steps be taken to counteract baleful influences on innocent victims. How imperative is it then that as colored women, we inculcate correct principles and set good examples for our own youth, whose little feet will have so many thorny paths of prejudice temptation, and injustice to tread. The colored youth is vicious we are told, and statistics showing the multitudes of our boys and girls who crowd the penitentiaries and fill the jails appall and dishearten us. But side by side with these facts and figures of crime I would have presented and pictured the miserable hovels from which these youth criminals come.

Make a tour of the settlements of colored people, who in many cities are relegated to the most noisome sections permitted by the municipal government, and behold the mites of humanity who infest them. Here are our little ones, the future representatives of the race, fairly drinking in the pernicious example of their elders, coming in contact with nothing but ignorance and vice, till at the age of six, evil habits are formed which no amount of civilizing or Christianizing can ever completely break. Listen to the cry of our children. In imitation of the example set by the Great Teacher of men, who could not offer himself as a sacrifice, until he had made an eternal plea for the innocence and helplessness of childhood, colored women are everywhere reaching out after the waifs and strays, who without their aid may be doomed to lives of evil and shame. As an organization, the National Association of Colored Women feels that the establishment of kindergartens is the special mission which we are called to fulfill. So keenly alive are we to the necessity of rescuing our little ones, whose noble qualities are deadened and dwarfed by the very atmosphere which they breathe, that the officers of the Association are now trying to secure means by which to send out a kindergarten organizer, whose duty it shall be both to arouse the conscience of our women, and to establish kindergartens, wherever the means therefore can be secured.

And so, lifting as we climb, onward and upward we go, struggling and striving, and hoping that the buds and blossoms of our desires will burst into glorious fruition ere long. With courage, born of success achieved in the past, with a keen sense of the responsibility which we shall continue to assume, we look forward to a future large with promise and hope. Seeking no favors because of our color, nor patronage because of our needs, we knock at the bar of justice, asking an equal chance.

QUESTIONS

(1) What are some of the evidence presented by Terrell that black women had little hope of escaping what Terrell calls the "womanhood of the race"?

(2) Despite the obstacles that black women faced, how was it possible for black women to obtain an education and a career?

(3) Black women had to confront the discriminatory practices of race and gender amalgamation. Was Terrell optimistic about the future of race relations in the United States?

(4) In addressing the position of black women, why did Terrell begin her speech by referring to the women's suffrage and the anti-slavery movement?

(5) What were some of the examples of progress that black women made during and after emancipation?

16 WHAT's In A NAME? Womanism, Black Feminism and Beyond

PATRICIA HILL COLLINS

Patricia Hill Collins is at present a distinguished university professor in the Department of Sociology at the University of Maryland, College Park. Before joining the faculty at Maryland in 2005, Collins was the chair of the Department of African American Studies at University of Cincinnati where she started her career as an assistant professor in 1982. Collins authored many scholarly works. Her first book, *Black Feminist Thought: Knowledge, Consciousness, and the Politics of Empowerment*, was published in 1990. It won the C. Wright Mills award, the distinguished publication award by the Association of Women in Psychology, and the Letitia Woods Brown Memorial Book Prize by the Association of Black Women Historians. Collins' other key works include *Fighting Words: Black Women and the Search for Justice*, 1998; *Black Sexual Politics: African Americans, Gender, and the New Politics of Racism*, 2005; and *From Black Power to Hip Hop: Racism, Nationalism, and Feminism*, 2006. Her article, "WHAT's In A NAME? Womanism, Black Feminism and Beyond," is presented below. In this article, Collins points to how both womanism and Black Feminism are used to define and explain black women's experience outside the first and second waves of feminism.

BLACK WOMEN ARE AT A DECISION POINT that in many ways mirrors that faced by African Americans as a collectivity. Building on the pathbreaking works by Toni Cade Bambara, Ntozake Shange, Angela Davis, Toni Morrison, June Jordan, Alice Walker, Audre Lorde and other black women who "broke silence" in the 1970s, African American women in the 1980s and 1990s developed a "voice," a self-defined, collective black women's standpoint about black womanhood (Collins 1990). Moreover, black women used this standpoint to "talk back" concerning black women's representation in dominant discourses (hooks 1989). As a result of this struggle, African American women's ideas and experiences have achieved a visibility unthinkable in the past.

But African American women now stand at a different historical moment. Black women appear to have a voice, and with this new-found voice comes a new series of concerns. For example, we must be attentive to the seductive absorption of black women's voices in classrooms of higher education where black women's texts are still much more welcomed than black women ourselves. Giving the illusion of change, this strategy of symbolic inclusion masks how the everyday institutional policies and arrangements that suppress and exclude African Americans as a collectivity remain virtually untouched (Carby 1992; Du Cille 1994). Similarly, capitalist market relations that transformed black women's writing into a hot commodity threaten to strip their works of their critical edge. Initially, entering public space via books, movies, and print media proved invigorating. But in increasingly competitive global markets where anything that sells will be sold regardless of the consequences, black women's "voices" now flood the market. Like other commodities exchanged in capitalist markets, surplus cheapens value, and the fad of today becomes the nostalgic memory of tomorrow.

While a public voice initially proved dangerous, black women's coming to voice ironically fostered the emergence of a new challenge. The new public safe space provided by black women's success allowed longstanding differences among black women structured along axes of sexuality, social class, nationality, religion, and region to emerge. At this point, whether African American women can fashion a singular "voice" about the black woman's position remains less an issue than how black women's voices collectively construct, affirm, and maintain a dynamic black women's self-defined standpoint. Given the increasingly troublesome political context affecting black women as a group (Massey and Denton 1993; Squires 1994), such solidarity is essential. Thus, ensuring group unity while recognizing the tremendous heterogeneity that operates within the boundaries of the term "black women" comprises one fundamental challenge now confronting African American women.

CURRENT DEBATES about whether black women's standpoint should be named "womanism" or "black feminism" reflect this basic challenge of accommodating diversity among black women. In her acclaimed volume of essays, *In Search of Our Mothers' Gardens*, Alice Walker (1983) introduced four meanings of the term "womanist." According to Walker's first definition, a "womanist" was "a black feminist or feminist of color" (xi). Thus, on some basic level, Walker herself uses the two terms as being virtually interchangeable. Like Walker, many African American women see little difference between the two since both support a common agenda of black women's self-definition and self-determination. As Barbara Omolade points out, "black feminism is sometimes referred to as womanism because both are concerned with struggles against sexism and racism by black women who are themselves part of the black community's efforts to achieve equity and liberty" (Omolade 1994, xx).

But despite similar beliefs expressed by African American women who define themselves as black feminists, as womanists, as both, or, in some cases, as neither, increasing attention seems devoted to delineating the differences, if any between groups naming themselves as "womanists" or "black feminists." The name given to black women's collective standpoint seems to matter, but why?

In this paper, I explore some of the theoretical implications of using the terms "womanism" and "black feminism" to name a black women's standpoint. My purpose is not to classify either the works of black women or African American women themselves into one category or the other. Rather, I aim to examine how the effort to categorize obscures more basic challenges that confront African American women as a group.

Womanism

ALICE WALKER'S MULTIPLE DEFINITIONS of the term "womanism" in *In Search of Our Mothers' Gardens*, shed light on the issue of why many African American women prefer the term womanism to black feminism. Walker offers two contradictory meanings of "womanism." On the one hand, Walker clearly sees womanism as rooted in black women's concrete history in racial and gender oppression. Taking the term from the Southern black folk expression of mothers to female children "you acting womanish," Walker suggests that black women's concrete history fosters a womanist worldview accessible primarily and perhaps exclusively to black women. "Womanish" girls acted in outrageous, courageous, and willful ways, attributes that freed them from the conventions long limiting white women. Womanish girls wanted to know more and in greater depth than what was considered good for them. They were responsible, in charge, and serious.

Despite her disclaimer that womanists are "traditionally universalist," a philosophy invoked by her metaphor of the garden where room exists for all flowers to bloom equally and differently, Walker simultaneously implies that black women are somehow superior to white women because of this black folk tradition. Defining womanish as the opposite of the "frivolous, irresponsible, not serious" girlish, Walker constructs black women's experiences in opposition to those of white women. This meaning of womanism sees it as being different from and superior to feminism, a difference allegedly stemming from black and white women's different histories with American racism. Walker's much cited phrase, "womanist is to feminist as purple to lavender" (1983, xii) clearly seems designed to set up this type of comparison – black women are "womanist" while white women remain merely "feminist."

This usage sits squarely in black nationalist traditions premised on the belief that blacks and whites cannot function as equals while inhabiting the same territory or participating in the same social institutions (Pinkney 1976; Van Deburg 1992). Since black nationalist philosophy posits that white people as a group have a vested interest in continuing a system of white supremacy, it typically sees little use for black integration or assimilation into a system predicated on black subjugation. Black nationalist approaches also support a black moral superiority over whites because of black suffering.

Walker's use of the term womanism promises black women who both operate within these black nationalist assumptions and who simultaneously see the need to address "feminist" issues within African American communities partial reconciliation of these two seemingly incompatible philosophies. Womanism offers a distance from the "enemy," in this case, whites generally and white women in particular, yet still raises the issue of gender. Due to its endorsement of racial separatism, this interpretation of womanism offers a vocabulary for addressing gender issues within African American communities without challenging the racially segregated terrain that characterizes American social institutions.

This use of womanism sidesteps an issue central to many white feminists, namely, finding ways to foster interracial cooperation among women. African American women embracing black nationalist philosophies typically express little interest in working with white women – in fact, white women are defined as part of the problem. Moreover, womanism appears to provide an avenue to foster stronger relationships between black women and black men, another very important issue for African American women regardless of political perspective. Again, Walker's definition provides guidance where she notes that womanists are "committed to survival and wholeness of entire people, male and female" (xi). Many black women view feminism as a movement that at best, is exclusively for women and, at worst, dedicated to attacking or eliminating men. Sherley Williams takes this view when she notes that in contrast to feminism, "womanist inquiry ... assumes that it can talk both effectively and productively about men" (1990, 70). Womanism seemingly supplies a way for black women to address gender oppression without attacking black men.

Walker also presents a visionary meaning for womanism. As part of her second definition, Walker has a black girl pose the question "Mama, why are we brown, pink, and yellow, and our cousins are white, beige, and black?" (xi). The response of "the colored race is just like a flower garden, with every color flower represented," both criticizes colorism within African American communities and broadens the notion of humanity to make all people people of color. Reading this passage as a metaphor, womanism thus furnishes a vision where the women and men of different colors coexist like flowers in a garden yet retain their cultural distinctiveness and integrity.

This meaning of womanism seems rooted in another major political tradition within African American politics, namely, a pluralist version of black empowerment (Van Deburg 1992). Pluralism views society as being composed of various ethnic and interest groups, all of whom compete for goods and services. Equity lies in providing equal opportunities, rights, and respect to all groups. By retaining black cultural distinctiveness and integrity, pluralism offers a modified version of racial integration premised not on individual assimilation but on group integration. Clearly rejecting what they perceive as being the limited vision of feminism projected by North American white women, many black women theorists have been attracted to this joining of pluralism and racial integration in this interpretation of Walker's "womanism." For example, black feminist theologian Katie Geneva Cannon's (1988) work *Black Womanist Ethics* invokes this sense of the visionary content of womanism. As an ethical system, womanism is always in the making – it is not a closed fixed system of ideas but one that continually evolves through its rejection of all forms of oppression and commitment to social justice.

Walker's definition thus manages to invoke three important yet contradictory philosophies that frame black social and political thought, namely, black nationalism via her claims of black women's moral and epistemological superiority via suffering under racial and gender oppression, pluralism via the cultural integrity provided by the metaphor of the garden, and integration/assimilation via her claims that black women are "traditionally universalist" (Van Deburg 1992). Just as black nationalism and racial integration coexist in uneasy partnership, with pluralism occupying the contested terrain between the two, Walker's definitions of womanism demonstrate comparable contradictions. By both grounding womanism in the concrete experiences of African American women and generalizing about the potential for realizing a humanist vision of community via the experiences of African American women, Walker depicts the potential for oppressed people to possess a moral vision and standpoint on society that grows from their situation of oppression. This standpoint also emerges as an incipient foundation for a more humanistic, just society. Overall, these uses of Walker's term "womanism" creates conceptual space that reflects bona fide philosophical differences that exist among African-American women.[1]

ONE PARTICULARLY SIGNIFICANT FEATURE of black women's use of womanism concerns the part of Walker's definition that remains neglected. A more troublesome line for those self-defining as womanist precedes the often cited passage,

---

[1] For a detailed treatment of Alice Walker's and other black feminist writers' connection to black nationalist politics, see Dubey (1994).

The Words of My People

The words of my people
So incorrect by the white man's definition
But so beautiful to my ear
I's seen, gon' be, lordy please have mercy
These words are deeply embedded in my history
They have passed down countless stories
From generation to generation
The words ... of my people.

By Billie Williams, Jr.

"committed to survival and wholeness of entire people, male and female" (xi). Just before Walker offers the admonition that womanists, by definition, are committed to wholeness, she states that a womanist is also "a woman who loves other women, sexually and/or nonsexually" (xi). The relative silence of womanists on this dimension of womanism speaks to black women's continued ambivalence in dealing with the links between race, gender and sexuality, in this case, the "taboo" sexuality of lesbianism. In her essay "The Truth That Never Hurts: Black Lesbians in Fiction in the 1980s," black feminist critic Barbara Smith (1990) points out that African American women have yet to come to terms with homophobia in African American communities. Smith applauds the growth of black women's fiction in the 1980s, but also observes that within black feminist intellectual production, black lesbians continue to be ignored. Despite the fact that some of the most prominent and powerful black women thinkers claimed by both womanists and black feminists were and are lesbians, this precept often remains unacknowledged in the work of African American writers. In the same way that many people read the Bible, carefully selecting the parts that agree with their worldview and rejecting the rest, selective readings of Walker's womanism produce comparable results.

Another significant feature of black women's multiple uses of womanism concerns the potential for a slippage between the real and the ideal. To me, there is a distinction between describing black women's historical responses to racial and gender oppression as being womanist, and using womanism as a visionary term delineating an ethical or ideal vision of humanity for all people. Identifying the liberatory potential within black women's communities that emerges from concrete, historical experiences remains quite different from claiming that black women have already arrived at this ideal, "womanist" endpoint. Refusing to distinguish carefully between these two meanings of womanism thus collapses the historically real and the future ideal into one privileged position for African American women in the present. Taking this position is reminiscent of the response of some black women to the admittedly narrow feminist agenda forwarded by white women in the early 1970s. Those black women proclaimed that they were already "liberated" while in actuality, this was far from the truth.

Black Feminism

AFRICAN AMERICAN WOMEN who use the term black feminism also attach varying interpretations to this term. As black feminist theorist and activist Pearl Cleage defines it, feminism is "the belief that women are full human beings capable of participation and leadership in the full range of human activities – intellectual, political, social, sexual, spiritual and economic" (1993, 28). In its broadest sense, feminism constitutes both an ideology and a global political movement that confronts sexism, a social relationship in which males as a group have authority over females as a group.

Globally, a feminist agenda encompasses several major areas. First and foremost, the economic status of women and issues associated with women's global poverty, such as educational opportunities, industrial development, environmental racism, employment policies, prostitution, and inheritance laws concerning property, constitute a fundamental global women's issue. Political rights for women, such as gaining the vote, rights of assembly, traveling in public, office holding, the rights of political prisoners, and basic human rights violations against women such as rape and torture constitute a second area of concern. A third area of global concern consists of marital and family issues such as marriage and divorce laws, child custody policies, and domestic labor. Women's health and survival issues, such as reproductive rights, pregnancy, sexuality, and AIDS constitute another area of global feminist concern. This broad global feminist agenda finds varying expressions in different regions of the world and among diverse populations.

Using the term "black feminism" positions African American women to examine how the particular constellation of issues affecting black women in the United States are part of issues of women's emancipation struggles globally (Davis 1989; James and Busia 1994). In the context of feminism as a global political movement for women's rights and emancipation, the patterns of feminist knowledge and politics that African American women encounter in the United States represent but a narrow segment refracted through the dichotomous racial politics of white supremacy in the United States. Because the media in the United States portrays feminism as a for-whites-only movement, and because many white women have accepted this view of American apartheid that leads to segregated institutions of all types, including feminist organizations, feminism is often viewed by both black and whites as the cultural property of white women (Caraway 1991).

DESPITE THEIR MEDIA ERASURE, many African American women have long struggled against this exclusionary feminism and have long participated in what appear to be for-whites-only feminist activity. In some cases, some black women have long directly challenged the racism within feminist organizations controlled by white women. Sojourner Truth's often cited phrase "ain't I a woman" typifies this longstanding tradition (Joseph 1990). At other times, even though black women's participation in feminist organizations remains largely invisible, for example, Pauli Murray's lack of recognition as a founding member of NOW, black women participated in feminist organizations in positions of leadership. In still other cases, black women combine allegedly divergent political agendas. For example, Pearl Cleage observes that black feminist politics and black nationalist politics need not be contradictory. She notes, "I don't think you can be a true Black Nationalist, dedicated to the freedom of black people without being a feminist, black people being made up of both men and women, after all, and feminism being nothing more or less than a belief in the political, social and legal equality of women" (1993, 180).

Using the term "black feminism" disrupts the racism inherent in presenting feminism as a for-whites-only ideology and political movement. Inserting the adjective "black" challenges the assumed whiteness of feminism and disrupts the false universal of this term for both white and black women. Since many white women think that black women lack feminist consciousness, the term "black feminist" both highlights the contradictions underlying the assumed whiteness of feminism and serves to remind white women that they comprise neither the only nor the normative "feminists." The term "black feminism" also makes many African American women uncomfortable because it challenges black women to confront their own views on sexism and women's oppression. Because the majority of African American women encounter their own experiences repackaged in racist school curricula and media, even though they may support the very ideas on which feminism rests, large numbers of African American women reject the term "feminism" because of what they perceive as its association with whiteness. Many see feminism as operating exclusively within the terms white and American and perceive its opposite as being black and American. When given these two narrow and false choices, black women routinely choose "race" and let the lesser question of "gender" go. In this situation, those black women who identify with feminism must be recoded as being either non-black or less authentically black. The term "black feminist" also disrupts a longstanding and largely unquestioned reliance on black racial solidarity as a deep tap root in black political philosophies, especially black nationalist and cultural pluralist frameworks (Dyson 1993). Using family rhetoric that views black family, community, race and nation as a series of nested boxes, each gaining meaning from the other, certain rules apply to all levels of this "family" organization. Just as families have internal naturalized hierarchies that give, for example, older siblings authority over younger ones or males over females, groups defining themselves as racial-families invoke similar rules (Collins 1998). Within African American communities, one such rule is that black women will support black men, no matter what, an unwritten family rule that was manipulated quite successfully during the Clarence Thomas confirmation hearings. Even if Anita Hill was harassed by Clarence Thomas, many proclaimed in barber shops and beauty parlors, she should have kept her mouth shut and not "aired dirty laundry." Even though Thomas recast the life of his own sister through the framework of an unworthy welfare queen, in deference to rules of racial solidarity, black women should have kept our collective mouths shut. By counseling black women not to remain silent in the face of abuse, whoever does it, black feminism comes into conflict with codes of silence such as these.

SEVERAL DIFFICULTIES accompany the use of the term "black feminism." One involves the problem of balancing the genuine concerns of black women against continual pressures to absorb and recast such interests within white feminist frameworks. For example, ensuring political rights and economic development via collective action to change social institutions remains a strong focal point in the feminism of African American women and women of color. Yet the emphasis on themes such as personal identity, understanding "difference," deconstructing women's multiple selves, and the simplistic model of the political expressed through the slogan the "personal is political," that currently permeate North American white women's feminism in the academy can work to sap black feminism of its critical edge. Efforts of contemporary black women thinkers to explicate a long-standing black women's intellectual tradition bearing the label "black feminism" can attract the attention of white women armed with a different feminist agenda. Issues raised by black women not seen as explicitly "feminist" ones, primarily issues that affect only women, receive much less sanction. In a sense, the constant drumbeat of having to support white women in their efforts to foster an anti-racist feminism that allows black women access to the global network of women's activism diverts black women's energy away from addressing social issues facing African American communities. Because black feminism appears to be so well-received by white women, in the context of dichotomous racial politics of the United States, some black women quite rightfully suspect its motives.

Another challenge facing black feminism concerns the direct conflict between black feminism and selected elements of black religious traditions. For example, the visibility of white lesbians within North American feminism overall comes into direct conflict with many black women's articles of faith that homosexuality is a sin. While individual African American women may be accepting of gays, lesbians and bisexuals as individuals, especially if such individuals are African American, black women as a collectivity have simultaneously distanced themselves from social movements perceived as requiring acceptance of homosexuality. As one young black woman queried, "why do I have to accept lesbianism in order to support black feminism?" The association of feminism with lesbianism remains a problematic one for black women. Reducing black lesbians to their sexuality, one that chooses women over men, reconfigures black lesbians as enemies of black men. This reduction not only constitutes a serious misreading of black lesbianism – black lesbians have fathers, brothers, and sons of their own and are embedded in a series of relationships as complex as their heterosexual brothers and sisters – it simultaneously diverts attention away from more important issues (Lorde 1984). Who ultimately benefits when the presence of black lesbians in any black social movement leads to its rejection by African Americans?

The theme of lesbianism and its association with feminism in the minds of many African Americans also overlaps with another concern of many African American women, namely their commitment to African American men. Another challenge confronting black feminism concerns its perceived separatism – many

African Americans define black feminism as being exclusively for black women only and rejecting black men. In explaining her preference for "womanism," Sherley Ann Williams notes, "one of the most disturbing aspects of current black feminist criticism (is) its separatism – its tendency to see not only a distinct black female culture but to see that culture as a separate cultural form having more in common with white female experience than with the facticity of Afro-American life" (1990, 70). This is a valid criticism of black feminism, one that in my mind, must be addressed if the major ideas of black feminism expect to avoid the danger of becoming increasingly separated from African American women's experiences and interests. But it also speaks to the larger issue of the continuing difficulty of positioning black feminism between black nationalism and North American white feminism. In effect, black feminism must come to terms with a white feminist agenda incapable of seeing its own racism as well as a black nationalist one resistant to grappling with its own sexism (White 1990). Finding a place that accommodates these seemingly contradictory agendas remains elusive (Christian 1989).

Beyond Naming

AFRICAN AMERICAN WOMEN'S EFFORTS to distinguish between womanism and black feminism illustrates how black women's placement in hierarchical power relations fosters different yet related allegiances to a black women's self-defined standpoint. While the surface differences distinguishing African American women who embrace womanism and black feminism appear to be minimal, black women's varying locations in neighborhoods, schools, and labor markets generate comparably diverse views on the strategies black women feel will ultimately lead to black women's self-determination. In a sense, while womanism's affiliation with black nationalism both taps an historic philosophy and a set of social institutions organized around the centrality of racial solidarity for black survival, this position can work to isolate womanism from global women's issues. At the same time, while black feminism's connections to existing women's struggles both domestically and globally fosters a clearer political agenda regarding gender, its putative affiliation with whiteness fosters its rejection by the very constituency it aims to serve.

NO TERM CURRENTLY EXISTS that adequately represents the substance of what diverse groups of black women alternately call "womanism" and "black feminism." Perhaps the time has come to go beyond naming by applying main ideas contributed by both womanists and black feminists to the over-arching issue of analyzing the centrality of gender in shaping a range of relationships within African American communities. Such an examination might encompass several dimensions.

First, it is important to keep in mind that the womanist/black feminist debate occurs primarily among relatively privileged black women. Womanism and black feminism would both benefit by examining the increasing mismatch between what privileged black women, especially those in the academy, identify as important themes and what the large numbers of African American women who stand outside of higher education might deem worthy of attention. While these African American women physically resemble one another and may even occupy the same space, their worlds remain decidedly different. One might ask how closely the thematic content of newly emerging black women's voices in the academy speak for and speak to the masses of African American women still denied literacy. Black women academics explore intriguing issues of centers and margins and work to deconstruct black female identity while large numbers of black women remain trapped in neighborhoods organized around old centers of racial apartheid. Talk of centers and margins, even the process of coming to voice itself, that does not simultaneously address issues of power leaves masses of black women doing the dry cleaning, cooking the fast food, and dusting the computer of the sister who has just written the newest theoretical treatise on black women.

Second, shifting the emphasis from black women's oppression to how institutionalized racism operates in gender-specific ways should provide a clearer perspective on how gender oppression works in tandem with racial oppression for both black women and men. This shift potentially opens up new political choices for African Americans as a group. Just as feminism does not automatically reside in female bodies, sexism does not reside in male ones. It may be time to separate political philosophies such as black nationalism, Afrocentrism, and feminism, from the socially constructed categories of individuals created by historical relations of racism and sexism. Black men cannot have black women's experiences but they can support African American women by advocating anti-racist and anti-sexist philosophies in their intellectual and political work (see, e.g., Marable 1983; hooks and West 1991; and Awkward 1995). Focusing on gender as a structure of power that works with race should provide the much needed space for dialogues among black women, among black men, and between black women and men.

This approach promises to benefit the black community as a collectivity because it models sensitivity to the heterogeneity concerning not only gender, but class, nationality, sexuality, and age currently operating within the term "black community." Thus, the womanism/black feminism debate also provides an excellent opportunity to model a process of building community via heterogeneity and not sameness. For African American women, breathing life into Alice Walker's seemingly contradictory meanings of "womanist" and "black feminist" means engaging in the difficult task of working through the diverse ways that black women have been affected by interlocking systems of oppression. Some black women will have to grapple with how internalized oppression has affected them because they are poor while others must come to terms with the internalized privilege accompanying their middle and upper-class status. Other black women must grapple with the internalized privileges that accrue to them because they engage in heterosexual behaviors or how American citizenship provides them rights denied to women elsewhere in the Diaspora. Working through the interconnected nature of multiple systems of oppression and potential ways that such intersectionality might foster resistance becomes significant in moving quite diverse African American women forward toward Walker's visionary term "womanism." A commitment to social justice and participatory democracy provide some fundamental ground rules for black women and men concerning how to relate across differences.

FINALLY, DESPITE THE PROMISE of this approach, it is important to consider the limitations of womanism, black feminism, and all other putatively progressive philosophies. Whether labeled "womanism," "black feminism," or something else, African American women could not possibly possess a superior vision of what community would look like, how justice might feel, and the like. This presupposes that such a perspective is arrived at without conflict, intellectual rigor, and political struggle. While black women's particular location provides a distinctive angle of vision on oppression, this perspective comprises neither a privileged nor a complete standpoint. In this sense, grappling with the ideas of heterogeneity within black women's communities and hammering out a self-defined, black women's standpoint leads the way for other groups wishing to follow a similar path. As for black women, we can lead the way or we can follow behind. Things will continue to move on regardless of our choice.

REFERENCES

- Awkward, Michael. 1995. *Negotiating Difference: Race, Gender, and the Politics of Positionality* (University of Chicago Press).
- Cannon, Katie G. 1988. *Black Womanist Ethics* (Atlanta: Scholar's Press).
- Caraway, Nancie. 1991. *Segregated Sisterhood: Racism and the Politics of American Feminism* (Knoxville: University of Tennessee Press).
- Carby, Hazel. 1992. "The Multicultural Wars," in *Black Popular Culture*, ed. Michele Wallace and Gina Dent (Seattle: Bay Press), pp. 187–199.
- Christian, Barbara. 1989. "But Who Do You Really Belong To – Black Studies or Women's Studies?," *Women's Studies* 17, no. 1–2: 17–23.
- Cleage, Pearl. 1993. *Deals With the Devil and Other Reasons to Riot* (New York: Ballantine Books).
- Collins, Patricia Hill. 1990. *Black Feminist Thought: Knowledge, Consciousness, and the Politics of Empowerment* (New York: Routledge).
- Collins, Patricia Hill. 1998. "Intersections of Race, Class, Gender, and Nation: Some Implications for Black Family Studies," *Journal of Comparative Family Studies* 29, no. 1 (1998): 27–36.
- Davis, Angela. 1989. *Women, Culture, and Politics* (New York: Random House).

- Dubey, Madhu. 1994. *Black Women Novelists and the Nationalist Aesthetic* (Bloomington: Indiana University Press).
- Du Cille, Ann. 1994. "The Occult of True Black Womanhood: Critical Demeanor and Black Feminist Studies," *Signs* 19, no. 3: 591–629.
- Dyson, Michael. 1993. *Reflecting Black: African-American Cultural Criticism* (Minneapolis: University of Minnesota Press).
- hooks, bell. 1989. *Talking Back: Thinking Feminist, Thinking Black* (Boston: South End Press).
- hooks, bell and Cornel West. 1991. *Breaking Bread: Insurgent Black Intellectual Life* (Boston: South End Press).
- James, Stanlie and Abena Busia (eds.). 1994. *Theorizing Black Feminisms* (New York: Routledge).
- Joseph, Gloria I. 1990. "Sojourner Truth: Archetypal Black Feminist," in *Wild Women in the Whirlwind*, ed. Joanne Braxton and Andree Nicola McLaughlin (New Brunswick, NJ: Rutgers University Press), pp. 35–47.
- Lorde, Audre. 1984. *Sister Outsider* (Trumansburg, NY: The Crossing Press).
- Marable, Manning. 1983. "Grounding with My Sisters: Patriarchy and the Exploitation of Black Women," in *How Capitalism Underdeveloped Black America* (Boston: South End Press), pp. 60–104.
- Massey, Douglas S. and Nancy A. Denton. 1993. *American Apartheid: Segregation and the Making of the Underclass* (Cambridge, MA: Harvard University Press).
- Omolade, Barbara. 1994. *The Rising Song of African American Women* (New York: Routledge).
- Pinkney, Alphonso. 1976. *Red, Black, and Green: Black Nationalism in the United States* (Cambridge University Press).
- Smith, Barbara. 1990. "The Truth That Never Hurts: Black Lesbians in Fiction in the 1980s," in *Wild Women in the Whirlwind*, ed. Joanne Braxton and Andree Nicola McLaughlin (New Brunswick, NJ: Rutgers University Press), pp. 213–245.
- Squires, Gregory D. 1994. *Capital and Communities in Black and White: The Intersections of Race, Class, and Uneven Development* (Albany, NY: SUNY Press).
- Van Deburg, William L. 1992. *New Day in Babylon: The Black Power Movement and American Culture, 1965–1975* (University of Chicago Press).
- Walker, Alice. 1983. *In Search of Our Mothers' Gardens* (New York: Harcourt, Brace Jovanovich).
- White, E. Frances. 1990. "Africa on My Mind: Gender, Counter Discourse and African-American Nationalism," *Journal of Women's History* 2, no. 1: 73–97.
- Williams, Sherley Ann. 1990. "Some Implications of Womanist Theory," in *Reading Black, Reading Feminist: A Critical Anthology*, ed. Henry Louis Gates. New York: Meridian, pp. 68–75.

QUESTIONS

(1) According to Collins, what are the various ways that black women's experience, for the most part, must be analyzed within a black feminist framework?

(2) There are debates about whether a black woman's standpoint should be called womanism or black feminist. Why do you think Collins argues that naming is less important than recognizing how both womanism and Black Feminism draw attention to the issues that are important to black women?

(3) What are some of the differences and similarities between womanism and Black Feminism?

(4) How important is standpoint theory for discussing and analyzing black women's lived experience?

(5) If a womanist is a black feminist, how did Black Feminism in the early 1970s disrupt and bring new perspective to feminism and the narrow feminist agenda advanced by white women that did not take into account the issue of difference in relation to race, gender, and class amalgamation?

17 To Be Black, Male, and "Feminist" – Making Womanist Space for Black Men

GARY L. LEMONS

Gary L. Lemons at present is a professor in the English Department at the University of South Florida. He holds a PhD from New York University (NYU) in English and American literature, with an Advanced Certificate in Museum Studies also from NYU. His most recent book, *Caught in the Spirit! Teaching for Womanist Liberation*, was published in 2017. Other works include *Black Male Outsider, a Memoir: Teaching as a Pro-Feminist Man*, 2008; and *Womanist Forefathers: Frederick Douglass and W. E. B. Du Bois*, 2009. Lemons' article, "To Be Black, Male, and 'Feminist' – Making Womanist Space for Black Men," which appears below, draws on the historical impact that castration and lynching have had on the black male psyche in constructing their identity. Thus, the necessity for black feminists to make a womanist space for black men to be feminists and strive for the equality of all people is paramount.

> Womanist ... A black feminist or feminist of color ... [c]ommitted to survival and wholeness of entire people, male and female ... Womanist is to feminist as purple to lavender.[1]
>
> Alice Walker

> If black men and women take seriously Malcolm [X]'s charge that we must work for our liberation 'by any means necessary,' then we must be willing to explore the way feminism as a critique of sexism, as a movement to end sexism and sexist oppression, could aid our struggle to be self-determining.[2]
>
> bell hooks

bell hooks says in "Reconstructing Black Masculinity" that "[c]ollectively we can break the life threatening choke-hold patriarchal masculinity imposes on black men and create life sustaining visions of a reconstructed black masculinity that can provide black men ways to save their lives and the lives of their brothers and sisters in struggle" (113). Toward the work of political

---

[1] Excerpted from Alice Walker's definition of "womanist" in *In Search of Our Mothers' Gardens* (New York: Harcourt Brace Jovanovich, 1983).

[2] From "Reconstructing Black Masculinity," in *Black Looks: Race and Representation* (Boston: South End Press, 1992).

(re)unification of the genders in black communities today, black men must acknowledge and begin to confront the existence of sexism in black liberation struggle as one of the chief obstacles impeding its advancement. Making womanist space for black men to participate in allied relation to feminist movement to oppose the oppression of women means black men going against the grain of the racist and sexist mythology of black manhood and masculinity in the US. Its underlying premise rooted in white supremacist patriarchal ideology continues to foster the idea that we pose a racial and sexual threat to American society such that our bodies exist to be feared, brutalized, imprisoned, annihilated—made invisible.

It has been the fear of emasculinization originating in the history of black male lynching where the power of white (male) supremacy performed itself in the ritual act of castration (the violent sexual dismembering of our bodies) as a tool "to put/ keep us in our place" expressly because we were black and male—to "feminine" us. Thus, it is the fear of feminization in the minds of many black men that has led us to over-determine our sexuality, believing the idea that our identity as men resides only in the power of our penises. Against the inhumanity of our past—we must create a place/space to make ourselves over again in our own image. It must not be one reconstructed in the very mythology which sexually demonized our bodies as the scourge of white womanhood, but rather one which frees us to be black in the most radically revolutionary manner, to be male in the most non-oppressive, anti-sexist way, to be feminist in the most supportive, non-patriarchal way to bring about an end to the domination, subordination, and mistreatment of women exactly because they are women.

I believe womanism, as Alice Walker conceived it, to be a liberatory location for remaking black manhood toward a male identity that transgresses the boundaries of patriarchy—freeing us from the oppressive racist/sexist, sexually "othered" space we occupied in the past. Theorizing a womanist space for black men means focusing on the historical impact castration and lynching have had on the black male psyche and on ways we construct our identity as men. It may begin to tell us why many black men have internalized the racist sexual myths of black manhood and masculinity such that images of "black macho" and the super sexual "buck/ stud" have prevailed in black communities as legitimate representations of black male power. hooks maintains that "[B]lack men who are most worried about castration and emasculation are those who have completely absorbed white supremacist patriarchal definitions of masculinity" ("Reconstructing Black Masculinity," 93). The black buck stereotype, conceived in the white racist imagination during the period of slavery, signified that every black male (who did not fit the "Uncle Tom," older non-sexualized type) stood as the symbol of the sexually brutalizing phallus operating always already as a sexual threat to the purity of white womanhood—thus the need for castration.

As a controlling image in the contemporary period, phallic representations of black masculinity in the Black Power Movement of the 1960s manifested themselves in popular culture via the performance of hyper-masculinity as witnessed in the popularity of blaxploitation films in the 1970s (a genre made famous by the movie *Shaft* and a host of others featuring the "superfly" or the hyper-cool black male stereotype). Yet the mythology of black machismo remains grounded in the black man as super-sexual savage created to control black men during slavery.[3] The (re)production and perpetuation of a hyper-sexualized, hard black manhood/masculinity in white supremacist capitalist media is fed by stereotypical portrayals of black males. The very sexually over-determined images that have "essentially" typed us through history are played out repeatedly on the contemporary scene in the arena of popular culture, where the "dick-clutching" posture of many black male rappers has obtained as a status symbol of male power in Hip-hop.

I defy the notion that black manhood and masculinity is about a "dick thing." Progressive black men renouncing sexist, misogynist, and patriarchal practice against women—that is the taproot of the "dick thing" mentality—begin to mediate the painful historical memory of our own dehumanization. Challenging the white supremacist stereotype of the "super dick" (that so many black men have internalized as the symbol of black male power) means resisting the racist/sexist sexual mythology created to control us. It would have us believe that we are no more than one big collective "walking, brutalizing phallus." When we begin to interrogate its oppressive power over us, we start to perceive the interrelated ways racism and male supremacist privilege work together to dehumanize all black men. Understanding the link between white privilege and male privilege—realizing that empowered images of black manhood do not rest in the reclamation of lost phallic power (the pre-eminent fallacy of manhood thinking in general)—black men come to experience transformative, liberatory power as men. When we begin to claim our bodies as our own—beyond the bounds of white supremacist capitalist patriarchal control—we no longer have to fear that our penises will be cut off for being black and male. When we fully realize this, we confront the psychic/sexual wound/violation that castration/lynching represents, discovering that our quest for power in the myth of the "big black dick" is a self-dehumanizing act—physically, psychologically, and spiritually. Black men coming to feminist consciousness signifies a radical departure from the racist/sexist ideology of black manhood/masculinity that has consumed many of us. Black men moving to reclaim our womanist/feminist past contest the power of the phallus in our lives and the lives of women, toward truly liberatory meanings of manhood.

---

[3] In *Soul on Ice* and *Sex and Racism in America*, respectively, both Eldridge Cleaver and Calvin Hernton offer provocative versions of US race, gender sexual hierarchy in which the racist sexualization of the black male operates.

Theorizing Black Men as Pro-Feminist Comrades

In this essay, I address the problematics of being a black male feminist focusing on African-American men's historic relation to feminism and their relationship to black liberation struggle and issues of sexism, patriarchy, misogyny. Examining the interrelation of these modes of female oppression to racism in the light of black feminist critique of the multiplicity of oppression in the history of black women's lives in the United States, I call for the creation of a political space for black men "in" feminism grounded in the history of the fight African-Americans waged for race and gender rights.

In the process, I address a set of questions which strike at the core of contemporary black resistance to feminism, while critically asserting the need for contemporary black men (and women) to come together in "womanist" solidarity to reclaim black male commitment to a liberatory movement rooted in struggle against racism and sexism. Can black people in the US reconceive a freedom movement beyond the imperatives of male identity toward a progressive platform which opposes not only racism, sexism, and classism—but homophobia as well? Can feminist and anti-racist strategies share the same political agenda in the spirit of coalition movement?

In a period when white supremacist groups are re-emerging in the form of a militia movement, when a new black manhood movement predicated on the black patriarchal capitalist ideas of Louis Farrakhan—can a progressive coalition movement against domination be forged that transgresses the borders of identity politics to affect a truly liberatory ideology that embraces a multiplicity of struggle? Can the academy be a site of oppositional struggle where progressive educators employ the classroom as a strategic location for liberatory education practice? And finally, what difference can a black male feminist make toward a vision of "wholeness" in black communities, where every individual woman, man, and child is valued and cared for? Addressing these questions, as a black male feminist, I envision a space in feminism where black men can work to empower themselves in feminist solidarity—working in the tradition and spirit of their womanist legacy.

Today black men must begin remembering their feminist past, one in which the fight against racist oppression was integrally linked to women's liberation struggle. Comprehending the power of this crucial fact, we will have to rethink the meaning of contemporary black liberation struggle. Beyond the exclusionary politic of anti-racist strategizing based solely on a masculinist recuperation of manhood, black men must begin resisting sexist propaganda that tells us wrongfully that to be fully empowered as black men we should strive to "atone" for its loss. Progressive black people in the US, calling out sexist and misogynist practice perpetrated by black men, create counter-hegemonic black male and female space where locations of race, gender, and sexual healing are created. At this particular historical moment, considering the fact that there is an emerging movement around the repatriarchalization of black masculinity, black men in particular need to recognize the vital link between the histories of feminist movement and black liberation movement connected to womanist concerns—acting to reconnect politically the integral line that connects both struggles. Only then will black men achieve a status of dignity and self-worth that is not always already tied to patriarchy—constructing an integrative, holistic movement against the dehumanizing power of patriarchal thinking.

In 1925, Amy Jacques Garvey, editor of the "Women's Page" of the *Negro World* and wife of Marcus Garvey, declared—

> We are tired of hearing Negro men say, "There is a better day coming" while they do nothing to usher in the day. We are becoming so impatient that we are getting in the front ranks and serve notice that we will brush aside the halting, cowardly Negro leaders ... Mr. Black Man watch your step! ... Strengthen your shaking knees and move forward, or we will displace you and lead on to victory and glory. (quoted in Giddings, 195)

Exhorting black men to act more aggressively toward racial progress or be "displace[d]" by more radically mobilized black women, Amy Garvey wrote without regard to the disposition of the black male ego. From the rise of black feminism in the second half of the 19th century and the fervor of its movement in the 1920s, through its re-emergence in the writings of contemporary black women novelists, critics, poets, theorists, and academics—black women feminists have determined for themselves a course of action often set against the grain of black racial and gender party lines. Always having to weigh their actions with regard to notions of race solidarity and the defense of themselves as women, black feminists share a history of liberation struggle cultivated in a political (inter)relation of racism and sexism.

In the text above Amy Jacques Garvey (author)itatively calls into question black male power (without compromising the movement for racial liberation). (Re)writing the destiny of black women in liberation struggle, she proclaims the power of black female agency. Yet when black women have written or spoken out in critique of black male status, privilege, and/or sexism—black men have accused them of perpetuating white supremacist emasculation of the black male. In the contemporary period, feminist black women writers continue to be "object" of anti-feminist rhetoric. Thinking about the *Black Scholar* essay Robert Staples wrote in 1979 which initiated "The Debate on Black Sexism," I maintain that the critique he wrote opposing black feminist writings by Michele Wallace and Ntozake Shange foreshadowed subsequent attacks on Alice Walker, Gayl Jones, Gloria Naylor, Toni Morrison, and Paule Marshall, among others, through the 1980s and '90s marked by the onslaught of black male criticism against the film version of Terry McMillan's recent novel *Waiting to Exhale*.

The anti-womanist response many black men voiced against the film echoed the negative reaction expressed toward the cinematic representation of *The Color Purple*, Alice Walker's epistolary novel of black female search for self-empowerment. Scoring big at the box office during the first weeks it played, *Waiting to Exhale* generated significant dialogue among black women and men on the current state of gender relations in black communities. Yet many black men contested male representation in the film asserting that once again a black woman had misrepresented them, focusing on negative images. Viewing it as nothing more than black male bashing, they saw no redeeming value to "airing the dirty laundry of black people." Listening to a radio program in which callers discussed their views of the film, I found myself wondering why every male who phoned in severely lambasted McMillan for having "(mis)treated black men in such stereotypical ways." A couple of weeks earlier, one black man I encountered one afternoon while sitting on a bus came on equipped with a copy of *Waiting to Exhale* in his hand ranting to black female passengers that he had to read "another male-bashing-book by a sister." Rather than challenge my black "brother" to rethink his misguided notion of black women writers, I sat in silence remembering the outspoken manner in which I had defended the book and film version of *The Color Purple* more than a decade ago.

As a black feminist man (having declared my political affiliation to feminism some years ago as the only [black] male student in a graduate women's feminist organization the manner in which I have articulated a pro-feminist positionality has taken many turns—some representing a radical "out" posture, others affecting a more subversive stance. In part, this essay works to oppose black male anti-feminist contempt and mistrust of contemporary black women writers as my work is an attempt to recover and reaffirm the history of black men in pro-feminist alliance with black and white women begun in the Woman Suffrage Movement. It also functions to assert the idea that black feminist critique of sexism and misogyny in black communities is not about "black male bashing" —but about black women confronting the reality of patriarchy acted out by black men. The "black male bashing" attitude only perpetuates popular media sensationalization of black life grounded in the myth of a black gender war. Creating space for progressive dialogues on the prevalence of black sexism need not be governed by male supremacist thinking as if the black male ego remains too fragile for the rigor of critique, even as black women labor under the myth of the matriarch, a castrating "superwoman." Recovering black men's pro-feminist past acts to engender a politic of intervention whereby black men (and women) come to understand the necessity of feminist critique in liberation struggle as a critical means to empower all black people.

Black Women Writing to Liberate Themselves: Breaking a Tradition of Silence

If the first wave of American feminism in the 19th century represented the struggle of black women to be recognized as "women"–the second movement for women's liberation set the stage for a renaissance of black women writers who employed literature as a vehicle for self-empowerment. Misguidedly, the liberatory writings of black women have become the targets of black male anti-feminists precisely because many believe that the sole aim of black female writers is to bash them. Critical dialogue during and since "The Debate on Black Sexism" has continued around what black male detractors of feminism consider the emasculation of black men by "angry black feminists," Robert Staples calls Wallace and Shange. Black men opposed to feminism, such as Ishmael Reed, have accused black women writers of complicity with white women feminists toward the racist castration of all black men.

Black women writers have been accused of breaking faith with a standing agreement with their male counterparts and black female representation of black men said to be counter-productive to African-American struggle against racist oppression. Yet few of the black male critics of black women writers are willing to acknowledge the reality of sexism in black communities. In "Family Plots: Black Women Writers Reclaim Their Past," Thulani Davis articulates the perceived attack on black men this way–

> Contemporary [women] writers are being accused of pillorying black men, promoting homosexuality, ignoring sociological overviews of black oppression – and they're often pegged as the first black writers to commit such sins. (14)

To the extent that black women have embraced feminism, many black anti-feminists believe it has led them into acts of betrayal through a "(Ms.)representation" of black men. The price black women writers pay is expulsion from the Tradition of ("racial uplift") writing hereto dominated by African-American male writers. According to Mel Watkins in "Sexism, Racism and Black Women Writers,"

> Those black women writers who have chosen black men as a target have set themselves outside a tradition that is nearly as old as black American literature itself. They have, in effect, put themselves at odds with what seems to be an unspoken but almost universally accepted covenant among black writers. (36)

The "unspoken covenant" to which Watkins refers resides in myth. Black writers have never had such an unstated agreement. In African-American literary history, prescriptive notions of representation have traditionally met opposition (example: the Harlem renaissance). To suggest (as Watkins does later in his article) that the Harlem renaissance was a period during which "the earliest fiction by American blacks, produced by the Talented Tenth school of writers ... [was] characterized by [its] emphasis on establishing humane, positive images of blacks" (36) reveals a limited knowledge of the period's literary crisis regarding the representation of blacks in fiction. Watkins completely ignores the many black female and male writers who contested the provincialism, sexism, and homophobia of the black middle class. Watkins' claim that contemporary African-American women writers initiated a trend toward negative images of black men ignores those less than positive portrayals created by a number of black male writers. Like Watkins, Robert Staples would have us believe Shange and Wallace were the first (rightly) "angry black feminists." How would black men like Mel Watkins and Robert Staples read the feminist writings of Frederick Douglass and W. E. B. Du Bois? Would they be called "angry black feminists?" Apparently, contemporary black men who oppose feminism have no knowledge of Shange and Wallace's historical black male womanist counterparts.

(Re)constructing a Black Male Feminist Past, Toward a Black Womanist Future

Considering the difference race makes in relation to black men and feminism, my analysis of black male feminism is situated in the historical light of African-American male participation in the Woman Suffrage Movement. It forms the basis for theorizing black male feminism as a site of resistance to anti-womanist thinking and a location for gender solidarity, where transformative ideas of black manhood and masculinity in support of women's rights work against the ideology of male supremacy. Contesting black male attacks on black feminists—from Michele Wallace and Ntozake Shange in the late 1970s to Alice Walker and Terry McMillan in the following decades—black men understanding the longstanding relationship between black women and men in coalition struggle for woman suffrage in the 1920s disrupts the contemporary myth that all black men are anti-feminists. (Re) establishing a black men's womanist history represents an important step toward ending the myth of feminism as an (alien)ating force in black lives.

On the one hand, racial imperatives articulated in the framework of race and cultural nationalism since the 1960s—during the rise of the Black Power Movement and most recently in the call for black male repatriarchalization by Louis Farrakhan with the Million Man March—"blackness" has again become synonymous with "maleness," reinscribing a male-centered view of race that always already ignores issues of sexism. On the other, in the 60s issues of gender equality and women's rights led the agenda of the Women's Liberation Movement, principally dominated by middle class white women. And for many white women feminists still, the relation of men to feminism continues to be articulated in terms of gender alone, excluding the impact race has had and continues to have on gender relations in the US. By the end of the Black Power Movement, just as racial injustice had come to be identified mostly with the plight of the black male, so at the height of the Women's Liberation Movement the oppression of women had come to be associated with women who were white and middle class.

Reflecting on the race and gender politics of the 1960s, I have come to view the Black Power Movement and the second wave of feminism as important clarifying moments in my evolution as a black male feminist teacher in the 1990s. But like black women feminists advocating the struggle against racism, black men supporting women against sexism find ourselves on the margins of both black liberation and women's movements. Often having to confront the question: Are you "black" first or "feminist?" we find ourselves walking a race/gender tightrope always having to negotiate a position of split allegiance. For black women feminists, emphasis on their status as women in many black communities has been equated with a betrayal of race solidarity and lesbianism (as if heterosexual affiliation alone should determine one's affinity to blackness).

The absence of a large-scale political pronouncement of black men in support of anti-sexist activism suggests that in the contemporary period something called "black male pro-feminism" is invisible. And in many ways, being black and male in feminist alliance means being an "invisible (wo)man"—not a woman but neither a man in traditional phallocentric terms. Without oversimplifying this condition, perhaps, there is a kind of gender/race ambiguity that informs the idea of black male feminist positionality. But, as I have stated before, it is the idea of feminism connected to a perverse notion of the feminine that in the historical memory of black men conjures up images of feminization, castration, and ultimately death which may partly account for contemporary black male anti-feminism. Thus, in white supremacist capitalist patriarchal culture, to many black men feminism represents a threat to their vision of black masculinity and manhood—of familial and cultural authority, responsibility, nationhood, and "manliness." Many view feminism in synonymous relation to white supremacy that attempts to reenact the sexual "un-marring" of black men as the prime spectacle in the contemporary period of a "high tech" lynching.

Yet we can no longer use the myth of feminism as a racist ploy to emasculate black men while we assert our power as men to oppress women. Progressive black men, whether or not we advocate feminism, ought to begin divesting ourselves of male privilege in support of black women. Opposing sexism and misogyny, we embrace our history of pro-feminist alliance in women's rights struggle. Confronting the fear of the feminine that feminism represents to many men, black men begin to formulate effective, liberatory strategies of gender empowerment in black communities which affirm the rights of all women. Moreover, as we insist upon our right to be treated with dignity and respect in this society, we do so not because we are men but because we are human beings. Black men need to know that feminism—as a belief rooted in the right of women to lead non-oppressive, non-objectified lives—is not racist, sexist, or classist. We must vigorously denounce black male anti-feminist rhetoric that reduces the feminism of black women to a diatribe against black men.

If black women feminists are "angry" with black men (to recite Robert Staples' choice of words), then we need to ask why—without the cloak of self-pity that so many of us wear as we hide behind the wall of sexist denial to defend our oppressive behavior and misogynist ways. We can no longer construct ourselves as innocent victims of racism—castrated by "our" women who have no sympathy for the battle we wage against the (white) "Man" who refuses us a bigger slice of patriarchal pie. Black men in the Woman Suffrage Movement speaking and writing in feminist alliance rejected the "black-man-as-victim" status as they fought to obtain social, economic, and political rights for black men and women—while working to secure certain rights for women particularly based on the condition of gender oppression across the boundaries of race. Why can't we?

Black Men Speaking and Writing in Feminist Alliance

Fundamentally, it must be stated that from Frederick Douglass to W. E. B. Du Bois, feminist movement in black communities has had a significant impact on the representation of African-Americans in black discourse. The emergence of a black female intelligentsia in the last decade of the 19th century was preceded by the rise of Douglass as one of the century's most recognized black intellectuals, and followed by Du Bois as the major arbiter of the intellectual and artistic movement known as the Harlem renaissance. In the African-American literary tradition these men stand as acknowledged leaders of the "race," but each in his own right commanded more than one discursive field in which he spoke and wrote on the subject of women's rights. To view Douglass and Du Bois only as race leaders obscures and diminishes their distinguished careers as advocates of women's rights. To overlook their active participation in the developing stage of black women's intellectual and political enterprise (from which African-American feminist movement emerged) represents a grave oversight. Frances Ellen Harper, Pauline Hopkins, Anna Julia Cooper, and Ida B. Wells, among others, constituted a feminist intellectual body of which Frederick Douglass and W. E. B. Du Bois were an integral part.

As pro-woman speakers and writers, these men fit within the black feminist tradition at the incisive juncture of black women's political and social activism, characterized in the writings of the "Woman's Era." I assert the importance of the pro-woman position Douglass and Du Bois held partly to counter the phallocentric identification of blackness, though at times both men represented themselves in rather traditionally patriarchal ways. In recovering the women's rights discourse of Douglass and Du Bois as models of black male pro-feminism, I employ it to counterpose contemporary black male anti-feminist sentiment. I argue that the vision of liberation struggle these men constructed around a race/gender coalition politic holds transformative possibilities for black liberation movement today. The liberatory nature of feminist writings by Douglass and Du Bois rests precisely on the conjoinment of gender and race issues. This way of thinking is representative of the ideals early coalition strategists conceived in linking abolitionism to feminism. Douglass, Elizabeth Cady Stanton, and Susan B. Anthony among others viewed gender and race oppression in coterminous relation (notwithstanding the racist ideology of the Woman Suffrage Movement). Therefore, a movement to oppose gender and race oppression could constitute a much more politically viable and powerful location from which to strategize black enfranchisement and the political freedom of women.

Relying on black feminists theorizing race, gender, and class as interlocking systems of oppression, I look to the work of Paula Giddings, Angela Davis, and hooks on the history of black women and men in feminist movement to clarify the dual positions Douglass and Du Bois occupied as race spokesmen and advocates of women's rights. As standpoints determining their views of black liberation, race/gender duality inform the complex ideological structure of the men's feminist writings. Grasping the strategy Douglass and Du Bois conceived to advance the struggle of black people enables contemporary black men to reconceptualize a movement in resistance to white supremacy which encompasses strategies that oppose the oppression of women.

While the history of joint movement involving black and white people against racism and sexism in the US presents less than a glowing model of success, as a feminist I believe progressive feminism (founded on the liberation of all people, female and male) remains a crucial site in which to foster a coalition politic–linking political resistance to gender, race, class, and sexual oppression (across the boundaries of identity politics). I believe the infusion of coalition politics, informed by feminist thinking, in black people's movement for liberation would transform the dynamics of gender relations in black communities such that no one–regardless of sex, sexual preference, and/or class–is excluded from the battle for black people to live as whole beings. In the process, black men interrogating meanings of manhood (beyond white supremacist patriarchal denial of black male humanity) come to view feminism as a life-sustaining way of thinking that enhances rather than threatens our lives. As woman suffragists and advocates of women's rights, Frederick Douglass and W. E. B. Du Bois have much to offer us as black male feminists.

"(Black) Men in Feminism?" The "Ins" and "Outs" of (White) Male Feminism

In the 1980s male feminism was debated in *Men in Feminism* (1987), edited by Alice Jardine and Paul Smith. Centering on the theoretical problematics of male feminism, essays in the anthology focused on issue of men's relation (or nonrelation) to feminist theory. Given the ever-increasing presence of male critical and theoretical discourse on women, a volume such as *Men in Feminism* possessed the potential to be crucially important to a continuing dialogue on where men stand in relation to feminism. But it woefully failed. The essays, for the most part, exclude a discussion of race and sexuality. The volume includes not one essay by a woman or man of color. What references there are to black men and women are only incidental. The relation of men of color to feminism is never addressed. We remain invisible at nearly every level of discussion. Only one essay written by a white gay man overtly engages "men in feminism" and male sexuality. Jardine and Smith blame the virtual absence of gay and non-white perspectives on their "trouble locating intellectuals, who, having shown interest in the question, would offer ... a gay or black perspective on the problem." Rather than simply confess to the failure of their search, they point to academia's lack of institutional commitment to diversity in its hiring practices (vii–viii).

I seriously question how extensively the editors looked for the "Other" perspective when by 1987 bell hooks had already written on the relationship of men of color to feminism in *Feminist Theory: From Margin to Center*, 1984. In spite of its glaring silence on the subject of black men and feminism, conceptually *Men in Feminism* raises a fundamental question as to whether male feminists can work to empower women in non-patriarchal ways. In "Male Feminism," Stephen Heath addresses this question asserting that "[m]en's relation to feminism is an impossible one ... politically. Men have a necessary relation to feminism ... and that relation is also necessarily one of a certain exclusion ... no matter how 'sincere,' 'sympathetic' or whatever, we are always in a male position which brings with it all the implications of domination and appropriation ..." (1). The idea that men cannot in feminist alliance with women politically subvert the power of male supremacy is like saying white people in anti-racist solidarity with black people cannot divest themselves of white supremacist thinking.

Considering the institutionalization of women's studies in the academy and the proliferation of feminist scholarship by men (mostly white), I too am suspicious of male presence into this arena—particularly when so much of it appears appropriative, motivated by professional advancement. Yet male feminism situated in activist relation to feminist movement demonstrates a necessary engagement in theory and practice. Otherwise, the "in" space of "feminist" men construct can only be patriarchal—one of control, penetration, and violation. Discovering and writing about the lives of Douglass and Du Bois as woman suffragists has helped me to free myself from the kind of paralyzing male feminist theorizing trap that Stephen Heath sets up. If all feminist men concluded as he does that our relation to feminism is indeed an impossible one, we would never get on with the task at hand—to end sexism and the oppression of women. The history of black male pro-feminist relation to women's movement against sexism shows that despite the patriarchal baggage all men carry, we can be men without being oppressors of women.

(Black) male feminism as a politic of intervention (opposing sexism in black communities) represents a crucial step toward educating men on the ill-effects of male domination. According to bell hooks, the struggle against sexist oppression will be most successfully fought when men undergo feminist transformation—only when we are challenged by women to understand that the oppression of women is a form of self-oppression. Women can no longer afford to theorize men on the margin of feminism when sexist practice impacts the lives of women daily as its victims and men as its perpetrators. Women accepting progressive men as feminist allies will end the stigma of feminist movement as a separatist enterprise. While separatist thinking may free women from the presence of men, it does not eradicate sexism in the society at large. Instead, it mirrors the very sexist behavior feminist women seek to end.

"Re-membering" in Feminist Solidarity, Renewing Progressive Partnerships between Black Women and Men

As the 1960s brought forth with it a renaissance of black women writers, so it gave birth to a new generation of black female scholar/critics who would become the architects of a black feminist theory and criticism. From the re-emergence of feminism in black communities in the 1960s, came some of today's most outspoken black feminists. Of them, bell hooks, more than any other has addressed the necessity of black men in feminist movement. "Men: Comrades in Struggle" (in *Feminist Theory: From Margin to Center* critically addressed the need for men's political engagement in feminism. In one of her most radical essays on the subject, "Feminist Focus on Men" (from *Talking Back: Thinking Feminist, Thinking Black*, 1989)—she calls for women scholars to begin writing on men:

> Now we [women] can acknowledge that the reconstruction and transformation of male behavior, of masculinity, is a necessary and essential part of feminist revolution … While it is critical that male scholars committed to feminist struggle do scholarship that focuses on men, it is equally important that women scholars focus on men. (127, 132)

Putting into practice that which she advocates, hooks works in the tradition of 19th and early 20th-century black feminist coalition struggle. *Yearning: Race, Gender, and Cultural Politics* (1990) includes "Black Women and Men: Partnership in the 1990s," a dialogue between herself and Cornel West. *Breaking Bread: Insurgent Black Intellectual Life* (1991), co-authored with West, opens with the essay above as the basis for what represents a book-length continuation of the conversation the two began earlier. As intellectual "partners" discussing the challenge of integrating radical intellectualism into the struggle against racism, sexism, and the economic and cultural exploitation of African-Americans, they become comrades of the mind negotiating—

> [T]he point of connection between black women and men [that is the] space of recognition and understanding, where we know one another so well, our histories, that we can take the bits and pieces, the fragments of who we are, and put them back together, re-member them. (19)

In "re-member[ing]" black women and men's histories, hooks and West remember the legacy of those gone before them, who fought for the liberation of black people. That hooks and West would frame their coming together in the tradition of African-American intellectualism brings a new, even more lucid understanding of a historic exchange between black women and men. Well known dialogues have been recorded between Frederick Douglass and black women intellectuals including Sojourner Truth, Frances Harper, and Ida B. Wells-Barnett, among others. Dialogues have been documented which took place between W. E. B. Du Bois and Mary Church Terrell, Anna Julia Cooper, and Jessie Fauset—as well as those he had with a number of other black female thinkers of his day. *Breaking Bread* is about maintaining and preserving the historical continuity of black intellectual life. In the company of Douglass and Du Bois, bell hooks and Cornel West find their dialogue solidly grounded in a long history of black female/male "partnership" in feminist movement.

Claiming the feminist positionality of Douglass and Du Bois as a critical standpoint from which to call contemporary black men into renewed dialogue with black women on the status of gender relations in black communities, as a feminist black male college professor teaching African-American literature, I have constructed a cluster of courses in which the focus is the examination of the gender, race, class, and sexual politics of black people in the US. Teaching as a feminist, I aim my courses (while focusing on the experiences of black Americans) to engender the anti-racist/anti-sexist agenda Douglass and Du Bois conceived. The remainder of this essay works to explain the performance of anti-racist-feminism in my education practice—where the classroom is employed as a space not only for teaching progressive race and gender politics but for creating a liberatory location in which students learn about the transformative power of human rights activism.

From Theory to Practice: Teaching Feminism to Re-member

Committed to progressive feminist movement as articulated by hooks, I envision teaching as a process of "re-membering" in which African-American literary narratives become agents of social healing, across the boundaries of race, gender, class, and sexuality. Many students interested in ways these categories intersect come to my classes seeking an approach to understand the complex relation between them. I set up the political struggle of black Americans recounted in fiction, poetry, and/ or essay form as a model for liberation politics.

Over the past five years, I have developed a course repertory grounded in feminism.[4] Working from my background in African-American literature, the courses I teach apply a sociological perspective to the representation of black female/male gender relations rather than a strictly traditional "literary" interpretation. This approach illustrates the juncture where the personal, political, and pedagogical meet to establish the classroom as a space of feminist activism, where teaching black literature serves a liberatory purpose.

But it is the standpoint from which I perform an anti-racist/feminist pedagogy in the classroom that distinguishes my teaching as a male feminist. Thinking about ways to contest male privilege, sexism, and patriarchal hegemony and the power of the maternal in my life as a man, a husband, a father, and a teacher—I have come to draw upon the style, attitudes, and critical thinking about life experience my mother passed on to me. For me, performing a black male feminist positionality in the classroom means tapping into the maternal as a transformative space in which to nurture the development of critical consciousness in my students. I work to achieve a relationship with them associated with a maternal posture rather than paternal, patriarchal, or traditionally masculine-identified interaction. Following

---

[4] For example, students in a course I teach called "Black Female Representation in the Harlem Renaissance" focus on the politics of gender and race in the US during the 1920s. They study fictional accounts of "mixed-race" women in the African-American literary genre known as the "novel of passing." Examining the impact of miscegenation on the female body, students call into question "race" as an inherently natural category while analyzing the interrelated ways white supremacy, male privilege, classism, and homophobia function to shape the destiny of "biracial" women. Female and male students reading, discussing, and writing about the dilemma of "the tragic mulatta" come to understand the value of progressive feminist critique to engage the multiple oppression she experiences. Interrogating the fallibility of racial categorizing and the fallacy of whiteness, they comprehend the oppression of women as bound up in complex matrix of competing power relations. Moreover, they come to understand that all forms of domination are interconnected. I suggest to them that for individuals concerned with issues of social justice, coalition politics rooted in feminist movement can be a powerful force toward mobilizing people across borders. For me, the classroom serves as a viable site for the development of critical consciousness that values coalition building that resists the dehumanization of all people. Teaching in the spirit of feminist black men like Frederick Douglass and W. E. B. Du Bois advocating feminism who have come before me, I put into practice the anti-racist-feminist legacy they created.

Sally Ruddick's progressive line of thought that "a man who engages in mother-ing to some extent takes on the female condition and risks identification with the feminine" (45), I claim the act of "mothering" as a liberatory location to employ the maternal as a strategy of nurturance in my pedagogical practice in opposition to ways of the Father.

Growing up in a patriarchal household where my father's experience as a mil-itary officer informed the masculine rigidity of its day-to-day operation—as an often withdrawn timid little boy, I came to fear, despise, and later resist his notions of manhood, manliness, and masculinity. But in reflection, I was never drawn to the idea of male supremacy. More than anything, I identified with my mother's condition as black woman who, as a house-keeper/cook for a period in her life working tirelessly at the whims of elite white women, always had to enter the back door of their elegantly appointed homes to perform her duties as a servant. But it is my mother's sharp tongue, her resolute will to struggle, her critical understanding of the way race shaped her experience as a black female working class mother and wife that have informed how and what I teach. Teaching students (male students in particular) to resist anti-feminist ideas that men embracing feminism necessarily means a loss of a masculinity, I hold to Ruddick's idea that: "The fear of becoming 'feminine' ... is a motivating force behind the drive to master women and whatever is 'womanly' ... [G]rown men should confront the political meaning of 'femininity' and their own fear of the feminine. A man does not, by becoming a mother, give up his male body or any part of it. To be sure, by becoming a mother he will, in many social groups, challenge the ideology of masculinity" (45).

It stands to reason that men who embrace feminist thinking risk having their masculinity called into question; this is the point exactly. A man advocating and teaching feminism means taking risks—breaking through barriers of man-hood and masculinity inscribed in patriarchy, where qualities of nurturance and mothering are devalued. The maternal, as Ruddick insists, possesses transgendered capabilities.

Since my first course in feminism nearly ten years ago in graduate school when I read *Feminist Theory: From Margin to Center* for the first time, hooks' progres-sive vision of feminist movement against all forms of domination has shaped and guided my vision of the classroom as a space for liberatory education practice. But feminism itself remains a contested ideology in and outside the classroom not only because it subverts patriarchal power but also because it is bound up in complicated issues of race, class, and sexuality. For any teacher—whether female or male, black or not, gay or straight—employing progressive feminist politics to teach against white supremacy and male domination represents a transgres-sive act. Anti-racist feminist practice in the classroom requires risk-taking by the teacher and student. Often it means speaking from the personal, a space loaded with ideological baggage in need of exposure and examination.

When declaring to students that I am a feminist, they always react in complex ways, depending upon their race, gender, and sexual affiliations. But a feminist black man in (or outside) the classroom is an oddity. First of all, I am at odds with many white students' fear of black men and racist attitudes about black people in general. Secondly, I am at odds with many black students whose rage against and contempt for all white people blind them to the possibilities of progressive coalition movement across racial boundaries in resistance to racism, when we begin to de-essentialize "blackness." I am also at odds with male students especially (of color and not) who buy into male supremacist ideas of manhood and masculinity. They view me as a traitor to mankind a misanthrope of the worst kind!

As a black man teaching feminism as a strategy to combat racism, I take risks in the classroom posing a particular challenge to essentialized meanings of black liberation and racial solidarity linked to narrow ideas of black manhood and masculinity. Like black women feminists, my commitment to black struggle against racism is called into question by students of color who (always few in number at my institution) argue that "feminism is a white woman's thing." As a black man teaching in a predominately white, private institution who advocates an end to male privilege, sexism, and misogyny from a particularly "black" feminist perspective, my color and gender pose problems for white students in my classes. While white male presence in them is rare, those white men they do attract are often in the process of coming to grips with their fear of "blackness" —especially that personified in negative stereotypes of black men. Similarly, white women in my classes, whether feminist or not, respond to me in ways that suggest they too are working to figure out their own relationship to a "feminist black man." Feminist students who are female (of color and not), suspicious of men's motives for teaching and claiming feminist alliance, often display attitudes of distrust toward the notion of a male feminist. Generally, in the minds of both white students and students of color, I represent an image of black manhood and masculinity out of synch with the racist and sexual mythologies inscripted on the black male body over the course of time. I am not a Sambo, an Uncle Tom, a buck, a rapist, or a dope-dealer. But I am a black man who must downplay the fact of my tallness (6'4") and my "loud" voice (which I have been told by white females in my classes that these aspects of my identity frighten them)—because I am specifically "black and "male."

By the same token, disclaiming a patriarchal nationalist black masculinity (as represented by the ideas of Farrakhan dramatically played out in the Million Man March), I am viewed by many black male students as not only having sold out my blackness but my manhood as well because I critically opposed the March and most of its "Mission Statement." I maintain that a major contributing factor to the failure of black liberation movement in the 1960s had to do with its over-emphasis on issues relating to the needs of black men that excluded those of black women. The inability of the movement to sustain a successful oppositional stance and resistance to white supremacy and white supremacist capitalist patriarchal exploitation of black culture resided in the fact that many black men who participated in the movement viewed the struggle against racism solely in male-identified terms as I have already argued.

Black students in my classes (often because they feel threatened by implicit and explicit acts of racism perpetrated by white administrators, faculty members, and staff persons in a predominately white university setting) resist my claim that anti-racist ideology must be affected through a number of radical strategies—beyond the limited perspective of black male identity politics. Toward bell hooks' liberatory vision of "education as the practice of freedom," I claim a pedagogical strategy rooted in the politics of progressive feminist movement against all forms of domination, where teachers committed to coalition building cross race, gender, class, and sexual borders teach students ways to oppose the dehumanization of all people.

Contemporary black men actively calling into question male supremacy represents a potentially powerful voice for rethinking black masculinity. Transformative strategies of black liberation linked to a liberatory vision of black manhood and masculinity reflect a critically oppositional view of black men's racial oppression and the power we possess to oppress women precisely because we are men. When black men begin to construct a large-scale movement against racism and sexism, we embark upon a new path of struggle—one of feminist reclamation, not patriarchal atonement. Accepting our past as black men fighting racism as we waged with women the battle for gender rights, we claim a destiny beyond the bounds of patriarchy.

REFERENCES

- Cleaver, Eldridge. 1968. *Soul on Ice* (New York: Dell Publishing Co., Inc.).
- Davis, Thulani. 1987. "Family Plots: Black Women Reclaim the Past," *Voice Literary Supplement* (March): 14–17.
- Giddings, Paula. 1984. *When and Where I Enter: The Impact of Black Women on Race and Sex in America* (New York: Bantam Books).
- Hernton, Calvin. 1965. *Sex and Racism in America* (New York: Grove Press).
- hooks, bell. 1984. *Feminist Theory: From Margin to Center* (Boston: South End Press).
- hooks, bell. 1989. *Talking Back: Thinking Feminist, Thinking Black* (Boston: South End Press).
- hooks, bell. 1990. *Yearning: Race, Gender, and Cultural Politics* (Boston: South End Press).
- hooks, bell. 1992. *Black Looks: Race and Representation* (Boston: South End Press).
- hooks, bell and Cornel West. 1991. *Breaking Bread: Insurgent Black Intellectual Life* (Boston: South End Press).
- Jardine, Alice and Paul Smith (eds.). 1987. *Men in Feminism* (New York: Routledge).

- Ruddick, Sara. 1989. *Maternal Thinking: Toward a Politics of Peace* (New York: Ballantine Books).
- Staples, Robert. 1979. "The Myth of Black Macho: A Response to Angry Black Feminists," *The Black Scholar* (March–April): 24–32.
- Walker, Alice. 1983. *In Search of Our Mothers' Gardens* (New York: Harcourt Brace Jovanovich).
- Watkins, Mel. 1986. "Sexism, Racism and Black Women Writers," *The New York Times Book Review* (June): 36.

QUESTIONS

(1) What does it mean to be black, male, and feminist? And why is it important for a black male to claim a feminist identity?

(2) Is claiming a black male feminist identity a way of developing self-reflexivity that is necessary for coming to terms with black masculinity and simultaneously putting forward a critique of sexism and patriarchy that benefits all men in spite of race and social class background?

(3) Why is it not accurate to conflate womanism and feminism or to argue that womanism is a form of feminism? Can a black man be a womanist?

(4) Why is it important for black male feminists to continuously define themselves in relation to the activist history of black women in the spirit of the intersectionality of sexism and racism?

(5) What are some of the strategies that can be used to transform a college classroom into a space for liberatory educational practice that takes into consideration feminist activism?

PART VI
Past, Present, and Future Issues

ERICA F. COOPER

· ·

At the start of the twentieth century, Antonio Gramsci coined the term "ideology" to describe the methods of social control that are rooted in language and discourse. He revealed that ideology depends upon four interdependent processes: hegemony, naturalization, legitimization, and marginalization. Hegemony is achieved whenever the dominant beliefs, rules, norms, and practices within a culture are disseminated and publicly endorsed.[1] Marginalization is used to promote hegemony because it challenges and demonizes the beliefs and practices of all opposing or non-dominant groups. Naturalization and legitimization operate as the two remaining methods that are used to achieve hegemony. Public and private interactions collectively present the beliefs of the dominant group as natural and legitimate. In contrast, the beliefs that are opposing to the dominant group are ignored, distorted, and publicly denounced. Ultimately, protecting an ideology requires commitment and participation from all stakeholders even if they are unaware of how their participation is undeniably oppressive to themselves and others.

The manner in which a group views the world (its ideology) is determined by the features of the language used by its members. During all human interactions reality is co-constructed through the act of naming. For this reason, critical theorists have emphasized the relationship between language, power, and thought. They suggest that the act of naming is always ideological.[2] Language is strategic because it reveals the

---

[1] Antonio Gramsci, "The Intellectuals," in *Selections from the Prison Notebooks*, trans. and ed. Q. Hoare and G. N. Smith (New York: International Publishers, 1971), pp. 3–23. Available at: www.marxists.org/archive/gramsci/prison_notebooks/selections.htm.

ideological agenda of the group that controls its creation and usage. At the same time, the emergence of a new ideological discourse is rigorously resisted by the existing power structure. Similarly, non-dominant groups are denied access to developing the language that is used by mainstream society.

Why is language ideological? According to literary critic and rhetorical theorist, I. A. Richards, historical and contemporary socio-political and economic conditions influence the social construction of language and meaning.[3] The meanings that are derived from language are produced during our interactions with others. Cognition and behaviors are influenced by the intricate relationship between language, communication, and meaning.[4] Therefore, in the absence of language, thoughts would cease to exist. Additionally, since many linguistic communities speak different languages, they view and respond to the world differently.[5] Therefore, "reality" and knowledge are not discovered by humans. Instead, they only exist because they are created through (public or private) interactions.

In essence, language, as it is unveiled in social interactions, is hegemonic in cultivating and sustaining socially supported and socially oppressive ideologies. In this section, "Past, Present, and Future Issues," Cheryl I. Harris, Barbara J. Fields, and Kathleen Neal Cleaver deconstruct the structure of racist ideology by exploring the relationship between language, meaning, and thought. Historically, racism, rooted in the mainstream vernacular, has rigidly defined public and private relationships within the United States. Harris, Fields, and Cleaver explain how racist language obscures the similarities of lived experiences amongst members of the working class. Such language created illusions of difference based on dual yet dialectical notions of purity, white supremacy, and black inferiority. For over two hundred years, during intra- and inter-racial encounters, the economic interests of the ruling class have been preserved while the "white" working class is heavily exploited. To reinforce this point, each author critically examines the hegemonic processes connected with the rhetoric of white supremacy. By scrutinizing the essence of this ideology, the detrimental psychological effects of racism on black and white people are clearly revealed. Specifically, Harris, Fields, and Cleaver draw attention to ways in which

---

[2] See Cheris Kramarae, *Women and Men Speaking* (Rowley, MA: Newbury House, 1981); Michael McGee, "The 'Ideograph': A Link Between Rhetoric and Ideology," *Quarterly Journal of Speech* 66, no. 1 (1980): 1–16; and Ian Haney Lopez, "The Social Construction of Race: Some Observations on Illusion, Fabrication and Choice," *Harvard Civil Rights: Civil Liberties Law Review* 29 (1994): 1–62.

[3] C. K. Ogden and I. A. Richards, *The Meaning of Meaning: A Study of the Influence of Language upon Thought and the Science of Symbolism* (London: Kegan Paul, Trench, Trubner & Co, 1923).

[4] Edward Sapir, *Culture, Language and Personality* (Berkeley: University of California Press, 1958); Benjamin Lee Whorf, "Science and Linguistics" [1940], in *Language, Thought and Reality*, ed. John B. Carroll (Cambridge, MA: MIT Press, 1956), pp. 207–19.

[5] This is known as the concept of linguistic relativity from the Sapir-Whorf hypothesis. See Whorf, "Science and Linguistics."

the public endorsement of racial monikers by politicians, court justices, educators, and the "average" citizen naturalize and legitimize "white" people while injuring all who are non-white. The presence of racist language arbitrarily and artificially separates people on the basis of a socially constructed concept of "pure blood" that is proposed as ideal and natural. Collectively, these three chapters demonstrate what Kenneth Burke coined with the phrase, "language as symbolic action,"[6] or the ability of language to operate more than simply as a medium of conveying information. Harris, Fields, and Cleaver inform us about the hegemonic underpinnings of racist ideology that support dual and yet dialectical systems of racial subjugation and racial domination as well as racial inclusion and racial exclusion.

Cheryl I. Harris: Whiteness as Property

Racial identity is the term used to distinguish between groups and to determine civil and political rights. In Chapter 18, Cheryl Harris argues that historically (state and federal) judges and legislative assemblies designed laws and policies that legitimized the notions of "race," racial identity, and white supremacy within the United States. She explains how class tensions posed a real threat to those who benefited from the existing social system particularly after the Civil War. The emancipation of the slaves accelerated these fears and tensions. The "exigence"[7] of a potential class war threatened to destroy the significant financial benefits associated with an economic system dependent upon the exploitation of labor from the working class. Therefore, the danger of losing economic prosperity created an urgent need to contain a problem.

Harris argues that racism became the means of promoting a system of class exploitation. Socially constructed distinctions on the basis of this concept of "racial difference" were used to divide the working class while protecting and perpetuating this ideology as both natural and legitimate. As early as the colonial period, physical characteristics such as hair texture and color, facial features, and skin color were the standards used to define racial groups. Although courts and legislatures agreed to use physical appearance as the basis for defining racial classifications, this standard was difficult to enforce.[8] Therefore, other criteria such

---

[6] Kenneth Burke. *Language as Symbolic Action: Essays on Life, Literature, and Method* (Berkeley: University of California Press, 1966).

[7] This term is defined by Lloyd Bitzer as a problem or imperfection marked by urgency. Lloyd Bitzer, "The Rhetorical Situation," *Philosophy and Rhetoric* 1, no. 1 (1968): 1–11 (p. 3).

[8] Erica F. Cooper, "One 'Speck' of Imperfection–Invisible Blackness and the One-Drop Rule: An Interdisciplinary Approach to Examining *Plessy v. Ferguson and Jane Doe v. State of Louisiana*" (PhD, dissertation, Indiana University, 2008). See also Frank W. Sweet, "Timeline of B/W 'Racial' Determination in the United States," *BackinTyme Essays*, July 1, 2007. Available at: http://backintyme.com/essays/?p=34; and Frank W. Sweet, *The Notion of Invisible Blackness: Legal History of the Color Line* (Palm Coast, FL: Backintyme, 2005).

as the rule of association and simple blood quantum laws emerged in an effort to define racial groups with more clarity.[9] Unfortunately, creating a racial divide proved difficult because states were not uniform in selecting and enforcing criteria.[10] For example, some states used quantum laws and other states relied upon appearance and/or association. Even among the states using the same criterion there was variation. In the case of the quantum statutes, some states established 1/4th African ancestry as the marker for defining blackness and others used the 1/8th or 1/16th standard.[11] As a result, a person could be accepted as "black" in the eyes of the law in one state but white in another. As the threat of a potential class war became imminent during the nineteenth century, Harris concludes that there was an increasing need to establish a more rigid racial system to permanently divide laborers.

In response to this context, Harris describes how one-drop language, introduced into public and private conversations, created a bifurcated racial classification system as well as a social system of domination and oppression. The racial binary affected the meanings that society as a whole associated with "white" and "black." Eugenics "research" constructed race as an experience that was immutable, natural, and directly connected to a person's bloodline or genetics rather than simply physical appearance. Under these new guidelines racial groups became mutually exclusive. Similarly, court justices legitimized these new meanings in establishing legal precedent rooted in the newly constructed idea that one drop of black blood was a sufficient marker to distinguish between whites and non-whites. The presence of this "new" concept had significant effects on the social and political structure within the United States. Civil and social rights were granted or denied depending on the side of the color line in which a person was assigned. Harris states:

> Because legal recognition of a person as white carried material benefits, "false," or inadequately supported claims were denied like any other unsubstantiated claim in a property interest. Only those who could lay "legitimate" claims to whiteness could be legally recognized as "white," because allowing physical attributes, social acceptance, or self-identification to determine whiteness would diminish its value and destroy the underlying presumption of exclusivity.

It is clear that jurisprudence and science were hegemonic in establishing a distinct and rigid color line where whiteness was associated with purity and material

---

[9] See Cooper, "One 'Speck' of Imperfection," chapter 1.

[10] See Cooper, "One 'Speck' of Imperfection," chapter 2.

[11] Virginia established the first quantum law in 1705. One-eighth or more African ancestry determined who was black. However, by the end of the century, Virginia lowered the fraction to one-fourth. See Cooper, "One 'Speck' of Imperfection," chapter 1.

privileges and blackness was aligned with imperfection and restricted access. As a result of this linguistic shift, those who were not accepted as white under the one-drop doctrine were marginalized as white supremacy became the dominant ideology.

Harris uses the phrase "psychological wage of whiteness," to describe the ripple effect that occurred once workers recognized that their "whiteness" was valuable. These workers failed to question whether or not racial differences were legitimate and real or the effects that this system had upon non-whites. Instead, they began to voluntarily segregate themselves from non-white people believing that whites were more important and more highly valued within the society. According to Harris, the "psychological wage of whiteness," which was first addressed by W. E. B. Du Bois in *Black Reconstruction*, revealed the cognitive rather than material benefits that white workers acquired from embracing these tenets of white supremacy. Both Du Bois and Harris remind us that it has historically been the social commitment of *all* whites to uphold a rigid racial binary that contributed to the divisions among members of the working class. In exchange for their support, scientists, legislators, and courts perpetuated discourses of white supremacy to uplift the white worker. The assumption that racial differences are real and significant provided a cognitive distraction from the materiality of the economic subjugation and exploitation of capitalism amongst white workers.

In contrast to the white worker, Harris argues that the emergence of white supremacy had a tremendously negative effect on non-white people. "The hyper-valuation of whiteness" that simultaneously emerges is dialectically paired with the devaluation of "blackness" (or self-concept) among non-white people. As a part of the marginalization process, non-white people were induced to believe that there was no inherent value in their non-white identity. As the devaluation of "blackness" occurred within the larger society, black people were involuntarily placed in a position of racial subordination. In order to survive within this environment, Harris argues that black people were forced to reject their racial identity while attempting to "pass for white."

Barbara J. Fields: Whiteness, Racism, and Identity

In this chapter, Barbara Fields explores the delicate relationship between knowledge and language to demonstrate how what is "worth knowing" is directly connected to the basic tenets of white supremacy. In particular, Fields concludes that "whiteness" research perpetuates white supremacy. For example, researchers utilize racist monikers that emerged in response to the one-drop rule whenever they examine this topic. By using labels such as "white" or "black," "scholars" unapologetically naturalize the ideology of racism by uncritically accepting the racial bifurcation system that results from the meanings that have been attached to these terms for a century. For this reason, white supremacy is elevated without question each time scholarship including "racialized" language rooted in one-drop reasoning is used to describe or classify people. This language used in scholarship continues to endorse the validation of whiteness and at the same time subjugating the experiences of all who are non-white.

To support this observation, Fields offers examples of the relationship between language and thought. Researchers consistently refer to people who migrate from Europe to the United States as "white" and/or "immigrant." Consequently, this relationship has influenced the manner in which "immigrant" is now defined. This codification within academic discourse contributes to several "cognitive chain reactions." According to Fields, the word "immigrant" is never used when discussing the arrival of non-white people. For this reason, scholars have completely failed to acknowledge the arrival of non-white groups. However, when the arrival of these groups is discussed, Fields argues that researchers have linked their presence to slavery, illicit activities, and/or unlawful entry. In addition, the inability of researchers to more broadly define "immigration" naturalizes and legitimizes white supremacy and promotes the marginalization of non-white people. Therefore, blind endorsement of racist language and the clusters of meaning that emerge contribute to the negative impact of their research on non-white people while preserving white supremacy.

By problematizing the state of existing research, Fields challenges us to examine the impact of academic discourse on cognition and behavior. How can we address the disparity between the proposed objectives of research that is designed to interrogate the legitimacy of racism and the reality that it dismally fails to achieve those goals with significant damaging effects? If immigration is an experience that is limited to "whites" or those of European ancestry, why should we be surprised whenever "Americans" openly contest the arrival and the presence of those who are not white? In the United States, at the time of writing (2018), we are grappling with the implications of the very research that Fields criticizes. The current separation of children from their parents in deportation camps within the United States is directly related to the meanings that have been generated and disseminated publicly by academics and endorsed by politicians and courts regarding whiteness, immigration, and entitlement. Non-white people are not entitled to rights and privileges because they have never officially attained the "legally acceptable" status as "immigrants." Therefore, they are not worthy of any sympathy because they have no right to be here anyway. Will scholars ever reckon with the overlooking of non-whites' experiences? If "whiteness" scholars respond to this crisis, it must be done with a recognition of how the language influences cognitions. Lastly, once they are aware of the racially biased methods and medium, will scholars be willing to sever ties with the oppressive language that is limiting their perspective? If the naturalization and legitimization of white supremacy in academic research is exposed, the importance of developing new, non-racist language will become a new top priority that must be introduced into all discussions involving the arrival of white and non-white groups. One can certainly question whether or not scholars will ever take responsibility for their (un)conscious role in shaping public attitudes toward this issue.

In addition to establishing the ways in which academic discourse is hegemonic and promotes white supremacy, Fields also reminds us that the reactions to white supremacy from the average white and/or non-white person fosters the subordination of non-white people. On one hand, non-white people cannot avoid using the very language of white supremacy that fuels their own oppression whenever they attempt to describe or define themselves. To counteract the devaluation of "blackness," African Americans developed their own labels as a form of empowerment. Unfortunately, as Fields argues, this strategy of resistance did not challenge the dominant ideology. Instead, the new terms that emerged were just synonymous with the existing standard language. As African Americans believed that they were empowering themselves by developing their own monikers to define themselves, this act of "psychological" resistance in reality operated as an act of compliance. These terms created a false consciousness among African Americans as they were deceived into thinking that they had agency when defining and establishing the value of their racial identity. Unfortunately, they were completely unaware of how these terms perpetuated the material reality of their own racial subjugation. In essence, Fields provides a cautionary tale of how people of color co-sponsor the preservation of racism. African Americans (and other people of color) will never receive full cognitive emancipation or social equality as long as they remain entangled within this web of oppressive language, thought, and meaning.

If white supremacy forced people of color to devalue themselves, reject their social standing, and develop their own words to define themselves, what effect did it have on those who benefited from it? The "psychological wages" associated with white supremacy encouraged white workers to actively protect it. Fields expands on the discussion associated with the psychological wages of whiteness. She states that as members of the dominant group, white workers gained access to spaces that were restricted to those who were not white. They were allowed to laugh at the jokes that targeted other marginalized groups. Once "immigrant" was codified with "whiteness," all European "immigrants" were also invited to join the in-group upon their arrival. As soon as (white) European immigrants entered the United States they also immediately embraced racism. The psychological benefits of "belonging" to the "in-group" were a greater reward than interrogating the legitimacy of racism. Therefore, Fields argues that it is problematic for academics to suggest that racism is a substitute for race. By doing so, race becomes an attribute of racism rather than the symbolic act of racism. Due to the psychological effects of racism on both white and non-white people, Fields believes that "there is no voluntary and affirmative side to racism as far as its victims are concerned."

Kathleen Neal Cleaver: The Antidemocratic Power of Whiteness

Kathleen Cleaver deconstructs the ideological impact of white supremacy on the psyche of white people. She reveals how hegemony among "whites" regardless of socio-economic status is cultivated through their social interactions which promote racism. Although the aristocracy receives the most significant economic benefits from dividing the working class, Cleaver suggests that the ideology of white supremacy is most often wielded by other elements within the society. For example, during private and public discussions involving the ordinary citizen, white supremacy thrives and is reinforced. Cleaver believes that white workers imagined a relationship between race and labor that reflected the psychological and public wages associated with white supremacy.

Once society endorsed the codification between race and slave status during the eighteenth century, white workers began to describe themselves in distinct ways. For example, white workers created terms that defined labor in a hierarchical manner on the basis of white supremacy. As a result, whites were easily able to distinguish their work from the non-whites. During this process, white workers used the term "freedman" exclusively when they described people of European descent. In addition to aligning "free" status with European identity, white workers also stopped using terms that implied servitude or servant status such as "domestic worker" and/or "indentured servant" to describe themselves. Cleaver brings attention to the fact that the term "servant" was utilized by white workers only when describing the type of labor that was provided by people of color. This bold action was unprecedented because prior to the eighteenth century, "servant" status was not restricted to racial group membership.

According to Cleaver, the crafted meanings used among white workers were a reaction to the emergent ideological system of capitalism. In the transition from the agrarian way of life to a capitalist state, at least half of the "free" workforce in the United States was completely wage dependent. Whilst white workers recognized their own material reality of labor/class based slavery, the emancipation of black people heightened their insecurities. The expansion of the free labor force also brought changes to the socio-political landscape where former slaves contested their denial of the political rights that white workers had exclusively enjoyed. In response to the changing economic system, white workers cultivated the discourse of labor to promote white supremacy and manage the dissonance that they experienced from the unexpected and adverse effects of capitalism.

The white working class naturalized and legitimized the exploitation of non-white people and themselves through masking the material reality of wage dependency. In doing so, white workers undermined their ability to obtain liberation from their own economic exploitation and oppression. The psychological stress of capitalism obscured their own fears and subjugation. Cleaver argues that uniting with black workers with whom they shared common goals and interests was the only viable remedy to end the economic oppression of the white worker. Unfortunately, these workers remained psychologically invested in endorsing a white supremacist vision that protected the "oppressive system of capitalism and ruined democracy."

Although the action of white workers was hegemonic in marginalizing black people, the socio-economic status of the white worker did not improve. According to Cleaver, the public and psychological wages that they received from their compliance were rationalized as a viable substitute amongst white workers. Some whites were given public titles simply because they were white. The legitimacy of the political and judicial system was heavily dependent upon their support and they knew it. To enforce white supremacy, legislators and court justices needed to be elected into office. Without the support at the polls of white voters, the entire socio-political system would collapse. In compensation for their unwavering political support, Cleaver describes how white workers received lenient punishments for crimes, such as less jail time, or were released without any accompanying charges made against them. The punishments were particularly more lenient whenever whites were involved in altercations with people of color. The criminal justice system with the "blind" cooperation of courts and legislators often refused to hold white people accountable for their actions. The inactivity of the courts and lawmakers established an environment of lawlessness where white men, in particular, collectively preserved the social hierarchy that was cultivated by white supremacy.

The ability of racism to protect itself, according to Cleaver, is revealed by comparing how the working class during the nineteenth century and present day responded to the fears associated with capitalism. Cleaver believes that in the past, "masculinity" operated as a coping mechanism to manage the dissonance associated with wage dependency. As white workers actively sought to define the term "worker," its meaning incorporated "masculinity" and "whiteness." The resulting cluster of meaning impacted how people reacted to the terms individually and collectively. It was implied that workers were only "masculine," white men. In response to this paradigm shift, Cleaver proposes the thought-provoking question of how the disgruntled working class during the twenty-first century will realign their identity with notions of "white male superiority". Hence, we are forced to acknowledge a reality where "whatever connection exists between the racially charged political rhetoric of recent campaigns and the disturbing fragmentation and decline facing the industrial worker, the abiding significance attached to whiteness is clear." As whiteness continues to dominate discussions about race, class, and gender, the "antidemocratic politics" within the United States is more apparent.

Conclusion

These three chapters promote a dialogue designed to challenge us to consider the hegemonic nature of language. By introducing and defining "race based" terms, naturalization, legitimization, and marginalization still operate to preserve the ideology of white supremacy in the twenty-first century. According to Fields, white supremacy in the second half of the twentieth century did not reveal itself in the same manner as it had done in the past. The absence of slavery or Jim Crow legislation encouraged academics to assume that the United States had evolved into a post-racial society where racism was a thing of the past and where race had ceased to exist. However, Fields, Cleaver, and Harris remind us that language is ideological, seductive, and omnipotent. Contemporary social and political conversations about immigration and terrorism are ridden with white supremacist reasoning. Scholars, politicians, and other groups continuously promote the idea that anyone who is white has lawfully entered the United States and has a natural right to remain. White people are never publicly threatened and their presence is consistently legitimized and naturalized because it is never contested. In contrast, the arrival of non-white people is wrought with presumptions of illegality that leads to social hostility and paranoia. People of color are never afforded the right to have their arrival narratives heard or endorsed. Instead, their marginalization begins before they ever leave their countries of origin.

Similarly, as the violent actions of terrorism become more prevalent in the twenty-first century, the actions of white men are never aligned with this term even when they are responsible for the slaughter of large numbers of people. When white people are the perpetrators of violent criminal actions against persons of color (in particular), their actions are ignored and in many cases protected within the criminal justice system and courts because they are not deemed as criminal. For this reason, terrorism, as a term, is rarely if ever used in the presence of "whiteness." The fictitious mental image that the average person generates in response to the word "terrorist" is one where the perpetrator is a person of color who is unlawfully present and violent. Socially constructed uses of whiteness fail, as Fields declares, to "banish the troubling asymmetry that is the essence of racism."

Lastly, scholars must also recognize the role that they serve in naturalizing and legitimizing whiteness through the marginalization of non-white people. Cleaver criticizes scholarship for allocating too much attention to the obvious "targets of racism." Like white workers, racism has a direct effect on those who study it. It frames what they see and how they describe what it is that they see. Their failure to recognize the power of this ideology has resulted in their own legitimization of racism. They naturalize white supremacy whenever they describe and differentiate between people on the basis of race. Racist attitudes are revealed whenever they endorse or fail to interrogate the relationship between race and the rights afforded to whites. Without accepting the role that they serve in establishing an episte-mology of racism, academics will continue to validate white supremacy. Instead, responsible scholarship must also acknowledge that white supremacy has an effect on its perpetrators as well as its targets. Scholars must realize that they function as perpetrators as well. Collectively, Harris, Fields, and Cleaver remind us that racial domination will remain as long as citizens endorse and embrace this oppressive language and the meanings cultivated from it.

QUESTIONS

(1) According to the authors in this section, what was and continues to be the most pressing issue for race relations in the United States?
(2) How does whiteness influence democratic politics in the United States?
(3) How do we understand whiteness? Is whiteness the same as white supremacy?
(4) What connection might there be between "whiteness as property" and the formation of America's working-class history?
(5) After reading the authors of this section, how do you think that the problem of white supremacy can be solved in the United States?

FURTHER READINGS

- Charles Mills, *Blackness Visible: Essays on Philosophy and Race* (Ithaca, NY: Cornel University Press, 1998).
- Christel N. Temple, "Communicating Race and Culture in the Twenty-First Century: Discourse Post-Racial/Post-Cultural Challenge," *Journal of Multicultural Discourses* 5, no. 2 (2010): 45–63.
- Frantz Fanon, *Black Skin, White Masks*, trans. Charles Lam Markmann (New York: Grove Press, 1976).
- George Yancy (ed.), *What White Looks Like: African-American Philosophers on the Whiteness Question* (New York: Routledge, 2004).
- Hortense Spiller, *Black, White, and in Color: Essays on American Literature and Culture* (Chicago University Press, 2003).
- Lewis R. Gordon, *Fanon and the Crisis of European Man: An Essay on Philosophy and the Human Sciences* (New York: Routledge, 1995).
- Michelle Alexander, *The New Jim Crow: Mass Incarnation in the Age of Colorblindness* (New York: New Press, 2010).
- Naomi Zack, *White Privilege and Black Rights: The Injustice of U.S. Police Racial Profiling and Homicide* (Lanham, MD: Rowman & Littlefield, 2015).
- Robert Gooding-Williams, "Race, Multiculturalism, and Democracy," *Constellations: An International Journal of Critical and Democratic Theory* 5, no. 1 (1998): 18–41.
- Toni Morrison, *Playing in the Dark: Whiteness in Literary Imagination* (Cambridge, MA: Harvard University Press, 1993).

18 Whiteness as Property

CHERYL I. HARRIS

Cheryl I. Harris, at present, is the Rosalinde and Arthur Gilbert Foundation Chair in Civil Rights and Civil Liberties at the University of California, Los Angeles. Some of her key works include "Limiting Equality: The Divergence and Convergence of Title VII and Equal Protection," 2014; "Reading Ricci: Whitening Discrimination, Racing Test Fairness," 2010; and "Whitewashing Race: Scapegoating Culture," 2008. The extract reproduced below is taken from her famous article, "Whiteness as Property." Harris focuses on the historical role "whiteness as property" played and continues to play in the United States. And given that all whites are invested in "whiteness as property," Harris points out that it is a grave challenge for most whites to disaffiliate themselves from whiteness and white privilege.

Moreover, as it emerged, the concept of whiteness was premised on white supremacy rather than mere difference. "White" was defined and constructed in ways that increased its value by reinforcing its exclusivity. Indeed, just as whiteness as property embraced the right to exclude, whiteness as a theoretical construct evolved for the very purpose of racial exclusion. Thus, the concept of whiteness is built on both exclusion and racial subjugation. This fact was particularly evident during the period of the most rigid racial exclusion, as whiteness signified racial privilege and took the form of status property.

At the individual level, recognizing oneself as "white" necessarily assumes premises based on white supremacy: It assumes that black ancestry in any degree, extending to generations far removed, automatically disqualifies claims to white identity, thereby privileging "white" as unadulterated, exclusive, and rare. Inherent in the concept of "being white" was the right to own or hold whiteness to the exclusion and subordination of blacks. Because "[i]dentity is ... continuously being constituted through social interactions,"[1] the assigned political, economic, and social inferiority of blacks necessarily shaped white identity. In the commonly held popular view, the presence of black "blood"–including the infamous "one-drop"[2]–consigned a person

---

[1] Robert C. Post, "The Social Foundations of Defamation Law: Reputation and the Constitution," *California Law Review* 74 (1986), p. 709.

[2] F. James Davis, *Who Is Black?* (University Park, PA: Penn State University Press, 1991), p. 5 (citations omitted).

to being "black" and evoked the "metaphor ... of purity and contamination" in which black blood is a contaminant and white racial identity is pure.[3] Recognizing or identifying oneself as white is thus a claim of racial purity,[4] an assertion that one is free of any taint of black blood. The law has played a critical role in legitimating this claim.

White Legal Identity: The Law's Acceptance and Legitimation of Whiteness as Property

The law assumed the crucial task of racial classification, and accepted and embraced the then-current theories of race as biological fact. This core precept of race as a physically defined reality allowed the law to fulfill an essential function—to "parcel out social standing according to race" and to facilitate systematic discrimination by articulating "seemingly precise definition of racial group membership."[5] This allocation of race and rights continued a century after the abolition of slavery.[6]

The law relied on bounded, objective, and scientific definitions of race—what Neil Gotanda has called "historical race"[7]—to construct whiteness as not merely race, but race plus privilege. By making race determinant and the product of rationality and science, dominant and subordinate positions within the racial hierarchy were disguised as the product of natural law and biology rather than as naked preferences.[8] Whiteness as racialized privilege was then legitimated by science and was embraced in legal doctrine as "objective fact."

Case law that attempted to define race frequently struggled over the precise fractional amount of black "blood"—traceable black ancestry—that would defeat a claim to whiteness.[9] Although the courts applied varying fractional formulas

---

[3] Neil Gotanda, "A Critique of 'Our Constitution is Colorblind,'" *Stanford Law Review* 44 (1991), p. 26.

[4] See ibid. at p. 27.

[5] Robert J. Cottrol, "The Historical Definition of Race Law," *Law & Society Review* 21 (1988): 865–869.

[6] See ibid.

[7] Gotanda defines "historical race" as socially constructed formal categories predicated on race subordination that included presumed substantive characteristics relating to "ability, disadvantage, or moral culpability." Gotanda, "A Critique of 'Our Constitution is Colorblind,'" p. 4.

[8] See Cass R. Sunstein, "Naked Preferences and the Constitution," *Columbia Law Review* 89 (1980), pp. 1693–1694.

[9] See, for example, *People v. Dean*, 14 Mich. 406 (x866), in which the majority held that those with less than one-quarter black blood were white within the meaning of the constitutional provision limiting the franchise to "white male citizens," see ibid. at 425. The dissent argued that a preponderance of white blood should be sufficient to accord the status of whiteness. See ibid. at 435, 438 (Martin, C.J., dissenting).

in different jurisdictions to define "black" or, in the terms of the day, "Negro" or "colored," the law uniformly accepted the rule of hypodescent[10]—racial identity was covered by blood, and white was preferred.[11]

This legal assumption of race as blood-borne was predicated on the pseudo-sciences of eugenics and craniology that saw their major development during the eighteenth and nineteenth centuries.[12] The legal definition of race was the

---

[10] "Hypodescent" is a term used by anthropologist Marvin Harris to describe the American system of racial classification in which the subordinate classification is assigned to the offspring if there is one "superordinate" and one "subordinate" parent. Under this system, the child of a black parent and a white parent is black. Marvin Harris, *Patterns of Race in the Americas* (New York: Walker, 1964), pp. 37, 56.

[11] According to various court decisions of the nineteenth and early twentieth centuries, the term "negro" was construed to mean a person of mixed blood within three generations, see *State v. Melton & Byrd*, 44 N.C. (Busb.) 49, 51 (1852); a person having one-fourth or more of African blood, see *Gentry v. McMinnis*, 3 Dana (Ky.) 382, 385 (1835); *Jones v. Commission*, 80Va. 538, 542 (1885); a person having one-sixteenth or more of African blood, see *State v. Chavers*, 50 N.C. 1i, 14–15 (1857); *State v. Watters*, 25 N.C. (3Ired.) 455, 457 (1843); a person having one-eighth or more of African blood, see *Rice v. Gong Lum*, 139 Miss. 760, 779 (925); *Marre v. Marre*, 184 Mo. App. 198, 211 (1914); anyone with any trace of Negro blood, see *State v. Montgomery County School*, Dist. No. 16, 242 S.W. 545, 546 (1922). The term "colored" too had a range of legal meanings. See ii C.J. Colored 1224 (917). For a review of court decisions and statutes of nineteenth and early twentieth centuries delineating who is a "Negro" or who is colored, see Charles S. Mangum, *The Legal Status of the Negro* (Chapel Hill: University of North Carolina Press, 1940), pp. 1–17.

An example of the complexity of defining these terms is revealed in *State v. Treadaway*, 52 So. 500 (La. 1910), in which the Louisiana state supreme court exhaustively reviewed the various meanings of the words "negro" and "colored" in considering whether an "octoroon" – a person of one-eighth black blood – was a Negro within the meaning of a statute barring cohabitation between a person of the "white" race and a person of the "negro or black" race. See ibid. at 501–510. In examining the definitions propounded in various dictionaries, court decisions, and statutory law that used either term, the court concluded that "colored" denoted a person of mixed white and black blood in any degree, and a "negro" was a "person of the African race, or possessing the black color and other characteristics of the African." Ibid. at 531. Because "there are no negroes who are not persons of color; but there are persons of color who are not negroes," ibid., the court concluded that the statute did not include octoroons because they were not commonly considered "negroes," although they were persons of color, see ibid. at 537. The response of the Louisiana legislature was to reenact the statute with the identical language, except it substituted the word "colored" for the word "Negro." See Mangum, *Legal Status of the Negro*, pp. 5–6.

[12] For example, Samuel Morton, one of the principal architects of these theories, ascribed the basis of black and non-white racial inferiority to differences in cranial capacity, which purportedly revealed that whites had larger heads. Notwithstanding the gross breaches of scientific method and manipulation of data evident in Morton's theory (see Thomas F. Gossett, *Race: The History of an Idea in America* (Oxford University Press, 1963), pp. 73–74), his 1839 book, *Crania Americana*, was widely accepted as the scientific explanation of blacks' inability to mature beyond childhood, see Gossett, *Race*, pp. 58–59 (citing the remarks of Oliver Wendell Holmes, Sr., extolling Morton as a "leader" whose "severe and cautious ... researches" would provide "permanent data for all future students of Ethology"); see also Ronald Takaki, *Iron Cages: Race and Culture in 19th Century America* (Oxford University Press, 1990), p. 113 (citing the remarks of an Indiana senator in 1850 who spoke of the diminished brain capacity of blacks). These and

"objective" test propounded by racist theorists of the day who described race to be immutable, scientific, biologically determined—an unsullied fact of the blood rather than a volatile and violently imposed regime of racial hierarchy.

In adjudicating who was "white," courts sometimes noted that, by physical characteristics, the individual whose racial identity was at issue appeared to be white and, in fact, had been regarded as white in the community. Yet if an individual's blood was tainted, she could not claim to be "white" as the law understood, regardless of the fact that phenotypically she may have been completely indistinguishable from a white person, may have lived as a white person, and have descended from a family that lived as whites. Although socially accepted as white, she could not *legally* be white.[13] Blood as "objective fact" dominated over appearance and social acceptance, which were socially fluid and subjective measures.

But, in fact, "blood" was no more objective than that which the law dismissed as subjective and unreliable. The acceptance of the fiction that the racial ancestry could be determined with the degree of precision called for by the relevant standards or definitions rested on false assumptions that racial categories of prior ancestors had been accurately reported, that those reporting in the past shared the definitions currently in use, and that racial purity actually existed in the United States.[14] Ignoring these considerations, the law established rules that extended

---

other widely disseminated theories of black inferiority provided the rationale for the political and popular discourse of the time that argued that black equality and participation in the polity were impossible because blacks lacked the capacity to develop rational decision making. See Reginald Horsman, *Race and Manifest Destiny* (Cambridge, MA: Harvard University Press, 1981), pp. 116–157 (describing the permeation of "scientific" bases for racial inferiority into every aspect of American thought).

[13] See, e.g., *Sunseri v. Cassange*, 185 So. 1, 4–5 (La 1938). The case involved a suit by Sunseri to annul his marriage to Cassagne on the grounds that she had a trace of "negro blood." He contended that his wife's great-great-grandmother was a "full-blooded negress," and Cassagne herself asserted that she was Indian. See ibid. at 2. It was not disputed that all of Cassagne's paternal ancestors from her father to her great-great-grandfather were white men. See ibid. Moreover, Cassagne had been regarded as white in the community, as she and her mother had been christened in a white church, had attended white schools, were registered as white voters, were accepted as white in public facilities, and had exclusively associated with whites. See ibid. at 4–5. Nevertheless, because certificates and official records designated Cassagne and some of her relatives as "colored," the court concluded that she was not white and that thus there were sufficient grounds to annul the marriage. See *Sunseri v. Cassagne*, 196 So. 7, lo (La. 1940); see also *Johnson v. Board of Educ. of Wilson County*, 82 S.E. 832, 833–835 (1914) (refusing to allow the children of a "pure white" husband and a wife who was less than "one-eighth negro" to be admitted to white schools because of the presence of "negro blood in some degree," even assuming that the marriage was valid and not violative of the miscegenation statute).

[14] It is not at all clear that even the slaves imported from abroad represented "pure Negro races." As Gunner Myrdal noted, many of the tribes imported from Africa had intermingled with peoples of the Mediterranean, among them Portuguese slave traders. Other slaves brought to the United States came via the West Indies, where some Africans had been brought directly, but still others had been brought via Spain and Portugal, countries in which extensive interracial sexual

equal treatment to those of the "same blood," albeit of different complexions, because it was acknowledged that, "[t]here are white men as dark as mulattoes, and there are pure blooded albino Africans as white as the whitest Saxons."[15]

The standards were designed to accomplish what mere observation could not: "That even blacks who did not look black were kept in their place."[16] Although the line of demarcation between black and white varied from rules that classified as black a person containing "any drop of black blood"[17] to more liberal rules that defined persons with a preponderance of white blood to be white,[18] the courts universally accepted the notion that white status was something of value that could be accorded only to those persons whose proofs established their whiteness as defined by the law.[19] Because legal recognition of a person as white carried material benefits, "false" or inadequately supported claims were denied like any other unsubstantiated claim to a property interest. Only those who could lay "legitimate" claims to whiteness could be legally recognized as "white," because allowing physical attributes, social acceptance, or self-identification to determine whiteness would diminish its value and destroy the underlying presumption of exclusivity. In effect, the courts erected legal "No Trespassing" signs.

In the realm of *social* relations, racial recognition in the United States is thus an act of race subordination. In the realm of *legal* relations, judicial definition of racial identity based on white supremacy reproduced that race subordination at

---

relations had occurred. By the mid-nineteenth century it was, therefore, a virtual fiction to speak of "pure blood" as it relates to racial identification in the United States. See Gunnar Myrdal, *An American Dilemma: The Negro Problem and Modern Democracy* (New York: Harper & Row, 1962), p. 123.

[15] *People v. Dean*, 14 Mich. 406, 422 (r 866).

[16] Rayond T. Diamond and Robert J. Cottrol, "Codifying Caste: Louisiana's Racial Classification Scheme and the Fourteenth Amendment," *Loyola Law Review* 29 (1983), p. 281.

[17] For a history of the "one-drop" rule, see Davis, *Who Is Black?* According to Davis:
The nation's answer to the question "Who is black?" has long been that a black is any person with any known black ancestry. This definition reflects the long experience with slavery and later with Jim Crow segregation. In the South it became known as the "one-drop rule," meaning that a single drop of "black blood" makes a person black. It is also known as the ... "traceable amount rule," and anthropologists call it the "hypo-descent rule," meaning that racially mixed persons are assigned the status of the subordinate group. This definition emerged from the American South to become the nation's definition, generally accepted by whites and blacks alike. Blacks had no other choice. (Davis, *Who is Black?*, p. 5)

[18] See e.g., *Gray v. Ohio*, 4 Ohio 353, 355 (1831).

[19] The courts adopted this standard even as they critiqued the legitimacy of such rules and definitions. For example, in *People v. Dean*, 14 Mich. 406 (1886), the court, in interpreting the meaning of the word "white" for the purpose of determining whether the defendant had voted illegally, criticized as "absurd" the notion that "a preponderance of mixed blood, on one side or the other of any given standard, has the remotest bearing upon personal fitness or unfitness to possess political privileges," ibid. at 417, but held that the electorate that had voted for racial exclusion had the right to determine voting privileges, see ibid. at 46.

the institutional level. In transforming white to whiteness, the law masked the ideological content of racial definition and the exercise of power required to maintain it: "It convert[ed] [an] abstract concept into an entity."[20]

Whiteness as Racialized Privilege

The material benefits of racial exclusion and subjugation functioned, in the labor context, to stifle class tensions among whites. White workers perceived that they had more in common with the bourgeoisie than with fellow workers who were black. Thus, W. E. B. Du Bois's classic historical study of race and class, *Black Reconstruction*,[21] noted that, for the evolving white working class, race identification became crucial to the ways that it thought of itself and conceived its interests. There were, he suggested, obvious material benefits, at least in the short term, to the decision of white workers to define themselves by their whiteness: their wages far exceeded those of blacks and were high even in comparison with world standards.[22] Moreover, even when the white working class did not collect increased pay as part of white privilege, there were real advantages not paid in direct income: whiteness still yielded what Du Bois termed a "public and psychological wage" vital to white workers.[23] Thus, Du Bois noted:

> The [whites] were given public deference ... because they were white. They were admitted freely with all classes of white people, to public functions, to public parks ... The police were drawn from their ranks, and the courts, dependent on their votes, treated them with ... leniency ... Their vote selected public officials, and while this had small effect upon the economic situation, it had great effect on their personal treatment ... White schoolhouses were the best in the community, and conspicuously placed, and they cost anywhere from twice to ten times as much per capita as the colored schools.[24]

The central feature of this convergence of "white" and "worker" lay in the fact that racial status and privilege could ameliorate and assist in "evad[ing] rather than confront[ing] class exploitation."[25] Although not accorded the privileges of

---

[20] Stephen J. Gould, *The Mismeasure of Man* (New York: Penguin Books, 1981), p. 24.

[21] W. E. B. Du Bois, *Black Reconstruction* (photo. reprint 1976) (1935).

[22] *See* ibid., p. 634.

[23] Ibid., p. 700.

[24] Ibid., pp. 700–701.

[25] David Roediger, *The Wages of Whiteness* (London: Verso, 1991), p. 13. One of Roediger's principal themes is that whiteness was constructed both from the top down and from the bottom up. See ibid., pp. 8–11. His vigorous analysis of the role of racism in the construction of working class consciousness leads him to conclude that "the pleasures of whiteness could function as a

the ruling class, in both the North and South, white workers could accept their lower class position in the hierarchy "by fashioning identities as 'not slaves' and as 'not blacks.'"[26] Whiteness produced—and was reproduced by—the social advantage that accompanied it.

Whiteness was also central to national identity and to the republican project. The amalgamation of various European strains into an American identity was facilitated by an oppositional definition of black as "other."[27] As Hacker suggests, fundamentally, the question was not so much "who is white" but, rather, "who may be considered white," as the historical pattern was that various immigrant groups of different ethnic origins were accepted into a white identity shaped around Anglo-American norms.[28] Current members then "ponder[ed] whether they want[ed] or need[ed] new members as well as the proper pace of new admissions into this exclusive club."[29] Through minstrel shows in which white actors masquerading in blackface played out racist stereotypes, the popular culture put the black at "'solo spot centerstage, providing a relational model in contrast to which masses of Americans could establish a positive and superior sense of identity[,]' ... [an identity] ... established by an infinitely manipulable negation comparing whites with a construct of a socially defenseless group."[30]

[wage] for white worker ... [S]tatus and privilege conferred by race could be used to make up for alienating and exploitive class relationships." Ibid., p. 13. Roediger further argues that the conjunction of "white" and "worker" came about in the nineteenth century at a time when the non-slave labor force came increasingly to depend on wage labor. The independence of this sector was then measured in relation to the dependency of blacks as a subordinated people and class. See ibid., p. 20. The involvement of all sectors, including the white working class, in the construction of whiteness aids in explaining the persistence of whiteness in the modern period.

[26] Ibid., p. 13.

[27] "One of the surest ways to confirm an identity, for communities and individuals, is to find some way of measuring what one is not." Kai Erikson, *Wayward Puritans: A Study in the Sociology of Deviance* (New York: John Wiley, 1966), p. 64. Toni Morrison's study of the Africanist presence in US literature echoes the same theme of the reflexive construction of "American" identity:
It is no accident and no mistake that immigrant populations (and much immigrant literature) understood their Americanness as an opposition to the resident black population. Race in fact now functions as a metaphor so necessary to the construction of Americanness that it rivals the old pseudo-scientific and class-informed racisms whose dynamics we are more used to deciphering ... Deep within the word "American" is its association with race. To identify someone as South African is to say very little; we need the adjective "white" or "black" or "colored" to make our meaning clear. In this country, it is quite the reverse. American means white ... (Toni Morrison, *Playing in the Dark: Whiteness and the Literary Imagination* (Cambridge, MA: Harvard University Press, 1992), pp. 46–47).

[28] Andrew Hacker says that white became a "common front" established across ethnic origins, social class, and language. Andrew Hacker, *Two Nations* (New York: Scribner, 1992), p. 12.

[29] Ibid., p. 9.

[30] Roediger, *Wages of Whiteness*, p. 118 (quoting Alan W. C. Green, "'Jim Crow,' 'Zip Coon': The Northern Origin of Negro Minstrelsy," *Massachusetts Review* 2 (1970), p. 395).

It is important to note the effect of this hypervaluation of whiteness. Owning white identity as property affirmed the self-identity and liberty[31] of whites and, conversely, denied the self-identity and liberty of blacks.[32] The attempts to lay claim to whiteness through "passing" painfully illustrate the effects of the law's recognition of whiteness. The embrace of a lie, undertaken by my grandmother and the thousands like her, could occur only when oppression makes self-denial and the obliteration of identity rational and, in significant measure, beneficial.[33] The economic coercion of white supremacy on self-definition nullifies any suggestion that passing is a logical exercise of liberty or self-identity. The decision to pass as white was not a choice, if by that word one means voluntariness or lack of compulsion. The fact of race subordination was coercive and circumscribed the liberty to self-define. Self-determination of identity was not a right for all people, but a privilege accorded on the basis of race. The effect of protecting whiteness at law was to devalue those who were not white by coercing them to deny their identity in order to survive[34]

Whiteness, Rights, and National Identity

The concept of whiteness was carefully protected because so much was contingent upon it. Whiteness conferred on its owners aspects of citizenship that were all the more valued because they were denied to others. Indeed, the very fact of citizenship itself was linked to white racial identity. The Naturalization Act of

---

[31] I do not attempt here to review or state a position with regard to the profusion of theories that describe the relationship between liberty and property; that is beyond the scope of this inquiry. Rather, I use liberty in the Hohfeldian sense as a privilege, "a legal liberty or freedom," not involving "a correlative duty but the absence of a right on someone else's part to interfere." Stephen R. Munzer, *A Theory of Property* (Cambridge University Press, 1990), p. 18.

[32] In this respect, whiteness as property followed a familiar paradigm. Although the state can create new forms of property other than those existing at common law, "in each case that it creates new property rights, the state necessarily limits the common law liberty or property rights of other citizens, for conduct which was once legal now becomes an invasion or an infringement of the new set of rights that are established." Richard Epstein, "No New Property," Brooklyn Law Review 56 (1990), p. 754; see A. Leon Higginbotham, *In the Matter of Color: Race and the American Legal Process* (Oxford University Press, 1978), p. 13 (noting that, when the law establishes a right for a person, group, or institution, it simultaneously constrains those whose "preferences impinge on the right established").

[33] This problem is at the center of one of the early classics of black literature, *The Autobiography of an Ex-Coloured Man*, by James Weldon Johnson, the story of a black man who "passes" for white, crossing between black and white racial identities four times. See Henry L. Gates, Jr., Introduction to James W. Johnson, *The Autobiography of an Ex-Coloured Man* (New York: Vintage, 1989 [1912]), p. vi.

[34] I am indebted to Lisa Ikemoto for the insight regarding how whiteness as property interacts with liberty and self-identity.

1790 restricted citizenship to persons who resided in the United States for two years, who could establish their good character in court, and who were "white."[35] Moreover, the trajectory of expanding democratic rights for whites was accompanied by the contraction of the rights of blacks in an ever deepening cycle of oppression.[36] The franchise, for example, was broadened to extend voting rights to unpropertied white men at the same time that black voters were specifically disenfranchised, arguably shifting the property required for voting from land to whiteness.

QUESTIONS

(1) How did the law protect whites' interaction with "life, liberty, and pursuit of happiness" as self-evident truths that are spelt out in the Declaration of Independence?
(2) How did the Naturalization Act of 1790 institutionalize whiteness. Explain.
(3) Whiteness denotes who can enjoy white privilege. How did whiteness socially, economically, and politically, during and after slavery, impact blacks?
(4) How did whiteness define the legal status of blacks?
(5) How did whiteness denote who can enjoy white privilege and who cannot? Draw on the evidence that Harris provides.

---

[35] See Naturalization Act of 1790, ch. 3, § i, x Stat. 103, 103 (1790) (repealed 1795). As Takaki explains, this law "specified a complexion for the members of the new nation" and reflected the explicit merger of white national identity and republicanism. Takaki, *Iron Cages*, p. x. It was also another arena in which the law promulgated racial definitions as part of its task of allocating rights of citizenship. These decisions further reinforced white hegemony by naturalizing white identity as objective when in fact it was a constructed and moving barrier. As noted in *Corpus Juris*, a white person constitutes a very indefinite description of a class of persons, where none can be said to be literally white; and it has been said that a construction of the term to mean Europeans and persons of European descent is ambiguous. "White person" has been held to include an Armenian born in Asiatic Turkey, a person of but one-sixteenth Indian blood, and a Syrian, but not to include Afghans, American Indians, Chinese, Filipinos, Hawaiians, Hindus, Japanese, Koreans, negroes; nor does white person include a person having one fourth of African blood, a person in whom Malay blood predominates, a person whose father was a German and whose mother was a Japanese, a person whose father was a white Canadian and whose mother was an Indian woman, or a person whose mother was a Chinese and whose father was the son of a Portuguese father and a Chinese mother. 68 C. J. White 258 (1934) (citations omitted).
[36] See Diamond and Cottrol, "Codifying Caste," p. 262.

19 Whiteness, Racism, and Identity

BARBARA J. FIELDS

Barbara J. Fields is at present a professor of American history at Columbia University. She was the first black woman to receive tenure at Columbia University. Her research focus is specifically on the American South and nineteenth-century social history. She is well known for her article, "Slavery, Race and Ideology in the United States of America," 1990. She has authored several books including *Slaves No More: Three Essays on the Emancipation and Civil War*, 1995; and *Slavery and Freedom on the Middle Ground: Maryland during the 1970s*, 1984. Fields' more recent coauthored book with Karen Fields is titled *Racecraft: The Soul of Inequality in American Life*, 2012. The essay, "Whiteness, Racism, and Identity," reproduced below, examines how whiteness determines the position of African Americans in the United States.

Whiteness is the shotgun marriage of two incoherent but well-loved concepts: identity and agency. Racism—the assignment of people to an inferior category and the determination of their social, economic, civic, and human standing on that basis—unsettles fundamental instincts of American academic professionals who consider themselves liberal, leftist, or progressive. It is an act of peremptory, hostile, and supremely—often fatally—consequential identification that unceremoniously overrides its objects' sense of themselves. Racism thus unseats both identity and agency, if identity means sense of self,[1] and agency anything beyond conscious, goal-directed activity, however trivial or ineffectual.[2] The targets of

---

[1] Rogers Brubaker and Frederick Cooper have subjected *identity* to overdue historical and theoretical scrutiny, urging its replacement with more precise terms for the varied and often mutually exclusive ideas that it seems to cover. They warn against assuming that the current ubiquity of *identity* as a category of practice proves its validity as a category of analysis or even its existence, until recent times, as a category of practice. See "Beyond 'Identity,'" *Theory and Society* 29 (2000): 1–47.

[2] Perry Anderson has reminded us that *agency* in the sense of conscious, goal-directed activity, is an analytically empty concept unless one also specifies the nature of the goal and the relationship between the conscious intent of those who pursue it and its social result. Agency in choosing to marry at a certain age, for example, is not agency in bringing about the population growth or decline to which the choice contributes. Perry Anderson, "Agency," in *Arguments Within English Marxism* (London, 1980), 2–58.

racism do not "make" racism, nor are they free to "negotiate" it, though they may challenge it or its perpetrators and try to navigate the obstacles it places in their way. Even as racism exposes the hollowness of agency and identity, it violates the two-sides-to-every-story expectation of symmetry that Americans are peculiarly attached to. There is no voluntary and affirmative side to racism as far as its victims are concerned, and it has no respect for symmetry at all.

That is why well-meaning scholars are more apt to speak of *race* than of *racism.* *Race* is a homier and more tractable notion than *racism,* a rogue elephant gelded and tamed into a pliant beast of burden. Substituted for *racism, race* transforms the act of a subject into an attribute of the object. And because *race* denotes a state of mind, feeling, or being, rather than a program or pattern of action, it radiates a semantic and grammatical ambiguity that helps to restore an appearance of symmetry, particularly with the help of a thimblerig that imperceptibly moves the pea from *race* to *racial identity.*

Whiteness is just such a thimblerig. It performs a series of deft displacements, first substituting race for racism, then postulating identity as the social substance of race, and finally attributing racial identity to persons of European descent. By those maneuvers, it is possible to reinstate the orthodox pieties. *Whiteness* invests ordinary white people with agency (even if only in evil-doing), in the flabby sense that *agency* has acquired in American historical literature. Furthermore, by equating race with identity and attributing it to white persons, *whiteness* seems to banish the troubling asymmetry that is the essence of racism. The vagueness of the concept of identity and its usually undetected incursions back and forth across the border between individual and collective, subjective and objective, optional and compulsory,[3] have tempted scholars to collapse racism—a forcible and authoritative assignment of race—into racial identity.

Once racism, having passed through the buffer zone of whiteness, crosses the border into identity and voluntarism, it returns to its point of origin with an alias—*race*—and a new passport. The blurred photograph shows a neutral face, and the impostor goes surrounded by the benevolent trappings of agency. A brand becomes an identity, and those who wear the brand become agents in its burning into their own flesh (the helpful ambiguity of the word leaving delicately obscure

---

[3] As Brubaker and Cooper demonstrate, the concept of identity has grave shortcomings even when limited to individuals; particularly, its liability to reification and essentialism, which devotees have tried to correct by reducing the concept to a contradiction in terms. Defining it as contingent, fluid, and multiple may rescue it, at least nominally, from reification and essentialism, but only by raising the question of how, in that case, it is identity at all. In the transit from individual to collective, the concept becomes incoherent. Whatever one supposes to be the psychological, psychosocial, or psychoanalytic constituents of identity in the individual, they dissipate into feeble metaphor when transposed to the collective. Brubaker and Cooper, "Beyond Identity."

whether *agent* in this instance means initiator or instrument).[4] As one artless formulation has it: "'[R]ace,' as an embodied category of difference and a constructed aspect of identity, is not imposed by one group upon another ... [I]t is a product of an ongoing dialogue. ... 'Racial' identifications ... function as tools of both domination and resistance."[5] When the domestication of racism is complete, those to whom race has been attached as a stigma appear instead as its willing co-authors, their co-authorship apotheosized as an act of resistance.

Traveling under the alias of race or racial identity, racism remains, none the less, as despotic as ever, the alias masking its despotism. Since it remains racism, whatever the name on its passport, it forbids its objects to be other than members of a race. When a *New York Times* reporter refers to "Anglos, blacks, and Hispanics," it is not through ignorance that persons of African descent speak both English and Spanish, but because, once people are known to have African ancestry, no other characteristic is admissible as a public identification of them.[6] Nor can persons of African descent escape the consequences of the imposed identification by assertion or manipulation of their sense of self.[7] New York City police officers, having identified an African immigrant as a black man, killed him on the spot. There was no dialogue or negotiation, just as enslavement was no matter for dialogue or negotiation between owners and their property.[8]

Afro-Americans themselves have fought successively for different ways of naming themselves as a people: African, colored, Afro-American, Negro with capital letter, black (with or without capital letter), African-American. (The current

---

[4] *Agent* in English, as Perry Anderson points out, can carry the opposite connotations of active initiator or passive instrument, free agent or the agent of another. Anderson, "Agency," 18.

[5] Joanne Pope Melish, *Disowning Slavery: Gradual Emancipation and "Race" in New England, 1789–1860* (Ithaca, 1998), 3–4. Note the apologetic quotation marks around "race" and "racial" and the quiet shift from *identity* to *identification*.

[6] Rick Bragg, "Legacy of a Cuban Boy: Miami City Hall Is Remade," *The New York Times*, May 10, 2000, A20.

[7] The identification, it must be added, is not a simple matter of how they happen to look. Walter White, one-time head of the National Association for the Advancement of Colored People, looks like Dwight Eisenhower in the photograph at the front of his autobiography and was once assured that he was pure white by a white fellow passenger on a train who claimed to have a foolproof way to judge: "[I]f you had nigger blood," his companion explained, "it would show here on your half-moons." But face and fingernails notwithstanding, word got out about him while he was fact-finding in Phillips County, Arkansas, after a massacre there in the summer of 1919. "There's a damned yellow nigger down here passing for white and the boys are going to get him," an unknowing white train conductor told him as he was making good his getaway. White recounts the Phillips County episode in *A Man Called White: The Autobiography of Walter White* (New York, 1948), 51; the fingernail anecdote appears in Claude McKay, *A Long Way From Home* (San Diego, 1970), 110.

[8] See Adam Rothman's astringent comments on the obscuring vocabulary of encounter, exchange, and negotiation that is becoming conventional in scholarly discussions of slavery and empire, in "The Expansion of Slavery in the Deep South, 1790–1820" (PhD diss., Columbia University, 2000), 9.

jargon, *people of color*, does not belong to the series, being instead a semantic device to equate the unlike situations of Afro-Americans and other Americans of non-European origin.)[9] Rather than evidence of Afro-Americans' participation in the creation of race, the campaign for each name has been an attempt, particular to its time and circumstances, to name, define, or create a sense of peoplehood, in opposition to the prevailing racial (that is, racist) assignment. Each name, once accepted into the general public vocabulary, has simply become a variant word for Afro-Americans' race. A sense of peoplehood, nationhood, or comradeship in struggle may be available to others; but, for persons of African descent, all reduce to race, a life sentence for them and their issue in perpetuity.

Necessarily, the boundaries of the group for which African-descended people themselves have sought to define the terms of belonging and solidarity more or less coincide with the boundaries of the group that law and custom designate a race: It was precisely in order to escape racism that they sought their own definition of belonging and solidarity. But the only reason scholars conclude without thought or hesitation that every such proposed self-definition is an acquiescence in (or, as the tedious jargon has it, construction of) race is that the equation of self-definition and race for Afro-Americans—and for them alone—is an axiom, no more in need of proof than susceptible of it. In other words, the equation of Afro-Americans' peoplehood with race is a corollary of racism.

For purposes of defining kinship or social belonging or of asserting or enforcing group solidarity, European immigrants might think of themselves, and be thought of by society at large, in many ways—as Finns, Scots, Fenians, Knights of Columbus, *paesani, Turnverein* members, Forty-Eighters, or (as Professor Arnesen acutely reminds us) Democrats or Roman Catholics—without those designations' automatically reducing to race. But not Afro-Americans. Any individual or group self-definition or self-understanding that persons of African descent have developed while attempting to survive or oppose enslavement or demand freedom and citizenship has become race when translated into the general American idiom.

A chasm thus separates race as applied to European immigrants and as applied to persons of African descent. *Racialization* is the rotten plank by which whiteness scholars try to bridge the chasm. But the plank will not bear any weight. In the first place, *racialize*, like most adjectives passing for verbs, does not denote a precise action. What, exactly, do scientists, immigration officials, ballot reformers, intelligence testers, newspaper cartoonists, employers and potential employers, WASP

---

[9] It should not be necessary to add that distinguishing the situation of Afro-Americans from that of other Americans of non-European origin in no way denies or minimizes the bigotry, discrimination, and exploitation to which Americans of non-African, non-European origin have been subjected (as, indeed, have many Americans of European origin). It probably is necessary to add, however, that the situations of Americans of non-African, non-European origin can no more be equated with each other than with the situation of Afro-Americans.

snobs, and middle- and working-class nativists do when they racialize immigrants? The question itself is part of the answer: Not all racializers do the same thing when they racialize; and Professor Arnesen is right, therefore, to deplore the passive and stative constructions that so often obscure subject and action in the whiteness literature.

The rest of the answer, however, is what causes the plank bridge to collapse. Whatever the various racializers of European immigrants do, there is one thing none does, and that is to assign European immigrants to a biological category on the basis of the one-drop-of-blood or any-known-ancestry rule that applies to Afro-Americans. The rule itself forestalls anything of the kind, since it is designed to identify only one race; if applicable to a second, it can no longer identify the first. A recent illustration is the decision of a faction of Seminoles, apparently with the encouragement of federal government officials, to expel Afro-Seminoles from membership. African ancestry, it seems, outweighs both Seminole ancestry and two hundred years of shared history. The official terminology of *black Seminoles* and *blood Seminoles*, in its bare-faced absurdity, perfectly captures the one-drop rule, working away at the old stand.[10]

Whether as rough-and-ready ideology or as legal definition, racism in America has served, not to classify or categorize people, but to specify who is black and who is not. It is considered chic in some quarters to elide that fact, with the concept *racialize* disguising the elision. *Multi-racial* and its euphemistic synonym, *multicultural*, occupy a place of honor, on the supposition, presumably, that a blight becomes a blessing if widely enough diffused. Whatever their defects as historical analysis, they have become obligatory public gestures. Among breaches of propriety, defining race in "bipolar" terms ranks well ahead of wearing animal fur.[11] Nevertheless, bipolarity and asymmetry are the essential historical constituents of American racial ideology and of the actions that the ideology distills.

Inseparable from the bipolarity and asymmetry of American racial ideology is the "unmarked, unnamed status," "seeming normativity," "structured in-visibility," and "false universality" of those who are designated "not black." That is the datum the whiteness literature seeks to extinguish or overrule. Rather than explore what the absence of a mark or name means, whiteness scholarship mulishly insists upon inserting the mark and name, officiously making good the failure of people in the past to do it themselves, as Professor Arnesen properly complains. The point, it seems, is not to interpret the past but to change it. By its insistence upon marking

---

[10] William Glaberson, "Who Is a Seminole, and Who Gets to Decide?" *The New York Times*, January 29, 2001.

[11] During a symposium at a university in southern California, a senior historian of white women rebuked me for emphasizing the historical origin of American racial ideology in the enslavement of Afro-Americans—not, apparently, because she judged the argument invalid, but because she thought it unseemly to make in California.

and naming and making visible, whiteness scholarship first strews race and races everywhere and then, *mirabile dictu*, discovers them everywhere.

Race then becomes so ubiquitous as to lose determinate shape, as Professor Arnesen points out. "Race and races are American history," according to Matthew Frye Jacobson. "[T]o write about race in American culture is to exclude virtually nothing."[12] Jacobson prefaces his own observation with Oscar Handlin's parallel observation that "immigrants *were* American history."[13] Both are fallacious, and a notable blind spot in whiteness literature reveals how the two fallacies compound each other. Whereas exploring how European immigrants became white is all the rage, no one deems it pertinent to such exploration to ask how African and Afro-Caribbean immigrants became black.[14] Whiteness, according to its bards, may be identity; but blackness, as their silence confirms, is identification, authoritative and external. So unremarkable appears the alchemy by which African and Afro-Caribbean immigrants become black that they barely register as immigrants in the first place. The only Americans of African descent whom American historical literature routinely, if metaphorically, sees as immigrants are those who were not (American slaves and their descendants); while the Americans of African descent who actually were immigrants (voluntary migrants from Africa and the Caribbean) scarcely figure in the history of immigration and, on the rare occasions when they do, figure in it on a strictly segregated basis.[15]

---

[12] Matthew Frye Jacobson, *Whiteness of a Different Color: European Immigration and the Alchemy of Race* (Cambridge, MA, 1998), 11.

[13] Donna R. Gabaccia, "Nomads, Nations, and the Immigrant Paradigm," *Journal of American History* 86 (1999): 1115–1134, asks why American historians of America have produced a nation-of-immigrants model, while historians of France, Canada, Germany, Australia, and Argentina, with equal grounds for doing so, have not. Gabaccia attributes the peculiarity of the United States to its "long history of slavery as a source of significant national disunity."

[14] A few, not of the whiteness school, have done so with respect to post-1965 Caribbean immigrants. (None give detailed attention to nineteenth- and early twentieth-century migrations.) Like whiteness scholars, they remain trapped in the internal contradictions of identity as an organizing concept. They avoid systematic comparison with European immigrants and concern themselves with how Caribbean immigrants define themselves, to the neglect of how white Americans define them. For example, see Mary C. Waters, *Black Identities: West Indian Immigrant Dreams and American Realities* (New York, 1999); and Milton Vickerman, *Crosscurrents: West Indian Immigrants and Race* (New York, 1999).

[15] Winston James, in "Explaining Afro-Caribbean Social Mobility in the United States: Beyond the Sowell Thesis," *Comparative Studies in Society and History* (forthcoming), establishes that, while fascinated with slave disembarkation ports as metaphorical Ellis Islands for Afro-Americans, American historians have been virtually blind to the thousands of African and Afro-Caribbean immigrants who passed through the real Ellis Island. He also upbraids historians for their preoccupation with comparing Caribbean immigrants to Afro-American natives, evading the more appropriate comparison of Caribbean immigrants to European immigrants. See also Roy Bryce-Laporte, "Black Immigrants: The Experience of Invisibility and Inequality," *Journal of Black Studies* 3 (1972): 29–56.

Thus, in asking how immigrants acquire racial status in America, whiteness scholarship ignores the immigrants who, willy-nilly, acquire such status, fully named and marked, in order to focus on those whose racial status must be named and marked retroactively by historians. Not only does the question of African and Caribbean immigrants' transformation into black people not enter the reckoning; neither does the related question of how, in their own self-perception, African and Caribbean immigrants became Africans and Caribbeans, which most were not before they left home.[16] Immigrants from Europe underwent no comparable transformation. However they came to define themselves, or be defined by others, upon their arrival in America—as white people, Italians, Germans, or Jews, for instance—*European* was not one of the definitions.

The question of Afro-immigrants' becoming black is the only context in which that of Euro-immigrants' becoming white makes any sense at all; though the real issue is not how immigrants became white or black, but how persons not born and bred to it, whatever their ancestry, became oriented in the American world of black and white. When the dichotomy was not completely irrelevant in the immigrants' place of origin (as for most European immigrants), it would have been overlaid with other pairs—peasant/landlord, villager/chief, native/colonial, illiterate/educated, *indigène/évolué*, black/brown (or coloured)—that fundamentally distinguish it from the stark opposition that prevailed in the United States.

There is no mystery about how Afro-Caribbeans became oriented: by sudden encounter with a system of racism whose extent, depth, and depravity took even the best informed among them by surprise.[17] But, whereas Afro immigrants could not avoid confronting the apparatus and conventions of racism head-on, Euro-immigrants varied in the extent to which they were even aware of the apparatus, let alone acquainted at first hand with Afro-Americans. Whiteness is consequently a mixed bag, whose contents might, on one hand, be the use of the word *nigger* in children's games and, on the other hand, the wielding of bludgeon, torch, and firearm in pogroms against Afro-Americans. The first, as David Roediger illustrates by the example of his own boyhood, could coexist with admiration for Curt Flood, Bob Gibson, Lou Brock, Muhammad Ali, Tina Turner, and Smokey Robinson; it might eventuate in authorship of *The Wages of Whiteness*, rather than in Klan or Aryan Nation membership or anti-black violence.[18]

---

[16] Vickerman, *Crosscurrents*, 9–12, deals with the problem briefly and schematically. Winston James investigates how migrants from the British Caribbean to Britain became "Caribbeans" after reaching their destination. See "Migration, Racism, and Identity Formation: The Caribbean Experience in Britain," in *Inside Babylon: The Caribbean Diaspora in Britain*, ed. Winston James and Clive Harris (London, 1993), 231–287.

[17] Winston James, *Holding Aloft the Banner of Ethiopia: Caribbean Radicalism in Early Twentieth-Century America* (London, 1998), chapter 3, "Coming At Midnight: Race and Caribbean Reactions to America."

[18] David R. Roediger, *The Wages of Whiteness: Race and the Making of the American Working Class* (London, 1991), 3–5.

In any case, what may appear to be black/white relations often turn out, when probed, to rest on relations of power and rank among white persons. During the early 1920s, Rebecca Garvin, an Afro-American resident of Charleston, South Carolina, used to take her infant grandson for a daily outing around Colonial Lake in a lavishly adorned baby carriage. Each day a burly Irish policeman would see her and smile, until one day he approached close enough to see that the baby inside was a black boy, not—as the carriage had led him to suppose—a young white son or daughter of the Charleston aristocracy taking a promenade with his black mammy. At once the policeman turned hostile and tried to ban Rebecca Garvin from the area (which, under the law, he could not do). Whatever that Irishman's views about Afro-Americans and however they may have figured in his sense of self, his conduct in that instance had primarily to do with his relationship to his white superiors.[19]

The concept of whiteness cannot, therefore, solve what I take to be its central problem (at least as far as labor history is concerned): the source of working-class bigotry, often murderous, against persons of African descent. Indeed, as an organizing concept, whiteness leads to no conclusions that it does not begin with as assumptions. Whiteness is a racial identity; therefore, white people have a racial identity. Whiteness equals white supremacy; therefore, European immigrants become white by adopting white supremacy. Whiteness entails material benefits; therefore, the material benefits white people receive are a reward for whiteness.

Considering how whiteness scholars scourge others for assuming a built-in tendency toward solidarity among workers, they display a strikingly romantic vision of solidarity as the state of nature for white people. Exclusion from whiteness, they seem to assume, must account for any breach of solidarity. If a white man snubs another or calls him a hard name, let alone exploits or disfranchises him, the point at issue is bound to be the victim's racial bona fides. On the far side of the color line, it seems, universal brotherhood and equality prevail.

The wage that supposedly accrues to whiteness typifies the romanticism that besets whiteness scholarship. Even supposing Afro-Americans' access to resources reduced to zero, it would not follow that the resources thus freed would be sufficient for all white people to have a share. Nor would the exclusion of Afro-Americans from civic and material goods guarantee Euro-Americans' access to them, as white people of the laboring classes learned to their cost after disfranchisement in the South.[20] (Whether the denial of goods to Afro-Americans

---

[19] Mamie Garvin Fields and Karen E. Fields, *Lemon Swamp and Other Places: A Carolina Memoir* (New York, 1983), 9–10.

[20] In fact, most of them understood the danger from the outset, as J. Morgan Kousser has argued, and were not taken in by the blandishments of the disfranchisers. See *The Shaping of Southern Politics: Suffrage Restriction and the Establishment of the One-Party South, 1880–1910* (New Haven, 1974).

psychologically compensated white people for their own failure to obtain them is a question best left to those enamored of speculation that evidence can neither prove nor disprove.) Who receives what is denied to Afro-Americans depends on political contest. The contest might turn on which white people can best take advantage of power over Afro-Americans, or it might have little or nothing to do with Afro-Americans.

For example, the town-dwelling middle class in upstate South Carolina during the 1890s and 1900s sought to curtail lynching by expanding the definition of capital offenses and speeding the process of legal execution. Obviously, solicitude for the victims of lynching had nothing to do with it. The reformers were determined to restore law and order, which is to say rule by the right sort of white people under the right circumstances; their leverage over Afro-Americans in the penal system provided a handy means to that end.[21] In contrast, the denial of Afro-Americans cannot account for the publicly subsidized middle-class entitlements that became available to white working people in the post-World War Two period. If it did, white people ought to have enjoyed such entitlements from the dawn of the republic.

In 1909, a remarkably plain-spoken white Southerner disentangled the Negro Problem from race and the topics commonly equated with it: the supposed laziness, ignorance, criminality, or physical repulsiveness of Negroes. It was, he concluded, a matter of power:

> The problem, How to maintain the institution of chattel slavery, ceased to be at Appomattox; the problem, How to maintain the social, industrial, and civic inferiority of the descendants of chattel slaves, succeeded it, and is the race problem of the South at the present time. There is no other.[22]

W. E. B. Du Bois reached a similar conclusion in discarding the academic race dogma within which he had once sought to discover a space for the aspirations of Afro-American people. "[T]he black man," he eventually concluded, is simply "a person who must ride 'Jim Crow' in Georgia."[23]

The ideological formulation *race relations* skirted the considerable difficulties of stating the Negro problem within the forms of a purportedly democratic polity

---

[21] Stephen A. West, "From Yeoman to Redneck in Upstate South Carolina, 1850–1915" (PhD diss., Columbia University, 1998), chapter 7.

[22] Quincy Ewing, "The Heart of the Race Problem," *Atlantic Monthly* 103 (1909): 396. I am grateful to Cary Fraser for bringing this remarkable document to my attention.

[23] Quoted in Adolph L. Reed, Jr., *W. E. B. Du Bois and American Political Thought: Fabianism and the Color Line* (New York, 1997), 124. In chapter 7, Reed takes on two important tasks. First, he seeks to establish the proper place of the idea of "double consciousness," which has been reduced to a cliché, both in Du Bois's thinking and in that of his contemporaries. Second, he challenges scholars' habit of appealing to Du Bois's phrase in lieu of evidence for the existence of a generic racial consciousness among Afro-Americans.

and with respect to persons who were nominally citizens in that polity enjoying full political rights. *Race relations* so suited the liberal thought of the time, and has been so well able to accommodate the internal twists of liberal and neoliberal thought since, that it remains a vital part of the prevailing public language today.[24] It lingers on to cozen scholars who, instead of investigating it as an ideological device, accept it ingenuously as an empirical datum.[25] What race relations has accomplished on one side of the equation of racism, whiteness bids fair to accomplish on the other. With identity and agency displacing questions of political, economic, and social power, whiteness offers us endless variations on the theme of race that, reproducing their assumptions as conclusions, invariably end where they started.

QUESTIONS

(1) Given that whiteness is not the same as white supremacy, what are some of the problems these two concepts pose for blacks?
(2) Race is not the same as racism. What are some of the problems that arise when race is substituted for racism or vice versa?
(3) How, according to Fields, does whiteness as a structure and an identity come together to position blacks as inferior to whites?
(4) Using various cases from the chapter, explain how the one-drop rule assigns blacks to a biological category.
(5) According to Fields, immigrants in the United States do acquire some forms of racial status. Is there a difference between blacks from Caribbean, for example, and European immigrants?

---

[24] Michael R. West develops this argument in "The Education of Booker T. Washington: The Negro Problem, Democracy, and the Idea of Race Relations" (PhD diss., Columbia University, 2000). West dates the origin of *race relations* as a tactful formulation of the Negro Problem to the era of Booker T. Washington, who was its most talented and successful popularizer.

[25] Roediger illustrates its mystical hold when he chides me for analyzing the installation of wage labor relations between former slaves and former owners as the installation of wage labor relations between former slaves and former owners. Presumably, once people of African descent are concerned, the issue can only be race relations. See *Wages of Whiteness*, 7–8.

Kathleen Neal Cleaver at present is a senior lecturer at Emory School of Law. She started her undergraduate education at Oberlin College and later transferred to Barnard College. By 1966, she left college and obtained a secretarial job at the New York branch of the Student Nonviolent Coordinating Committee. From 1967 to 1971, Cleaver was the first communication secretary of the Black Panther Party. After years of exile in Algeria and France with her former husband Eldridge Cleaver, in 1975, she returned to the United States. In 1981, she returned to undergraduate studies at Yale University. Three years later, in 1984, she graduated with a BA in History. She continued her education and graduated from Yale Law School in 1989. After graduating, she worked for Cravath, Swain & Moore, a law firm in New York City. She taught at several universities including Yale University, Benjamin N. Cardozo School of Law, and Sarah Lawrence College. The essay below, "The Antidemocratic Power of Whiteness" is published by *Chicago-Kent Law Review* volume 70, issue 3, Symposium on the "Law of Freedom Part II: Freedom Beyond the United States," in April 1995. In this work, Cleaver shows how whiteness has shaped America's history, laws, and legal culture.

Like the formally neutral concept of "civil rights," "race" usually makes one think of blacks. To link the idea of race with the social construct of whiteness is uncommon. As a rule, white Americans no longer see race in relation to their own identity, and genuinely believe that racism[1] poses a problem for "others." Nobel prize winning author Toni Morrison finds it both poignant and striking that the academic concentration on racism's targets avoids studying the impact racism has on its perpetrators.[2] But this little noticed blindness does not stop with academic

---

[1] In America, racism is generally thought of as that intense, virulent form of hatred underlying the victimization of "outcast" groups. However, here I am using a broader definition in which racism consists of any set of beliefs that ascribe to real or imagined genetic characteristics a socially relevant character such that these differences can be legitimately used to rank and discriminate between social groups defined by race. See Pierre L. Van Den Berghe, *Race and Racism: A Comparative Perspective* 11 (2nd ed. 1978).

[2] Toni Morrison, *Playing in the Dark: Whiteness and the Literary Imagination* 11 (1992).

disciplines. A widespread failure to acknowledge that whiteness conveys internal meanings at the same time it fulfills anti-black functions helps frustrate programs that seek to eliminate racism's pernicious legacy.[3] Thus, *The Wages of Whiteness*, a sophisticated analysis of the significance of racism in the formation offers a welcome addition to the emerging literature interrogating whiteness.[4]

Labor historian David R. Roediger draws upon recent scholarship in social history, such as the study of gender roles, industrial discipline, and popular republicanism in examining the specific ways that beliefs in white racial superiority became part of the consciousness of working men, weaving mass culture, language and politics into his neo-Marxist analysis. Going beyond the obvious results in order to understand the motives of their choices, Roediger does not focus on the material benefits of 'white skin privilege.' Instead, he looks at the agency of working men themselves in constructing the meaning of whiteness. Understanding this process is crucial to Roediger because he shares African-American scholar W. E. B. Du Bois's conclusion concerning the deepest injury that white supremacy caused. Du Bois wrote that though "the consequences of [racist] thought were bad enough for colored people the world over," they were "even worse when one considers what this attitude did to the [white] worker ... He began to want, not comfort for all men but power over other men ... He did not love humanity and he hated niggers."[5] This passionate devotion to white supremacy holds a partial explanation for the failure of the post-Civil War Reconstruction and the collapse of its legal framework for black freedom.

Oliver Wendell Holmes once said that the lawyer's task was not done until "he had seen ... the birth and growth of society, and by the farthest stretch of his reason ... [understood] the philosophy of its being."[6] The most turbulent disputes from the American past have left their mark not only on the narrative of our history, but in the text of our laws, and on the form of our legal culture. These disputes, and their resolution, have entwined themselves into our public consciousness and thus become part of how we perceive the world around us. The abolition of slavery, and in turn segregation, provoked the most virulent disputes of all, but before

---

[3] The intense public controversy that has accompanied legally enacted programs to diminish preferences formerly accorded to whites, such as affirmative action, civil rights laws barring racial discrimination in employment, programs that promote diversity in professional school admissions, and the redrawing of the boundaries of electoral districts to conform to Voting Rights Act provisions, all testify to the recalcitrant nature of this problem, quaintly attributed to "white backlash."

[4] For an in-depth examination of the legal nature of whiteness as a form of property, see Cheryl I. Harris, "Whiteness as Property," 106 *Harv. L. Rev.* 1707 (1993).

[5] David R. Roediger, *The Wages of Whiteness* 6 (1991) (citing W. E. B. Du Bois, *The World and Africa: An Inquiry into the Part Which Africa Has Played in World History* 18–21 (1965)).

[6] *The Occasional Speeches of Justice Oliver Wendell Holmes* 22 (Mark D. Howe ed., 1962).

any careful understanding of that legacy has been reached, complex new changes are again throwing our social and legal world into turmoil. Judges, practitioners, and legal scholars all need a better grasp of the intricate relationships between beliefs in racial superiority and inferiority and the operation of our legal institutions. The brief, provocative examination in *The Wages of Whiteness* enhances that understanding.

Indebted to the dialectical study of race and class that W. E. B. Du Bois pioneered in his classic historical work *Black Reconstruction,*[7] Roediger adopted his theme from Du Bois's formulation that the status and privileges conferred on the basis of whiteness provided compensation for exploitative and alienating class relationships,[8] that even when white workers were paid a lowly wage, they were "compensated in part by a ... public and psychological wage."[9] Du Bois concluded that nineteenth century workers prized whiteness to such an extent that instead of joining with black workers with whom they shared common interests, they adopted a white supremacist vision that approved of capitalism and "ruined democracy."[10] White supremacy served as the unifying theme of the militant resistance that defeated Confederates mounted against the revolution that ended the political and legal structure of slavery. The triumph of white supremacy helped destroy the

---

[7] W. E. B. Du Bois, *Black Reconstruction in America 1860–1880* (1935).

[8] Roediger, *supra* note 5, at 12.

[9] 1 & at 12 (quoting Du Bois, *supra* note 7, at 700–701). The context in which Du Bois explained why the white Southern worker accepted such low pay is worth understanding more fully. He stated:

> The political success of the doctrine of racial separation, which overthrew Reconstruction by uniting the planter and the poor white, was far exceeded by its astonishing economic results. The theory of laboring class unity rests upon the assumption that laborers, despite internal jealousies, will unite because of their opposition to exploitation by the capitalists.
>
> Most persons do not realize how far this failed to work in the South, and it failed to work because the theory of race was supplemented by a carefully planned and slowly evolved method, which drove such a wedge between the white and black workers that there probably are not today in the world two groups of workers with practically identical interests who hate and fear each other so deeply and persistently and who are kept so far apart that neither sees anything of common interests.
>
> It must be remembered that the white group of laborers, while they received a low wage, were compensated in part by a sort of public and psychological wage. They were given public deference and titles of courtesy because they were white ... The police were drawn from their ranks, and the courts, dependent upon their votes, treated them with such leniency as to encourage lawlessness ...
>
> One can see ... why labor organizers ... made such small headway in the South. They were ... appealing to laborers who would rather have low wages upon which they could eke out an existence than see colored labor with a decent wage. White labor saw in every advance of Negroes a threat to their racial prerogatives ...
>
> Du Bois, *supra* note 7, at 700–701.

[10] Roediger, *supra* note 5, at 13 (quoting Du Bois, *supra* note 7, at 700).

legal transformation of the entire political system that Reconstruction initiated and eviscerated the laws of freedom that would have extended democracy to freed slaves.

Until the 1860s, the United States was not only an expanding nation but also a slaveholding republic. In the republican vision of a nation composed of small independent producers, suspicion ran deep both against the ranks of the power-ful *and* the powerless.[11] One rarely sung verse of *The Star Spangled Banner* that Francis Scott Key based on the British military's use of mercenaries and freed slaves to burn down the White House during the War of 1812 says:

> No refuge could save the
>   hireling and the slave
> from the terror of flight or
>   the groom of the grave.[12]

Back when this verse was penned in 1814, hireling was a term of disgrace. The radical ideal of republican government then eschewed dependency and elevated independence. Those gradations of dependency that whites experienced during the eighteenth century, such as apprenticeship, impressment, indentured servitude, farm tenancy and convict labor, Roediger argues, prevented the drawing of hard distinctions between an "idealized white worker and a pitied or scorned servile black worker."[13] Many eighteenth-century whites worked as servants, the same term used with the modifier "perpetual" or "negro" to describe blacks.[14] Racial atti-tudes during the eighteenth century, Roediger believes, were more contradictory and promiscuous than they later became given the galling varieties of "unfree-dom" whites experienced as well as the popular denunciation of "slavery" which flourished in anti-British rhetoric of the revolutionary era. From 1800 to 1860, the gradual transition into an economy in which wage labor became widespread, and the class of "hireling" expanded dramatically, produced problems for republican ideology.[15] Dependency on wages, however, was not merely compared unfavorably with the ideal form of labor but it also faced comparison with the genuine slave.[16]

Roediger explains the context in which the consciousness of a working class was developing in this way:

> On the one hand, the specter of chattel slavery—present historically in no other nation during the years of significant working class formation—made for a remarkable awareness of the dangers of dependency and a strong suspicion of paternalism. On the

---

[11] Ibid. at 44.
[12] Ibid. (quoting Francis Scott Key, *The Star-Spangled Banner* (1814)).
[13] Ibid. at 25.
[14] Ibid.
[15] Ibid. at 45.
[16] Ibid. at 46.

other hand, hard thought about 'the hireling and the slave' could make the position of the hireling comparatively attractive. The white hireling had the possibility of social mobility the Black slave did not. The white hireling was usually a political freeman, and the slave, and with very few exceptions, the free Black, were not. The comparison could lead to sweeping critiques of wage labor as 'white slavery,' but it could also reassure wage workers that they belonged to the ranks of 'free white labor.' ... [W]orking Americans therefore expressed soaring desires to be rid of the age-old inequities of Europe and any hint of slavery. They also expressed the rather pedestrian goal of simply not being mistaken for ... 'negers.' And they saw not nearly so great a separation between these goals as we do.[17]

Roediger argues that the particular constellation of social developments and attitudes that connected "white" with worker did not fully come together before the nineteenth century. Not until the 1860s did the process that reduced nearly one-half of the nonslave labor force to dependence upon wages and subjected them to new forms of capitalist discipline reach its completion.[18] Also by the 1860s those republican notions of political and economic independence that had inflamed the nation's imagination during the Revolutionary era were waning. According to historian Gordon Wood:

People in the early nineteenth century sensed that everything had changed ... [M]urder, suicide, theft, and mobbing became increasingly common responses to the burdens that liberty and the expectation of gain were placing on people ... Urban rioting became more prevalent and destructive than it had been. Street, tavern, and theater rowdiness, labor strikes, racial and ethnic conflicts—all increased greatly after 1800 ... America may have been still largely rural, still largely agricultural, but now it was ... perhaps the most thoroughly commercialized nation in the world.[19]

America's newly industrializing commercial empire in formation was something unprecedented. As new types of production and social relations emerged during the raucous transition to capitalism, the political rhetoric of the day wrestled to define the new working conditions variously called "wage slavery," "white slavery," or "free white labor."

Central to the nineteenth-century worker's devotion to whiteness was his assertion of maleness, with its perils and yearnings, and his uncertain claim to republican citizenship in the world of men.[20] Roediger's examination of the way laborers cherished the term 'freeman' is illuminating. "[I]n an urban society in which work and home became more radically separated and masculinity underwent extensive

---

[17] Ibid. at 46–47.
[18] Ibid. at 20.
[19] Gordon S. Wood, *The Radicalism of the American Revolution* 306–313 (1992).
[20] Roediger, *supra* note 5, at 11.

redefinition, its masculine ending may have had special appeal."[21] The word held the double meaning of economic and political independence. And in the antebellum era, "Blackness," Roediger explains, "almost perfectly predicted lack of the attributes of a freeman."[22] This surprises no one, but what Roediger's study clarifies is how important it is to emphasize that blacks were perceived as "*anticitizens,* as 'enemies rather than members of the social compact.'"[23] Thus, along with agitation to expand male suffrage to include all freemen went efforts to bar free blacks from exercising the franchise or to make the legal definition of freeman congruent with white adult males.[24]

The analysis of new meanings and words defining labor is an intriguing element of Roediger's study. The increasing use of the words "help" or "hired man" or "hired hand" to replace "servant" developed early in the nineteenth century. The decline in the willingness of white domestic workers to be called servants Roediger attributes to the egalitarian notions current in post-revolutionary America plus the obnoxious association between "servant" and the work slaves performed.[25] Roediger found that virtually all the evidence from the nineteenth-century sources shows that the new usages were initiated by the workers, not, as some historians have claimed, by their employers. He quotes James Fenimore Cooper's derisive observation that "[a] man does not usually hire his cook to *help* him cook his dinner, but to cook it herself."[26] Roediger describes the new terminology for household and farm laborers as the worker's means of asserting claims to greater dignity and freedom than the term servant permitted, given the link between servility, slavery, and blacks.[27]

Widespread repudiation of the term *master,* for which the Dutch word *boss* was substituted, was another innovation. Webster's 1829 dictionary, Roediger reports, did not yet include *boss.* And in 1837, James Fenimore Cooper bristled at the popular usage of "boss," claiming that "'the laboring classes of whites' moved by a desire not to be connected with 'negro slaves' had dispensed with the term *master* ... [But] they have resorted to the use of the word *boss,* which has precisely the same meaning in Dutch!"[28]

Tracing the transformation of slang terms into racist slurs more explicitly demonstrates the changing consciousness. As late as 1840, the connotation of

---

[21] Ibid. at 55.

[22] Ibid. at 56.

[23] Ibid. at 57.

[24] Ibid. at 58.

[25] Ibid. at 48–49.

[26] Ibid. at 48 (quoting James Fenimore Cooper, *The American Democrat; Or, Hints on the Social and Civic Relations of the United States of America* 122 (1838)).

[27] Ibid. at 49.

[28] Ibid. at 54.

'coon' was that of a country bumpkin or city slicker. Davy Crockett's coonskin cap became the symbol the Whig Party used to identify with rural folk during the 1840 Presidential campaign. Democrats denounced their Whig rivals as "coons" using epithets like "Whig coonism" and "Whig coonventions." New York City Democrats attacked the Whigs as a "Federal Whig Coon Party."[29]

Later in the century, the blackface minstrel character Zip Coon came to personify the stereotypical irresponsible, dandified free Northern black, and by the end of the nineteenth century the "coon song" craze reached such intensity that Zip's songs sold millions of copies of sheet music.[30] The popularity of minstrel songs and black-face entertainment provided urban wage earners with a sentimental, rowdy but safe form of rebellion. Explaining the phenomenal appeal after the Civil War of the "coon songs," Roediger cites the work of scholars who found that this appeal lay in the songs' projection onto emancipated blacks of those values and actions that aroused both fascination and fear among working class whites. Roediger writes, "Whatever his attraction, the performers and audience knew that they were *not* the Black dandy personified by Zip Coon."[31]

The elaborate cultural disguise of "blacking up" emphasized that those on stage performing were in reality white and that whiteness mattered.[32] All whites could participate in the central joke of the minstrel show, despite their own ethnic and religious diversity, and the minstrel farce presented them with an increasingly smug whiteness. The masking process, Roediger argues, holds the key to the genius of minstrel shows, for it allowed the performer to both display and then reject the natural self in the way he could so convincingly take on and then take off blackness.[33] It also, Roediger concludes, offered the working masses an illusory opportunity to retain the joys of preindustrial culture amidst the discipline and repression associated with industrialization, social mobility, and respectability.[34] These shows addressed the broadest tensions produced by the creation of the first American working class,[35] and the uninhibited wildness of the minstrel performances gave the men in the audience a representation of psychological perversity that was the antithesis of the qualities associated with capitalist acquisitiveness.[36]

The late nineteenth-century neologism "*miscegenation*," coined by the combination of the Latin words *miscere* ('to mix') and *genus* ('race'), also illustrated the way changes in language revealed the growing racist consciousness. Introduced

---

[29] Ibid. at 98.
[30] Ibid. at 98.
[31] Ibid. at 116.
[32] Ibid. at 117.
[33] Ibid. at 116.
[34] Ibid. at 118.
[35] Ibid. at 127.
[36] Ibid. at 118.

in an 1863 pamphlet, the term was created by Democrats who sought to smear their Republican opponents, insinuating in the pamphlet that pro-Republican abolitionists would bring about race mixing. The new word soon replaced the older term "amalgamation" in the virulent political rhetoric denouncing the impeding "mongrelization" of the United States.[37]

In *The Wages of Whiteness*, Roediger paraphrases the concept of *herrenvolk* democracy that sociologist Pierre L. van den Berghe applied to the ideology of nations such as the United States and South Africa that were democratic for the master race but tyrannical towards subordinated racial groups,[38] into "*herrenvolk* republicanism." "We should perhaps speak," Roediger writes, "of a *herrenvolk* republicanism, which read African-Americans out of the ranks of the producers and then proved more able to concentrate its fire downward onto the dependent and Black than upward against the rich and powerful."[39] The main strength of such an ideology was that *herrenvolk* republicanism reassured whites who constantly feared downward mobility, that no matter what else they lost, they could never lose their whiteness.[40] Since this nineteenth-century republicanism placed mainly negative demands on the state, it easily degenerated from its lofty hatred of slavery into a clear disdain for slaves, and then free Blacks, and then into mere racial pettiness.[41]

The later half of the nineteenth century, when recently emancipated slaves lost all the political gains that the Civil War amendments and the Civil Rights Acts[42]

---

[37] Ibid. at 155–156.

[38] Written in the 1960s, van den Berghe's explanation of the evolution of such regimes is based on the changes that followed the undermining of a paternalistic system of race and ethnic relations. He wrote:

> [In] the political sphere aristocratic, colonial, or white settler regimes became transformed into 'representative' governments with wider participation in the polity, though in South Africa and until recently in the United States the democratic process was still restricted to the dominant racial caste. However, even these *Herrenvolk* democracies are clearly different from the colonial government or the planter slave-owning oligarchy which preceded them, if only because they were legitimized in terms of an ideology that could be effectively used to challenge the racial *status quo*. Thus these *Herrenvolk* democracies contained the ideological seeds of their own destruction, providing the educated elite within the oppressed groups and the progressive minority of the dominant group with a set of values to deny legitimacy to the established order.
>
> Pierre L. van den Berghe, *Race and Racism* 126 (1978).

[39] Roediger, *supra* note 5, at 59–60.

[40] Ibid. at 60.

[41] Ibid.

[42] The Thirteenth Amendment abolished slavery throughout the United States, and authorized Congress to pass appropriate legislation to enforce its provisions. The Civil Rights Act of 1866 was the first enactment designed to protect the newly granted legal rights of emancipated blacks. The Fourteenth Amendment, ratified in 1868, was enacted to eliminate questions regarding the constitutionality of the 1866 Civil Rights Act. The Enforcement Act of 1870 and the Ku Klux Klan Act of 1871 were subsequently enacted to give federal courts the authority to intervene in the vigilante actions of Southern mobs who used terrorism to intimidate the enfranchised freed slaves

had won, receives little attention in Roediger's work, but it was that era that fully brought the *herrenvolk* republic into being. The official withdrawal of Federal troops from the defeated Confederacy in 1877 represented the final abandonment of most post-war Reconstruction reforms and guaranteed the resurgence of Southern Democrats. Once restored to power, these resentful Southern politicians used the legislatures, the courts, and Ku Klux Klan terrorism to impose vicious regimes of paternalism, peonage, and segregation on freed blacks. Roediger's analysis reveals that popular commitment to white supremacy was so entrenched by the time of Emancipation, that even fundamental alteration in the political position of blacks did not remove the ingrained perception of inferiority. "But if Northern white workers developed new attitudes toward people of color only slowly and contradictorily," Roediger writes, "emancipation made for much more consistent and dramatic changes in how such workers conceived of *themselves*."[43] The role assigned to blacks in the white worker's view of the world became more complex. According to Roediger, "whiteness" could no longer "be an unambiguous source of self-satisfaction ... No longer could the supposedly servile, lazy, natural and sensual African-American serve as so clear a counterpoint to white labor and so convenient a repository for values that white workers longed for and despised."[44]

The Irish immigrants' fierce appropriation of whiteness provides the paradigmatic case study for Roediger's theory. Early in the nineteenth century, it was an open question among the native born white Protestants whether these Celtic immigrants belonged to the white race.[45] Vilified, segregated, excluded and castigated, the "paddy" was believed to be an inferior race. "Bestial," "simian," "savage," and "wild" were descriptions repeatedly applied to Irish immigrants who was ridiculed as a "nigger" turned inside out.[46] The connections drawn between Blacks and Irish did not always favor the Irish.[47] The imperative driving Irish workers to define themselves as whites, despite their hatred of the British and distaste for their American descendants was that "public and psychological wage" that whiteness promised to desperate immigrants in an industrializing society that held them in contempt.

The millions of Irish forced to come to America during the Great Famine between 1845 and 1855 helped seal the later marriage between the Democratic Party and

---

and subjugate them again to white control. Following the enactment of the Fifteenth Amendment, which was ratified in 1870, Congress passed the Civil Rights Act of 1875.

The United States Supreme Court held that Act unconstitutional in The Civil Rights Cases, 109 U.S. 3 (1883), and this paved the way for the decision in *Plessy v. Ferguson*, 163 U.S. 537 (1896), that found no bar in the Fourteenth Amendment to race discrimination under the principle of "separate but equal."

[43] Roediger, *supra* note 5, at 175.

[44] Ibid.

[45] Ibid. at 133.

[46] Ibid.

[47] Ibid.

the Irish Catholics, who brought in thousands upon thousands of largely urban voters, and used their political strength to buy acceptance as "white." Yet Roediger cautions against seeing the embrace of whiteness in purely utilitarian terms.[48] He writes:

> For Irish-American Catholics, the anxieties and the desires resulting from a loss of a relationship with nature were particularly acute. Though gang labor, cottage industry and putting-out systems had some substantial currency in mid-century Ireland, no antebellum European immigrant group experienced the wrenching move from the preindustrial countryside to full confrontation with industrial capitalism in an urban setting with anything like the intensity of Irish Catholics ... Torn from their homes, they resettled in places remarkably different from Ireland. Not only relocated in cities, but in the most crowded quarters of them, Irish-Americans maintained only the most tenuous of ties to nature.[49]

In part, the Irish immigrant's anguish over the divorce from the rhythms of nature and the land were covered over by attacking preindustrial behaviors as "black," and the more frantically they sought to distance themselves from blacks, the more apparent became the mixture of fascination with their repulsion.[50] The attacks by pro-slavery Democrats on the antislavery positions of Republicans could not match the monomaniacal focus on race in the political appeals by and to Irish immigrants. Any advocacy of natural rights for blacks or abolition of slavery they attacked as "political amalgamation," and Irish politicians attacked the failure to keep free blacks out of 'white' jobs as the "amalgamation of labor."[51]

The analysis Roediger develops starts from a position black scholars and writers have long articulated: the race problem is a white problem.[52] And in Roediger's opinion the traditional theoretical approach to labor history will simply perpetuate an oversimplified view of race which sees whiteness as natural, until it recognizes how workers participated in the creation of their own racial identity.[53] Roediger points out that labor historians should be able to grasp the inconsistency of any theory that asserts that the industrial worker's racist views merely trickled down from the ruling class. This should be particularly clear now, given that neo-Marxist perspectives in which workers are seen as historical actors making their own choices and creating their own cultural forms dominate the study of the

---

[48] Ibid. at 150.

[49] Ibid. at 151.

[50] Ibid. at 154.

[51] Ibid.

[52] See, e.g., Ralph Ellison, "Beating that Boy," in *Shadow and Act* 99–100 (1964); W. E. B. Du Bois, *The World and Africa* ch. 2 (1965); James Baldwin, *The Price of the Ticket* 87–89, 251, 666 (1985); Morrison, *supra* note 2, at 64–66.

[53] Roediger, *supra* note 5, at 6.

working class.[54] Yet, the new labor history remains reluctant to acknowledge the worker's participation in the construction of "whiteness" and "white supremacy," clinging to variations on the presumption that economic relations produced racist attitudes.[55]

For Marxist historians, class remains the privileged category of analysis even when scholars acknowledge the deformations of race, for to them economic class seems to have greater objective validity and therefore more political importance.[56] Roediger is critical of this preference, and in his analysis it is the simultaneous structural formation of the working class with a systematic elaboration of its sense of whiteness that takes center stage. "[W]hiteness," in the broadest strokes, Roediger argues, "was a way in which white workers responded to a fear of dependency on wage labor and to the necessities of capitalist work discipline."[57] The most pressing task that social and cultural historians face, in Roediger's view, "is not to draw precise lines separating race and class but to draw lines connecting race and class."[58] The study of class must be reconceptualized, he argues, to recognize how race operates to create class consciousness.

Roediger's theoretical analysis of the meaning of whiteness to the worker's self concept will have lasting significance if its insights bring clarity to the remarkable power of racism to sustain itself. The structural economic crisis now disrupting our society is the most severe this nation has seen in a century.[59] If whiteness in the nineteenth century offered a way for the newly forming working class to express fears of dependency and anguish over the imposition of capitalist discipline,

---

[54] Ibid. at 9.

[55] Ibid. at 10.

[56] Under the heading of "Marxism and the White Problem," in his introduction, Roediger reflects upon the distinction historian Barbara Fields elaborated in her essay "Ideology and Race in American History." Ibid. at 7–8. Race, Fields argued, is an ideological as opposed to physical fact, and thus entirely the product of history, while the reality of class can assert itself independently of social consciousness. Thus, Fields concluded that since class has objective reality and race only a spurious objectivity, they are not equivalent concepts. Barbara J. Fields, "Ideology and Race in American History, in *Region, Race and Reconstruction* 150–151 (J. Morgan Kousser and James M. McPherson, eds., 1982).

However, for Fields, the historical dimension of race secures its permanent significance. She wrote:

> [Race] became the ideological medium through which Americans confronted questions of sovereignty and power because the enslavement of Africans and their descendants constituted a massive exception to the rules of sovereignty and power that were increasingly taken for granted. And, despite the changes it has undergone ... race has remained a predominant ideological medium because the manner of slavery's unraveling had lasting consequences for the relations of whites to other whites, no less than for those of whites to blacks. Ibid. at 168–169.

[57] Roediger, *supra* note 5, at 13.

[58] Ibid. at 11.

[59] See, e.g., Michael Harrington, *The New American Poverty* (1984).

is it predictable that the fears and agonies modern day workers face may also seek expression in resurgent white male superiority? Whatever connection exists between the racially charged political rhetoric of recent campaigns and the disturbing fragmentation and decline facing the industrial worker, the abiding significance attached to whiteness is clear.

This attachment to whiteness has far-reaching side effects, particularly in light of the way race polarizes everyone. As Professor Lani Guinier has observed, Americans "have learned to see race as an issue of blame and punishment."[60] In the polarized, winner-takes-all climate of our political debate, Guinier writes, it seems there is no longer any will to do more than blame race for our problems. In some instances, among those overwhelmed by the magnitude of problems that seem to defy solutions, she writes, there is a belief that the solutions are the problem.[61] The assault on blacks and the poor that characterizes our present debate inhibits the creation of any "approach that gives working-class whites and blacks, poor people of all hues and other political orphans a ... way to make common ground. ... No one tries to point out," she concludes, "that the interests of minorities and the poor are integral to our collective self-interests."[62] Clearly these spurious wages that white racism paid long ago continue to bedevil our democracy.

QUESTIONS

(1) Why, according to Cleaver, is it important not only to focus on the benefits of whiteness, but also on how the white working class in the nineteenth century constructed the meaning of whiteness?
(2) Why, for example, was the word "help" used to replace the word "servant"?
(3) In terms of whiteness, why should the study of class be re-conceptualized?
(4) Why, during the nineteenth century, did the white working class accept low wages from their employers?
(5) What are some of the effects of whiteness on democratic politics today?

---

[60] Lani Guinier, "Beyond Winner Take All: Democracy's Conversation," *The Nation*, Jan. 23, 1995, at 85.
[61] Ibid.
[62] Ibid. at 85–86.

Glossary

Abolitionists. People who, before the American Civil War, wanted slavery in the United States to end. Abolitionists believed that slavery violated basic human rights and freedom. Thus, they organized to make slavery illegal. They wrote and distributed a wide variety of anti-slavery literature in which they pointed to the atrocities of American slavery.

African Civilization Society (ACS) (1858–1869). ACS, with its headquarters in Brooklyn, New York, was established in 1858 by Henry Highland Garnet. It worked with black churches and schools. Some of the prominent members included Richard H. Cain, Reverend Amos N. Freeman, John Stella Martin, and Reverend Rufus L. Perry. The ACS sent teachers to the South to educate free blacks. The goal of the ACS, spelt out in its Constitution, was to civilize and Christianize Africa and the African people. The ACS saw itself as a major force in the demise of the African slave trade and promoting African self-governance and self-reliance. It was Garnet's vision that educated black Americans would move to Africa as cultural missionaries to lead the economic, political, and moral development of Africans.

African Female Benevolent Society (AFBS). On February 12, 1833, the AFBS was formed. Phebe Thuey was the President and Hannah Rich was the Vice President. Its purpose, as stated in its Constitution, was for its members to use their intellect to break down the barrier of prejudice and raise themselves to an equality "with those fellow beings who differ from [them] in complexion alone." At the fifteenth anniversary of the AFBS, in 1848, Reverend Henry Highland Garnet was the featured speaker. Garnet's speech was titled "The Past and Present Condition, and the Destiny of the Colored Race." In his speech, he bemoaned the evil of slavery. However, he did not advocate for African Americans to emigrate. He states, "America is my home, my country, and I have no other. I love whatever of good there may be in her institutions. I hate her sins. I loathe her slavery, and I pray Heaven that ere long she may wash away her guilt in tears of repentance."

African Slave Trade. The African Slave Trade, also known as the Atlantic Slave Trade or Transatlantic Slave Trade, began in the fifteenth century, after the Portuguese started their exploration on the coast of West Africa, which was followed by the British and French. At first, the numbers of Africans enslaved were small. In the middle of the seventeenth century, with the development of plantations on the newly contested Caribbean islands and American mainland, the trade grew immensely.

Afrocentrism. A cultural ideology or worldview that focuses on the history of blacks in Africa and the African diaspora. It is a response to Eurocentric attitudes about blacks and their historical contribution to civilizations. It revisits blacks' history with an African cultural and ideological focus. Afrocentrism deals primarily with self-determination and African agency and it is a Pan-African ideology in culture, philosophy, and history.

Agency. The capacity of individuals and groups to act in a given milieu by engaging with the social structure.

American Antislavery Society (AAS) (1833–1870). Founded in 1833 by William Lloyd Garrison and Arthur Tappan with its headquarters in New York City. Some of its members included Susan B. Anthony, Elizabeth Cady Stanton, Lucy Stone, and Samuel Cornish. The AAS published the *National Antislavery Standard*, a weekly newspaper, under the editorship of Lydia M. Child and David L. Child. Frederick Douglass, an escaped slave, was a leader of the AAS and often spoke at its meetings. By 1838, the AAS had 1,350 local charters and about 250,000 members. In 1839, the different approaches of its members to many concerns caused the ASA to be divided, with some members forming the American and Foreign Antislavery Society (AFAS) in 1840. The AAS was indeed controversial and sometimes met with a tremendous amount of violence. The AAS came to an end in 1870.

American and Foreign Antislavery Society (AFAS). Abolitionists including Samuel Cornish, William Jay, Amos Phelps, and Arthur and Lewis Tappan founded the AFAS in May 1840. These abolitionists were a part of the American Antislavery Society (AAS) and left the organization to form the AFAS because of their fundamental disagreement with William Lloyd Garrison on issues such as anarchism, established religion, and women's right to vote in the meetings' proceedings. Also, they disagreed with other members including James E. Birney and Elizur Wright Jr. over the belief that the AAS should found a new party and enter electoral politics. Throughout its existence, the AFAS produced pamphlets advocating its view. It had difficulties in recruiting new members. In 1855, it stopped holding its annual meeting and the executive committee's last meeting was held in 1859.

American Missionary Association. Founded on September 3, 1846, in Albany, New York. It was a Protestant-based Abolitionist Group. Its main purpose was to abolish slavery and to provide education for blacks. It also emphasized the promotion of equality and Christian values.

American Negro Academy (ANA) (1897–1920). The first organization in the United States to support the academic scholarship of blacks. Alexander Crummell was the first President of the Academy. It encouraged classical academic studies and liberal arts as a contrast to Booker T. Washington's approach to education, which emphasized industrial education for black youth.

American Revolution (1775–1783). The American Revolution is also known as the American Revolutionary War or the American War of Independence. The war arose from increasing conflicts between inhabitants of the thirteen American colonies and the colonial government, which represented the British crown. In April 1775, conflicts between British troops and colonial militiamen in Lexington and Concord initiated the armed conflict, and by the following summer, the rebels were waging a full-scale war for their independence. In 1778, France entered the American Revolution on the side of the colonists, turning what had basically been a civil war into an international battle. In 1781, with the aid of the French, the Continental Army forced the British to surrender at Yorktown, Virginia. The Americans had effectively won their independence, though fighting would not formally end until 1783. The American Revolution fought by the American colonies against Britain influenced political ideas and revolutions around the world, as an inexperienced, largely divided nation won its freedom from the highest military force of its time.

Anthony, Susan B. (1820–1906). Anthony was born in Adams, Massachusetts, and was raised in a Quaker household with a long activist tradition. She worked as a teacher for fifteen years. She then became active in the Temperance movement, which advocated against the consumption of alcohol. However, because she was a woman, she was not allowed to speak at the gatherings. In 1852, Anthony joined the women's movement and dedicated herself to women's suffrage. She also advocated for the abolition of slavery. Anthony traveled and lectured throughout the United States. In her lectures, she advocated for the right of women to own their own property, retain their own earnings, and form women's labor organizations. In 1900, with the help of Anthony's persuasion, the University of Rochester began to admit women.

Apartheid Government of South Africa. In 1948, after the National Party acquired power in South Africa, its all-white government instantaneously started to enforce existing policies of racial segregation under a system of legislation that it called apartheid. In 1994, when the African National Congress Party gained power in South Africa and Nelson Mandela became the President of South Africa, apartheid came to an end.

Aryan Nation. A white supremacist religious organization, whose origin was premised on the teaching of Wesley A. Smith, an important figure in the early Christian Identity Movement. From the late 1970s to 2001, its headquarters were in Hayden, Idaho. Until 1998, Richard Girnt Butler was the leader of the organization. Neuman Britton took over the leadership until 2001, then Harold Ray Redfeairn of Ohio took over the role. Under Redfeairn's leadership, Dave Hall, a Federal Bureau of Investigation informant, joined the organization, and exposed the organization's illegal activities. Redfeairn was expelled from the organization by Butler. When Butler died in 2004, the future of the organization was uncertain. Morris L. Gulett, the self-proclaimed leader of the organization, closed the organization's headquarters in Converse, LA, and announced his retirement from the Aryan Nation.

Assimilation. Assimilation in the United States has several meanings. Taking its meaning from the American sociologist Henry Pratt Fairchild, assimilation is associated with Americanization or the melting pot theory. Also, some scholars believed that assimilation and acculturation were synonymous. It involves the minority group members assimilating or conforming to the norms and values of the majority group.

Atlanta Compromise. In 1885, Booker T. Washington, who was then the president of Tuskegee Institute, and other African American leaders made an agreement with Southern whites that Southern blacks would submit to white political rule. In return, Southern whites would make sure that blacks received basic education provided by the educational charities founded by Northern whites. In addition, blacks were to be protected by due process in the laws. In return, blacks would not agitate for equality and justice. This agreement is known as the Atlanta Compromise, which was greatly criticized by W. E. B. Du Bois, William Monroe Trotter, and other black leaders who believed that blacks should fight for civil rights.

Atlantic Slave Trade. Also known as the Transatlantic Slave Trade, which existed from the sixteenth to the nineteenth century. It entailed the transportation of enslaved Africans from central and western Africa by slave traders to the Americas and the Caribbean where Africans were sold as slaves. A small number of Africans were directly captured by the slave traders during the coastal raids. The slave trade employed the triangle slave route and its middle passage to ship Africans to the New World. These economies relied on secure labor to produce products to be sold to Europe. In the sixteenth century, the Portuguese was the first nation to be involved in the slave trade. The Atlantic Slave Trade was abolished in the British Empire by the Abolition of the Slave Trade Act of 1807.

Bancroft, George (1800–1891). Bancroft started his education at Phillips Exeter Academy. At the age of thirteen, he started his undergraduate education at Harvard University and graduated when he was seventeen. He moved to Germany and completed his doctoral degree at the University of Göttingen in 1820. He spent some years touring Europe. After he returned to the United States, in 1844, Bancroft was the Democratic candidate for the governorship of Massachusetts. In 1845, he was appointed to James Knox Polk's cabinet as Secretary of the Navy where he served until 1846. During his short tenure, he established the United States Naval Academy at Annapolis, creating a legacy of education and leadership. He was an American historian and statesman and was prominent in promoting education in his home state Massachusetts.

Baraka, Amiri (1934–2014). Baraka, born Everett LeRoi Jones in Newark, New Jersey, was an African American poet and professor. He taught at many universities including SUNY at Buffalo and SUNY at Stony Brook. Some of his nonfiction works include *Home: Social Essay*, 1965; *Poetry for the Advanced*, 1979; and *The Essence of Reparations*, 2003.

Battle of Liberty Place (Battle of Canal Place). This was an attempted insurrection on September 14, 1874 in New Orleans, which was then the capital of Louisiana, by the Crescent City White League also known as the White Man's League, an American white paramilitary organization of the Democratic Party, which was made up largely of Confederate veterans, who were against the Reconstruction era Louisiana state government. During the attempted insurrection, the White League fought against the outnumbered New Orleans Metropolitan Police and state militia. The White League held the statehouse, armory, and downtown area for three days, withdrawing before the arrival of federal troops who restored the elected government. No insurgents were charged in this attempted insurrection.

Black Feminism. A movement that became popular in the 1960s as a response to the sexism of the Civil Rights Movement and the racism of the feminist movement. Proponents of Black Feminism point out that black women are positioned differently than white women because, for example, racism, sexism, and classism amalgamate to oppress black women in specific ways. This draws attention to the concept of intersectionality, which, in 1989, was coined by black legal scholar Kimberlé

Crenshaw in her article, "Demarginalizing the Intersection of Race and Sex: A Black Feminist Critique of Antidiscrimination Doctrine, Feminist Theory and Antiracist Politics."

Black Lives Matter. In 2013, after the acquittal of George Zimmerman in the fatal shooting of Trayvon Martin, an African American teenager, the movement was co-founded by black community organizers Alicia Garza, Patrisse Cullor, and Opal Tometi. The movement holds meetings and speaks out against the police killing of blacks, racial profiling, police violence, and racial inequality in the American criminal justice system. Black Lives Matter became nationally recognized for its street demonstration after the police killing of Michael Brown in Ferguson, Missouri and Eric Garner in New York City in 2014. It continues to campaign against police violence and systematic racism towards blacks.

Black Nationalism. A social and political moment that was prominent in the 1960s and the 1970s. It arose as a response to America's racism and has created an oppositional space for black political discourse. And while its emphasis is on blacks separating from whites in order to be self-sufficient, Black Nationalism has a long intellectual tradition. In 1852, Martin R. Delany, in his book *The Condition, Elevation, Emigration, and Destiny of the Colored People of the United States, Politically Considered*, advocated for the self-sufficiency of blacks and called for "emigration of the colored people of the United States" to Liberia. Also, in the years between Reconstruction and World War I, one of the main advocates for the self-sufficiency of blacks in the United States was Bishop Henry McNeal Turner of the African Methodist Episcopal Church.

Black Panther Party (BPP). A political organization formed in October 1966 in California by Huey Newton and Bobby Seale. It comprised black militants whose function was to monitor the Oakland Police Department and challenge police brutality in Oakland, California. The BPP was involved with shoot-outs with police in California and New York City. In 1969, community social programs became the primary activity of the organization such as its involvement with the Free Breakfast for Children Program and community health clinics to address issues such as food injustice in black communities. The BPP was under investigation by the FBI. J. Edgar Hoover who was then the director of the FBI called the BPP "the greatest threat to the internal security of the country." In 1974, Newton and eight other BPP members were arrested by the police. Newton, in order to avoid conviction, exiled to Cuba. Elaine Brown was appointed as the first chairwoman of the party. When Newton returned to the United States, in 1977, one of the female BPP members endured a harsh discipline involving a beating, which was authorized by Newton. Precisely for this reason, Brown resigned from the organization and moved to Los Angeles, CA. The membership of the BPP was decreasing and in 1982, the BPP's sponsored school closed.

Black Power Movement of the 1960s. It originated during the criticism of the Civil Rights Movement. It was a political movement that employed various forms of activism, both violent and peaceful, to achieve a form of Black Power aimed at self-determination. It was influenced by black leaders such as Malcolm X and the Black Panther Party, a revolutionary and socialist organization founded in 1968 by Bobby Seale and Huey Newton.

Blaxploitation. A term coined in the early 1970s to refer to black action films, which feature black actors in leading roles. The films were often condemned by their critics for reinforcing and perpetuating stereotypes of blacks and for the glorification of violence, especially in black communities. Blaxploitation arose at a critical juncture for the Hollywood film industry. The 1971 film *Sweet Sweetback's Baadasssss Song*, written, produced, and directed by Melvin Van Peebles kicked off the genre.

Blumenbach, Johann Friedrich (1752–1840). Blumenbach was a German physicist, physiologist, and anthropologist. He was the first to explore the study of mankind in his work on natural history. His teachings in comparative anatomy were applied to his classification of human races into five categories. In 1776, Blumenbach was appointed as an extraordinary professor of medicine and an inspector of the museum of natural history in Göttingen. The philosopher Immanuel Kant was strongly influenced by Blumenbach's biological concept of formative forces in developing his idea of organic purpose. Whereas Kant has a heuristic concept in mind in order to explain mechanical causes, Blumenbach perceived of causation as entirely resident in nature.

Bonaparte, Napoleon (1769–1821). Napoleon, known as Napoléon I, born on the island of Corsica, was a French military leader and emperor. He conquered much of Europe in the early nineteenth century and rose rapidly through the ranks of the military during the French Revolution (1789–1799). In a 1799 coup d'état, after seizing power in France, Napoleon crowned himself emperor of France in 1804. He successfully waged war against many European nations and expanded his empire. In 1812, he launched a disastrous French invasion of Russia, and two years later, renounced the throne and was exiled to the island of Elba. In his Hundred Days Campaign in 1815, he briefly returned to power. After a terrible defeat at the Battle of Waterloo, Napoleon surrendered once again and was exiled to the secluded island of St. Helena, where he died when he was only 51 years old.

Bourbon Democracy. It was based on the practice of the members of the Democratic Party, the Bourbon democrats, which was not a term used by them. The term "bourbon" was used, principally, by critics complaining of traditional perspectives. Bourbon Democracy was based on the ideologies of conservatism and classical liberalism, and supported the presidential candidates Charles O'Connor and Samuel J. Tilden in 1872 and 1876 respectively and President Glover Cleveland in 1884–1888 and 1892–1896. The Bourdon democrats were promoters of laissez-faire capitalism, which included opposition to high tariffs as a form of protectionism that the Republicans advocated.

Buffoon. A person whose outlandish behavior is a source of amusement for others.

Bushman. This term referred to the San or Saan people who are members of the Khoikhoi-speaking indigenous people of the southern African region – Botswana, Namibia, Angola, Zambia, Zimbabwe, Lesotho, and South Africa – and the hunter-gatherers and the first people to occupy this region.

Butler, Benjamin (1818–1893). In 1838, Benjamin Butler graduated from Colby College in Maine. In 1840, he was admitted to the Massachusetts Bar, where he started a large criminal practice. In 1853, he was elected to the Massachusetts House of Representatives and then, in 1859, to the Senate of the Commonwealth. While in office, he attended the Democratic convention where he voted for Jefferson Davis to run for the presidential nomination, as well as candidates including John C. Breckinridge. Butler, in 1839, entered the Massachusetts Militia and, in 1855, was promoted to brigadier general even though he had no official military training. Benjamin Butler was a general in the American Civil War (1861–1865) and became one of the most disliked generals of the war, offending many on both sides of the war. He returned to politics and after serving several unsuccessful campaigns, he was elected governor of Massachusetts in 1882, and was a presidential candidate during the election of 1884.

Calhoun, John C. (1782–1850). Calhoun was an American statesman and political theorist from South Carolina. He was educated at Yale University. He later returned to South Carolina and served in South Carolina's legislature. He served three terms in the House of Representatives. He was a strong supporter of the war of 1812 fought between America, Great Britain, and their respective allies to defend American honor against British infractions of American independence and neutrality during the Napoleonic Wars. From 1817 to 1825, he was the Secretary of War under President James Monroe. In 1825, he ran for president. He was vice president to John Quincy Adams, and to Andrew Jackson. Calhoun is largely remembered for defending slavery and advancing the concept of state rights.

Capital Punishment. It is also known as the death penalty and is a government sanctioned practice whereby a person is put to death by the state as a punishment for a crime. The sentence that

someone be punished in such a manner is referred to as a death sentence, whereas the act of carrying out the sentence is known as an execution.

Capitalism. An economic system in which ownership of the means of production, distribution, and exchange of wealth are in the hands of private individuals and corporations. Other general characteristics that are central to capitalism include capital accumulation, wage labor, a price system, voluntary exchange, and a competitive market. Various forms of capitalism in practice include free market or laissez-faire capitalism, welfare capitalism, and state capitalism. Most existing capitalist economies are mixed economies, which combine free markets with government intervention into the economy.

Césaire, Aimé (1913–2008). Césaire, born in Basse-Pointe, Martinique, was a Francophone and French poet, author, and politician. In the 1930s, he was one of the founders of the Négritude movement, a literary movement born out of the intellectual environment of black writers in Paris in the 1930s and 1940s, coming together to assert their cultural identity through the French language. In 1945, with the support of the French Communist Party, Césaire was elected the mayor of Fort-de-France. Many of his works were translated from French into several languages.

Christophe, Henri (1767–1820). Christophe was an African slave who was the key leader in the Haitian Revolution (1791–1804), which succeeded in gaining independence from France in 1804. The following year, 1805, Christophe, under Jean-Jacques Dessalines, assisted in the seizing of Santo Domingo, today the Dominican Republic, who in the Treaty of Basel of 1795, acquired the colony from Spain. After Dessalines was assassinated in 1806, Christophe fled to the Plain-du-Nord and created a separate government. On February 17, 1807, he was elected president of the State of Haiti where he was backed by General Jean-Pierre Boyer. In 1811, he declared Haiti a Kingdom and had himself crowned by Corneil Breuil, the archbishop of Milot.

Cinque, Joseph (1814–1879). Cinque, also known as Sengbe Pieh, was born in Sierra Leone. He was married with three children and was a farmer. In 1839, he was captured illegally by African slave traders and sold to a Portuguese slave trader Pedro Blanco. He was kept as a prisoner on the Portuguese slave ship *Tecora*, which violated the treaties prohibiting the international slave trade. Eventually, Cinque was taken to Cuba and was sold with other captured people to Spaniards José Ruiz and Pedro Montez. The Spaniards transported the captives on the *Amistad* with an intention to sell them as slaves to work on the sugar plantation. On June 30, 1839, Cinque led a revolt and killed the ship's captain and the cook. In the revolt, two slaves died and two sailors escaped. After two months, when the ship arrived in Long Island, New York, Cinque and the other Africans were charged with mutiny and murder and were taken to New Haven, Connecticut, to await trial. Despite the lies that the Spaniards espoused, the case was ruled in the district and circuits court in favor of the Africans. It was then appealed to the Supreme Court. In March 1840, the Court ruled for the Africans to regain their freedom since they had been kidnapped and sold illegally. In 1842, Cinque and the other Africans returned to Africa.

Civil Rights. The political, social, and economic rights that each citizen has by virtue of being a citizen in the United States, and which are fundamentally upheld by law. The meaning of the phase is shaded by its most common reference to the civil rights of blacks and non-whites in the United States. In the United States, any state which gives constitutional or legal guarantees to its citizens confers their civil rights.

Civil Rights Act of 1875. It was sometimes called the Enforcement Act or Force Act, which was signed into law by President Ulysses Grant on March 1, 1875 as a reaction to the violations of the civil rights of African Americans. The Act was a United States federal law that was enacted during the Reconstruction era "to protect all citizens in their civil and legal rights" in equal treatment in public transportation, public facilities, and to prohibit exclusion of any citizen from jury service. The Act was not enforced effectively.

Civil Rights Movement. A movement campaigning for the full recognition of the rights of African Americans from the 1950s through to the 1970s, whose leaders included the Reverend Dr. Martin Luther King. Some key moments include: the 1954 Supreme Court ruling in *Brown v. Board of Education* that ruled school segregation of blacks and whites unconstitutional; in 1955, the bus boycott organized in Montgomery, Alabama, after Rosa Parks was arrested for refusing to give up her seat to a white man; and demonstrations and sit-ins at diners where blacks were refused entry. The activism of the movement helped in the passing of the Civil Rights Act of 1964 and the passing of the Voting Rights Act of 1965. The civil rights period was one of great convulsion for the United States, especially in the Southern states.

Civil War (1861–1865). It was fought in the United States because of a longstanding controversy about the prohibition of slavery. It started in April 1861 when Confederates attacked Fort Sumter in South Carolina shortly after the inauguration of President Abraham Lincoln on March 4, 1861. The nationalists of the Union proclaimed loyalty to the United States Constitution. They faced secessionists from the seven Confederate states of America – South Carolina, Mississippi, Florida, Alabama, Georgia, Louisiana, and Texas – who advocated for states' rights to expand slavery. The 54th Massachusetts Infantry Regiment, comprising 178,975 black men was formed in 1863 to fight in the Civil War.

Clarke, John Henrik (1915–1998). Clarke was born in Union Springs, Alabama. From 1969 to 1986, he was a professor and the founding chair of Black and Puerto Rican Studies at Hunter College, City University of New York. Other universities that he taught included Cornell University, the New School for Social Research, University of Ghana, and the University of Ibadan, the oldest university in Nigeria. He promoted study of the African American experience and the need for the insertion of African accomplishments in world history. Besides teaching and lecturing, he co-founded the *Harlem Quarterly*, and was the book review editor of the *Negro History Bulletin*, the associate editor of *Freedomways*, and a feature writer for the *Pittsburg Courier.*

Colfax Massacre. The massacre occurred on April 13, 1873 in Colfax, Louisiana. It followed the hotly contested Louisiana governor's race of 1872 in which the Republicans won the election by a small margin, which, of course, angered the Democrats. As a result, the Democrats organized a white militia to challenge the mostly black militia that was under the control of the Republican governor. On April 13, 300 armed white men including members of the White Camelia and the Ku Klux Klan attacked the court house building. Many of the black defenders fled while others surrendered. Nonetheless, about 150 blacks were killed including forty-eight who were murdered after the battle. After order was reestablished by the New Orleans police and the federal troops, ninety-seven white militia men were arrested and charged with violation of the Enforcement Act that was passed between 1870 and 1871.

Colored Female Religious and Moral Reform Society. An African American women's club organized in Salem, Massachusetts, by forty women in 1818, religious in its stance. These women created their own constitution published in the *Liberator*, an abolitionist newspaper. The members faithfully promised to "be charitably watchful over each other" and worked to get sickness and death benefits for women. The members of the club were required to take a vow of secrecy.

Colorism. A term coined by Alice Walker in her 1983 book, *In Search of Our Mothers' Gardens*, in which she defines colorism as the preference for light-skinned blacks by blacks or in her words, "prejudicial or preferential treatment of same raced people based on their color." It is not a synonym for racism, as a system in place for the benefit of whites, when colorism is internalized by members of the black community.

Color-line. The color-line was originally used in reference to the racial segregation that existed in the United States beginning in the Reconstruction period. In 1881, Frederick Douglass published "The Color line" in the *North American Review*. The phrase gained fame when W. E. B. Du Bois, in *The Souls of Black*

Folk published in 1909, stated: "The problem of the twentieth century is the problem of the color-line."

Combahee River Collective (1974–1980). The Collective was a black feminist lesbian organization that was active in Boston, Massachusetts, starting in 1974, and was founded by Barbara Smith, after Smith, with other delegates, attended the first regional meeting of the National Black Feminist Organization (NBFO) in New York City in 1973 and realized that the NBFO's vision for social change was not very radical. The Collective is famous for the development of the *Combahee River Collective Statement*, a primary document of the history of contemporary Black Feminism, which was to address the needs of black lesbians and also to organize on behalf of black feminists. For the Collective, Black Feminism was "the logical political movement to combat the manifold and simultaneous oppression that all women of color face."

Commonwealth. The meaning of the term "commonwealth" in the fifteenth century meant public welfare. It expanded in the seventeenth century to mean "a state in which the supreme power is vested in the people" in a democratic state. Lately, the term has been used to name some fraternal associations of nations, most particularly the Commonwealth of Nations, an organization predominantly comprising previous territories of the British Empire.

Compromise of 1877 (or Compromise of 1876). An unwritten deal that settled the intensely disputed debate of 1876 concerning who was to be the President of the United States. Republican Rutherford B. Hayes was awarded the presidency over Democrat Samuel J. Tilden on the condition that Hayes would withdraw federal troops in South Carolina, Florida, and Louisiana for Republican government of these states to stay in power. It resulted in the federal government withdrawing troops from the South, which ended the Reconstruction period.

Cooper, Anna Julia (1858–1964). Cooper, born a slave in Raleigh, North Carolina, was a teacher, writer, and activist who advocated education for African Americans and women. In 1867, two years after the Civil War, Cooper started her formal education at the St. Augustine Normal School and Collegiate Institute that was built for former slaves. In 1877, she married George A. G. Cooper and after his death in 1879, she attended Oberlin College. In 1884, she earned a BA and, in 1887, an MA in Mathematics. Before moving to Washington, DC to teach at the Washington colored high school, just after graduation, she worked at Wilberforce University and St. Augustine's. In Washington, DC she met Mary Church Terrell who was also a teacher. Cooper and Terrell both boarded at Alexander Crummell's home. In 1892, Cooper published her first book, *A Voice from the South by a Black Woman of the South*, in which she argues that the education of black women is necessary for the uplifting of the entire black race.

Cosmopolitanism. Early proponents of cosmopolitanism included the Stoics such as Cicero. The Stoics rejected the idea that a person should be defined by one's city of origin, as was typical of Greek males at the time. Rather, the Stoics insisted that people were "citizens of the world." In Greek etymology, "world," in its original sense, meant "cosmos" or "universe." The Stoics' idea of being "a citizen of the world" captures the meaning of cosmopolitanism as "the need to recognize and act on one's membership in a global community of human beings."

Critical Race Theory (CRT). A theoretical framework in the social sciences that uses critical theory to provide the analytical and ethical foundation for the study of society and culture as they relate to categories such as race, law, and power. In the 1980s, as an offshoot of critical legal studies, CRT started as a theoretical movement within American law schools with scholars such as Derrick Bell, Kimberlé Crenshaw, Mari Matsuda, and Patricia Williams. Two of the main concerns of CRT are: (1) to examine white supremacy and power and how both are maintained over time and the role that the law plays in this process; and (2) to examine some of the options that are necessary to transform the relationship between the law and the maintenance of the power structure that works in the interests of the dominant group.

Cruse, Harold (1916–2005). Cruse, an American academic, was born in Petersburg, Virginia. He was an outspoken social critic and a professor of African American Studies at the University of Michigan until the mid-1980s. After publishing, in 1967, *The Crisis of the Negro Intellectual*, in 1968, he was invited to lecture at the University of Michigan and taught in the African American Studies program. He was one of the first African American Studies professors, and one of the first to be granted tenure without holding a degree.

Cultural Anthropology. A branch of anthropology that deals with the study of culture in all of its aspects and uses the methods, concepts, and data of archeology, ethnography, and ethnology to examine cultural variation among human beings. In analyzing cultures, the cultural anthropologist engages in fieldwork or participant observation, interviews, and surveys. Cultural anthropology contrasts with social anthropology.

Cultural Pluralist. The American philosopher Horace Kallen is credited for coining the term "cultural pluralism" in his essay, "Democracy Versus the Melting Pot" published in *The Nation* in 1915. Cultural pluralism is when people of non-dominant cultures are encouraged to maintain their cultural traditions and practices within the larger society.

Damocles. A figure presented in a moral anecdote about "the sword of Damocles." The anecdote tells the tale of how Damocles told King Dionysius how fortunate he was to have so much power and authority and be surrounded with magnificence and glory. Dionysius offers to switch places with Damocles for a day so that Damocles can experience first-hand Dionysius' fortune, which Damocles accepts. He sits on the king's throne and is surrounded by all of the luxury. However, Dionysius arranges for a huge sword to be hung above the throne held at the pommel only by a single hair of a horse's tail. Realizing that being a king with great power and fortune also comes with great danger, Damocles no longer wants to sit on the throne and begs the king to be allowed to leave.

Declaration of Independence. A statement adopted on July 4, 1776 by the Second Continental Congress meeting at the Pennsylvania State House in Philadelphia. It announced the thirteen states, no longer under British rule, which would found the new nation, the United States of America.

Democracy. A system of government in which the citizens exercise power directly or through representatives elected from among themselves to form a governing body such as a parliament, a legislated elected body of government. Democracy is often referred to as "rule of the majority."

Dessalines, Jean-Jacques (1758–1806). Dessalines was born in Central West Africa and was transported to the French colony of Saint-Dominigue (Haiti), the French West Indies, as a slave. He was given the name Jean-Jacques Duclos, which was the name of his master. He became a field hand and then was promoted to a foreman. At the age of 30, he was sold to a free black man named Dessalines, and his last name was changed to Dessalines. When the slave rebellion broke out in 1791, Dessalines escaped from the plantation, and joined with Toussaint L'Ouverture in a ferocious battle to free slaves on the island, which, over time, led to the independence of Haiti. In the battle, Dessalines positioned himself as a lieutenant and was nicknamed "the tiger." The French Republic, in 1793, declared an end to slavery in France and in all of the French colonies. However, many whites lobbied France to get slavery reinstated and Napoleon sent troops to restore French rule on the island, which resulted the battle of Crête-à-Pierrot. In 1802, L'Ouverture was captured and arrested. With the help of Dessalines, blacks and mulattoes joined forces, and the French ceded and left the island. In 1804, Dessalines declared independence and appointed himself emperor of Haiti. Haiti became the first black independent republic of the world.

Emancipation Proclamation. A presidential proclamation and executive order issued by President Abraham Lincoln on January 1, 1863, after the government issued a series of warnings under the Second Confiscation Act, which were laws passed during the Civil War, in the summer of 1862, allowing Confederate supporters sixty days to surrender or face confiscation of their land and slaves. The proclamation based on the President's constitutional authority as commander-in-chief of the armed forces declared that all slaves in the rebellious states "shall be then, thenceforward, and forever free."

Enforcement Act of 1871. Also known as the Civil Rights Act of 1871, which was passed by President Ulysses S. Grant on April 20, 1871. It was an act of the United States Congress, empowering the president to stop the writ of habeas corpus so as to combat the Ku Klux Klan (KKK) and other white supremacist groups and prevent them attacking and killing blacks in detention. It was the last of three enforcement acts passed during the Reconstruction era by the United States Congress from 1870 to 1871. The Act was also intended to combat the actions of the KKK and other white supremacist against groups of black men who wanted to vote.

Environmental Racism. A term used to explain and describe environmental injustice within a racialized content that is present in socially marginalized racial minority communities subject to a large amount of exposure to pollutants and the denial of these communities to access ecological benefits including natural resources, clean air, and water.

Epictetus (AD 55–135). Epictetus was a Greek philosopher who was born a slave in Hierapolis Phrygia (present-day Pamukkale, Turkey). He lived in Rome until his banishment. He then went to live in Nicopolis in Northern Greece for the remainder of his life. For Epictetus, philosophy was a way of life and not just a theory. For him, all external events are beyond our control. Precisely, for this reason, we should unquestionably accept whatever happens. And since one is responsible for one's action, such action can be examined and controlled by self-discipline. His teachings were recorded and published by his student Arrian of Nicomedia in his *Discourses of Epictetus* and *Enchirdion* or *Handbook of Epictetus.*

Equiano, Olaudah (1747–1797). Equiano, known as Gustavus Vassa, was abducted and became a slave. About six months after his abduction, Equiano was brought to the coast of Nigeria where he was placed on a slave ship; the first time he saw white men. The ship landed in Barbados and all the slaves were sold except for the young Equiano. Two weeks later, he was shipped off to the English colony of Virginia, where he was purchased and put to work. Less than a month later, he had a new master, Michael Henry Pascal, a lieutenant in the Royal Navy. He worked for Pascal for seven years and then moved to England where he educated himself and under Pascal's command traveled the world on various ships. Equiano, in 1776, bought his freedom. In England, he became an active abolitionist and a leading member of the Sons of Africa, a small abolitionist group of free Africans in London. Equiano lectured about the cruelty of British slave owners and spoke out against slavery. He was involved in the resettling of former slaves. In 1789, Equiano published *The Interesting Narrative of the Life of Olaudah Equiano, or Gustavus Vassa, the African*, in which he describes the horrors of the Middle Passage.

Ethnology. A branch of anthropology that compares and analyzes the characteristics of different people and the relationship between them. Ethnology (*ethnologia*) is credited to Adam Franz Kollár because of his use of the term in his 1783 book, *Historiae jurisque publici regni ungariae amoenitates I–II*, published in Vienna. The aims of ethnology involve the reformulation of human history, the interpretation of cultural invariants such as the incest taboo and cultural change, and the origination of generalizations about human nature, a concept, since the nineteenth century, which has been disputed by philosophers including Hegel and Marx. In the United States, ethnology has developed along independent routes of examination and pedagogical principles with cultural anthropology.

Eugenics. A set of beliefs and practices aimed at improving the genetic quality of a human population. In 1883, eugenics was developed by Francis Galton. In the early twentieth century, starting in the United Kingdom, eugenics movements emerged and spread to most European countries, Canada, and the United States. In the latter, especially, the eugenics movement was based on biological determinism and the supposed genetic superiority of the Anglo-Saxon. Later, the eugenics movement became associated with Nazi Germany and the Holocaust. The movement gained prominence under Adolph Hitler's leadership and was geared towards complementing the Nazi racial policies asserting the superiority of the Aryan race and claiming scientific legitimacy.

Farrakhan, Louis (1933–). Farrakhan was born Louis Eugene Walcott in the Bronx, New York City, and was formerly known as Louis X. He is an American religious leader, an African American activist, and social commentator. He is the leader of the Nation of Islam, a religious group in the United States. In October 1995, he organized the Million Man March in Washington, DC in which he encouraged black men to renew their commitments to their families and communities. He is at the center of controversies that deem him anti-Semitic, which he has emphatically denied.

Fauset, Jessie (1882–1961). Fauset, born in Camden County, New Jersey, was an African American editor, poet, novelist, and educator. In 1905, she graduated with a BA in Classical Languages from Cornell University and, later, received an MA in French from the University of Pennsylvania. For a while, Fauset taught Greek and Latin at Dunbar High School in Washington, DC, for black students. In 1919, she left teaching and became the editor of *The Crisis*, a literary magazine founded by W. E. B. Du Bois. She worked as an editor until 1927 and then took up a teaching position at DeWitt Clinton High School in the Bronx until 1944. During this time, she continued to write and publish her novels. Her novels include *Plum Bun*, 1928; *The Chinaberry Tea*, 1931; and *Comedy: American Style*, 1931.

Faustin I (1782–1867). Also known as Faustin Soulouque, Faustin was a career officer and general in the Haitian army. In 1847 he was elected as the President of Haiti. In 1849, under the name Faustin I, he was declared Emperor of Haiti. He quickly dismissed the army's ruling elites and placed black loyalists in many administrative positions. Also, he created a secret police and personal army. In the same year, he established a black nobility in Haiti. However, his efforts to reconquer the neighboring Dominican Republic weakened his power and a scheme led by General Fabre Nicolas Geffrard forced him to resign in 1859. Geffrard then became President of Haiti in 1859.

Federal Constitution. A document that was drafted and ratified for the purpose of setting up a system of federalism. Federalism gives the national, state, and local government their own specific powers which are spelt out in the Constitution, which was effective on March 4, 1789.

Feminism. An ideology advocating for women's rights based on the equality of the sexes. It is a movement with a long history. The basic position of feminism is a conscious stand in opposition to male defamation and mistreatment of women. In the United States, the first wave of feminism started with the suffragists and their campaign for the right of women to vote. The second wave of feminism started in the 1960s and consists of liberal, Marxist, socialist, and radical feminists. Their focus was to put an end to gender oppression. The third wave of feminism includes Black Feminism whose focus is to draw attention to the intersectionality of identity categories as oppressive for black women. Today, the fourth wave of feminism is in opposition to sexual harassment and violence against women. In short, it is concerned with equality and justice for all women.

Feminist Consciousness. This refers to an awareness of women's inequality and the need to resist and address such inequality by using a feminist perspective. It aims to have an effect on how gender inequality is defined and addressed.

Fifteenth Amendment. The Fifteenth Amendment to the American Constitution was ratified on February 3, 1870. It granted to black men the right to vote by declaring that the "rights of citizens of the United States to vote shall not be denied or abridged by the United States or by any state on account of race, color, or previous condition of servitude." The promise of the Fifteenth Amendment would not be fully realized for almost a century. Through the laws that were implemented by the Southern states such as poll taxes, literacy tests, and the grandfather clause, black men were effectively disenfranchised.

Fifth Amendment. The fifth of the first ten amendments of the United States Constitution, which is called the Bill of Rights, enacted in 1791. It guarantees citizens that due process will be observed by governing authorities in the event of their arrest or trial. Of significance is a person's right to avoid self-incrimination, which is referred to as "taking the fifth."

First Amendment. One of the most important amendments to the United States Constitution. It comprises several rights of citizens of a liberal democratic polity. These include freedom of religion, of speech, of press, and the right of individuals to assemble and petition the government. This amendment, as a part of the Bill of Rights, was to lessen the worries of those who dreaded the emergence of an imperious central government. In the twenty-first century, the Supreme Court, drawing on the "due process" phrasing of the Fourteenth Amendment has contended that the First Amendment freedoms are also safeguarded from weakening by the states.

Fourteenth Amendment. This amendment to the United States Constitution was adopted on July 9, 1868. It granted citizenship to all persons born or naturalized in the United States including former slaves, and equal protection of the laws.

Fourth of July. The federal holiday in the United States commemorating the adoption of the Declaration of Independence on July 4, 1776.

Franklin, Benjamin (1706–1790). Franklin was born on Milk Street in Boston Massachusetts, and was a scientist, politician, and a founding father of the United States. He attended Boston Latin School, but did not graduate. While working as an apprentice to his brother James, a printer, he learned the printing trade. When he was denied publication in the *New England Courant*, a newspaper founded by James, Franklin adopted a pseudonym, and his letters were published. From an early age, Franklin was an advocate of free speech. He wrote in one of his letters: "Without freedom of thought, there can be no such thing as wisdom and no such thing as public liberty without freedom of speech." Eventually, he would help to draft the Constitution. In addition, he negotiated the 1783 Treaty of Paris ending the American War of Independence.

Free Soil Party (1848–1852). A short-lived political party in the United States that took part in the presidential elections of 1848 and 1852 and some state elections. Its focus was to contest the expansion of slavery into the Western territories. To this end, one of its main arguments was that free men in the United States constituted a morally and economically superior system, which conflicts with slavery. As such, it worked to fight against existing laws that discriminated against free blacks in states such as Ohio.

Freedmen's Aid Society. Founded by the American Missionary Association in 1861 during the American Civil War and primarily supported by the Congregational, Presbyterian, and Methodist churches in the North. After the Civil War, it founded schools and colleges for the freed slaves in the South. It provided assistance and training for teachers in the North to move to the South to train freed slaves as nurses, teachers, and other professionals. In the 1920s, it was reorganized and renamed the Board of Education for Negroes.

Freedmen's Bureau. After the Civil War, the Freedmen's Bureau, also known as the US Bureau of Refugees, was established on March 3, 1865 by Congress to help former black slaves and poor whites during the Reconstruction period. The Freedmen's Bureau provided food, housing, and medical aid to the poor. In addition, it provided schools and offered legal aid to former slaves. Due to the shortage of funding and pressure from the white Southerners, and President Andrew Johnson taking up office in April 1865 after the assassination of President Abraham Lincoln, the Freedmen's Bureau was prevented from carrying out its program. In 1872, Congress got rid of the Bureau.

Fugitive Slave Bill. The Fugitive Slave Bill or the Fugitive Slave Act allowed for the capturing and returning of runaway slaves within the territory of the United States. In 1793, the first Fugitive Slave Act statutes were enacted, which authorized local governments to seize and return slaves to their masters. It also imposed penalties on anyone who helped slaves to escape. There was widespread resistance to the Slave Act and, as a part of the Compromise of 1850 between Southern slave-holding interests and Northern Free-Soilers, the United States Congress, on September 18, 1850, added further provisions to the Fugitive Slave Bill regarding runaway slaves. For one, it imposed harsher punishments for those who interfered with their capture. The Fugitive Slave Bill was among the most controversial bills of the nineteenth century, and many Northern states passed special legislation to sidestep its provisions. In 1864, the Fugitive Slave Bill was repealed by Congress.

Garrison, William Lloyd (1805–1879). Garrison, born in Newburyport, Massachusetts, to immigrant parents from the British colony New Brunswick, which,

today, is a province of Canada, was a journalist, suffragist, and abolitionist. At age twenty-five, he joined the abolitionist movement. For a brief time, he was involved with the American Colonization Society, a group established in 1816 by Robert Finley to support the migration of free blacks to Africa and, from 1821 to 1822, to found the colony of Liberia. He was the editor of the abolitionist newspaper *The Liberator*, which, in 1831, he founded with Isaac Knapp. In 1870, he became a noticeable voice for the woman suffrage movement.

Giddings, Paula. She currently holds the position of the Elizabeth A. Woodson 1922 Professor of Afro-American Studies at Smith College. Some of her works include *When and Where I Enter: The Impact of Black Women on Race and Sex in America*, 1984; *Burning All Illusions: Writings from the Nation on Race, 1866–2002*, 2002; and *Ida, A Sword Among Lions: Ida B. Wells and the Campaign Against Lynching*, 2008. She is a writer and an American historian whose work focuses on the conditions of blacks and black women in the United States.

Glissant, Édouard (1928–2011). Glissant, born in Sainte-Marie Martinique, was a French writer, philosopher, and literary critic. In 1946, Glissant left Martinique and went to Paris where he studied ethnography at Musée de l'Homme and received a PhD. Afterwards, he studied history and philosophy at the Sorbonne. With Paul Niger, he established the separatist Front Antillo-Guyanais pour l'Autonomie party in 1959. He was barred by Charles de Galle from leaving France between 1961 and 1965. He returned to Martinique in 1965 and founded the Institut Martiniquais d'Études, as well as *Acoma*. From 1995, Glissant was a distinguished professor of French at the CUNY Graduate Center. Many of his writings have been translated from French to English.

Globalization. Globalization is the freedom of multinationals and the expansion of their economic activities across political boundaries of nation states. Many multinationals view the world as a single market for the products in which they specialize. Globalization, the tacit recognized advancement of capitalism, is accelerated by the multiplicity of global communications networks, financial services, transportation, and the global linkage of financial markets. Globalization is described as the development of global markets for standardized products produced for profit for multinational corporations. Proponents of globalization claimed that globalization is inevitable and there are no coherent alternatives to globalization.

Gramsci, Antonio (1891–1937). Gramsci was an Italian Marxist philosopher and politician. In 1911, he began his studies at the University of Turin where he joined the Socialist Party and formed a leftist group within the Party, and in May 1919, he created the newspaper *L'Ordine Nuovo* (*The New Order*). He was the founder of the Italian Communist Party in 1924. After his party was outlawed by Benito Mussolini's fascist regime, Gramsci was arrested and imprisoned in 1926. In prison, in spite of the rigorous censorship, Gramsci carried out an extraordinary and wide ranging historical and theoretical study of Italian society and strategy for change, known as the *Prison Notebooks*, which included topics such as Italian history and nationalism, the French revolution, fascism, and high and popular culture. Gramsci is best known for the theory of cultural hegemony, which describes and explains how the state and the ruling capitalist class, the bourgeoisie, use cultural institutions to uphold, reinforce, and maintain power in capitalist society. Plagued with poor health and too ill to be moved, he died on April 27, 1937, soon after he was due to be released from prison on April 21, 1937.

Hall, Stuart (1932–2014). Hall, born in Kingston, Jamaica, lived and worked in England. He was a cultural theorist and sociologist. In the 1950s, he was a founder of the *New Left Review*. In 1964, Hall joined the Centre for Contemporary Cultural Studies at Birmingham University and became its director in 1974. He is credited with broadening the scope of cultural studies to include race and gender issues. In 1979, he left Birmingham University and became a professor of sociology at the Open University from where he resigned in 1997. His published works include his famous 1996 essay, "Cultural Identity and Diaspora," in which he examines how blacks, especially Caribbean blacks' cultural identities, have been impacted by the African diaspora.

Hamilton, Alexander (1755–1804). Hamilton, born in the British West Indies, Charlestown Nevis, to a single mother, came to America as a teenager. He was an American statesman and one of the founding fathers of the United States. Hamilton attended King's College, now Columbia University in New York City. He never graduated. The college was closed during the British occupation of the city during the Revolutionary War. At the start of the war in 1775, Hamilton joined a militia company. In 1776, he raised a provincial artillery company in which he was appointed the captain. He soon became the senior aid to General Washington. After the war, he was elected as a representative to the

Congress of the Federation, a unicameral body with executive and legislative function. Hamilton resigned to practice law and founded the Bank of New York, the first national bank. He was a member of the Continental Congress, an author of the Federalist Papers, and a supporter of the American Constitution. He was troubled by the personal political scandal that surrounded him. In July 1804, he was shot and killed by Vice President Aaron Burr.

Harlem Renaissance. A social, cultural, and artistic explosion that took place in Harlem in the 1920s. As a literary movement, it was known as the "new Negro movement," which was named after Alain LeRoy Locke's 1925 anthology. The Harlem Renaissance grew out of the changes that had taken place in the black community since the abolition of slavery and the expansion of many black communities in the North. The Harlem Renaissance was an overt racial pride movement in terms of intellect and production, literature, music, and art that would represent the New Negro who was surrounded with a new dignity and refused to succumb to the policies and practice of the Jim Crow laws.

Harper, Francis Ellen (1825–1911). Harper, born free in Baltimore, Maryland, was a black abolitionist, suffragist, poet, and author. She was a member of the Woman's Christian Temperance Union. In 1883, she became superintendent of the Colored Section of the Philadelphia and Pennsylvania Section of the Woman's Christian Temperance Union (WCTU). Her career as a political speaker and political activist began even before she joined the WCTU. In 1853, she joined the American Anti-Slavery Society founded by William Lloyd Garrison. However, before joining the organization, she helped escaped slaves along the Underground Railroad on their way to Canada. In 1896, she helped to establish the National Association for Colored Women and served as Vice President. At the age of 20, she published her first book of poetry. When she was 67 years old, she published the acclaimed book *Lola Leroy or Shadows Uplifted.*

Hawkins, John (1532–1595). Admiral Sir John Hawkins was an English slave trader and was involve in the Triangle Trade, which, in the sixteenth century involved providing colonies with goods from England in exchange for African slaves. He made three voyages. In 1562, he sailed with three ships, the *Pinta, Nina,* and *Santa Maria,* to the Caribbean and traded 301 slaves that he and his men hijacked from a Portuguese slave ship. His second voyage, in 1564, was financed by Queen Elizabeth I. He sailed with Frances Drake, his second cousin, to the West African coast. He took many African slaves but only 400 survived when they reached Borburata on the western Venezuela coast. His third voyage began in 1567 and ended in 1569. Hawkins and Drake acquired many more slaves from the traders in Africa and increased their human cargo by capturing the Portuguese slave ship *Madre de Dias* (Mother of God). About 400 slaves on this trip were taken across the Atlantic to Santo Domingo, Margarita Island, and Borburata.

Hayes, Rutherford B. (1822–1893). In 1845, Hayes earned a law degree from Harvard University and went on to practice law in Ohio. He was an opponent of slavery and, in the 1850s, he joined the Republican Party in its opposition against the expansion of slavery. Shortly after the Civil War, he signed up to fight for the Union. In 1864, he was nominated for Congress. Five years later, in 1869, Hayes moved to Cincinnati where he would own a striving law practice. Hayes was the nineteenth President of the United States from 1877 to 1881. Hayes reached a compromise known as the Compromise of 1877 to be President. The Compromise of 1877 marked the end of Reconstruction in the same year.

Haytian Revolution (Haitian Revolution) (1791–1803). The largest and most successful slave rebellion led by Toussaint L'Ouverture. The slaves not only ended slavery but also French colonial rule in Saint-Dominigue. By 1801, L'Ouverture prolonged the revolution beyond Saint-Dominigue, conquering the neighboring Spanish colony of Santo Domingo. In 1803, when the French troops withdrew from the western part of the island, the colony declared its independence as Hayti (Haiti).

Helvetian Settlement. In 1845, 108 people from one of the cantons of Switzerland settled in New Glarus in Wisconsin, three years before Wisconsin became a state on May 29, 1848. It was referred to as the Helvetian Settlement. It preserved its culture in terms of language, religion, and customs.

Herrenvolk. The more general meaning of this term is that of a "master race," a race that considers itself superior to all other races. The term gained prominence in Nazi Germany.

Hill, Anita (1956–). Hill, an African American woman, is a university professor of social policy, law, and women's studies at Brandeis University. In 1991, Hill became a national figure when she accused Clarence Thomas, a US Supreme Court nominee, of sexual harassment when he was her boss at the United States Department of Education and the Equal Employment Opportunity Commission.

Hopkins, Pauline (1859–1930). Hopkins, born in Portland Maine, was a black playwright, novelist, and columnist. In 1900, she published "The Mystery Within Us," which appeared in *Colored American Magazine.* In 1902, she became editor of the magazine. During this period, she authored three novels, *Hagar's Daughter: A Story of Southern Caste Prejudice*, 1901; *Winona: A Tale of Negro Life in the South and Southwest*, 1902; and *Of One Blood: The Hidden Self*, 1903. In 1915, she was the first black editor of the *New Era Magazine*, a leading journal at that time. In 1918, when the journal folded, she took a job as a stenographer at the Massachusetts Institute of Technology and worked there for the rest of her life.

Hottentot. A term used by European travelers, especially the Dutch settlers, in Southern Africa to describe the Khoikhoi peoples who are native to southwestern Africa. Traditionally, the Khoikhoi practiced nomadic pastoral agriculture, which involved the raising of livestock. There is a click that is characteristic of the Khoikhoi language. In an imitation of the sound, the settlers referred to this as Hottentot.

Huxley, Thomas Henry (1825–1895). Huxley was an English biologist of the second half of the nineteenth century who specialized in comparative anatomy. He was a noted follower of the thought of Charles Darwin. His most famous work, *Evidence as to Man's Place in Nature*, was published in 1863. He developed the new evolutionary conception by focusing on man and ape in order to account for the human being as an animal.

Identity Politics. Practices of politics grounded on the requirement that an identity be recognized, be accommodated for, or form the basis of a collective movement of some kind. Usually (for historical reasons), these are distinguished from class-based politics and nationalist movements even though these were clearly also politics linked to identity like, for example, the Civil Rights Movement. Rather the term generally refers to a movement fostered around identities such as race, gender, ethnicity, sexuality, and disability where the demand is for recognition and acceptance of difference and for inclusion into the majority. Identity politics has now extended itself to multiculturalism and the politics of cultural recognition.

Ideology. A set of ideas that form the basis of political and economic systems and policy. Feminism, womanism, Marxism, conservatism, and liberalism, for example, are called ideologies. An ideology gives some account of how political and economic systems have come to be as they are and some indications of where these systems are heading, and also provides a guide for political action to maintain or challenge these systems. In the United States, distinctive forms of liberalism and conservatism have defined much of the ideological debates pertaining to American politics and have influenced mainstream ideas.

Immigration. The permanent moving of individuals and groups from one country to another, which is a basic fact of human history. In the United States, the major waves of immigration were during the colonial period, the first part of the nineteenth century, and from the 1880s to the 1920s. Many immigrants came to the United States to pursue better opportunities. From the seventeenth to the nineteenth centuries, many Africans were forcibly brought to the United States as slaves. Numerous Chinese immigrants came to the United States to work on the railroads. The first important federal legislation controlling immigration was the Chinese Exclusion Act of 1882. Individual states controlled immigration before the 1892 opening of Ellis Island, the country's first federal immigration station. In 1965, new immigration laws terminated the quota system that preferred European immigrants. At present, most of the immigrants to the United States are from Asia and Latin America.

Imperialism. The domination or control by one country or group of people over others, in ways assumed to be at the expense of the latter. Imperialism is rooted in the psychology of rulers of empires and the effects of surviving pre-capitalist social relations and not the economic interests of nations or class. This action is linked to colonialism in which an empire extended its power by forcefully acquiring territories. In addition, imperialism is viewed by some as an outgrowth of popular nationalism, a function of the need to support the welfare state, which helps to calm the working class, a feature of capitalist states.

Indentured Servant. During the colonial period in the United States, many indentured servants arrived in Virginia. They were men, women, and children who signed a contract by which they agreed to work for a certain number of years in exchange for transportation to Virginia and the provision of food, clothing, and shelter. Adults often served for four to seven years and children served much longer. With a long history in England, during the seventeenth century, indentured servitude was the primary means by which the plantations in Virginia were staffed. By the end of the seventeenth century, the number of new servants in Virginia decreased. The planters' need for labor was met by enslaved Africans.

Interest Group. An organization of people that shares a common interest and works together to promote and protect that interest and to pressure the government so that the interest of the group can be incorporated into the political agenda. Interest groups vary in size, aims, and strategies. The National Organization of Women (NOW) is one example of an interest group.

Internalized Oppression. A situation in which marginalized groups use against themselves the norms and values of the majority group that are used to oppress them. In trying to conform to the majority group expectations, the minority group will discriminate against members of their group by applying these values.

Intersectionality. A ground-breaking and developing field of study that offers a critical investigative optic to question racial, ethnic, class, ability, age, and gender inequalities. In fact, these various identity categories do not act independently but merge in discursive and non-discursive ways in the daily lives of black women and other women of color. In looking at these categories in their amalgamative mode, one can identify how power relations are organized, contested, and operated at the personal and the communal levels. Intersectionality draws our attention to the binding significance of the structures of discrimination transmogrifying knowledge as well as social institutions.

Islamophobia. Exaggerated fear and prejudice against Islamic religion and Muslims that is perpetuated and upheld by negative stereotypes about Muslims, especially when interpreted as a geopolitical force or the source of terrorism. It existed before the September 9, 2001 attacks, but has increased since then and today, especially in Western democratic nations, it is a serious problem for Muslims and people who are perceived as Muslims.

Jacobs, Harriet, Ann (1813–1897). Jacobs was born into slavery in Edenton, Carolina. Her parents Delilah and Elijah Jacobs were both slaves. The Jacobs family included John Jacobs, Harriet Jacobs' younger brother, and they lived with her maternal grandmother. Jacobs' mother died when she was six years old and she went to live with her slave owner Margaret Herniblow. Herniblow taught Jacobs to read and sew. When Herniblow died in 1825, Jacobs became the slave of Herniblow's three-year-old niece, the daughter of Dr. James Norcom who tried to force Jacobs into a sexual relationship with him. Notwithstanding all the threats from Norcom, Jacobs entered into a relationship with a white lawyer Samuel Treadwell Sawyer. She had two children with Sawyer who eventually purchased the two children as well as Jacobs' brother John. Eventually, Jacobs ran away. She hid in her grandmother's home for about seven years and then escaped to the North. She lived and worked in New York City and Boston until her freedom was purchased in 1852. Between 1853 and 1858, Jacobs wrote *Incidents in the Life of a Slave Girl* published in 1861 under her pseudonym Linda Brent.

Jefferson, Thomas (1743–1826). Jefferson, an American statesman, one of the founding fathers of the United States, and the principal author of the Declaration of Independence, was born in Virginia, where he graduated from the College of William and Mary. After graduation, he practiced law for a short period and, at times, defended slaves that sought their freedom. From 1797 to 1801, he was Vice President under John Adams. From 1801 to 1809, Jefferson served as the third president of the United States. Jefferson owned several slave plantations. When his wife Martha died in 1782, he had a relationship with his slave Sally Hemings. In 1785, Jefferson published the influential *Notes on the State of Virginia* in which, among other concerns, he expressed his belief that blacks whether by nature or nurture were inferior to whites.

Jim Crow Laws. These were laws of government practices in the Southern states of United States designed to separate blacks and whites in public and private facilities, and were reinforced in the "separate but equal" doctrine stemming from the 1896 landmark case *Plessy v. Ferguson*. These laws were used to preserve segregated schools, public transportation, and housing. In 1954, *Brown v. Board of Education* declared the "separate but equal" doctrine unconstitutional.

Johnson, James Weldon (1871–1938). Johnson, born in Jacksonville, Florida, attended Atlanta University, and after graduation took a job as a high school principal in Jacksonville. He was encouraged by his mother to study English Literature and the European musical traditions. On the occasion of President Abraham Lincoln's birthday, he wrote the song "Lift Every Voice And Sing." Because the song was indeed popular in black communities, it was known as the Black Anthem. After moving to New York in 1901, where he gained some success as a song writer for Broadway, he took a job as a US consul in Venezuela in 1906. During this time, he published some poems in *The Century Magazine* and *The Independent*. In 1912, Johnson anonymously published his novel, *The Autobiography of an Ex-Colored Man*, which explores in depth the issue of racial identity and the impact of denying one's blackness on the psyche. In 1920, he organized for the National Association for the Advancement of Colored People (NAACP). Johnson continued his writing. In 1922, he edited *The Book of American Negro Poetry*.

Jones, Gayl (1949–). Jones, born in Lexington, Kentucky, is an African American writer. In 1971, she graduated from Connecticut College with a BA in English and an MA in Creative Writing in 1973. In 1975, she earned her doctoral degree from Brown University. Her 1975 novel, *Corregidora*, explores the links between slavery and the lives of blacks in the United States. Her other writings include *Eva's Man*, 1976; *White Rat*, 1977; *The Healing*, 1998; and *Mosquito*, 1999.

Jones, Leroy (1958–). Jones is a jazz trumpeter from New Orleans. He took up trumpet playing when he joined his elementary school band. When he was thirteen years old, Jones joined guitarist Danny Baker's Fairview Baptist Brass Band. Jones spent four years in the city's popular St. Augustine High School Band. After graduating, he formed the Hurricane Brass Band, which along with the Fairview Band provided talent for another group, the Dirty Dozen Brass Band. With Eddie "Cleanhead" Vinson, he toured Canada. Later, he joined Della Reese, which led to international concert tours that resulted in Jones performing in Southeast Asia for a three-year period.

Jordan, June (1936–2002). Jordan, a Caribbean poet, essayist, and activist, was born in Harlem, New York. She graduated from Barnard College. She taught at several universities including City College of New York, Yale University, and State University of New York at Stony Brook. From 1989 to 2002, she was a professor in the Department of English, Women's Studies, and African American Studies at the University of California, Berkeley. Her writings include *Who Look at Me*, 1969; *Some Changes*, 1971; *Passion*, 1980; and *On Call: Political Essays*, 1985.

King, Martin Luther (1929–1968). King was born in Atlanta, Georgia. He attended segregated public schools in Georgia, graduating from high school at the age of fifteen. In 1948, King received his BA from Morehouse College. After three years of theological study at Crozer Theological Seminary in Pennsylvania, he was elected president of a largely white senior class. In 1951, he was awarded a BD degree. With a fellowship won at Crozer, he enrolled in graduate studies at Boston University, where, in June 1955, he received his doctoral degree. It was in Boston that King met and married Coretta Scott. King was the leader of the Civil Rights Movement. He founded and was involved in several other organizations such as Southern Christian Leadership Conference, the Albany Movement, and the Student Nonviolence Coordinating Committee. King put forward the doctrine of nonviolent civil disobedience. Also, he was involved in several marches and demonstrations. In 1955, he led the boycott in Montgomery, Alabama, after Rosa Parks was arrested for refusing to give up her bus seat to a white man. In his 1959 book, *The Measure of Man*, King condemns the racial injustices in the Western world and points to man's need for God's love. In 1963, King was monitored by the FBI and his phone was tapped. King fought for blacks to have the right to vote and to enjoy civil rights and liberties. In his campaign against segregation and economic inequality in Birmingham, Alabama, King was once again arrested and was also jailed. From his cell, he composed the now famous *Letter from Birmingham Jail* in which he responded to the call of the movement to pursue legal channels for social change. On April 4, 1968, King was assassinated by James Earl Ray.

Knights of White Liners. In 1876, some of the Confederate veterans formed a group called the Knights of White Liners. They murdered many blacks. After aligning themselves with the Democratic Party, they forced the Republican Party to withdraw federal troops from the South.

Ku Klux Klan. Commonly called the KKK, the Klan was founded in 1865. By 1870, the KKK extended into almost every Southern state and became a base for white Southern opposition to the policies of the Republican Party during Reconstruction, which were directed at instituting political and economic equality for blacks. Its members waged an anti-establishment movement that intimidated and directed constant violence at black and white Republican leaders. Even though Congress, in the 1870s, passed laws designed to restrain KKK terrorism, the organization saw that its primary goal, which was the reinstatement of white supremacy, was achieved through Democratic victories in state legislatures across the South. After a period of decline, in the early twentieth century, the KKK, through violent activities such as burning crosses and staging rallies, parades, and marches denouncing immigrants, blacks, Catholics, Jews, and organized labor, was once again active. Also, the Civil Rights Movement of the 1960s saw an outpouring of KKK action, including bombings of black schools and churches and violence in opposition to black and white activists in the South.

Lacedaemonians. Natives or inhabitants of Lacedaemonia, an area of ancient Greece comprising the city of Sparta and its surrounding area.

LGBTQ Community. Also referred to as the gay community, which comprises lesbians, gays, bisexual, queer, and transgender people. The community celebrates pride, diversity, individuality, and sexuality. Not all LGBTQ individuals consider themselves to be a part of the community.

Liberty Party. In the 1840s, a minor political party in the United States, with some of its branches surviving into the 1860s. The party, at the beginning, supported the abolition of slavery. It later broke away from the American Anti-Slavery Society (AASS) and promoted the view that the Constitution was an anti-slavery document, which was in opposition to AASS leader William Lloyd Garrison's view that the Constitution should be condemned as a pro-slavery document.

Lincoln, Abraham (1809–1865). Abraham Lincoln, an American statesman and lawyer, won the election in 1860 as the first Republican president on a platform promising to keep slavery out of the territories. Seven slave states in the Deep South seceded and created a new nation, the Confederate States of America. Owing to President Lincoln's role as protector of the Union during the Civil War and emancipator of the slaves spelt out in the Emancipation Proclamation, which held that all slaves "shall be then, thenceforward, and forever free," he is considered as one of America's greatest heroes. Lincoln was assassinated on April 14, 1865 by John Wilkes Booth.

Lorde, Audre (1934–1992). Lorde, a writer, poet, feminist, and gay and lesbian activist, was born in New York City and grew up in Harlem. In 1959, she received a BA from Hunter College and an MA in Library Science in 1961 from Columbia University. From 1969 to 1970, Lorde taught at Lehman College in the Department of Education. From 1970 to 1981, she was a professor of English at John Jay College of Criminal Justice where she unsuccessfully fought for the creation of a Black Studies Department. In 1981, she took a job at Hunter College as the distinguished Turner Hunter Chair. In late 1981, Lorde was one of the founders of the Women's Coalition of St. Croix, an organization that was dedicated to assisting women who have survived sexual abuse and intimate partner violence. In the late 1980s, she assisted in the establishment of the Sisterhood in Support of Sisters in South Africa to help black women who were impacted by apartheid and other kinds of injustice.

L'Ouverture, Toussaint (1743–1803). L'Ouverture, a free black man and a Jacobin, from the most influential political faction during the French Revolution, was the well-known leader of the Haitian Revolution. He began his military career as a leader of the 1791 slave rebellion in Saint-Dominigue, a prosperous slave colony, which, by 1800 was transformed into the first free colonial society to have explicitly rejected race as the basis for social ranking. Against the wishes of Napoleon Bonaparte, L'Ouverture, under Saint-Dominigue's Constitution, was proclaimed governor for life.

Malcolm X (1925–1965). Malcolm X, born Malcolm Little in Omaha, Nebraska, was the fourth of seven children. From the age of fourteen until he was twenty-one, he lived with his half-sister Ella Little-Collins in Roxbury, an African American community in Boston, Massachusetts. Afterwards, he spent a short time in Flint, Michigan. In 1943, he moved to Harlem in New York City. Two years later, in 1945, he returned to Boston and was engaged in a series of burglaries that targeted white homes.

In 1946, he was arrested and sent to Charleston State Prison where he started to serve his eight-to-ten-year sentence. In prison, with the influence of a convict named John Bembry, Malcolm X developed an enormous appetite for reading. And it was while he was in prison that his siblings wrote to him about the Nation of Islam. After some resistance, Malcolm X soon embraced the teachings of the Nation of Islam. When he was paroled in August 1952, after a meeting with Elijah Mohammed in Chicago, Malcolm X became the assistant minister of the Nation's Temple Number 1 in Detroit. In March 1954, he expanded Temple Number 12 in Philadelphia, and two months later, he was selected to lead Temple Number 7 in Harlem, where the membership rapidly increased. Not long after, he was targeted by the FBI. In January 1959, he married Betty Sanders and they went on to have six children. During 1962 and 1963, some events caused Malcolm X to reassess his involvement with the Nation of Islam and Elijah Mohammed. On March 8, 1964, Malcolm X publicly announced that he was leaving the Nation of Islam. He then founded Muslim Mosque Inc. and the Organization of African American Unity. After Malcolm X traveled to Mecca and saw Muslims of all races interacting as equals, he was convinced that through Islam, racial problems could be eliminated. On February 21, 1965, Malcolm X was assassinated.

Maroon Negroes. These were self-liberating Africans who escaped slavery in Jamaica and established communities in the eastern parishes. They fought the British to retain their independence. At the end of the Maroon War (1730–1739), the British realized that the defeat of the guerrilla army of the Maroons was impossible. As a result, the British made peace with the Maroons through the peace treaties of 1739 and 1740. The treaties recognized the freedom of the Maroons and granted them land in return for their capturing of runaway slaves.

Marquis de Lafayette, Gilbert du Motier (1757–1834). Lafayette was a French aristocrat and military officer who fought in the American Revolutionary War. He later returned to France and, in 1787, he was appointed to the Assembly of Notables. He was elected as a member of the Estates-General of 1789. After the formation of the National Constituent Assembly, along with Thomas Jefferson, Lafayette helped with writing of the Declaration of the Rights of Man and of the Citizen. Inspired by the United States Declaration of Independence in its invoking of natural law to establish the basic principles of a democratic state, Lafayette advocated for the end of slavery.

Marshall, Paule (1929–). Marshall was born in Brooklyn, New York into an immigrant family from Barbados. In 1954, she graduated cum laude and Phi Beta Kappa from Hunter College with a major in English Literature. She then began to write feature stories for *Our World*, a black publication. In 1959, she published her first novel, *Brown Girl, Brownstones*, which examined the black immigrant experience in the United States and the coming of age of a West Indian girl. Her writings include *Souls Clap Hands and Sing*, 1961; *Reena*, 1962; *The Chosen Place, the Timeless People*, 1969; *Praisesong for Widows*, 1983; and *Daughters*, 1991. Marshall's writings are rooted in black cultural history. Her focus on black women characters addresses contemporary issues from a black feminist perspective. She points to the oppressive systems that are in place impacting blacks and black women in a specific way.

Mayflower. A merchant ship that set sail from Plymouth in England in September 1620 for the New World. Normally, the *Mayflower*'s cargo was wine and dry goods but on this trip the ship carried 102 passengers, all hoping to start a new life on the other side of the Atlantic. Many of the passengers, fleeing religious persecution from King James of England, were Protestant separatists who, later on, were referred to as the Pilgrim Fathers. The culmination of the voyage led to the signing of the Mayflower Compact, the first governing document of Plymouth, Massachusetts, which was written by the men of the *Mayflower*. It established a basic form of democracy with each member contributing to the welfare of the community. With deaths and survival in the harsh New England winters, this voyage has become an iconic narrative in some of the original records of American history.

Mercer Cook, Will (1903–1987). Mercer, born in Washington, DC, was an African American diplomat and professor. He was the first American ambassador to Gambia and, at the same time, he was also the ambassador to Senegal. He held teaching positions at institutions such as Howard University, Atlanta University, and the University of Haiti. After working in Haiti, he returned to Howard University. He continued to write about Haiti and translated works from French to English including the writings of Leopold Senghor, a well-known French author and president of Senegal.

Million Man March. On October 16, 1995, a gathering of about 850,000 black men gathered at the National Mall in Washington, DC to address the problems of black communities and call for har-

mony and the renewal of these communities. This gathering was organized and hosted by Louis Farrakhan, the leader of the Nation of Islam, and was joined by many black religious groups, institutions, and organizations. The Million Man March came together not only as a rally of black men but also to build, what many saw, as a movement towards the future revitalization of blacks in the United States. Besides the keynote address by Farrakhan, many other prominent black speakers addressed the gathering, including Maya Angelou, Jesse Jackson, Benjamin Chavis Muhammed, Rosa Parks, and Stevie Wonder.

Minerva Literary Society. In 1834, a group of black women who were interested in literature and poetry, in order to promote self-education through what the group referred to as "polite literature," organized the Minerva Literary Society. The Society started with a membership of thirty women and then expanded. It held weekly meetings, which consisted of programs of readings and recitations of original prose, poetry, and essays.

Minstrel Show. A show developed in the early nineteenth century in the United States as a form of racially charged entertainment. Each show involved comic skits, variety acts, dancing, and music performance that parodied black people in America.

Miscegenation. A term referring to the mixing of people from different racial groups through marriage, cohabitation, sexual relations, and procreation. Laws banning interracial marriage and sex were known as anti-miscegenation laws. In the United States, these laws were first introduced in the slave-holding colonies of Virginia and Maryland in 1691 and 1692 respectively. Eventually, anti-miscegenation laws were introduced in the colonies and states where slavery did not exist. It was not until in 1964, in the case *McLaughlin v. Florida* and then again in *Loving v. Virginia* in 1967, that the Supreme Court ruled that state laws prohibiting miscegenation were unconstitutional.

Mississippi Freedom Democratic Party (Freedom Democratic Party). An American party founded in 1964 in the era of the Civil Rights Movement by Fannie Lou Hamer, Ella Baker, and Bob Moses as an offshoot of the populist Freedom Democratic Organization in Mississippi. It was organized by both blacks and whites to challenge the establishment of the Mississippi Democratic Party, which allowed only the participation of whites. African Americans made up 40 percent of the population in Mississippi.

Morgan, Lewis Henry (1818–1881). Morgan, an American ethnologist and chief creator of scientific anthropology, was known especially for establishing the study of kinship systems and for his widespread theory of cultural evolution. In the early 1840s, Morgan developed a profound interest in First Nations Americans and over his lifetime championed their struggles against colonialism and oppression. While studying the social history and culture of the Iroquois group, Morgan was adopted by First Nations in Seneca. He continued his study of First Nations in Northern Michigan and considered that if the First Nations' cultural system was also to be found in Asia, the Asiatic origins of First Nations might be shown. His considerations were compiled in his 1871 work, *Kinship, System of Consanguinity and Affinity of the Human Family*, which led Lewis to develop his theory of cultural evolution set forth in his 1877 work, *Ancient Society, or Researches in the Line of Human Progress from Savagery through Barbarism to Civilization.*

An attorney by profession, from 1844 to 1862, Morgan practiced law at Rochester, New York. From 1861 to 1868, he served in the New York State Assembly and from 1868 to 1869 in the Senate.

Morrison, Toni (1931–). Morrison, born in Lorain, Ohio, a Nobel and Pulitzer Prize winner, is a black novelist, essayist, and professor. In 1953, she graduated from Howard University with a BA in English. In 1955, she graduated with an MA in English from Cornell University. Her teaching appointments included Texas Southern University, Howard University, Rutgers University, and State University of New York. In 1984, she was the Albert Schweitzer Chair at the University of Albany, SUNY. From 1989 until her retirement in 2006, Morrison held the Robert F. Goheen Chair in the Humanities at Princeton University. Her novels include *The Bluest Eyes*, 1970; *Sula*, 1973; *Songs of Solomon*, 1977; *Paradise*, 1997; *A Mercy*, 2008; *Home*, 2012; and *God Help the Child*, 2015. Morrison's novels are recognized for their impressive themes, exquisite language, and meticulous portrayals of African American characters. Her most recent nonfiction book, *The Origin of Others* was published in 2017. In this work, one of the questions that she explores is what race is and why it matters in the United States.

Mott, Lucretia (1793–1880). Mott, one of the leading voices of the abolitionist and feminist movements of her time, was born in Nantucket, Massachusetts. Raised in a Quaker community, she became a member of the society's ministry and adopted its anti-slavery views. Mott helped form the Philadelphia Female Anti-Slavery Society in 1833 and, later, was among the founders of the American women's rights movement. Mott's feminist philosophy was outlined in her 1850 work, *Discourse on Women*, in which she addressed the restrictions on women participating in the public sphere and argued for equal economic opportunity and voting rights for women. After helping to establish Swarthmore College in 1864, Mott served as the first president of the American Equal Rights Association, an organization that advocated for universal suffrage. In 1868, Mott resigned from the organization.

Multiculturalism. In the United States, multiculturalism is the recognition and celebration of non-dominant cultures. And since multiculturalism involves the acknowledgment and promotion of cultural pluralism, it celebrates and seeks to protect cultural variety, for example, minority languages and customs. At the same time, it focuses on the unequal relationship between dominant and non-dominant cultures.

Murray, Pauli (1910–1985). Murray, born in Baltimore, was an American civil rights activist, women's rights activist, lawyer, and an episcopal priest. She was raised in Durham, North Carolina by her maternal grandparents. Murray worked as a janitor, typist, elevator operator, waitress, a reporter for the *Carolina Times*, for the Works Projects Administration (WPA), a teacher in the New York City Remedial Reading Project, professor, and an attorney. In 1933, she graduated with a BA in English from Hunter College. Afterwards, she attended Howard Law School and graduated in 1944, first in her class. In 1942, she joined the Congress of Racial Equality. Later, she graduated with an MA in Law at UC, Berkeley. In 1965, she graduated with a Doctor of Judicial Science degree from Yale University. She was the first African American to receive such a degree. Murray published articles, essays, and poems. She received a tenured professorship at Brandeis University in the American Studies Department. She left Brandeis University to attend the seminary. After three years of study, she was the first African American woman to be ordained an episcopal priest. Her published autobiographies include *Proud Shoes: The Story of an American Family*, 1956; *Song in a Weary Throat: An American Pilgrimage*, 1987; and *Black Activist, Feminist, Lawyer, Priest, and Poet*, 1989.

Napoleonic Wars (1799–1815). A series of wars that were fought under the leadership of Napoleon Bonaparte between France and several European powers formed into various coalitions and financed and usually led by Great Britain. The wars stemmed from the unresolved dispute associated with the French Revolution of 1789–1799 and its resultant conflicts, which are often categorized into five conflicts, each termed after the coalition that fought Napoleon. These five conflicts were the Third Coalition, 1805; the Fourth Coalition, 1806–1807; the Fifth Coalition, 1809; the Sixth Coalition, 1813; and finally, the Seventh Coalition, 1815.

National American Woman Suffrage Association. Formed on February 8, 1890 with the main purpose to work on suffrage for women in the United States. It was created by the merger of the National Woman Suffrage Association and the American Woman Suffrage Association.

National Association for the Advancement of Colored People (NAACP). A civil rights organization created in 1909 and America's oldest and largest civil rights organization. It was formed in New York City by black and white activists partly as a reaction to the 1908 Springfield race riot in Illinois. Its founding members included W. E. B. Du Bois, Ida B. Wells, Archibald Grimke, and Mary Church Terrell. In its Charter, the NAACP undertook to advocate for equal rights for all people, to end racial prejudice, and to "advance the interest of colored citizens" concerning voting rights, legal justice, and educational and employment opportunities. The first president of the NAACP was a white lawyer, Moorfield Storey. The only black person on the initial leadership team was Du Bois. He served as director of publications and research. In 1910, Du Bois started *The Crisis*, which became the leading publication for black writers. *The Crisis* came to an end in October 1923.

National Association of Colored Women. An American organization that was formed in July 1896 by Ida B. Wells, Mary Church Terrell, and Frances Harper at the first annual convention of the National Federation of Afro-American Women in Washington, DC. The president was Mary Church Terrell. Some of its objectives included working for the economic, moral, religious, and social welfare of women and youths; to defend the rights of women and youths; to encourage interracial understanding so that justice and goodwill may occur among all people; and to biennially hold educational workshops at the convention.

National Black Baptist Convention (NBC). Founded in Atlanta, Georgia, in 1885 when the leaders of the American National Baptist Convention, the Baptist Foreign Mission Convention, and the National Baptist Educational Convention joined to form the National Baptist Convention. It is the largest African American Christian denomination in the United States whose headquarters are at the Baptist World Center in Nashville, Tennessee.

National Black Political Assembly (NBPA). The NBPA, formerly known as the Gary Convention, was held on March 10, 1972, in Gary, Indiana. The NBPA gathered around 10,000 African Americans to discuss and examine black communities that were impacted by the economic crisis and ways that this crisis could be dealt with in black communities. The NBPA issued the Gary Declaration, which stated that the American political system was failing black Americans and that the only way to tackle this problem was to switch to an independent black politics. For the NBPA, it was important that more black politicians be elected to office, and to increase black representation, and develop an agenda for political change.

National Negro Convention Movement (NNCM) (1831–1864). The NNCM was founded by a group of prominent Northern free black men, with its first meeting, in 1831, in Philadelphia, Pennsylvania. One impetus for the first meeting in Philadelphia was the Cincinnati Riots of 1829, which emerged from the proposal by city leaders to get rid of Cincinnati's black population because of the conflict that emerged over job competition between black and white men. In the protest against anti-black violence, discrimination, and slavery, black leaders organized throughout the Midwest and Northeast. In the first decade of meetings, there was growing interracial cooperation between black and white abolitionists. However, with the enactment of the Fugitive Slave Law in 1850, the movement's focus was on developing a Black Nationalist political consciousness. Given that it was clear in the members' minds that the United States would never promote the equality of blacks, the movement debated about the need for blacks to emigrate to Canada, Liberia, and the Caribbean. The last meeting of the NNCM was in 1864, in Syracuse, New York.

National Organization for Women (NOW). NOW was founded in 1966 by Betty Friedan, Pauli Murray, and other feminists, with a commitment to take action to bring women into full participation and equal partnership with men in the mainstream of society in the United States. It was mainly a white middle-class women's initiative, with a program that many feminists today would pronounce as "reformist." At the time, when combined with the newly felt agitation of radical women emerging from the Civil Rights Movement and anti-war protests, NOW's results can be seen as revolutionary, especially for middle- and upper-class white women.

Natural Rights. These are rights which people have by nature without the interference of contract, or in the absence of political and legal institutions. Thus, natural rights, or what are today called human rights, are attributable to individuals without distinction of time and place. A contrast may be drawn with positive rights, that is, those rights awarded or promised by a legal system.

Naturalization Act of 1790. Known as the Nationality Act, it was the first statute in the United States to codify naturalization law. It restricted citizenship to "any alien being a free white person" of good character who has been in the United States for at least two years. Therefore, it excluded all non-whites, indentured servants, and slaves.

Naylor, Gloria (1950–2016). Naylor, born in Harlem, New York, was a black American novelist. In 1981, she earned her BA in English at Brooklyn College and in 1983 her MA in African American Studies at Yale University. Influenced by the works of other African American novelists including Zora-Neale Hurston, Toni Morrison, and Alice Walker, in 1982, Naylor published her first novel, *The Women of Brewster Place*, which in 1983 won the National Book Award. Her novels include *Linden Hills*, 1985; *Mama Day*, 1988; and *Bailey's Café*, 1992. Naylor taught writing and literature at many institutions including George Washington University, Boston University, New York University, and Cornell University.

Neoliberalism. The resurgence of nineteenth-century ideas associated with laissez-faire economic liberalism, which include privatization, contracting out, and the restructuring of the Keynesian welfare state. Starting with the Reagan administration, neoliberalism has been the defining political economic model of the United States government. In fact, the government's neoliberal policies not only represent the interests of business (with its enactment of free trade agreements, welfare-to-work programs, and workfare), but also provide further security guaranties to US capital in its search for cheap labor and lower production costs.

Neo-Marxist. This term relates to forms of twentieth-century political philosophy that arose from the adaptation and extension of Marxism and Marxist thought to accommodate or challenge modern concerns such as the global economy, the capitalist welfare state, the stability of liberal democracies, and the current world order centered on human rights and international corporations. It incorporates into its analysis other intellectual traditions such as critical theory and psychoanalysis.

New England Anti-Slavery Society (NEAS). NEAS was founded on January 1, 1832 in Boston, Massachusetts by its principal member William Lloyd Garrison who established the goals and philosophy of NEAS. For NEAS, slavery was immoral and its members advocated for an immediate end to slavery. It opposed the objective of the American Colonial Society (ACS) for free blacks to emigrate to Africa. NEAS worked with the General Colored Association of Boston, which was founded before NEAS. NEAS sponsored many lectures and published *The Liberator.* In January 1833, NEAS was expanded, and the American Anti-Slavery Society was created. In 1835, NEAS was reorganized into the Massachusetts Anti-Slavery Society.

Ninth Crusade (1271–1272). This is sometimes lumped together with the eighth crusade. It was the last major medieval crusade to the Holy Land. Edward I of England had been accompanied on his crusade by Cardinal Theobaldo Visconti, who, in 1271, became Pope Gregory X. The Ninth Crusade failed mainly because the crusading spirit was nearly nonexistent in Europe, and because of the increasing power of the mamluks in Egypt.

Nous Avons Changer Tout Cela. A French phrase originating in Molière's 1666 play *Le Médecin malgré lui*, meaning "we have to change all that." It is a facetious criticism directed at someone who lays down the law on everything and talks contemptuously of customs.

Oligarchy. A society governed by a small group of people who govern in their own interests. Historically, oligarchy was often tyrannical, relying on public obedience or oppression to exist. The ancient Greek philosopher Aristotle pioneered the use of the term as a synonym for rule by the wealthy. Today, the common term used in that context is plutocracy.

One-Drop Rule. Historically, prominent in the United States, the one-drop rule was a social and legal standard of racial classification. Because blacks were regarded as inferior to whites, the one-drop rule stated that anyone with one drop of black blood was considered black. The concept progressed over the course of the nineteenth century and became codified into law in the twentieth century.

Oppression. A term used to describe and explain the circumstances and experience of subordination and discrimination inflicted on marginalized groups. Race theorists use the term to examine and analyze the causes, nature, and primacy of black oppression. The sort of experience they apply the concept of oppression to and how they believe oppression stemming from race relates to other struggles for change is significant.

Pan-Africanism. In the United States, Pan-Africanist ideas promulgated by Martin Delany, Alexander Crummell, and Edward Blyden started to circulate in the mid-nineteenth century. Delany, for one, took into consideration the unequal treatment of blacks in the United States and contended that blacks could not prosper alongside whites. Thus, he promoted the idea that blacks should separate from the United States and create their own nation. Crummell and Blyden considered Africa as the best place for the creation of this new nation for blacks. Inspired by Christian missionary enthusiasm, Crummell and Blyden argued that blacks in the New World should return to their homelands in Africa and transform and enlighten the inhabitants there. Historically, Pan-Africanism has often taken the shape of a political or cultural movement. There are many varieties of Pan-Africanism. In its narrow political manifestation, it envisions a unified African nation where all people of the African diaspora can live in harmony.

Participatory Democracy. Another word for direct democracy in which there is a large participation of the constituents in the direction and operation of the political system. It strives to create opportunities for all members of a democratic polity to make consequential contributions to decision making, and seeks to expand and increase the variety of people who have access to such chances.

Payne, Daniel A. (1811–1893). Payne, a minister, historian, poet, and abolitionist, was born in Charleston, South Carolina, to free and deeply religious parents. At an early age, he began to write and teach. In 1829, when he was only nineteen years old, he started his first school in Charleston, where he taught for six years, until 1835, when the South Carolina legislature made it illegal to teach slaves to read or write. After his school was forced to close, Payne moved to the North, where, in 1850, he published a collection of poetry. His work expresses his concern for "moral purity" and "holy virtue." Payne was very active in the Temperance movement and other Christian efforts aimed at enhancing social reform. In 1881, he helped found the Bethel Literary and Historical Association. In this Association, Payne and other African American activists studied African American literature and history and celebrated the cultures of Africa. Through his long ministry with the African Methodist Episcopal Church and subsequent presidency of Wilberforce University, Payne followed a demanding program of self-directed study. Payne worked his entire life to disprove the pro-slavery theory that African Americans did not have the capacity to be full American citizens because they were inferior beings.

Phaedrus. A text by Plato, written around the same time as his *Republic* and *Symposium* in *c.* 370 BC. It is a dialogue between Plato's protagonist Socrates and Phaedrus, an interlocutor in numerous dialogues. The *Phaedrus* is apparently about love. However, the conversation in the dialogue revolves around the art of rhetoric and how it should be practiced. Also, it examines subjects as diverse as metempsychosis, the transmigration of the soul and especially its reincarnation after death, and erotic love.

Pharaoh. In ancient Egypt, the most powerful person and the political and religious leader of the Egyptian people holding the titles "Lord of the two lands" and "High Priest of Every Temple." In biblical times, the Israelites were enslaved in Egypt; under the leadership of Moses who was adopted by an Egyptian princess, Pharaoh's daughter, the Israelites escaped.

Phillips, Wendell (1811–1884). Phillips, an abolitionist, orator, and attorney, was born in Boston, Massachusetts. In 1831, he graduated from Harvard University and in 1833 he graduated from Harvard Law School. He was the president of the American Anti-Slavery Society and resigned in 1865 at the end of the Civil War. Phillips like William Lloyd Garrison believed that the Union would have to be dissolved to accomplish the goals of the abolitionists.

Phrenology. The study of the skull as suggestive of mental faculties, character traits, and racial characteristics. Starting in the eighteenth century, it was hypothesized by Frantz Joseph Gall, a Viennese doctor. Phrenology enjoyed an enormous amount of popular support well into the twentieth century but, later on, was completely condemned by scientific research.

Plessy v. Ferguson. The landmark decision of the Supreme Court in 1896 which upheld the constitutionality of racial segregation in the doctrine of "separate but equal." The case developed from an event, in 1892, in which Homer Plessy, a black man, refused to sit in a car for blacks on the train. Disallowing Plessy's argument that his constitutional rights were infringed, the Supreme Court ruled that a state law that "implies merely a legal distinction" between blacks and whites did not go against the Thirteenth and Fourteenth Amendments. After the *Plessy* decision, separate public accommodations based on race were encouraged and its reasoning was not overturned until 1954 in the case *Brown v. Board of Education.*

Plymouth Colony (1620–1691). An English colonial venture in North America. The first settlement of the Plymouth Colony was an area that was previously surveyed and named by Captain John Smith. The settlement served as the capital of the colony and developed as the modern town of Plymouth, Massachusetts.

Politics of Respectability. Rather than challenge mainstream attitudes for failing to accept the fact that cultures and individuals are different, the politics of respectability or as it is sometimes called respectability politics, is the effort of marginal groups to police their own members and to make sure that their social values are compatible with mainstream values. In the context of black American history, the politics of respectability was embraced as a way of trying to deliberately set aside and undermine those cultural and moral practices that were thought to be disrespected by the mainstream society, par-

ticularly in the milieu of family life and good manners. The politics of respectability can be traced to black scholars and activists including W. E. B. Du Bois and Booker T. Washington.

Pompey (106–48 BC). Gnaeus Pompeius Magnus, known in English as Pompey or Pompey the Great, was a military and political leader of the late Roman Republic. Throughout his long career on the battlefield, Pompey showed extraordinary military talents. Some of his military accomplishments were highlighted when he fought in Africa and Spain, suppressed the slave revolt of Spartacus, cleared the Mediterranean of pirates, and occupied Armenia, Syria, and Palestine. When Pompey's senatorial forces were attacked by Caesar's smaller army, they were completely overcome, and Pompey fled to Egypt. When Pompey arrived in Egypt, he hoped that King Ptolemy, his earlier client, would support him. However, the Egyptian king feared offending the victorious Caesar and refused to help Pompey. On September 28, Pompey was asked to leave his ships and come ashore at Pelusium, to which he complied. He was treacherously struck down and killed by one of Ptolemy's officers.

Popular Culture. In the early twentieth century, categories such as politics, entertainment, sports, news, fashion/clothes, technology, and the use of slang, especially in Western countries, emerged to influence and fashion people's ideas, attitudes, and perspectives within the mainstream of culture, which is referred to as popular culture. Highly promoted by mass media, popular culture continues to permeate the everyday lives of people in these societies and is now the emerging global mainstream of the twenty-first century.

Prince, Mary (1788–1833). Prince, born in Bermuda to an enslaved family, was a

British abolitionist and autobiographer. Prince was sold to many cruel owners and underwent terrible treatment from her masters. Eventually, she ended up in Antigua as a slave to the Wood family. Prince, in December 1826, married Daniel James, a former slave who had bought his freedom and worked as a carpenter and cooper. The marriage resulted in a cruel beating by her master. Two years later, in 1828, she traveled to England with her owners. Eventually, she ran away and found freedom in England, but could not return to her husband. Prince crusaded against slavery and worked alongside the Anti-Slavery Society. She was employed by Thomas Pringle, an abolitionist writer and secretary of the Anti-Slavery Society. Prince was the first woman to present an anti-slavery petition to Parliament. Also, she was the first black woman to write and publish an autobiography, *The History of Mary Prince: A West Indian Slave*, a key part of the anti-slavery campaign. Her book made people in Britain aware that, although the slave trade had been made illegal, life for blacks on the plantations continued to be full of cruelty and terrors.

Progressive Era. A period of widespread social activism and political reform across the United States from the 1890s to the 1920s. The progressive reformers drew support from the urban college-educated middle class. Some of their objectives were to end corruption in government, control business practices, address health hazards, and improve working conditions for poor people. In addition, the progressives rallied for the public to have more direct control over government. They thought this could be achieved, for example, through direct primaries to nominate candidates for public office and direct election of senators.

Puritan. A member of a group of English Protestants in the late sixteenth and seventeenth centuries called Puritans. Under restrictions from church and crown, the Puritans arrived in the English colonies in the New World, a migration that laid the foundation for the religious, intellectual, and social order of New England, which has resonated throughout American life ever since.

Race Prejudice. A negative feeling or attitude, which might result in discriminatory action towards a group of people based on their race.

Racial Separatism. Also referred to as racial segregation. For example, in the United States, under the Jim Crow Laws, racial separatism was practiced.

Racialization. A process whereby racial identities are assigned to blacks and other non-whites. In the United States, during the colonial period, for example, racialization was a process used by the colonists to render blacks inferior to whites so that it was easier to enslave blacks.

Racism. A system of advantage based on race, which is manifested personally, culturally, and institutionally that works to the advantage of the dominant group, which is white. All whites benefit from racism, even whites that are against racism and are working to put an end to racism in all its multidimensional forms.

Ratzel, Friedrich (1844–1904). Ratzel was a German geographer and ethnographer. He was influenced by Charles Darwin as well as by the German zoologist and philosopher Ernst Heinrich Haeckel. His work *Lebensraum* published in 1909 is about biogeography, which provided a foundation for German geopolitics, the expansion of the biological concept of geography. Ratzel's most famous work is *Anthropogeographie*, which was completed between 1872 and 1899, in which Ratzel examines the effects of different features and geographical location on people's lifestyles.

Reconstruction (1865–1877). The period that began at the end of slavery in 1865. In an effort to reinvigorate white supremacy, under the administration of President Andrew Johnson, in 1865 and 1866, new Southern state legislatures passed restrictive "black codes" to regulate and control the labor and conduct of previous slaves and other African Americans. In early 1867, under the Reconstruction Act of 1867, Southern states had to ratify the Fourteenth Amendment, which broadened the definition of citizenship granting "equal protection" to former slaves under the Constitution. Congress passed the Freedmen's Bureau and Civil Rights Bills and sent them to President Johnson for his signature. President Johnson vetoed the Bills. Ignoring President Johnson's veto, the 1868 Civil Rights Act became law. In February 1869, Congress approved the Fifteenth Amendment, which guaranteed that a citizen's right to vote would not be denied "on account of race, color or previous conditions of servitude." The KKK was a vigilant force opposing the rights of blacks. In 1871, President Ulysses Grant took some measures against the KKK's actions. White supremacy was gradually reinvigorated, however, and support for Reconstruction decreased. In 1875, with the Democratic Party controlling the House, and the KKK conducting a campaign of violence to take control of Mississippi, President Grant refused to send federal troops, which signaled the end of federal support for Reconstruction state governments. With the election of Rutherford B. Hayes, who reached a compromise to be President, the Democrats controlled the House. The Compromise of 1877 marked the end of Reconstruction in the same year.

Republican Government. In the United States, it is a government whose political authority comes from the citizens. Power is given to the government by its citizens as is inscribed in the Constitution and through its elected representatives.

Republicanism. In the United States, in the eighteenth century, republicanism was founded and first practiced by the founding fathers and was the guiding philosophy and a major part of their civic thought. It emphasized liberty and inalienable individual rights as central values. It rejected monarchy, aristocracy, and inherent power, making the people sovereign.

Rights of Man. A book written by Thomas Paine in 1791. It includes thirty-one articles and postulates that when a government fails to protect the natural rights of its citizens, political revolution is admissible. In this sense, the rights of man defend the French Revolution against Edmund Burke's claim, in *The Reflections on the Revolution in France*, that the revolution was demolishing the fabric of a good society.

Robinson, Cedric (1940–2016). Robinson, born in Oakland California, was a professor in the Department of Black Studies and the Department of Political Science at the University of California, Santa Barbara (UCSB). He also taught at the University of Michigan, Binghamton University, where, in 1973, he accepted his first tenured appointment, and at the State University of New York. With Corey Dublin, a student then at UCSB, Robinson created the *Third World News Review* on the campus and community radio station KCSB-FM 91.9. His books include *An Anthology of Marxism*,

2001; *Black Marxism: The Making of a Black Tradition*, 1983; and *Terms of Order: Political Science and the Myth of Leadership*, 1980.

Rose, Ernestine (1810–92). Rose, a feminist and abolitionist, was born in Piotrków Trybunalski, Poland as Ernestine Louise Potowska to a wealthy Jewish family. At the age of fourteen, she renounced the Jewish laws and customs that relegated women to an inferior status. Her mother died when she was sixteen, and she inherited a large amount of property. After her father arranged for her to marry a man the same age as him and signed over her inheritance as the dowry, she took her inheritance claim to a Polish court and won a legal endorsement of it. The following year, Rose left Poland, leaving most of her inheritance to her father, to live in Berlin, the Netherlands, and Paris respectively. When Rose was twenty-one, she moved to England. In 1834, she married William E. Rose and moved to the United States where she would focus her attention on the promotion of equal rights for women and the abolition of slavery. Eventually, she and her husband left the United States to live in England. She returned to the United States in 1873 to attend a convention of the National Women Suffrage Association where she gave a lecture.

Sambo. During the era of slavery, sambo was a name given to blacks to denote them as apologetic and subservient. However, after World War II, there was an increasing sensitivity to racial stereotyping and the term is considered as demeaning and insulting to blacks.

Sancho, Ignatius (1729–1780). Sancho was born on a slave ship. After both his parents died, he was taken to England. While in Greenwich, he worked for three maiden sisters. John Montagu, 2nd Duke of Montagu was impressed by Sancho's intellect and encouraged him to read and lent him books from his personal library. After a while, Sancho felt suffocated in Greenwich and, in 1749, he ran away to the Montagus. Sancho worked as a butler at Montagu House where he immersed himself in music, reading, writing, and poetry. He was the first black to vote in a British election. At the height of the debate about slavery, in 1776, Sancho wrote to the Irish novelist and Anglican clergyman Laurence Sterne, urging him to write against slavery and press for the abolition of the slave trade.

Second Amendment. Influenced by the English Bill of Rights of 1689, the Second Amendment was adopted on July 15, 1791 as a part of the amendments contained in the Bill of Rights. It is basically the right to keep and bear firearms. It was once described by Sir William Blackstone as an auxiliary right, which maintains and upholds the natural rights of an individual to self-defense and resistance to oppression and their civic duty to act in defense of the state. Today, the Second Amendment has been subject to renewed academic examination and judicial interests. For example, in the 2008 case *District of Columbia v. Heller*, the Supreme Court declared that the amendment protects an individual's right to possess and carry firearms.

Separate But Equal. A legal doctrine in United States constitutional law according to which racial segregation did not violate the Fourteenth Amendment. Under this doctrine, it was recognized that as long as the facilities provided to blacks and whites were equal, the state and local government could allow services, facilities, public accommodation, housing, education, employment, transportation, and medical care to be segregated by race. Separate but equal was confirmed in the 1896 landmark case *Plessy v. Ferguson*. As a result of the 1954 case *Brown v. Board of Education*, the separate but equal doctrine was deemed unconstitutional and overturned.

Sexism. A social relation in which men have power over women. It is premised on the behavior, policy, language, or other action of men which conveys the cultural, institutionalized, systematic, far-reaching, or constant view that women are inferior, which works to the advantage of men. Internalized sexism presents itself when women express these actions and views.

Shange, Ntozake (1948–2018). Shange, born Paulette L. Williams, in Trenton, New Jersey was a black American playwright and feminist. She graduated with a BA from Bernard College and an MA from the University of Southern California both in American Studies. She is well known for her 1975 Obie Award winning play, *For Colored Girls Who Have Considered Suicide/When the Rainbow is Enuf*. It tells the stories of seven women who have suffered discrimination in a racist and sexist society. Her other plays include *A Photograph: A Study of Cruelty*, 1977; *Black and White: Two Dimensional Planes*, 1979; *From Okra to Greens/A Different Kind of Love Story*, 1983; and *Whitewash*, 1994.

Shibboleth. The modern use of the word derives from the Hebrew Bible in the Book of Judges, chapter 12, and applied to the Ephraimites whose dialect included a differently sounding first consonant to the word shibbólet. The narrative is that after around 1370–1070 BC, the inhabitants of Gilead inflicted a military defeat upon the invading tribe of Ephraim. The surviving Ephraimites tried to cross the Jordan river to return to the territory where they lived and the Gileadites tried to prevent them by safeguarding the river's passages. In order to identify and kill the Ephraimites, the Gileadites asked them to say the word shibbólet. Because of their dialect, when saying the word shibbólet, it sounded to Gileadites as if they were saying "sibbolet," which exposed their identity as Ephraimites. Shibbólet is any custom or traditions, particularly a speech pattern, that distinguishes one group of people (the in-group) from others (the out-group).

Smith, Adam (1723–1790). Smith was a Scottish philosopher and political economist. He laid down the foundations of classic free market economy theory. He is well known for his book *An Inquiry into the Nature and Causes of the Wealth of Nations*, in which he demonstrates how the pursuit of self-interest could lead to the public benefit if undertaken in the context of a free and competitive market. What he calls the "invisible hand" guides the totality of exchanges such that, in the end, everything would balance out and everyone gets what each wants.

Social Contract. It is concerned with the origins of society and the legitimacy of the authority of the state over the individual. The social contract is an agreement between the ruled and rulers, which defines the rights and duties of each. Social contract theorists of the seventeenth and eighteenth centuries included Hugo Grotius, Thomas Hobbes, John Locke, Jean-Jacques Rousseau, and Immanuel Kant, who, in different ways, tried to solve the problems of political authority and people's natural rights.

Social Justice. This refers to the necessities of justice allied to the basis of social existence. The term has been criticized as involving redundancy because justice is unavoidably a social or interpersonal concern. Indeed, what is typically proposed by the term is a concern for the necessities of justice applied to social welfare and issues arising from sharing a common existence and, in this sense, social justice is necessarily a matter of distributive justice, a belief or set of beliefs explaining what justice requires when resources are justly distributed amongst people. The main emphasis of social justice is on the foundational character of justice in social life.

Spartans. Citizens of Sparta, a notable city-state in ancient Greece. After defeating Athens in the Peloponnesian War, 431–404 BC, Sparta gained power. The Spartans' culture was so harsh that the word "spartan" has become synonymous with a harsh way of life. Spartan society was carefully created around an austere moral code and a sense of duty. Male Spartans, at the age of seven, entered the agōgē, the educational system, which emphasized discipline, physical strength, and the importance of the Spartan state and where they received a military training. In addition, they studied reading, writing, music, and dancing, on their way to becoming accepted as full citizens. It is believed that females received similar education. However, for the girls, there was less emphasis on military training. In 371 BC, at the Battle of Leuctra, the Spartans were defeated by the Thebans and their empire experienced a long period of decline.

Spencer, Herbert (1820–1903). Spencer, after reading Charles Darwin's *On the Origin of Species*, coined the phrase the "survival of the fittest" in his 1864 book, *Principles of Biology*. The phrase proposes natural selection, which is the difference in survival and reproduction of individuals due to their different phenotype, the key mechanism of evolution. Spencer extended the theory of evolution into the realm of sociology and ethics. He also made use of Lamarckism, that is, the idea that the organism can pass on characteristics that it has acquired during its lifetime to its offspring.

Standpoint Theory. This theory takes into consideration a feminist perspective. It argues that knowledge stems from social position. Thus, it denies that established science is objective and proposes that research and theory have overlooked and downgraded women and feminist ways of thinking and knowing. Standpoint theory was devised by feminist theorist Sandra Harding. However, the theory materializes from a Marxist argumentation that people from an oppressed group have access to knowledge that is not accessible to those from an advantaged class. Starting in the 1970s, feminist writers inspired by this Marxist insight began to examine how inequalities between women and men impact knowledge production. Their work is linked to epistemology, a branch of philosophy that assesses the nature and acquisition of knowledge, and emphasizes that knowledge is always socially positioned. In a society stratified by gender and other identity categories such as race, class, sexuality, and disability, one's social position structures what one can realize. Black feminist Patricia Hill Collins anticipated a form of standpoint theory that underscored the standpoint of black women in the United States.

Stanton, Elizabeth Cady (1815–1902). Stanton, a suffragist, civil rights activist, and abolitionist, was born in Jonestown, New York. Until the age of sixteen, she attended Jonestown Academy where she studied Latin, Greek, and French. When she married Henry Stanton, they moved to Boston where her husband had joined a law firm. She became involved in the abolitionist movement and the women's rights movement. In 1848, she helped organize the world's first women's rights convention and, in 1863, formed the National Women's Loyal League with Susan B. Anthony. In 1870, seven years later, they established the National Woman Suffrage Association. Late in her life, she supported liberal divorce laws and reproductive self-determination and became an increasingly ostracized voice among women reformers. However, her efforts helped bring about the eventual passage of the Nineteenth Amendment in 1920, which gave women the right to vote.

Stone, Lucy (1818–1893). Stone, an orator, suffragist, and abolitionist, was born at Coy's Hill in West Brookfield, Massachusetts. In 1839, Stone attended Mount Holyoke Seminary for just one term. Four years later, she enrolled at Oberlin College. Stone recognized that Oberlin did not offer a level playing field for women. Thus, it denied Stone the opportunity to pursue her passion for public speaking. Nonetheless, in 1847, Stone graduated with honors and was the first woman from Massachusetts to earn a Bachelor's degree. She devoted her life to improving the rights of American women and supported the Women's National Loyal League, which was founded by Susan B. Anthony and Elizabeth Cady Stanton on May 14, 1863. In 1866, she helped found the American Equal Rights Association. She also organized the State Woman's Suffrage Association of New Jersey and was elected its president. Stone spent her life working on rights for women.

Student Nonviolence Coordinating Committee (SNCC). A civil rights group that was formed to give younger blacks a voice in the Civil Rights Movement. It was the concern of Ella Baker, who was then the director of the Southern Christian Leadership Conference (SCLC), that the SCLC, led by Martin Luther King Jr., was out of touch with younger blacks who desired the movement to make faster progress in gaining equal rights for blacks. In the wake of the Greensboro sit-in at a lunch counter that was barred to blacks, Baker, in April 1960, facilitated the first meeting of SNCC and encouraged its members to look beyond integration to broader social change. Baker tried to convince them that King's doctrine of nonviolent civil disobedience was a political tactic rather than a way of life. When Stokely Carmichael was elected the chair of SNCC in 1966, he reoriented the organization towards Black Power. SNCC soon became one of the most radical branches of the movement.

Terrorism. The term "terrorism" originated during the French Revolution of the eighteenth century. After the 1983 Beirut barracks bombing, the term "terrorism" became more widely used in mainstream discourse during the Ronald Reagan administration (1981–1989), and again after the attacks in New York City and Washington, DC in September 2001, and in Bali on October 12, 2002. Amongst academics and the government, terrorism has no agreed upon definition but is often used in a disapproving sense to define and explain aggressive actions committed by politically encouraged self-appointed substate groups. However, if such actions are carried out on behalf of a generally accepted cause, say the Maquis seeking to undermine the government of Vichy

France, then the term is typically side-stepped. In fact, one country's terrorist is another country's freedom fighter.

The Liberator (1831–1865). An American abolitionist newspaper, which was founded in 1831 by William Lloyd Garrison and Isaac Knapp.

The Talented Tenth. In 1896, the term was created by Northern white liberals and was then publicized by W. E. B. Du Bois in his influential essay "The Talented Tenth" published in 1903 in *The Negro Problem*, a collection of essays written by African Americans. Du Bois used the term to describe and explain the possibility, through classical education or becoming directly involved in social change, that one of every ten black men would become leaders of blacks throughout the world.

Thirteenth Amendment. On December 6, 1865, the Thirteenth Amendment to the Constitution, officially abolishing slavery in the United States, declared that "Neither slavery nor involuntary servitude, except as a punishment for crime whereof the party shall have been duly convicted, shall exist within the United States, or any place subject to their jurisdiction."

Thomas, Clarence. Thomas, a Justice of the Supreme Court of the United States, was born in Pinpoint, Georgia but grew up in Savannah, Georgia where he lived with his maternal grandparents. He graduated from the College of Holy Cross and Yale Law School. In 1991, he was only narrowly confirmed to the Supreme Court because he was accused of sexual harassment by lawyer Anita Hill in a public hearing. Thomas is conservative and supports small government while opposing more liberal benchmarks like affirmative action and gay marriage.

Tocqueville, Alexis de (1805–1859). Tocqueville, a French sociologist and politi-cal theorist, traveled to the United States in 1831 to study its prisons. In 1835 and 1840 respectively, he ended up writing two volumes of *Democracy in America*, one of the most influential books of the nineteenth century. With its forthright explanations of equality and individualism in the United States, Tocqueville's concerns were with the civic dimension of democracy and sociological problems engendered by democratic life. For him, democracy "serves the well-being of the greatest number."

Totalitarianism. A dictatorial form of centralized government that controls every feature of state and private behavior. Although the term was intended to describe fascist and communist regimes, totalitarianism is essentially connected with features of the former Soviet Union.

Transwomen. These people were categorized as males when they were born. The term "transwomen" is not always interchangeable with that of "transsexual women," although the two terms are often used in this way. Medical treatment in the transition for transwomen includes estrogen hormone replacement therapy.

Truth, Sojourner (1797–1883). Sojourner Truth, born Isabelle Baumfree in Swartekill, Ulster County, New York, was a slave and she and her family lived on Colonel Hardenbergh's estate in Esopus, New York, which was once under Dutch rule. Truth grew up speaking Dutch. After Hardenbergh's death, Truth, who was then nine years old, was sold to John Neely and later was sold to John Dumount who resided at West Park, New York. It was during this time that Truth learnt to speak English. After Dumont failed to fulfill his promise to free Truth, in 1826, she escaped from slavery with her infant daughter, a year before slaves were freed in New York. She devoted her life to the abolition of slavery. She also helped to recruit black troops for the Union army. Truth is well known for the "Ain't I A Woman?" speech.

Turner, Henry McNeal (1834–1915). Henry Turner was born near Abbeville, South Carolina. His parents were free blacks. His father died when he was young and he was forced to work picking cotton with slaves. After running away from home as a teenager, Turner first found employment as an office boy in a law firm. In 1851, he became an itinerant minister in the Methodist Episcopal Church and seven years later joined the African Methodist Episcopal (AME) Church in St Louis, Missouri where he became a minister. Turner's rise in the church was rapid. He became the twelfth elected minister.

Turner, Nat (1800–1831). Nat Turner was a black American slave who, in August 1931, with slaves and free blacks led the only effective, sustained slave rebellion in Southampton, Virginia. Spreading terror throughout the white South, his action set off a new wave of oppressive legislation, which prohibited the education, movement, and assembly of slaves and stiffened the severity of pro-slavery, anti-abolitionist convictions that persisted in that region until the American Civil War.

Uncle Tom. The title character in *Uncle Tom's Cabin*, an anti-slavery novel published by Harriet Beecher Stowe in 1852, which, according to Will Kaufman, laid the groundwork for the Civil War. Uncle Tom is also used as a derogatory epithet for an excessively subservient person, particularly when that person is aware of his or her status as lower class because he or she is black.

Universal Negro Improvement Association (UNIA). An organization founded in 1914 by Marcus Garvey, which was devoted to the elevation of racial pride, economic self-sufficiency for blacks, and the creation of an independent black nation in Africa. The influence of the UNIA spread in many urban black communities such as Harlem in New York City. After Garvey was indicted and convicted of fraud in the handling of funds that was raised to establish a black steamship line, he was pardoned by President Calvin Coolidge and deported to Jamaica. The UNIA never recovered from Garvey's deportation. Nonetheless, the UNIA did influence many individuals and groups on both sides of the Atlantic.

Van Evrie, John H. (1814–1896). Van Evrie was an American physician and a defender of slavery. He attacked abolitionists in a number of works. He was best known for being the editor of the *Weekly Day Book* and authored several books on slavery and race, which reproduced scientific racism. His writings emphasized the inferiority of blacks when compared to whites. Scientific racism was used as a justification for discrimination towards blacks.

Voluntarism. The term "voluntarism" was introduced by Ferdinand Tönnies in his philosophical writings. It refers to a metaphysical or psychological arrangement that assigns to the will a larger role than that attributed to intellect.

Wallace, Michele (1952–). Wallace, a black feminist author, cultural critic, and educator, was born in New York City. Wallace earned her BA in English and Creative Writing from City College in 1974. She received an MA in English from City College in 1990 and a PhD in Cinema Studies from New York University in 1999. In 1978, aged 26, she published her first book, *Black Macho and the Myth of the Superwoman*, creating a maelstrom of disagreement in the black community and beyond because Wallace declared that the Black Power movement of the 1960s was the black man's pursuit of his own power. She also asserted that the movement was determined by the desire to avenge, not equality. In addition, Wallace drew attention to black men's attraction to white women and examined whether a black man could truly love a black woman. In 1990, a new edition of *Black Macho* was released with a long introduction by Wallace titled "How I Saw It Then, How I See It Now," detailing her views concerning the controversy. Her writings include *Invisibility Blues: From Pop to Theory*, 1990; *Passing, Lynching and Jim Crow: A Genealogy of Race and Gender in U.S. Visual Culture, 1895–1929*, 1999; and *Dark Designs and Visual Culture*, 2004. At present, Wallace is a professor of English at the City College of New York and the Graduate Center of the City of New York.

War Amendments. Also known as the Reconstruction Amendments, the Thirteenth, Fourteenth, and Fifteenth Amendments of the United States Constitution. These amendments were adopted between 1865 and 1870, five years after the Civil War.

War on Poverty. This is the unofficial name that was introduced by President Lyndon B. Johnson during his State of the Union Address on January 8, 1964 in response to the poverty rate, which, in the United States, was about 19 percent. Congress passed the Equal Opportunity Act, which established the Office of Economic Opportunity to manage the local application of federal funds targeted to reduce poverty. As part of his poverty reduction strategies, President Johnson expanded the federal government's role in healthcare and education. These programs were part of the "Great Society" intended to end poverty.

Ward, Artemas (1727–1800). Ward was a major in the Worcester County militia in the French and Indian War (1754–1763). When the war ended, he returned to serve the general court and was placed on a taxation committee with Samuel Adams and John Hancock. He was removed from the assembly because he was an outspoken Patriot. Ward participated in the Siege of Boston and directed troops even though he was sick and in bed. He was appointed the head of Connecticut and New Hampshire militia forces during the siege. When Congress created a Continental Army, Ward was a major-general in the army. Under the Washington administration, Ward had a notable military career until he became ill and resigned in 1777.

Washington, George (1732–1799). George Washington, the son of a prosperous planter in Virginia, was an American statesman and soldier. He fought in the French and Indian War (1754–1763). During the American Revolutionary War (1775–1783), Washington was the commander-in-chief of the Continental Army and led the colonial forces to victory, which made him a hero. In 1783, with a peace treaty signed between Great Britain and the United States, Washington returned to Mount Vernon and to his family life. In 1787, he was asked to attend the Constitutional Convention in Philadelphia and head the committee to draw up the new Constitution. His remarkable management persuaded the committee members that Washington was the most qualified person to become the President of the United States. The first presidential election was held on January 7, 1789. Washington won the election and became the first President of the United States.

Washington, Madison (dates unknown). Madison Washington, an enslaved cook, on board the brig *Creole*, transporting 134 other slaves from Virginia for sale in New Orleans instigated a slave revolt on November 7, 1841. Washington led seventeen of the slaves on board in a rebellion. They killed one of the slave traders on board and injured some of the crew. Taking control of the *Creole*, they demanded that it sail to Nassau, which was under British control. Because, in 1839, Great Britain had abolished slavery in its nation and colonies, despite the protest of the United States, the British refused the demand of the United States for their return. However, the British took Washington and the seventeen slaves into custody and charged them with mutiny. The Admiralty court heard the case and ruled in favor of Washington and the other men. In April 1842, they were freed.

Welfare Queen. In the United States, "welfare queen" was a derogatory term used to talk about women who were engaged in welfare fraud, an act of illegally using state welfare systems by using, withholding, or giving (false) information to obtain more funds than would otherwise be given. During the early 1960s, welfare fraud was talked about in widely read magazines such as *Reader's Digest*. In 1974, the media started to report on welfare fraud and the term "welfare queen" originated. Since then, the term has remained a stigmatizing label that is, for the most part, directed at black single mother welfare recipients.

Wheatley, Phyllis (1753–1784). Wheatley, born in West Africa, was sold in slavery when she was seven or eight years old and brought to North America. She was purchased by John Wheatley as a personal servant to his wife and lived with the Wheatleys in Boston, Massachusetts. They educated Wheatley and she soon mastered Latin and Greek, going on to write highly celebrated poetry. She published her first poem in 1767 and her first volume of verse, *Poems on Various Subjects, Religious and Moral*, in 1773. Shortly after the publication of her book, in the same year, she was freed from slavery. She was the first published black female poet. After the deaths of the Wheatleys, she married John Peters, a free black grocer. In 1778, Peters was imprisoned for debt. Wheatley struggled financially because she was unable to find a publisher for her second volume of poems. For the remainder of her life, she gained employment as a scullery maid in a boarding house to support herself and her son.

Whig Party. A political party that was active in the middle of the nineteenth century in the United States. It emerged in the 1830s and was led by Henry Clay in opposition to the policies of President Andrew Jackson. The party supported the supremacy of Congress over the Presidency and supported policies that would enhance manufacturing, and was immediately ridiculed by the Jacksonian Democrats as a party devoted to the interests of wealth and aristocracy, a charge it never could entirely dismiss. Yet during the party's brief life, it managed to win backing from different groups including business, planters, reformers, and the emerging urban middle class and to hold its own in presidential elections. The essential political philosophy of the American Whig Party was not straightforwardly related to the British Whig Party and was opposed to absolute monarchy.

White Supremacy. With roots in scientific racism this is a racist ideology based on the view that whites are superior to blacks and other people of color. Thus, whites should be dominant over blacks and other races. The doctrine of white supremacy in the United States was enshrined in laws such as the Jim Crow laws that maintained, perpetuated, and upheld the social, political, and institutional domination of whites.

Whiteness. Unraced and unmarked, whiteness is a structure as well as an identity. In terms of the latter, whiteness is denoted in terms of anti-racist, racist, poor whites, and elite whites. Whiteness as a system bestows on all whites unearned white skin privilege.

Whiteness Studies. An interdisciplinary form of inquiry into the nature and causes of whiteness and white privilege. In the United States, it developed in the late twentieth century. The first wave of whiteness studies was pioneered by W. E. B. Du Bois. Drawing a great deal on how the grammar of whiteness works, as a guarantor for unearned, impeccable privileges, prearranged for whites and straightforwardly tied to apparent benefits, W. E. B. Du Bois, in his theorization, labels this phenomenon the "public and psychological wages" of whiteness. The second wave of whiteness studies focuses on naming whiteness as "an essential something" and on making whiteness visible to whites.

Williams, Fannie Barrier (1855–1944). Williams was born in Brockport, New York, and attended Brockport public school. After graduating, she attended the Brockport Normal School, a teacher's college, which is now SUNY Brockport, and graduated in 1870. She was the first black person to graduate. In 1875, Williams moved to Washington, DC, to teach and joined the emerging education movement. She was an educator and a political activist. She focused specifically on rights for blacks and women and lectured frequently on the need for suffrage for all women, especially black women. Williams was the only black woman selected to attend the National American Woman Suffrage Association convention in 1907. She was famous for her efforts to have blacks officially represented on the board of the World's Columbia Exposition held in Chicago in 1893. "The Intellectual Progress of the Women of the United States since the Emancipation Proclamation" was one of the two addresses Williams gave at the Exposition.

Woman Suffrage Movement. Developing from the larger movement for women's rights, the claim for women's suffrage began to gather strength in 1840s. The Seneca Falls Convention in 1848, which was the first women's rights convention, approved a resolution in favor of women's suffrage notwithstanding opposition from some of its organizers who thought that the idea was too extreme. However, in 1850, at the National Women's Rights Convention, suffrage was an important aspect of the movement's activities. The first national suffrage organizations were established in 1869, one led by Elizabeth Cady Stanton and Susan B. Anthony and the other by Susan Stone. In 1890, these two organizations finally came together as the National American Suffrage Organization, with Anthony as the leader. In the early 1870s, the suffragists made several attempts to vote, and when they were turned away, they filed lawsuits with the hope that the Supreme Court would rule that women had a constitutional right to vote. In 1872, when Anthony did vote, she was arrested and charged for voting, which provided the movement with renewed impetus. Much of the movement's energy was directed towards women's suffrage.

Womanism. A social theory based on the discontentment of black feminists with the second-wave feminist movement for not taking into consideration the history and experience of black women. Black feminist writer Alice Walker is credited with coining the term "womanism" as a clear distinction from feminism.

Working Class. In the United States, this is a class of people dependent on physical labor. They are employed for hourly wages, especially as manual workers and industrial workers. To be a member of the working class is to have some symbols of status such as wearing heavy protective clothes at work, being subject to firm regulation on the job, having to clock in and out of work at fixed times, and working in unionized jobs. Working-class jobs are categorized into four groups: unskilled laborers, artisans, factory workers, and contracting out workers who are, for the most part, contracted to work at home or in workshops. In the United States, the notion of the working class departs from the Marxist conceptualization of the working class as anyone who is not the owner of the means of production (the ruling class) and in turn sells his or her labor for money.

World War I (Great War) (1914–18). The war began in Europe on July 28, 1914 after the assassination of Archduke Franz Ferdinand, the heir to the Austro-Hungarian Empire. During the war, the central powers, Germany, Austria-Hungary, Bulgaria, and the Ottoman Empire fought against the Allied powers Great Britain, France, Russia, Italy, Romania, Japan and the United States. By the time the war was over on November 11, 1918, and the Allied powers claimed victory, more than sixteen million people were dead.

Writ of Habeas Corpus. Habeas corpus is a Latin term that literally means to "produce the body." It is a court order to a person or agency holding someone in custody to deliver the imprisoned individual to the court issuing the order and to present valid reasons why that person should be detained. In addition to the federal government, many states in the United States recognize the writ of habeas corpus and the government cannot suspend it except in extreme circumstance such as during times of war.

Xenophobia. Accurately the word means the fear of foreigners or strangers. Xenophobia is frequently used to refer to attitudes of disgust or hatred rather than mere fear of the "other." Feelings based on xenophobia have always played a part in how groups and communities are perceived. Xenophobia resists the conceptual universalism of many of the prevailing movements of ideas such as liberalism and socialism and has developed into more dogmatic ideological and structural forms of racism and nationalism, for instance. Xenophobic predispositions appear to express themselves when familiar structures and traditions seem to have broken down; for instance, in Western Europe after 1918 and Eastern Europe after the collapse of the Soviet Union and communism in the 1990s. Xenophobic predispositions were directed towards immigrants and racialized ethnic groups who were citizens of these societies.

Index